WMSCI 2019

The 23rd World Multi-Conference on Systemics, Cybernetics and Informatics

July 6 - 9, 2019 – Orlando, Florida, USA

PROCEEDINGS

Volume I

Edited by:

Nagib Callaos
Bruce Peoples
Belkis Sánchez
Michael Savoie

Organized by

International Institute of Informatics and Systemics

Member of the International Federation for Systems Research (IFSR)

COPYRIGHT

PROGRAM COMMITTEE

Chairs: Michael Savoie (USA)
C. Dale Zinn (USA)

Adamopoulou, Evgenia	National Technical University of Athens	Greece
Alam, Delwar	Daffodil International University	Bangladesh
Alanís Urquieta, José D.	Technological University of Puebla	Mexico
Alhayyan, Khalid N.	Institute of Public Administration	Saudi Arabia
Altamirano, Patricio	Institute of Advanced National Studies (IAEN in Spanish)	Ecuador
Andersen, J. C.	The University of Tampa	USA
Ascacivar Placencia, Yanelli Karen	Mecoacc	Peru
Batos, Vedran	University of Dubrovnik	Croatia
Bermúdez Juárez, Blanca	Meritorious Autonomous University of Puebla	Mexico
Bernikova, Olga	St. Petersburg State University	Russian Federation
Bönke, Dietmar	Reutlingen University	Germany
Bubnov, Alexey	Institute of Physics of the Czech Academy of Sciences	Czech Republic
Cárdenas, José	University of Guayaquil	Ecuador
Carreño Escobedo, Jorge Raúl	Universidad Nacional Mayor de San Marcos	Peru
Castro, John W.	University of Atacama	Chile
Chen, Jingchao	University Donghua	China
Chiang, Po-Yun	The Ministry of National Defense	Taiwan
Chou, Te-Shun	East Carolina University	USA
Chukwu, Ozoemena Joseph	Riga Technical University	Latvia
Ciemleja, Guna	Riga Technical University	Latvia
Cilliers, Liezel	University of Fort Hare	South Africa
Dantas de Rezende, Julio F.	Federal University of Rio Grande do Norte	USA
Dasilva, Julian	Barry University	USA
Doherr, Detlev	University of Applied Sciences Offenburg	Germany
Dyck, Sergius	Fraunhofer Institute of Optronics, System Technologies and Image Exploitation	Germany

Edwards, Matthew E.	Alabama A&M University	USA
Eremina, Yuliya	Riga Technical University	Latvia
Fagade, Tesleem	University of Bristol	UK
Farah, Tanjila	North South University	Bangladesh
Florescu, Gabriela	National Institute for Research and Development in Informatics	Romania
Fries, Terrence P.	Indiana University of Pennsylvania	USA
Gaile-Sarkane, Elina	Riga Technical University	Latvia
Gourisetti, Sri Nikhil Gupta	Pacific Northwest National Laboratory	USA
Gvatua, Salome	Riga Technical University	Latvia
Haba, Cristian-Gyözö	"Gheorghe Asachi" Technical University of Iasi	Romania
Haferkorn, Daniel	Fraunhofer Institute of Optronics, System Technologies and Image Exploitation	Germany
Hanacek, Petr	Brno University of Technology	Czech Republic
Hassan, Md. Maruf	Daffodil International University	Bangladesh
Hendel, Russell J.	Towson University	USA
Hilkevics, Sergejs	Ventspils University of Applied Sciences	Latvia
Ho, Sophia Shi-Huei	University of Taipei	Taiwan
Hsiao, Jung	SMS Infocomm Corporation	USA
Hu, Wen-Chen	University of North Dakota	USA
Ismail, Zainab Z.	University of Baghdad	Iraq
Jakubik, Maria	Haaga-Helia University of Applied Sciences	Finland
Jaros, Jiri	Brno University of Technology	Czech Republic
Jenq, John	Montclair State University	USA
Jenq, Priscilla	Carnegie Mellon University	USA
Jiménez, Ricardo	Barry University	USA
Kabwende, Benjamin Ngongo	Riga Technical University	Latvia
Khan, Salam	Alabama A&M University	USA
Kocmanova, Alena	Brno University of Technology	Czech Republic
Lamr, Marián	Technical University of Liberec	Czech Republic
Lapina, Inga	Riga Technical University	Latvia
Leclerc-Sherling, Christine	ASTRACS	USA
Lo, Yen-Fen	Shih Chien University	Taiwan
Lo, Yen-Hsi	Shih Chien University	Taiwan
Lu, Shen	University of South Florida	USA
Makarov, Alexander	Institute for Microelectronics- TU Wien	Austria
Matin, Mohammad Abdul	North South University	Bangladesh
Mechan Méndez, Víctor	Universidad Nacional Mayor de San Marcos	Peru

Mendoza Rojas, Hubert James	Universidad Nacional Mayor de San Marcos	Peru
Meyer, Heiko	Gefasoft AG	Germany
Miyazaki, Jun	Komazawa University	Japan
Mohammed, Ali J.	Ministry of Construction and Housing	Iraq
Moraes, Altino José M. de	Brazilian Ministry of Planning- Budget and Management	Brazil
Mylrea, Michael	Pacific Northwest National Laboratory	USA
Naito, Katsuhiro	Aichi Institute of Technology	Japan
Nemecek, Petr	Newton College	Czech Republic
Oganisjana, Karine	Riga Technical University	Latvia
Oliveira, Álvaro	UFRN	Brazil
Omer, Ako K.	Koya Univeristy	Iraq
Orantes-Jiménez, Sandra D.	Instituto Politécnico Nacional	Mexico
Ozolins, Modris	Riga Technical University	Latvia
Pando Álvarez, Rosa	Universidad Nacional Mayor de San Marcos	Peru
Pastirčáková, Kateřina	Jan Perner Transport Faculty- University of Pardubice	Czech Republic
Pavlakova Docekalova, Marie	Brno University of Technology	Czech Republic
Peng, Michael Yao-Ping	Hsuan Chuang University	Taiwan
Pickard, John	East Carolina University	USA
Placencia Medina, Maritza	Universidad Nacional Mayor de San Marcos	Peru
Quintana Salinas, Margot Rosario	Facultad de Medicina- Universidad Nacional Mayor de San Marcos	Peru
Redkin, Oleg	St. Petersburg State University	Russian Federation
Rodríguez, Nancy	Autonomous University of Madrid	Spain
Sánchez Flores, Guillermo	Technological University of Puebla	Mexico
Sander, Jennifer	Fraunhofer Institute of Optronics, System Technologies and Image Exploitation	Germany
Santos, Irani	SEMPLA-Prefeitura de Natal	Brazil
Scappini, Reinaldo	National Technological University	Argentina
Schaetter, Alfred	Pforzheim University	Germany
Segall, Richard S.	Arkansas State University	USA
Selberherr, Siegfried	Technische Universität Wien	Austria
Shah, Syed Zubair A.	Jamia Millia Islamia	India
Shiraishi, Yoshiaki	Kobe University	Japan
Silva-Valencia, Javier	Universidad Peruana Cayetano Heredia	Peru
Simberova, Iveta	Brno University of Technology	Czech Republic

Singh, Harwinder	Guru Nanak Dev Engineering College	India
Skrbek, Jan	Technical University of Liberec	Czech Republic
Sohn, Han Suk	New Mexico State University	USA
Souza, Mônica L.	Intellectos	Brazil
Sturgill, Ronda	The University of Tampa	USA
Šulc, Jaromír	Jan Perner Transport Faculty- University of Pardubice	Czech Republic
Sulema, Yevgeniya	National Technical University of Ukraine	Ukraine
Sun, Baolin	Wuhan University	China
Sverdlov, Viktor	Institute for Microelectronics- TU Wien	Austria
Szygenda, Stephen A.	Suuthern Methodist University	USA
Tanaka, Katsuyuki	Aichi Institute of Technology	Japan
Tartari, Simone	Intellectos	Brazil
Terzidis, Orestis	Karlsruhe Institut of Technology	Germany
Tintin, Romel	Institute of Advanced National Studies (IAEN in Spanish)	Ecuador
Tsubaki, Michiko	University of Electro-Communications	Japan
Velázquez-Araque, Luis	University of Guayaquil	Ecuador
Vrána, Stanislav	Czech Technical University in Prague	Czech Republic
Windbacher, Thomas	Technische Universität Wien	Austria
Yang, Zining	ACERTAS	USA
Yoshida, Naofumi	Komzawa University	Japan
Zaman, Moniruz	Daffodil International University	Bangladesh
Zaretsky, Esther	Givat Washington Academic College of Education	Israel

ADDITIONAL REVIEWERS

Abariga, Samuel	Division of Epidemiology and Biostatistics	USA
Abbas, Ghulam	Ghulam Ishaq Khan Institute	Pakistan
Abd Jelil, Radhia	Higher Institute of Fashion Professions of Monastir	Tunisia
Abdel Hafez, Hoda	Suez Canal University	Egypt
Abdul, Hamed	University of Management and Technology	Pakistan
Abe, Jair Minoro	Paulista University	Brazil
Aboalsamh, Hatim	King Saud University	Saudi Arabia
Abreu, António	Higher Education Polytechnic Institution of Engineering	Portugal
Abrukov, Victor	Chuvash State University	Russian Federation
Abu Omar, Mohammad	Al-Quds Open University	Palestine
Abuhejleh, Ahmad	University of Wisconsin-River Falls	USA
Acharya, Sushil	Robert Morris University	USA
Agarwal, Arun	Siksha `O` Anusandhan Deemed to be University	India
Agrebi, Maroi	University of Polytechnique Hauts-de-France	France
Agulhari, Cristiano Marcos	State University of Campinas	Brazil
Ahmed, Shamsuddin	Islamic University of Medinah	Saudi Arabia
Aiordachioaie, Dorel	Tokyo Institute of Technology	Japan
Akdeniz, Rafet	Namik Kemal University	Turkey
Aksamija, Zlatan	University of Illinois at Urbana-Champaign	USA
Aksoy, Mehmet S.	King Saud University	Saudi Arabia
Alafaireet, Patricia	University of Missouri	USA
Alexik, Mikulas	University of Zilina	Slovakia
Al-Hamouz, Sadeq	The World Islamic Sciences and Education University	Jordan
Al-Hamzah, Khawlah Hussein Ali	Basrah University	Iraq
Ali, Kamal	Jackson State University	USA

Aliguliyev, Ramiz	Institute of Information Technology, Azerbaijan National Academy of Sciences	Azerbaijan
Alkhatib, Ghazi	King Fahd University of Petroleum and Minerals	Saudi Arabia
Als, Adrian	University of the West Indies	Barbados
Alsmadi, Izzat	Yarmouk University	Jordan
Amornyotin, Somchai	Mahidol University	Thailand
Analide, Cesar	University of Minho	Portugal
Andina, Diego	Universidad Politécnica de Madrid	Spain
Andrade Ramos, Ana Luisa	University of Aveiro	Portugal
Arato, Peter	Budapest University of Technology and Economics	Hungary
Arinyo, Robert Joan	Polytechnic University of Catalonia	Spain
Ariton, Viorel	Danubius University	Romania
Aruga, Masahiro	Tokai University	Japan
Asadi, Saeid	University of Queensland	Australia
Asemi, Asefeh	Corvinus University of Budapest	Hungary
Asproni, Giovanni	European Bioinformatics Institute	UK
Aveledo, Marianella	Simon Bolivar University	Venezuela
Aydogan, Hasan	Selcuk University, Technology Faculty, Campus Selcuklu Konya	Turkey
Aziz, Soulhi	National School of Mineral Industry	Morocco
Bagheri, S.	Eindhoven University of Technology	Netherlands
Bagnoli, Franco	University of Florence	Italy
Bai, Zhengyao	Yunnan University	China
Bakar, Ab Rahim	University Putra Malaysia	Malaysia
Baker, John	Johns Hopkins University	USA
Bakmaz, Bojan	University of Belgrade	Serbia
Balas, Valentina	Aurel Vlaicu University of Arad	Romania
Balicki, Jerzy	Warsaw University of Technology	Poland
Banerji, Sanjay	Amrita Vishwa Vidyapeetham University	India
Bang, Jørgen	University of Aarhus	Denmark
Barb, Adrian	Penn State University	USA
Barba, Leiner	Popular University of Cesar	Colombia
Barsoum, Nader	Curtin University of Technology	Malaysia
Bäßler, Ralph	BAM Federal Institute for Materials	Germany
Batos, Vedran	University of Dubrovnik	Croatia
Baudin, Veronique	Laboratory for Analysis and Architecture of Systems	France
Becejski Vujaklija, Dragana	University of Belgrade	Serbia

Belahcen, Anouar	Aalto University School of Science and Technology	Finland
Bernabé, Gregorio	University of Murcia	Spain
Bernardi, Ansgar	German Research Center for Artificial Intelligence	Germany
Bernardino, Jorge	Institute of Engineering of Coimbra	Portugal
Bernick, Philip	Hathority, LLC	USA
Bettaz, Mohamed	Philadelphia University	Jordan
Bidarra, José	Aberta University	Portugal
Biernat, Krzysztof	Automotove Industry Institute	Poland
Bigan, Cristin	Ecological University of Bucharest	Romania
Bilbao, Javier	University of the Basque Country	Spain
Bist, Ankur Singh	Krishna Institute of Engineering and Technology, Ghaziabad	India
Blaha, Martin	University of Defence	Czech Republic
Boenke, Dietmar	Reutlingen University	Germany
Bojcetic, Nenad	University of Zagreb	Croatia
Bolboaca, Sorana Daniela	Iuliu Hatieganu University of Medicine and Pharmacy Cluj-Napoca	Romania
Borangiu, Theodor	Polytechnic University of Bucharest	Romania
Bordignon, Alex Laier	Pontifical Catholic University	Brazil
Botti-Salitsky, Rose	University of Massachusetts Dartmouth	USA
Bubnov, Alexey	Academy of Sciences of the Czech Republic	Czech Republic
Bucchiarone, Antonio	Institute of Information Science and Technologies	Italy
Buchalcevova, Alena	University of Economics, Prague	Czech Republic
Caldararu, Florin	Ecological University of Bucharest	Romania
Caldeira, Filipe	Polytechnic Institute of Viseu	Portugal
Camargo, Maria Emilia	University of Caxias do Sul	Brazil
Canbolat, Huseyin	Yildirim Beyazit University	Turkey
Cardoso, Eduardo	Monterrey Institute of Technology and Higher Education	Mexico
Carmo, Elisangela Gisele Do	Paulista State University	Brazil
Carmona, Samuel	Development and Medical Innovation Center	Spain
Carretero, Jesús	University Carlos III of Madrid	Spain
Challa, Radhakumari	Sri Sathya Sai Institute of Higher Learning	India
Chang, Chin-Chih	Chung Hua University	Taiwan
Chang, Weng-Long	National Kaohsiung University of Applied Sciences	Taiwan
Chang, Ya-Hui	National Taiwan Ocean University	Taiwan

Chaudhari, Narendra	Indian Institute of Technology Indore	India
Chen, Jingchao	DongHua University	China
Chen, Jyi-Ta	Southern Taiwan University	Taiwan
Chen, Lisa Y.	I-Shou University	Taiwan
Chen, Yil	Huafan University	Taiwan
Chen, Zhe	Northeastern University	China
Cherinka, R.	The MITRE Corporation	USA
Chiou, Richard	Drexel University	USA
Chorikavil Thomas, Jose	Central Plantation Crops Research Institute	India
Chou, Tsung-Yu	National Chin-Yi University of Technology	Taiwan
Chou, Tung-Hsiang	National Kaohsiung University of Science and Technology	Taiwan
Chuvakin, Anton	Gartner for Technical Professionals	USA
Cialdea, Donatella	University of Molise	Italy
Cirella, Jonathan	RTI International	USA
Comite, Ubaldo	University of Calabria	Italy
Corcuera, Pedro	University of Cantabria	Spain
Cortés Zaborras, Carmen	University of Malaga	Spain
Cunha, Idaulo J.	Intellectos	Brazil
D`Ulizia, Arianna	National Research Council	Italy
Da Rugna, Jerome	University Jean Monnet of Saint-Etienne	France
Dalla Vecchia, Alessandro	Federal University of Rio Grande do Sul	Brazil
Danjour, Miler Franco	Federal Institute of Education, Science and Technology of Rio Grande do Sul	Brazil
Dash, Sujata	North Orissa University	India
De Aquino, Andre L. L.	Federal University of Alagoas	Brazil
De la Puente, Fernando	University of Las Palmas de Gran Canaria	Spain
Deakins, Eric	University of Waikato	New Zealand
Desilva, Mauris	3D PARS (US) and 3D PARS Limited (UK)	USA
Dhamdhere, Vidya	G. H. Raisoni College of Engineering and Management	India
Dhingra, Arvind	Guru Nanak Dev Engineering College	India
Dizdaroglu, Bekir	Karadeniz Technical University	Turkey
Do Nascimento Morais, António J.	Open University	Portugal
Doherr, Detlev	University of Applied Sciences Offenburg	Germany
Doma, Salah	Alexandria University	Egypt
Donko, Dzenana	University of Sarajevo	Bosnia and Herzegovina
Druzovec, Marjan	University of Maribor	Slovenia

Duchen, Gonzalo	National Polytechnic Institute	Mexico
Dugarte Peña, Germán Lenin	Charles III University of Madrid	Spain
Dursun, Sukru	Selcuk University	Turkey
Dvornik, Josko	University of Split	Croatia
Ebadati, Omid Mahdi	Kharazmi University	Iran
El Oualkadi, Ahmed	Abdelmalek Essaadi University	Morocco
Elçi, Atilla	Aksaray University (Emeritus)	Turkey
Elías Hardy, Lidia Lauren	Higher Institute of Technologies and Applied Sciences	Cuba
El-Kashlan, Ahmed	Academy for Science and Technology	Egypt
Elmahboub, Widad M.	Hampton University	USA
Encabo, Eduardo	University of Murcia	Spain
Englmeier, Kurt	University of Applied Sciences Schmalkalden	Germany
Ercan, M. Fikret	Singapore Polytechnic	Singapore
Erins, Ingars	Riga Technical University	Latvia
Falkowski-Gilski, Przemyslaw	Gdansk University of Technology	Poland
Farhaoui, Yousef	Moulay Ismail University	Morocco
Farias, Patricia	Federal University of Pernambuco	Brazil
Félez, Jesús	Technical University of Madrid	Spain
Feng, Tao	Aramco Service Company	USA
Feraco, Antonio	Nanyang Technological University	Singapore
Fernandes, Márcia	Federal University of Uberlândia	Brazil
Fernandes, Paula Odete	Polytechnic Institute of Bragança	Portugal
Ferreira, Andrea	Federal University of Paraíba	Brazil
Figueroa de La Cruz, Mario M.	National Technological University	Argentina
Finkbine, Ronald	Indiana University Southeast	USA
Fiorini, Rodolfo A.	Polytechnic University of Milan	Italy
Fisser, Erwin	Soa Aids Nederland	Netherlands
Flammia, Madelyn	University of Central Florida	USA
Floyd, Raymond	Innovative Insights, Inc.	USA
Foglia, Pierfrancesco	University of Pisa	Italy
Fox, Richard	Northern Kentucky University	USA
Frejlichowski, Dariusz	West Pomeranian University of Technology	Poland
Fujdiak, Radek	Brno University of Technology	Czech Republic
Furst, Jacob D.	DePaul University	USA
Furukawa, Susumu	University of Yamanashi	Japan
Gandhewar, Nisarg	SB Jain Institute of Technology, Managment & Research	India

Garai, Gautam	Saha Institute of Nuclear Physics	India
García, Alberto Eloy	University of Cantabria	Spain
Garcia Bedoya, Olmer	State University of Campinas	Brazil
García Marco, Francisco J.	University of Zaragoza	Spain
García-Aracil, Adela	Polytechnic University of Valencia	Spain
García-Ramírez, José Miguel	University of Granada	Spain
Gedviliene, Genute	Vytautas Magnus University	Lithuania
Genser, Robert	Institute for Handling Devices and Robotics	Austria
George, Alan	Montana State University	USA
Ghayoumi, Mehdi	Kent State University	USA
Ghosh, Uttam	Vanderbilt University	USA
Giampapa, Joseph	Carnegie Mellon University	USA
Gini, Giuseppina	Polytechnic of Milan	Italy
Gnatyuk, Volodymyr	V.E. Lashkaryov Institute of Semiconductor Physics of the National Academy of Sciences of Ukraine	Ukraine
Gnudi, Adriana	University of Bergamo	Italy
Gobron, Stephane	Iwate University	Japan
Gouyon, David	University of Lorraine	France
Grouverman, Valentina	Research Triangle Institute	USA
Guedes de Souza, Sergio	Federal University of Rio de Janeiro	Brazil
Gueorguieva, Natacha	City University of New York	USA
Gui, M. W.	National Taipei University of Technology	Taiwan
Gulbahar, Yasemin	Ankara University	Turkey
Györödi, Cornelia	University of Oradea	Romania
Haddad, Hisham	Kennesaw State University	USA
Hajduk, Zbigniew	Rzeszow University of Technology	Poland
Ham, Chan	Kennesaw State University	USA
Hamie, Ali	University of Brighton	UK
Hanakawa, Noriko	Hannan University	Japan
Haruvy, Nava	Netanya Academic College	Israel
Hashimoto, Shigehiro	Kogakuin University	Japan
Hieber, Hartmann	International Consulting Bureaux	Germany
Hilkevics, Sergejs	Ventspils University of Applied Sciences	Latvia
Hishiyama, Reiko	Waseda University	Japan
Holmqvist, Mona	Kristianstad University College	Sweden
Hong, Sungbum	Jackson State University	USA
Hong, Tzung-Pei	National University of Kaohsiung	Taiwan
Hsu, Ching-Hsien	Chung Hua University	Taiwan

Huget, Marc-Philippe	University of Liverpool	UK
Hunek, Wojciech P.	Opole University of Technology	Poland
Ilunga, Masengo	University of South Africa	South Africa
Imbalzano, Giovanni	MPI	Italy
Inci, Ahmet Can	Bryant University	USA
Inkinen, Tommi	University of Helsinki	Finland
Intakosum, Sarun	King Mongkut's Institute of Technology Ladkrabang	Thailand
Ionescu, Adela	University of Craiova	Romania
Ishikawa, Hiroshi	Niigata University of International and Information Studies	Japan
Ivasic-Kos, Marina	University of Rijeka	Croatia
Izydorczyk, Jacek	Silesian University of Technology	Poland
Jacobson, Jon A.	University of Michigan	USA
Jakóbczak, Dariusz	Politechnika Koszalinska	Poland
Jalal, Laassiri	Ibn Tofail University	Morocco
Janota, Aleš	University of Žilina	Slovakia
Jaoua, Ali	University of Qatar	Qatar
Jara Guerrero, Salvador	University of Michoacan	Mexico
Jaramillo-Núñez, Alberto	National Institute of Astrophysics, Optics and Electronics	Mexico
Jastrzebska, Agnieszka	Warsaw University of Technology	Poland
Jenq, John	Montclair State University	USA
Joshi, Dheeraj	National Institute of Technology Kurukshetra	India
Julião, Rui Pedro	New University of Lisbon	Portugal
Kabassi, Katerina	Technological Education Institute of the Ionian Islands	Greece
Kachanova, Tamara L.	Saint-Petersburg State Electrotechnical University "LETI"	Russian Federation
Kalganova, Tatiana	Brunel University	UK
Kaneko, Itaru	Tokyo Polytechnic University	Japan
Kaneko, Yoshihiro	Gifu Univiersity	Japan
Kaur, Kiran	University of Malaya	Malaysia
Kawaguchi, Masashi	National Institute of Technology, Suzuka College	Japan
Kawarazaki, Noriyuki	Kanagawa Institute of Technology	Japan
Kemmerich, Thomas	University College Gjøvik	Norway
Kenk, Mourad A.	Computer Science Department, Faculty of Science, South Valley University	Egypt
Keswani, Bright	Gyan Vihar University	India

Khademi, Aria	Pennsylvania State University	USA
Khalifa, Abdul Jabbar	Al-Nahrain University	Iraq
Khudayarov, Bakhtiyar	Tashkent Institute of Irrigation and Agricultural Mechanization Engineers	Uzbekistan
Kim, Eung Sang	Korea Electrotechnology Research Institute	South Korea
Kim, Hyunju	Wheaton College	USA
Kinser, Jason	George Mason University	USA
Kiriazov, Petko	Bulgarian Academy of Sciences	Bulgaria
Knipp, Tammy	Florida Atlantic University	USA
Kohir, Vinayadatt V.	Indian Institute of Technology	India
Kopparapu, Sunil Kumar	Tata Consultancy Services Limited	India
Korsakiene, Renata	Vilnius Gediminas Technical University	Lithuania
Koul, Saroj	Acadia University	Canada
Kouroupetroglou, Georgios	University of Athens	Greece
Kozlovskis, Konstantins	Riga Technical University	Latvia
Kozma, Tamas	University of Debrecen	Hungary
Kreisler, Alain	University Paris 06	France
Kroumov, Valeri	Okayama University of Science	Japan
Krovvidy, Srinivas	Fannie Mae	USA
Kucuksille, Ecir	Suleyman Demirel University	Turkey
Kumar, Prashant	Shivaji University	India
Kumar, Shashi Kumar	Bangalore University	India
Kumar Pandey, Sumit	Jharkhand Rai University	India
Kurtulus, Kemal	Istanbul University	Turkey
Kushida, Takayuki	Tokyo University of Technology	Japan
Lai, Yeu-Pong	Chung Cheng Institute of Technology	Taiwan
Lakhoua, Mohamed Najeh	University of Carthage	Tunisia
Lasmanis, Aivars	University of Latvia	Latvia
Latawiec, Krzysztof J.	Opole University of Technology	Poland
Law, Rob	Hong Kong Polytechnic University	Hong Kong
Ledesma Orozco, Sergio E.	Guanajuato University	Mexico
Lee, Chang Won	Hanyang University	South Korea
Lee, DoHoon	Pusan National University	South Korea
Lee, Jong Kun	Changwon National University	South Korea
Lee, Kyung Oh	Sun Moon University	South Korea
Lee, Yih-Jiun	Chien Kuo Technology University	Taiwan
Lee, Yusin	National Cheng Kung University	Taiwan
Li, Weigang	University of Brasilia	Brazil
Lim, Hwee-San	Science University of Malaysia	Malaysia

Lin, Hong	University of Houston Downtown	USA
Lin, Shu-Chiung	Tatung University	Taiwan
Lipikorn, Rajalida	Chulalongkorn University	Thailand
Lipinski, Piotr	Technical University of Lodz	Poland
Loffredo, Donald	University of Houston-Victoria	USA
Lopes da Silva, Paulo A.	Military Engineering Institute	Brazil
López de Lacalle, Luis Norberto	University of the Basque Country	Spain
López Román, Leobardo	University of Sonora	Mexico
Lorenzo, Carla	National University of San Juan	Argentina
Lyridis, Dimitrios	National Technical University of Athens	Greece
Lyudmila, Mihaylova	Lancaster University	UK
Magnani, Lorenzo	University of Pavia	Italy
Mainguenaud, Michel	Institut National des Sciences Appliquées	France
Malollari, Ilirjan	University of Tirana	Albania
Mandal, Pratap Chandra	Indian Institute of Management, Shillong	India
Mao, Xiao-Bing	Wuhan University of Technology	China
Marappan, Raja	SASTRA University	India
Marcelino, Roderval	Federal University of Santa Catarina	Brazil
Marinova, Rossitza	Concordia University of Edmonton	Canada
Marlowe, Thomas J.	Seton Hall University	USA
Marra, Cirley Barbosa	Universidade Federal do Sul da Bahia	Brazil
Martínez Rebollar, Alicia	Polytechnic University of Valencia	Spain
Marx Gómez, Jorge	University Oldenburg	Germany
Masum, Salahuddin Mohammad	Daffodil International University	Bangladesh
Mateen, Ahmed	University of Agriculture Faisalabad	Pakistan
Matsuda, Michiko	Japanese Standards Association	Japan
Maymir-Ducharme, Fred A.	IBM US Federal	USA
McConnell, Rodney	University of Idaho	USA
McMahon, Ellen	National-Louis University, College of Management and Business, Retired	USA
Memon, Imran	Zhejiang University	China
Mendes Gomes, Luis	University of the Azores	Portugal
Merten, Pascaline	Free University of Brussels	Belgium
Metrolho, Jose	Polytechnic Institute of Castelo Branco	Portugal
Mihai, Dan	University of Craiova	Romania
Milcic, Diana	University of Zagreb Faculty of Graphic Arts	Croatia
Mishra, Deepak	Indian Institute of Space Science and Technology	India

Misurec, Jiri	Brno Univerzity of Technology	Czech Republic
Moin, Lubna	Pakistan Naval Engineering College	Pakistan
Monti, Marina	National Research Council	Italy
Morgan, Theresa	Wudang Research Association	USA
Morshed, Ahmed Hisham	Ain Shams University	Egypt
Mozar, Stefan	Electrical Testing Services Pty Ltd.	Australia
Mróz-Gorgoń, Barbara	Wroclaw University of Economics	Poland
Muñoz García, Ana Celina	Los Andes University	Venezuela
Mylonas, Phivos	Ionian University	Greece
Nag, Abhijit	The University of Memphis	USA
Nagaiah, Narasimha	University of Central Florida	USA
Nagarkar, Mahesh	SCSM College of Engineering	India
Nagy, Endre L.	Society of Instrument and Control Engineers	Japan
Navas Delgado, Ismael	University of Malaga	Spain
Nayyar, Anand	KCL Institute of Management and Technology	India
Neaga, Elena Irina	University of Wales Trinity st David	UK
Nemec, Juraj	Matej Bel University	Slovakia
Neumüller, Moritz	Vienna University of Economics and Business	Austria
Newsome, Mark	Hewlett-Packard Company	USA
Niculescu, Virginia	Babes-Bolyai University	Romania
Nievola, Julio Cesar	Pontifical Catholic University of Paraná	Brazil
Nikolarea, Ekaterini	University of the Aegean	Greece
Novikov, Oleg	Tomko	Russian Federation
Nugroho, Heru	Telkom University	Indonesia
Núñez, Jose Luis	Technical University of Madrid	Spain
Objelean, Nicolae	State University of Moldova	Moldova, Republic of
Occelli, Sylvie	Economic Social Research Institute of Piemonte	Italy
Odella, Francesca	University of Trento	Italy
Odetayo, Michael	Coventry University	UK
Odhiambo, Marcel O.	Vaal University of Technology	South Africa
Olson, Patrick C.	National University	USA
Ong, Sim-Heng	National University of Singapore	Singapore
Ortiz Sosa, Lourdes Maritza	Andres Bello Catholic University	Venezuela
O'Sullivan, Jill	Farmingdale State College	USA
Oszust, Mariusz	Rzeszow University of Technology	Poland
Ow, Hock	University Malaya	Malaysia

Paiva, Teresa	Guarda Polytechnic Institute	Portugal
Pal, Tandra	National Institute of Technology, Durgapur	India
Park, Se Hyun	Chung-Ang University	South Korea
Parrilla Roure, Luís	University of Granada	Spain
Patel, H	University of Bridgeport	USA
Patel, Kuntalkumar P.	S. V. Institute of Computer Studies	India
Paul, Stephane	Thales Research	France
Pereira, Elisabeth T.	University of Aveiro	Portugal
Pereira, Rafael	Federal University of Santa Maria	Brazil
Periyasamy, Pitchapillai	Sree Saraswathi Thyagaraja College	India
Perjési-Hámori, Ildikó	University of Pécs	Hungary
Petrillo, Antonella	University of Naples Parthenope	Italy
Phakamach, Phongsak	North Eastern University	Thailand
Pickl, Stefan	Bundeswehr University Munich	Germany
Pieterse, Vreda	University of Pretoria	South Africa
Pilvere, Irina	Latvia University of Agriculture	Latvia
Pingitore, Alessandro	Council National Research, Clinical Physiology Institute	Italy
Plakitsi, Katerina	University of Ioannina	Greece
Poh, Elsa	Eastern Michigan University	USA
Polenakovikj, Radmil	Ss. Cyril and Methodius University Business Start-up Centre	Macedonia
Poniszewska-Maranda, Aneta	Lodz University of Technology	Poland
Poobrasert, Onintra	National Electronics and Computer Technology Center	Thailand
Poveda, Geovanny	Technical University of Madrid	Spain
Prasad, P. M. K.	GVP College of Engineering for Women, Visakhapatnam	India
Prykarpatsky, Anatoliy K.	Ivan Franko State Pedagogical University	Ukraine
Pshehotskaya, Ekaterina	InfoWatch	Russian Federation
Qabazard, Adel M.	Kuwait Institute for Scientific Research	Kuwait
Quadro, Martín	National University of Córdoba	Argentina
Quan-Haase, Anabel	University of Western Ontario	Canada
Quist-Aphetsi, Kester	Ghana Telecom University College	Ghana
Rachev, Boris	Technical University of Varna	Bulgaria
Rahmes, Mark	Harris Corporation	USA
Rahouma, Kamel	Technical College in Riyadh	Egypt
Rashid, Kasim	Amman University	Canada

Reichwald, Julian	Cooperative State University Baden-Wurttemberg Mannheim	Germany
Reis, Arsénio	University of Trás-os-Montes e Alto Douro	Portugal
Reis, Rosa	Porto Superior Institute of Engineering	Portugal
Renes-Arellano, Paula	University of Cantabria	Spain
Reuter, Matthias	Clausthal University of Technology	Germany
Reyes-Méndez, Jorge J.	University of Toronto	Canada
Riihentaus, Juhani	Docent (retired), University of Eastern Finland	Finland
Ripon, Shamim	East West University	Bangladesh
Rivza, Peteris	Latvia University of Agriculture	Latvia
Rizki, Mateen	Wright State University	USA
Rizzo, Rosalba	University of Messina	Italy
Rodi, Anthony	California University of Pennsylvania	USA
Rodrigues, Nelson	Polytechnic Institute of Bragança	Portugal
Rodríguez Florido, Miguel Ángel	University of Las Palmas de Gran Canaria	Spain
Rodríguez-Piñero, Piedad Tolmos	Rey Juan Carlos University	Spain
Rojas, Arturo	National University of Engineering	Peru
Rolland, Colette	University of Paris 1 Pantheon-Sorbonne	France
Romansky, Radi	Technical University of Sofia	Bulgaria
Romero, Luis Felipe	University of Sonora	Mexico
Romli, Fairuz	Universiti Putra Malaysia	Malaysia
Ros, Frederic	Orleans University	France
Rößling, Guido	Darmstadt University of Technology	Germany
Rot, Artur	Wroclaw University of Economics	Poland
Rout, Deepak	National Institute of Technology Goa	India
Roveda, Loris	University of Applied Sciences and Arts of Southern Switzerland	Switzerland
Rowe, Neil	Naval Postgraduate School	USA
Ruiz Rey, Francisco J.	University of Malaga	Spain
Ruiz Zamarreño, Carlos	Public University of Navarra	Spain
Rutkowski, Jerzy	Silesian University of Technology	Poland
Ščeulovs, Deniss	Riga Technical University	Latvia
Sadri, Houman	University of Central Florida	USA
Salazar, Antonio	Simon Bolivar University	Venezuela
Saleh, Magda M.	Alexandria University	Egypt
Salim, Siham	National Research Center	Egypt
Samcovic, Andreja	University of Belgrade	Serbia

Sanna, Andrea	Polytechnic University of Turin	Italy
Santagati, Cettina	University of Catania	Italy
Santos, Jorge	Polytechnic Institute of Porto	Portugal
Sarma, Himangshu	University of Bremen	Germany
Sasakura, Mariko	Okayama University	Japan
Sastry G, Hanumat	University of Petroleum and Energy Studies	India
Selberherr, Siegfried	Technische Universität Wien	Austria
Selim, Haysam	University of Nevada Las Vegas	USA
Seme, David	University of Picardie Jules Verne	France
Sencu, Razvan	University of Manchester	UK
Serôdio, Carlos M. J.	University of Trás-os-Montes and Alto Douro	Portugal
Shang, Yilun	Tongji University	China
Shanker, Udai	Indian Institute of Technology Roorkee	India
Shieh, Chin-Shiuh	National Kaohsiung University of Applied Sciences	Taiwan
Shieh, Hsin-Jang	National Dong Hwa University	Taiwan
Shin, Jungpil	University of Aizu	Japan
Shing, Chen-Chi	Radford University	USA
Shiraishi, Masatake	Ibaraki University	Japan
Shojafar, Mohammad	University Sapienza of Rome	Italy
Siddique, Zahed	University of Oklahoma	USA
Silva, Geraldo	Estadual Paulista University	Brazil
Simion, Gabriela	University Politehnica of Bucharest	Romania
Singh, Vijander	Netaji Subhas University of Technology (Formerly NSIT)	India
Siriopoulos, Costas	Zayed University	United Arab Emirates
Sllame, Azeddien M.	University of Tripoli	Libya
Sokolov, Sergey	Keldysh Institute for Applied Mathematics	Russian Federation
Sornkaew, Thanakorn	Ramkhamheang University	Thailand
Sotirov, Sotir	University "Prof. Dr Asen Zlatarov"	Bulgaria
Sousa, António	Institute of Biomedical Engineering	Portugal
Spalek, Seweryn	Silesian University of Technology	Poland
Srotyr, Martin	Czech Technical University in Prague	Czech Republic
Stasytyte, Viktorija	Vilnius Gediminas Technical University	Lithuania
Steinbacher, Hans-Peter	University of Applied Science Kufstein	Austria
Štork, Milan	University of West Bohemia	Czech Republic
Stosic, Lazar	Institute of Management and Knowledge, External Associate Coordinator for Serbia, Skopje, Macedonia	Serbia
Straub, Jeremy	North Dakota State University	USA

Strugar, Ivan	University of Zagreb	Croatia
Suárez-Garaboa, Sonia Mª	University of A Coruña	Spain
Subba Reddy, N. V.	Manipal Institute of Technology	India
Subban, Ravi	Department of Computer Science, School of Engineering and Technology, Pondicherry University	India
Subramoniam, Suresh	College of Engineering	India
Sundaram, Aruna	A.M Jain College	India
Sureerattanan, Nidapan	Independent	Thailand
Sutherland, Trudy	Vaal University of Technology	South Africa
Suviniitty, Jaana	Aalto University School of Technology	Finland
Swart, William	East Carolina University	USA
Szabó, Csaba	Technical University of Kosice	Slovakia
Tadepalli, Gopal	Anna University	India
Tadisetty, Srinivasulu	Kakatiya University	India
Tam, Wing K.	Zodicom Technology Pty Limited	Australia
Tansel, Abdullah Uz	City University of New York	USA
Tao, C. W.	National Ilan University	Taiwan
Taraghi, Zohreh	Mazandaran University of Medical Scienses	Iran
Taylor, Stephen	Sussex University	UK
Teixeira Pinto, Leonel	Federal University of Santa Catarina	Brazil
Tenreiro Machado, J. A.	Institute of Engineering of Porto	Portugal
Thapliyal, Mathura	Hemvati Nandan Bahuguna Garhwal University	India
Thompson, Laura	Keiser University	USA
Thurasamy, Ramayah	Science University of Malaysia	Malaysia
Tiwari, Rahul	Medi-Caps University, Indore M.P.	India
Tomar, Ravi	University of Petroleum	India
Trifas, Monica	Jacksonville State University	USA
Truyol, Albert	Academy of Environment ENSMSE et ENSHG	France
Tsai, Chang-Lung	Chinese Culture University	Taiwan
Tsaur, Woei-Jiunn	Da-Yeh University	Taiwan
Tseng, Juin-Ling	Minghsin University of Science and Technology	Taiwan
Tsiligaridis, John	Heritage University	USA
Tu, Shu-Fen	Chinese Culture University	Taiwan
Ucal, Meltem	Kadir Has University	Turkey
Ulovec, Andreas	University of Vienna	Austria
Unalan, Halit Turgay	Anadolu University	Turkey

Vallejo, Marta	Heriot-Watt University	UK
Vallejo Gutiérrez, José Refugio	University of Guanajuato	Mexico
Varughese, Joe	Northern Alberta Institute of Technology	Canada
Vasilache, Simona	University of Tsukuba	Japan
Vázquez, Ernesto	Autonomous University of Nuevo Leon	Mexico
Vegh, Laura	Technical University of Cluj-Napoca	Romania
Velaga, Sreerama Murthy	GMR Institute of Technology	India
Venkateswarlu, Somu	KL University	India
Venu Gopal, S.	Vardhaman College of Engineering	India
Vimarlund, Vivian	Linköping University	Sweden
Vintere, Anna	Latvia University of Agriculture	Latvia
Vityaev, Evgenii E.	Sobolev Institute of Mathematics SB RAS	Russian Federation
Vizureanu, Petrica	"Gheorghe Asachi" Technical University of Iasi	Romania
Wada, Shigeo	Tokyo Denki University	Japan
Waghmare, Vishal	Department of Computer Science, Vivekanand College, Kolhapur	India
Wataya, Roberto Sussumu	Adventist University Center of Sao Paulo	Brazil
Wei, Wei	Zhejiang University	China
Wei, Xinzhou	New York City College of Technology	USA
Whatley, Janice	University of Salford	UK
Whitbrook, Amanda M.	University of Nottingham	UK
Wielki, Janusz	Opole University of Technology	Poland
Wolfengagen, Viacheslav	Institute for Contemporary Education JurInfoR-MSU	Russian Federation
Wu, Tung-Xiung (Sean)	Shih Hsin University	Taiwan
Wu, Wen-Yen	I-Shou University	Taiwan
Xochicale Rojas, Hugo A.	DeSiC - Desarrollo de Sistemas de Cómputo	Mexico
Yang, Fengfan	Nanjing University of Aeronautics and Astronautics	China
Yang, Hung Jen	National Kaohsiung Normal University	Taiwan
Ye, Xin	California State University San Marcos	USA
Yoon, Changwoo	Electronics and Telecommunications Research Institute	South Korea
Yussupova, Nafissa I.	Ufa State Aviation Technical University	Russian Federation
Zafar, Sherin	University Faridabad	India
Zargayouna, Mahdi	Inrets Institute and Paris-Dauphine University	France
Zaridis, Apostolos	University of the Aegean	Greece
Zaveri, Jigish	Morgan State University	USA

Zavialova, Tatiana V.	National Research Technical University	Russian Federation
Zdunek, Rafal	Wroclaw University of Technology	Poland
Zeheb, Ezra	Israel Institute of Technology	Israel
Zelinka, Tomas	Czech Technical University in Prague	Czech Republic
Zemliak, Alexander	Autonomous University of Puebla	Mexico
Zhang, Haiqiang	Beijing Jiaotong University	China
Zhang, Wei	AI Foundations, IBM Research	USA
Zhang, Xiaozheng Jane	California Polytechnic State University	USA
Zhang, Yanlong	Manchester Metropolitan University	UK
Zhong, Cheng	Guangxi University	China
Zoch, Stephen	Houston Community College	USA
Zogla, Irena	Professor Emeritus, the University of LatviaSenior researcher, Rezekne Academy of Technologies	Latvia

ADDITIONAL REVIEWERS FOR THE NON-BLIND REVIEWING

Abdulrahaman, Ribwar	Koya University	Iraq
Acosta, Patricia	Universidad de las Americas	Ecuador
Acosta Guzmán, Ivan Leonel	Universidad de Guayaquil	Ecuador
Adamopoulou, Evgenia	National Tecnhical University of Athens	Greece
Adekunle, Yinka	Babcock University	Nigeria
Aderhold, Daniel	Universidad Peruana de Ciencias Aplicadas	Peru
Ahn, Dohee	Chung-Ang University	South Korea
Akdeniz, Rafet	Namik Kemal University	Turkey
Al-Masri, Alaaeddin	An-Najah National University	Palestine
Alsaqqar, Awatif	Aurok University	Iraq
Alvarado, Luz Deicy	Universidad Distrital Francisco José de Caldas	Colombia
Armas, Jimmy	Universidad Peruana de Ciencias Aplicadas	Peru
Armoush, Ashraf	An-Najah National University	Palestine
Barbosa, Cátia	Federal University of Minas Gerais	Brazil
Barbosa, Cátia Rodrigues	Universidade Federal de Minas Gerais	Brazil
Bauer, Thomas A.	University of Vienna	Austria
Belardi, Aldo Artur	Centro Universitário FEI	Brazil
Benova, Eleonora	Comenius University	Slovakia
Berleant, Daniel	University of Arkansas at Litte Rock	USA
Bernardi, Ansgar	German Research Center for Artificial Intelligence	Germany
Bernardino, Jorge	Institute of Engineering of Coimbra	Portugal
Bezhani, Eda	University Aleksander Moisiu	Albania
Blackmore, Chris	The Open University	UK
Bönke, Dietmar	Reutlingen University	Germany
Buchelli Perales, Orivel Jackson	Universidad Nacional de Trujillo	Peru
Buonopane, Gerald	Seton Hall University	USA
Burcham, Joan	Arkansas State Univesity	USA

Bustos García De Castro, Pablo	Universidad de Extremadura	Spain
Cantu, José	Universidad Autonoma de Nuevo Leon	Mexico
Casagni, Michelle	MITRE	USA
Cashel-Cordo, Peter	University of Southern Indiana	USA
Castañeda, Pedro	Universidad Peruana de Ciencias Aplicadas	Peru
Castek, Jill	University of Arizona	USA
Chen, Jong-Chen	National Yunlin University of Science and Technology	Taiwan
Chen, Zhikui	Dalian University of Technology	China
Collar, Emilio	Western Connecticut State University	USA
Costa, Ivanir	Universidade Nove de Julho	Brazil
Crepeau, John	University of Idaho	USA
Cunha, Izabella	Federal University of Minas Gerais	Brazil
Darwish, Mahmoud	Navajo Technical University	USA
Dave, Leena	RTI International	USA
De Magalhães, Candida Alzira	Universidade Federal de Roraima	Brazil
Decker, Tim	University of Siegen	Germany
Demaidi, Mona	An-Najah National University	Palestine
Demstichas, Kostas	Institute of Communication and Computer Systems	Greece
Denicol, Alexandre	Intellectos	Brazil
Dhiman, Rohtash	Deenbandhu Chhotu Ram University of Science and Technology	India
Dhir, Vijay	Sant Baba Bhag Singh University	India
Do Nascimento Morais, António J.	Open University	Portugal
Drews Jr., Paulo	Universidade Federal do Rio Grande	Brazil
Drumm, Christian	FH Aachen University of Applied Sciences	Germany
Duque, Néstor	Universidad Nacional de Colombia	Colombia
Egesoy, Ahmet	Ege University	Turkey
Egoavil Ayala, Miguel Sebastian	Universidad Peruana Cayetano Heredia	Peru
El Breidi, Farid	University of Southern Indiana	USA
Espejo, Raul	Syncho Reserach Ltd.	UK
Fang, Wen-Chang	National Taipei University	Taiwan
Fazlagic, Jan	Poznan University of Economics and Business	Poland
Fertalj, Kreso	University of Zagreb	Croatia

Figueiredo, Josiel	Federal University of Mato Grosso	Brazil
Florescu, Gabriela	National Institute for Research and Development in Informatics	Romania
Franco, José Ricardo Queiroz	Universidade Federal de Minas Gerais	Brazil
Gardea, Carlos	National Autonomous University of Mexico	Mexico
Ghosh, Joydeep	Indian Institute of Technology Bombay	India
Gimenez, Edson	Instituto Nacional de Telecomunicações	Brazil
Gregus, Michal	Comenius University	Slovakia
Ham, Chan	Kennesaw State University	USA
Hilário, Ronderson	Federal University of Minas Gerais	Brazil
Hinojosa, Moises	Universidad Autonoma de Nuevo Leon	Mexico
Hjelseth, Eilif	Norwegian University of Technology	Norway
Hofmann, Sara	University of Bremen	Germany
Hong, Jinglan	Shandong University	China
Hong, Seongtae	Sangmyung University	South Korea
Hosain, Shazzad	North South University	Bangladesh
Ismail, Yasser	Southern University and A&M College	USA
Ison, Ray	The Open University	UK
Ivanovs, Andrejs	Riga Stradinsh University	Latvia
Jacobs, Gloria	University of Arizona	USA
Jenčová, Edina	Technical University of Košice	Slovakia
Jencova, Edina	Faculty of Aeronautics of the Technical University of Kosice	Slovakia
Jiang, Wuhua	HeFei University of Technology	China
Jilek, Miroslav	Czech Technical University in Prague	Czech Republic
Kali, Yassine	Ecole de Techologie Superieure	Canada
Kämper, Klaus-Peter	FH Aachen University of Applied Sciences	Germany
Katrib, Miguel	University of Havana	Cuba
Khan, Farhan	National University of Sciences and Technology	Pakistan
Krishna, Rama	National Institute of Technical Teachers Training and Research	India
Lastre Aleaga, Arlys Michel	Universidad Tecnológica Equinoccial	Ecuador
Lee, Chung-Wei	University of Illinois at Springfield	USA
Lee, Meng-huang	Shih Chien University	Taiwan
Li, Jie	Shanghai Maritime University	China
Li, Ruqiong	Shanghai Normal University	China
Lin, Wayne	TakMing University of Science and Technology	Taiwan

Lisitsyn, Pavel	St. Petersburg State University	Russian Federation
Lopez Garay, Hernan	Universidad de Ibagué	Colombia
Maciá, Francisco	Universidad de Alicante	Spain
Marrone, Dan	Farmingdale State College	USA
Mauricio, David	Universidad Nacional Mayor de San Marcos	Peru
Maxey, Christopher	University of Maryland	USA
Meeson, Reginald	Institute for Defense Analyses	USA
Meister, Darren	Ivey Business School	Canada
Melgarejo, Miguel	Universidad Distrital Francisco José de Caldas	Canada
Miklos, Jorge	Paulista University	Brazil
Modlic, Borivoj	University of Zagreb	Croatia
Molina Beltran, Ferney Alberto	Universidad Nacional	Colombia
Mujumdar, Sudesh	University of Southern Indiana	USA
Müller, Karl H.	Steinbeis Transfer Center New Cybernetics in Vienna	Austria
Murzaku, Ines	Seton Hall University	USA
Myers, Margaret	Institute for Defense Analyses	USA
Nag, Abhijit	The University of Memphis	USA
Nedjalkov, Mihail	Bulgarian Academy of Sciences	Bulgaria
Nunes, Daniel	Instituto Nacional de Telecomunicações	Brazil
Ogbonna, Chibueze	Babcock University	Nigeria
Okada, Hiraku	Nagoya University	Japan
Oliveira, Allan	Federal University of Mato Grosso	Brazil
Oliveros, Jacobo	Benemérita Universidad Autónoma de Puebla	Mexico
Ott, Elfriede	Ostfalia University of Applied Sciences	Germany
Pawlak, Mirosław	Adam Mickiewicz University	Poland
Perez Vielma, Maira	National Autonomous University of Mexico	Mexico
Perlis, Donald	University of Maryland	USA
Peter, Timm-Julian	University of Siegen	Germany
Pettenpohl, Heinrich	Fraunhofer ISST	Germany
Porto, Marcelo Franco	Universidade Federal de Minas Gerais	Brazil
Prasad, P. M. K.	GVP College of Engineering for Women, Visakhapatnam	India
Qamhieh, Manar	An-Najah National University	Palestine
Qian, Yu	Cortexica Company	UK
Rahman, Rummana	North South University	Bangladesh
Rana, Faisal	American university of Dubai	United Arab Emirates
Ravi, Kishore Kumar	Indian Institute of Technology Kharagpur	India

Reis, Arsénio	University of Trás-os-Montes e Alto Douro	Portugal
Resende Faria, Diego	Aston University	Spain
Richards, Matthew	The Boeing Company	USA
Rico-Ramirez, Miguel Angel	University of Bristol	UK
Rioga, Danielle	Federal University of Minas Gerais	Brazil
Roushdy, Mohamed	Ain Shams University	Egypt
Rozevskis, Uldis	University of Latvia	Latvia
Ruiz-Pinales, José	University of Guanajuato	Mexico
Rus Mansilla, Francisco	University of Málaga	South Sandwich Islands
Saad, Maarouf	Ecole de Techologie Superieure	Canada
Sahd, Lize-Marie	Stellenbosch University	South Africa
Saini, Himanshi	Deenbandhu Chhotu Ram University of Science and Technology	India
Saini, Manish	Deenbandhu Chhotu Ram University of Science and Technology	India
Salem, Sameh A.	National Telecom Regulatory Authority	Egypt
Samiah, Abdul	National University of Sciences and Technology	Pakistan
Sánchez, Francisco Javier	Universidad Autónoma Metropolitana Iztapalapa	Mexico
Sánchez Suárez, Elio Edwin	Universidad de Guayaquil	Ecuador
Sayed, Samir	National Telecom Regulatory Authority	Egypt
Serkovic, Laura	Universidad Nacional Autónoma de México	Mexico
Sexton, Natasha	Stellenbosch University	South Africa
Shahini-Hoxhaj, Remzie	Universiteti i Prishtines	Kosovo
Silva Balarezo, Mariana	Universidad Catolica de Trujillo	Peru
Singh, Amardeep	Punjabi University	India
Singh, Karan	Jawaharlal Nehru University	India
Singh, Sudhansu Sekhar	KIIT University	India
Smoot, Chris	Institute for Adanced Studies on Climate Change	USA
Sobrado, Eddie	Pontificia Universidad Católica del Perú	Peru
Stöcker, Pamela	FH Aachen University of Applied Sciences	Germany
Subedi, Kul	University of Memphis	USA
Tarhan, Ayça	Hacettepe University	Turkey
Tartaraj, Azeta	University Aleksander Moisiu	Albania
Tommasino, Pasquale	Sapienza University	Italy
Trifiletti, Alessandro	Sapienza University of Rome	Italy
Tripathi, Kumud	Indian Institute of Technology Kharagpur	India

Tsiligaridis, John	Heritage University	USA
Valdivia, César	Pontificia Universidad Católica del Perú	Peru
Velandia, Hernando	Universidad de Pamplona	Colombia
Verzilin, Dmitrii	Lesgaft State University of Sport and Health	Russian Federation
Villarreal Valerio, Julian Anibal	Universidad Nacional Mayor de San Marcos	Peru
Viskup, Pavel	Tomas Bata University	Czech Republic
Walker, Daniel	Tsunami Memorial Institute	USA
Wang, Jun-Ren	National Taiwan Sport University	Taiwan
Weber, Lyle	The King's University	USA
Wei, Xinzhou	New York City College of Technology	USA
Wesley, Joan	Jackson State University	USA
Woodcock, Timothy	Texas A and M University	USA
Xia, Guang	HeFei University of Technology	China
Yoon, Changwoo	Electronics and Telecommunications Research Institute	South Korea
Yoon, Seokhyun	Dankook University	South Korea
Yu, Jaehoon	Osaka University	Japan
Zavala-Rio, Daniel	Instituto Tecnológico y de Estudios Superiores de Monterrey	Mexico
Žibala, Dace	Rīga Stradiņš University	Latvia
Ziegler, Christian	Karlsruhe Institute of Technology	Germany

HONORARY PRESIDENTS OF PAST CONFERENCES
Bela Banathy
Stafford Beer
George Klir
Karl Pribram
Paul A. Jensen
Gheorghe Benga

HONORARY CHAIR
William Lesso
(1931-2015)

PROGRAM COMMITTEE CHAIRS
Michael Savoie
C. Dale Zinn

GENERAL CHAIR
Nagib Callaos

ORGANIZING COMMITTEE CHAIRS
Belkis Sánchez
Andrés Tremante

**CONFERENCES PROGRAM MANAGER /
PROCEEDINGS PRODUCTION CHAIR**
María Sánchez

OPERATIONAL ASSISTANTS
Jaime Noguera
Kilian Méndez

Special Track on Design and Modeling in Science, Education, and Technology: DeMset 2019
In the context of
The 23rd World Multi-Conference on Systemics, Cybernetics and Informatics: WMSCI 2019

GENERAL CHAIRS
Nagib Callaos
Hsing-Wei Chu

ORGANIZING COMMITTEE CHAIRS
Andrés Tremante
Belkis Sánchez

PROGRAM COMMITEE

Mohammad Siddique (USA)
C. Dale Zinn (USA)

Aldrette-Malacara, Alejandra	Popular Autonomous University of the State of Puebla	Mexico
Hendel, Russell J.	Towson University	USA
Ilunga, Masengo	University of South Africa	South Africa
Lau, Newman	Hong Kong Polytechnic University	Hong Kong
Martínez-Flores, José L.	Popular Autonomous University of the State of Puebla	Mexico
Mccann, Roy A.	University of Arkansas	USA
Oanta, Emil	Constanta Maritime University	Romania
Ophir, Dan	Afeka Tel Aviv Academic College of Engineering	Israel
Paiano, Roberto	University of Salento	Italy
Reetz, Edgar	Ilmenau University of Technology	Germany
Srivastava, Smriti	Netaji Subhas Institute of Technology	India
Vrána, Stanislav	Czech Technical University in Prague	Czech Republic
Wang, Chuan-Ju	National Taiwan University	Taiwan
Zaretsky, Esther	Givat Washington Academic College of Education	Israel

ADDITIONAL REVIEWERS

Ahmed, Shamsuddin	Islamic University of Madinah	Saudi Arabia
Aruga, Masahiro	Tokai University	Japan
Chen, Duanbing	University of Electronic Science and Technology of China	China
Chen, Hsiao-Ping	Grand Valley State University	USA
Deliyska, Boryana	University of Forestry, professor-retired	Bulgaria
Dvornik, Josko	University of Split	Croatia
Gini, Giuseppina	Politecnico di Milano	Italy
Ham, Chan	Southern Polytechnic State University	USA
Jawahar, P. K.	B.S.Abdur Rahman Crescent Institute of Science and Technology	India
Jenq, John	Montclair State University	USA
Lee, Chang Won	Hanyang University	South Korea

Leighty, Brian	Knowledge Sciences Inc.	USA
Lin, Kuei-Chih	Department of Electronic Engineering- Ming Chuan University	Taiwan
Mullins, Michael	Aalborg University	Denmark
Nour, Walaa	Tanta University	Egypt
Oh, SooCheol	Electronics and Telecommunications Research Institute	South Korea
Oya, Hidetoshi	Shonan Institute of Technology	Japan
Rodríguez Lozano, Gloria I.	National University of Colombia	Colombia
Santos, Joaquín	Simon Bolivar University	Venezuela
Sarfraz, Muhammad	Kuwait University	Kuwait
Savva, Andreas	University of Nicosia	Cyprus
Shankaranarayanan, Avinash	Royal Melbourne Institute of Technology Global	Australia
Silva, Paulo	Military Institute of Engineering	Brazil
Strefezza, Miguel	Simon Bolivar University	Venezuela
Sulema, Yevgeniya	National Technical University of Ukraine Kiev Polytechnic Institute	Ukraine
Vizureanu, Petrica	Technical University Iasi	Romania
Wu, Yufei	University of Trinidad and Tobago	Trinidad and Tobago
Yu, Yuanbin	JiLin University	China
Zaveri, Jigish	Morgan State University	USA
Zhang, Boquan	Guangdong University of Technology	China

ADDITIONAL REVIEWERS FOR NON-BLIND REVIEWING

Alsadoon, Abeer	Charles Sturt University Study Centres	Australia
Caraballo, Joshua	Latinos Salud	USA
Gallas, Mohamed-Anis	University of Mons	Belgium
Grodzki, Erika	Lynn University	USA
Liotta, Salvator-John	Université Libre de Bruxelles	Belgium
Nokovic, Bojan	Royal Bank of Canada	Canada
Prasad, Chandana	Charles Sturt University Study Centres	Australia

Special Track on Knowledge and Cognitive Science and Technologies: KCST 2019
In the context of
The 23rd World Multi-Conference on Systemics, Cybernetics and Informatics: WMSCI 2019

KCST 2019

GENERAL CHAIR
Nagib Callaos

ORGANIZING COMMITTEE CHAIRS
Belkis Sánchez
Andrés Tremante

PROGRAM COMMITEE

Abd El-Aziem, Mostafa	Arab Academy for Science and Technology	Egypt
Abe, Jair Minoro	Paulista University	Brazil
Adascalitei, Adrian	"Gheorghe Asachi" Technical University of Iasi	Romania
Bönke, Dietmar	Reutlingen University	Germany
Bubnov, Alexej	Academy of Sciences and the Czech Republic	Czech Republic
Florescu, Gabriela C.	National Institute for R&D in Informatics	Romania
Haba, Cristian-Gyozo	"Gheorghe Asachi" Technical University of Iasi	Romania
Jingchao, Chen	Donghua University	China
Kaczorek, Jerzy	Gdansk University of Technology	Poland
Kim, Kyungdeok	Uiduk University	South Korea
Koleva, Maria	Bulgarian Academy of Sciences	Bulgaria
López Román, Leobardo	University of Sonora	Mexico
Marlowe, Thomas	Seton Hall University	USA
Mostafaeipour, Ali	Yazd University	Iran
Obwegeser, Nikolaus	Vienna University of Economics and Business Administration	Austria
Ophir, Dan	Ariel University Center of Samaria	Israel
Pereira, Elisabeth	University of Aveiro	Portugal
Poobrasert, Onintra	National Electronics and Computer Technology Center	Thailand
Sulema, Yevgeniya	National Technical University of Ukraine	Ukraine
Sun, Baolin	Wuhan University	China
Wiszniewski, Bogdan	Gdansk University of Technology	Poland
Zaretsky, Esther	Hebrew University	Israel

ADDITIONAL REVIEWERS

Abd El-Aziem, Mostafa	Arab Academy for Science and Technology	Egypt
Ahmad, Siti Zulaiha	Universiti Teknologi MARA - Perlis Branch	Malaysia

Al-Radhi, Mohammed Salah	Budapest University of Technology and Economics	Hungary
Angeli, Chrissanthi	University of West Attica	Greece
Areitio, Gloria	University of The Basque Country	Spain
Ashoor, Asmaa Shaker	University of Babylon	Iraq
Bazzi, Ahmad	CEVA-DSP	France
Bhuvaneswaran, R. S.	Anna University	India
Carmo, Elisangela Gisele	Paulista State University	Brazil
Challita, Khalil	Notre Dame University - Louaize	Lebanon
Chen, Hsi-jen	National Cheng Kung University	Taiwan
Cozza, Vittoria	University of Padua	Italy
Das, Srijan	Institut National de Recherche en Informatique et en Automatique - Inria	France
Daunys, Gintautas	Siauliai University	Lithuania
Deliyska, Boryana	Technical University, Sofia	Bulgaria
Dhaliwal, Balwinder S	Guru Nanak Dev Engineering College	India
Fattahi, Jaouhar	Laval University	Canada
Fislake, Martin	University of Koblenz	Germany
Freitas, Maria	Federal University of Paraná	Brazil
Gandhi, Niketa	Machine Intelligence Research Labs	USA
Garnace, Reynaldo	Philippine Science High School Eastern Visayas Campus	Philippines
Janev, Valentina	The Mihajlo Pupin Institute	Serbia
Kanishcheva, Olga	National Technical University	Ukraine
Kostalova, Alena	Tomas Bata University in Zlin	Czech Republic
Kumar, Shashi Kumar. R.	Bangalore University	India
Lagasio, Valentina	Sapienza University	Italy
Lebre, Marie-Ange	Institut Pascal	France
Malikov, Andrey	North Caucasus Federal University	Russian Federation
Margelevicius, Mindaugas	Vilnius University	Lithuania
Orduña-Cabrera, Fernando	International Institute for Applied Systems Analysis (IIASA)	Austria
P Shenoy, Revathi	Manipal Academy of Higher Education	India
Rao, Ashwini	Mukesh Patel School of Technology Management and Engineering	India
Rocha, Alan	National Institute of Technical Teachers´ Training and Research	India
Romão, Luiz	University of the Region of Joinville	Brazil
Ruiz-Ojeda, Nicolas Enrique	Universidad Simón Bolívar	Venezuela
S, Haseena	Mepco Schlenk Engineering College	India
Sarv, Ene-Silvia	Tallinn University, freelance	Estonia
Saylan Kırmızıgül, Aslı	Erciyes University	Turkey
Senerchia, Rory	Johnson & Wales University	USA
Senette, Caterina	Italian National Research Council	Italy
Sengupta, Dipanjan	Intel Labs	USA
Sharma, Durga	MAISM under RTU India and AMIT, AMU MOEFDRE	India

Sidhom, Sahbi	University of Lorraine	France
Silva, Marcelo	Brazilian Federal Police	Brazil
Tintin, Romel	Institute of National Advanced Studies. The State Graduate University	Ecuador
Tropmann-frick, Marina	Hamburg University of Applied Sciences	Germany
Tuama, Amel	Northern Technical University	Iraq
Uddin, Ikram	University of Haripur	Pakistan
Vasiu, Radu	Polytechnic University of Timişoara	Romania
Wang, Juan	Delta Micro technology Inc	USA
Wataya, Roberto Sussumu	Adventist University Center of Sao Paulo	Brazil
Wu, Huaming	Tianjin University	China
Xochicale, Hugo Alberto	DeSiC - Desarrollo de Sistemas de Cómputo	Mexico
Xu, Haotian	Wayne State University	USA
Yang, Shanhu	University of Cincinnati	USA
Yao, Kunpeng	Ecole Polytechnique Fédérale de Lausanne	Switzerland
Zhao, Xuejiao	Nanyang Technological University	Singapore

ADDITIONAL REVIEWERS FOR NON-BLIND REVIEWING

Anciaux, Didier	Université de Lorraine	France
Barragan-Ocaña, Alejandro	Instituto Politecnico Nacional	Mexico
Caputo, Francesco	University of Campania Luigi Vanvitelli	Italy
Cherubino, Patrizia	BrainSigns srl	Italy
Choras, Michal	University of Technology and Environment	Poland
Di Lucchio, Loredana	Sapienza Università di Roma	Italy
Ghasemi, Hadi	University of Houston	USA
Guzman Cabrera, Rafael	Universidad de Guanajuato	Mexico
Heil, Dominik	Cranfield University	South Africa
Kurkowski, Miroslaw	Cardinal Stefan Wyszyński University in Warsaw	Poland
Lamanna, Giuseppe	University of Campania	Italy
Monteiro, Roberto	Cimatec	Brazil
Mukherjee, Dipti Prasad	Indian Statistical Institute	India
Persad, Aaron	Massachusetts Institute of Technology	USA
Santos, Alex Álisson Bandeira	Cimatec	Brazil
Shariatipour, Seyed	Coventry University	UK
Thomas, Llewelyn	LaSalle Ramon Llull University	Spain

Number of Papers Included in these Proceedings per Country

(The country of the first author was the one taken into account for these statistics)

Country	# Papers	%
TOTAL	88	100.00
United States	13	14.77
Peru	9	10.23
Germany	8	9.09
Japan	8	9.09
Latvia	8	9.09
Brazil	5	5.68
Mexico	5	5.68
Ecuador	3	3.41
Egypt	3	3.41
Taiwan	3	3.41
Austria	2	2.27
Canada	2	2.27
Poland	2	2.27
Belgium	1	1.14
China	1	1.14
Colombia	1	1.14
Costa Rica	1	1.14
Croatia	1	1.14
Czech Republic	1	1.14
Iraq	1	1.14
Italy	1	1.14
Norway	1	1.14
Pakistan	1	1.14
Paraguay	1	1.14
Russian Federation	1	1.14
Saudi Arabia	1	1.14
South Africa	1	1.14
South Korea	1	1.14
Spain	1	1.14
United Arab Emirates	1	1.14

Foreword

Our purpose in the 23rd World Multi-Conference on Systemics, Cybernetics and Informatics (WMSCI 2019) is to provide, in these increasingly related areas, a ***multi-disciplinary forum, to foster interdisciplinary communication*** among the participants, and to support the sharing process of diverse perspectives of the same trans-disciplinary concepts and principles.

Systemics, Cybernetics and Informatics (SCI) are increasingly being related to each other in almost every scientific discipline and human activity. Their common trans-disciplinarity characterizes and communicates them, generating strong relations among them and with other disciplines. They work together to create a whole new way of thinking and practice. This phenomenon persuaded the Organizing Committee to structure WMSCI 2019 as a multi-conference where participants may focus on one area, or on one discipline, while allowing them the possibility of attending conferences from other areas or disciplines. This systemic approach stimulates cross-fertilization among different disciplines, inspiring scholars, originating new hypothesis, supporting production of innovations and generating analogies; which is, after all, one of the very basic principles of the systems' movement and a fundamental aim in cybernetics.

WMSCI 2019 was organized and sponsored by the International Institute of Informatics and Systemics (IIIS, www.iiis.org), member of the International Federation of Systems Research (IFSR). The IIIS is a ***multi-disciplinary organization for inter-disciplinary communication and integration***, which includes about 5,000 members. Consequently, a main purpose of the IIIS is to foster knowledge integration processes, interdisciplinary communication, and integration of academic activities. Based on 1) the transdisciplinarity of the systemic approach, along with its essential characteristic of emphasizing *relationships* and *integrating* processes, and 2) the multi-disciplinary support of cybernetics' and informatics' concepts, notions, theories, technologies, and tools, the IIIS has been organizing multi-disciplinary conferences as a platform for fostering inter-disciplinary communication and knowledge integration processes.

Multi-disciplinary conferences are organized by the IIIS as support for ***both intra-*** and ***inter-disciplinary*** communication. Processes of intra-disciplinary communication are mainly achieved via traditional paper presentations in corresponding disciplines, while conversational sessions, regarding trans- and inter-disciplinary topics, are among the means used for inter-disciplinary communication. Intra- and inter-disciplinary communications might generate *co-regulative cybernetic loops*, via negative feedback, and *synergic* relationships, via positive feedback loops, in which both kinds of communications could increase their respective effectiveness. Figure 1 shows at least two cybernetic loops if intra- and inter-disciplinary are adequately related. A necessary condition for the effectiveness of Inter-disciplinary communication is an adequate level of **variety** regarding the participating disciplines. *Analogical thinking and learning processes* of disciplinarians depend on it; which in turn are potential sources of the creative tension required for cross-fertilization among disciplines and the generations of new hypotheses. An extended presentation regarding this issue can be found at www.iiis.org/MainPurpose.

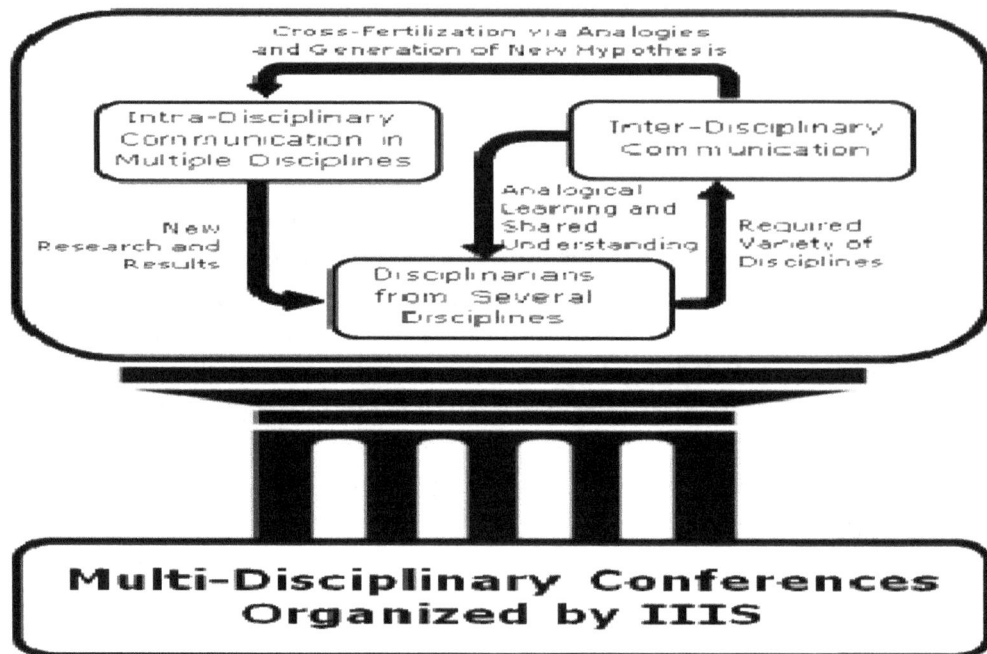

Figure 1

In the specific case of Systemics, Cybernetics and Informatics (SCI), the IIIS is an organization dedicated to contribute to the development of the Systems Approach, Cybernetics, and Informatics potential, using both: knowledge and experience, thinking and action, theory and practice, for:

a) The identification of synergistic relationships among Systemics, Cybernetics and Informatics, and between them and society.
b) The promotion of contacts among the different academic areas, through the transdisciplinarity of the systems approach.
c) The identification and implementation of communication channels among the different professions.
d) The supply of communication links between the academic and professional worlds, as well as between them and the business world, both public and private, political and cultural.
e) The stimulus for the creation of integrative arrangements at different levels of society, as well as at the family and personal levels.
f) The promotion of trans-disciplinary research, both on theoretical issues and on applications to concrete problems.

These IIIS objectives have oriented the organizational efforts of yearly WMSCI/ISAS/IMSCI/CISCI conferences since 1995.

On behalf of the Organizing Committee, I extend our heartfelt thanks to:

1. The 456 members of the different Program Committees, from 56 countries (including the PC members of the events organized in its context and jointly with WMSCI 2019). Almost all the members of the Program Committee are ***authors or co-authors sessions' best papers in previous conferences***, i.e. papers selected by the respective audience as the best paper of the session in which they were presented.
2. The 748 additional reviewers, from 83 countries, for their ***double-blind peer reviews***; and
3. The 232 reviewers, from 46 countries, for their efforts in making the ***non-blind peer reviews***. (Some reviewers supported both: non-blind and double-blind reviewing for different submissions).

The names and affiliation of both kinds of reviewers are listed in these proceedings. We extend our gratefulness to all of them. The scholarly quality of the authors and the reviewers is what define the quality of the conference and its respective proceedings. Consequently, our gratitude is to the members of the programs' committees, both kinds of reviewers and the collaborating authors.

A total of 1537 reviews made by 980 reviewers, from 86 counties, (who made at least one review) contributed to the quality achieved in WMSCI 2019. This means an average of 8.49 reviews per submission (181 submissions were received). ***Each registered author had access, via the conference web site, to the reviews that recommended the acceptance of their respective submissions***. Each registered author could also get information about: 1) the average of the reviewers' evaluations according to 8 criteria, and the average of a global evaluation of his/her submission; and 2) the comments and the constructive feedback made by the reviewers, who recommended the acceptance of his/her submission, so the author would be able to improve the final version of the paper.

In the organizational process of WMSCI 2019, about 181 articles were submitted. These pre-conference proceedings include about 88 papers that were accepted for presentation from 30 countries (41 countries taking into account the presentations in collocated events). I extend our thanks to the invited sessions' organizers for collecting, reviewing, and selecting the papers that will be presented in their respective sessions. The submissions were reviewed as carefully as time permitted; it is expected that most of them will appear in a more polished and complete form in scientific journals. This information about WMSCI 2019 is summarized in the following table, along with the other collocated events:

Conference	# of submissions received	# of reviewers that made at least one review	# of reviews made	Average of reviews per reviewer	Average of reviews per submission	# of papers included in the proceedings	% of submissions included in the proceedings
WMSCI 2019	181	980	1537	1.57	8.49	88	48.62%
IMSCI 2019	88	439	974	2.22	11.07	41	46.59%
WMSCI & IMSCI	269	1419	2511	1.77	9.33	129	47.96%
CISCI 2019	118	572	1205	2.11	10.21	65	55.08%
TOTAL	387	1991	3716	1.87	9.60	194	50.13%

All submissions were peer reviewed by the two-tier reviewing methodology of the International Institute of Informatics and Systemics (IIIS, www.iiis.org). As it might be noticed, from the table above, *9.6 reviews were made, in average, for each submission we received.* After the conference is over, the names of the reviewers will be published on the IIIS web site along with the titles of the papers each reviewer reviewed. This means that what had been a double-blind review, up to the conference, is transformed to single-blind review, after the conference is over. In this way, each author would have information about the names of the reviewers of his/her submission, but not vice-versa. Likewise, each author would know how many reviewers reviewed his/her submission and relate it to the average, being informed in the above table, of 9.6 reviews per paper.

Our two-tier reviewing methodology meet two different objectives of peer-review: 1) to improve the paper via non-anonymous reviewers (non-blind reviews) and 2) to improve the acceptance/non-acceptance decision of the Organizing Committee via traditional anonymous reviewers (double-blind reviews) A recommendation to accept, made by non-anonymous reviews, is a *necessary* condition, but it is *not a sufficient* one. A submission, to be accepted, should also have a majority of its double-blind reviewers recommending its acceptance. These two necessary conditions generate a more reliable and rigorous reviewing than any of those reviewing methods, based on just one of the indicated methods, or just on the traditional double-blind reviewing.

We extend our gratitude to the invited sessions' organizers: Dr. Shigehiro Hashimoto and Dr. Natalja Lace; as well as to the special track co-chairs and the co-editors of these proceedings, for the hard work, energy and eagerness they displayed preparing their respective sessions. We express our intense gratitude to Professor William Lesso (1931-2015) for his wise and timely, adequate and valuable tutoring, for his eternal energy, integrity, and continuous support and advice, as the Program Committee Chair of past conferences (since 1981), as well as for being a very caring old friend and intellectual father to many of us. We also extend our gratitude to Professor Belkis Sánchez, who brilliantly managed the organizing process.

Our gratitude to Professors Bela H. Banathy, Stafford Beer, George Klir, Karl Pribram, Paul A. Jensen, and Gheorghe Benga who dignified our past WMSCI conferences by being their Honorary Presidents. We also extend our gratitude to the following scholars, researchers, and professionals who accepted to deliver plenary workshops and/or to address the audience of the General Joint Plenary Sessions with keynote addresses.

We would like also to extend our gratefulness to Professor Shigehiro Hashimoto for his yearly support in the last 20 years as well as for his editorial work for the journal; as well as to Professor Grandon Gill, Dr. Jeremy Horne, Professor Thomas Marlowe and Professor Matthew E. Edwards for their continuous advice and support in the conferences they participated in, along the last 12 years; as well as in the conferences they were not able to participate in. Their advices and the kind of care they provided us with are highly valued and appreciated.

We also extend our gratitude to the following scholars, researchers, and professionals who accepted to deliver plenary workshops and/or to address the audience of the General Joint Plenary Sessions with keynote addresses.

Workshops and Conversational Sessions

Professor Thomas Marlowe, Seton Hall University, USA, Department of Mathematics and Computer Science, Program Advisor for Computer Science, Doctor in Computer Science and, Doctor in Mathematics.

Professor Stuart A. Umpleby, The George Washington University, USA, President of the Executive Committee of the International Academy for Systems and Cybernetics Sciences, Former President of The American Society of Cybernetics.

Professor Matthew E. Edwards, Alabama A&M University. USA, Professor of Physics and, Former Dean, School of Arts and Sciences, Director of IHSEAR: Institute of Higher Science Education Advancement, and Research.

Professor Tatiana Medvedeva, Siberian State University of Transport. Russia, Department of World Economy and Law Former Head of the Scientific and Practical Center for Business and Management.

Dr. Bruce E. Peoples, Innovations LLC, USA, Founder and CEO, Formerly at Université Paris 8, France, Laboratoire Paragraphe, Chair Emeritus of an ISO/IEC Standards Committee, Generated over 50 Invention Disclosures, 15 Patent Applications and 11 Patent Awards.

Professor William Swart, East Carolina University, USA, FMR. Dean of Engineering and Technology at New Jersey Institute of Technology, Provost and Vice President for Academic Affairs at East Carolina University, Researcher and Consultant at NASA's Space Shuttle.

Professor Richard Self, University of Derby, UK, The School of Computing and Mathematics, Senior Lecturer in Analytics and Governance.

Plenary Keynote Speakers

Professor Thomas Marlowe, Seton Hall University, USA, Department of Mathematics and Computer Science, Program Advisor for Computer Science, Doctor in Computer Science and, Doctor in Mathematics.

Professor Shigehiro Hashimoto, Kogakuin University, Japan, Councilor and Dean, Faculty of Engineering, Former Associate to the University President. Doctor of Engineering and Doctor of Medicine. Biomedical Engineering.

Professor Matthew E. Edwards, Alabama A&M University, USA. Professor of Physics and Former Dean of the School of Arts and Sciences. Director of IHSEAR: Institute of Higher Science Education, Advancement and Research.

Dr. Paul Page, Queen's University Belfast, UK, School of Electronics, Electrical Engineering & Computer Science, High Performance and Distributed Computing, Lecturer (Education) – Society & Community.

Professor Stuart A. Umpleby, The George Washington University, USA, President of the Executive Committee of the International Academy for Systems and Cybernetics Sciences, Former President of The American Society of Cybernetics.

Professor Tatiana Medvedeva, Siberian State University of Transport. Russia, Department of World Economy and Law Former Head of the Scientific and Practical Center for Business and Management.

Fr. Dr. Joseph Laracy, Seton Hall University, USA, College of Arts and Sciences, Department of Mathematics and Computer Science, Complex Systems, Differential Equations, and Dynamical Systems.

Dr. Russell Jay Hendel, Towson University, USA, Dept. of Mathematics. Researcher in Discrete Number Theory, the Theory of Pedagogy, Applications of Technology to Pedagogy, and the Interaction of Mathematics and the Arts.

Dr. David Cutting, Queen's University Belfast, UK, School of Electronics, Electrical Engineering and Computer Science, Course Director: BSc Software, Engineering with Digital Technology Partnership, Fellow of the Higher Education Academy.

Professor William Swart, East Carolina University, USA. FMR. Dean of Engineering and Technology at New Jersey Institute of Technology. Provost and Vice President for Academic Affairs at East Carolina University. Researcher and Consultant at NASA's Space Shuttle.

Professor Christian Greiner, Munich University of Applied Sciences, Germany, Associate Dean Applied Research, Professor at the Department of Business Administration.

Professor Mohammad Ilyas, Florida Atlantic University, USA, Department of Computer and Electrical Engineering and Computer Science, Former Dean of the College of Engineering and Computer Science; Member of Global Engineering Deans Council.

Mg. Philipp Belcredi, Comparative-Systemic Intervention, Austria, Owner and CEO, Former CEO of Pewag Chain. Inc.

Professor Wen-Chen Hu, University of North Dakota, USA, School of Electrical Engineering & Computer Science, Former (2010-2017) editor-in-chief of the International Journal of Handheld Computing Research (IJHCR).

Professor Thomas Peisl, Munich University of Applied Sciences. Germany, Professor of International Management and Strategy, Former Marketing Director at General Electric Europe.

Professor Maritza Placencia Medina, Departamento Académico de Ciencias Dinámicas de la Universidad Nacional Mayor de San Marcos, Peru, Facultad de Medicina, Centro de Investigaciones Tecnológicas.

Professor Andrés Tremante, Florida International University, USA, Department of Mechanical and Materials Engineering.

Invited Sessions Organizers

Professor Shigehiro Hashimoto, Kogakuin University, Japan. Councilor and Dean, Faculty of Engineering, Former Associate to the University President. Doctor of Engineering and Doctor of Medicine. Biomedical Engineering.

Professor *Dr. oec* Natalja Lace, Riga Technical University, Faculty of Engineering, Economy and Management. Head of Department of Corporate Finance and Economics.

Many thanks to Drs. Sushil Archarya, Esther Zaretsky, and to professors Michael Savoie, Hsing-Wei Chu, Mohammad Siddique, Friedrich Welsch, Thierry Lefevre, José Vicente Carrasquero, Angel Oropeza, and José Ferrer, for chairing and supporting the organization of conferences and/or special events or tracks in the context of, or collocated with, WMSCI 2019, and previous conferences. We also wish to thank all the authors for the quality of their papers, the Program Committee members and the additional reviewers for their time and their contributions in the respective reviewing processes.

Our gratefulness is also extended to the organizations that provided scientific, academic, professional, or corporate co-sponsorships in this conference and/of previous ones. The following are among these organizations:

Special Thanks to Dr. Jeremy Horne, Dr. Harvey Hyman, and Ms. Molly Youngblood Geiger (Google Partners Community Ambassador) for their efforts in helping us with the identification of above shown co-sponsors.

We extend our gratitude as well to professor Belkis Sanchez, Eng/Mg María Sánchez, Ms. Kilian Mendez, Mr. Jhonny Romero, Mr. Jaime Noguera, and Mr. Freddy Callaos for their knowledgeable effort in supporting the organizational process, maintaining the email lists, producing the hard copy and CD versions of the proceedings, developing and maintaining the software that supports the interactions of the authors with the reviewing process and the Organizing Committee, as well as for their support in the help desk, the promotional process, and their advising role in the promotion of the conference.

Professor Nagib C. Callaos, Ph. D.
WMSCI 2019 General Chair
www.iiis.org/Nagib-Callaos

WMSCI 2019
The 23rd World Multi-Conference on Systemics, Cybernetics and Informatics
Special Track on Design and Modeling in Science, Education, and Technology: DeMset 2019
Special Track on Knowledge and Cognitive Science and Technologies: KCST 2019

VOLUME I

CONTENTS

Knowledge and Information/Communications Technologies

Educational Research, Design, and Modeling

Qualitative Models and Modeling in Science and Engineering

Quantitative Models and Modeling in Science and Engineering

Research Design. Action-Research and Design.

Artificial Intelligence

Cognitive Science

Knowledge Science

Philosophy of Cognition

Authors Index

The Age of Academic Globalization

Sukjin KANG

Faculty of Business Management, Korea Aerospace University,
Goyang City, Gyeonggido 10540, South Korea

Seungryul LEE

Faculty of English, Korea Aerospace University,
Goyang City, Gyeonggido 10540, South Korea

Dongmyong LEE

Faculty of Business Management, Korea Aerospace University,
Goyang City, Gyeonggido 10540, South Korea

ABSTRACT

This paper explores the Logos, Pathos, Ethos, and "Lechus" of higher education across culture in the age of academic globalization. Instead of following a formal syllogism, Logos is reoriented to overcome neocolonialism supported by standardized massification and to create values and wealth by respecting and reconciling cultural differences with a new AND Logic. Academic globalization and higher education also need reorientation of Pathos. Empathy, or concern for the other lies at the center of this new reconceptualization. Here empathy signifies not only feeling what someone else feels but ethical action for the other. Through the practice of giving and taking, higher education can cultivate a new *otherish* Ethos. All these *otherlish* sequences primarily require unlearning attitudes and creative imaginative power in higher education. The significance of unlearning and educated imagination in the age of academic globalization will be explored through a new coined term, Lechus.

Keywords: Globalization, Higher Education, Logos, Pathos, Ethos, Lechus.

1. INTRODUCTION

The negative impacts of globalization have been widely discussed. Globalization frequently signifies McDonaldization under Anglo-Saxon capitalism and implies American hegemony. This term has been widely circulated since Theodore Levitt used the term in his article, "The Globalization of Markets," in the *Harvard Business Review* in 1983. This term also appears in articles concerning higher education across many countries. Philip G. Altbach points out that it involves information technology and the use of common language for communication. According to Altbach, the common language for scientific communication in the knowledge economy is English, arguing that higher education has been a major battlefield for achieving political and economic goals [1]. In addition, he argues that IT is the ultimate form of globalization which can be shared worldwide. Though recognizing that the power of English and IT is strong enough to dominate academic fields for knowledge production and its preservation, academic globalization needs more than English and IT, including the Internet, as tools to communicate, store, and retrieve information.

In establishing principles and models of higher education under academic globalization, McDonaldization, or the neo-colonization of Anglo-Saxon hegemony, has been a conundrum. How to establish cross-cultural or cross-national relationships without homogenization in the age of the Internet on an uneven playing field is a challenging issue. Academic globalization for better performance and fairness requires a reexamination of the Logos, Pathos, and Ethos of education in this globalized society.

Here Logos signifies neither a formal syllogism nor consistency. To the contrary, a new logic is founded upon accepting different values and systems, even contradictory ones to be globalized. Pathos here means to nurture a hybrid "love cat" rather than a "mad dog" [2]. Regrettably contemporary higher educations under competitive capitalist systems have emphasized the need to be a hero, or a winner in a game, and thus have generated mad dogs. Thus, Pathos will be reinterpreted to paying attention to the other in a blended form and be related to sympathetic action. Retaining consistency between knowledge and behavior has been a crucial ethical value, which is still significant in this global era. Yet a new connection economy requires more than the conformation of action to knowledge. Action based ethics may necessitate a review of the knowledge action gap. Under the term, emergent knowledge, an attempt will be made to establish a new relationship between knowing and doing. In addition, the significance of unlearning and educated imagination will be discussed under Lechus, a hybrid neologism. An unlearning attitude and imagination do not exactly fit into triadic form, and thus, another section will be added to explore the true sense of academic globalization: unlearning and dreaming education.

2. RECONCILIATION, CULTURAL DIFFERENCE, AND INTEGRATIVE THINKING

The main benefit from globalization is efficiency, or the increase of profit or competitiveness through economies of scale and learning effects. Standardized globalization offers maximum benefits and increases profitability through mass production. Localization lies in the other pole, which emphasizes the pressures for local responsiveness and individual difference of tastes and preferences. Localization respects differences across nation and culture, yet requires higher costs to meet local demand. In the middle lies glocalization, coined by Sony chairman Akio Morita, a kind of compromise or looking in both directions.

Considering the significance of monetary pressure in highly competitive environments, standardized globalization or compromising glocalization seems inevitable, and higher education is no exception. Yet, contemporary mass production systems in education result in growing inequality and domination, irrevocable homogenization, and poor creativity. Without dominative and even neo-colonial standardization or a half-hearted compromise, higher education can retain a sustainable position and nurture global talent by creating wealth from conflicting values.

Value creation through reconciliation holds the key here. Concerning business, some scholars including Fons Trompenaars, attempt to create wealth through reconciling value difference and to provide a training ground for reconciliation. Trompenaars identifies seven fundamental dimensions of culture. Among them, five dimensions are from an American sociologist, Talcott Parson's five relationships among people: universalism versus particularism, individualism versus communitarianism, neutral versus affective, specific versus diffuse, achievement versus ascription [3]. The other two dimensions are adopted from anthropologists and other sociologists such as Edward Hall and Tom Cottle, and they concern attitudes with regard to time and the environment: sequential verses synchronic, and mechanic versus cybernetic. Whereas the major task of anthropologists and sociologists is to identify cultural differences, that of business management is to harness the differences in order to create wealth and value.

An additional task of higher education is to develop **people's reconciling skills through** training in cross-cultural situations, which can be elaborately organized in international business situations in higher education. Through the case study of the Missouri Computational Company, for instance, students practice reconciling individualism and communitarianism. Reconciliation may start from competitive individualism, yet after its connection to communitarian cooperation, it is reconciled into "coopetition." The same consequence can be achieved counterclockwise, from cooperation to competition [4]. To understand other cultures and to reconcile cultural differences are prerequisite, and above all, to cultivate an integrative mindset is crucial.

Bill Gates's creative capitalism, in fact, is the culmination of an integrative mindset. As he points out, systems innovation rather than technological innovation is necessary in order to improve the majority of human life [5]. He proposed a new system in which both making a profit and gaining recognition work together. This hybrid engine of self-interest and moral sentiment for others is more powerful than maximizing self-interest or caring for others alone. This "AND" logic is fully realized in Daniel **Lubetzky's** snack company, KIND. The guiding principle of KIND is "AND" − both tasty and healthy, both financial success and social contribution, both thinking with the workplace and transcending it [6]. This **company's vision** is not only inspiring but also productive, for its social contribution outdoes non-profit business organizations and its financial achievement exceeds other snack companies which pursue their interests alone.

Concerning the intellectual components of intercultural education, understanding similarities and differences across cultures has been placed at the center, thus to learn the language, history, or religious or business practices of another country has been emphasized in higher education. Yet in the age of academic globalization, Global Logos should mean more than cultural awareness, or understanding other cultures. Intercultural Global Logos should incorporate integrative thinking, the capability to hold two opposing ideas in mind, and embracing different and even contradictory cultures. Higher education needs to be based upon reconciliation and integrative thinking across cultures to foster contemporary global leaders who can make profits and create values without depending upon McDonaldization.

3. ATTENTION ECONOMY AND EMOTIONAL EMPATHY

Proposing creative capitalism as an alternative form of traditional capitalism, Bill Gates asks us to pay attention to care for the other, proclaiming that even the father of capitalism and bearer of self-interest, Adam Smith, opens his *The Theory of Moral Sentiment* with a clear manifestation of human sympathy. Traditional capitalism is based upon the assumption that the foundation of human judgment is self-interest, or the desire to maximize our profits. Yet in fact, maintaining current social systems based upon principles of authoritative economics is virtually impossible or highly costly as behavioral economists have demonstrated. For instance, financial incentives alone cannot make firefighters or soldiers risk their lives. Human beings are not *econs* to judge and move with reason alone [7].

Logocentric Western academic cultures and intellectual traditions put Logos or rationality before Pathos or emotion, for the former seems to be stable, fixed, and controllable. They have occupied a privileged position all throughout the history of the West, whether they are designated *eidos, telos, ousia*, reason, logos, or conscience. Yet these centers cannot hold their positions without seemingly supplementary opposites. By the end of the 20th century, the significance of emotion had been recovered in almost all disciplinary studies. Daniel Goleman proclaims that man is a rationalizing animal, not a rational one [8]. Thanks to neuroscience we understand the function of the limbic systems and the significance of human emotion. The disruptive nature of emotion has been exaggerated, and made the myth of an emotion-free state desirable. Understanding the myth of rationality and restoring positive emotion in everyday life are current issues. And the main concern here among human emotions is empathy, for this fundamental human trait most seriously requires attentions in a modern context.

Firstly, empathy means to notice and understand the perspective of the other. This perceptive aspect of empathy is particularly significant for contemporary human beings in an urban trance. Herbert Simon says "what information consumes is rather obvious: it consumes the attention of its recipients. Hence a wealth of information creates a poverty of attention" [9]. Simply paying more attention to the other is itself a great virtue in this era, considering the following the second aspect of empathy related to mirror neuron.

Secondly, empathy is about the capacity to feel what others feel. It concerns the capacity of reading dynamics and managing them. Human brains are interconnected through so-called mirror neurons, through which we feel as the other feels. Empathy frequently promotes loyalty and turns out to be beneficial in establishing relationships.

The empathy discussed here can be associated with the conception of love by Tim Sanders. Sanders suggests that love is interchangeable with terms like caring, charity, and compassion. Love means being able to help others to grow. Sharing intangibles with partners with "The Love Cat Way" is valuable, especially in the information age. The first step of "The Love Cat Way" is to build knowledge for those who struggle to succeed in this knowledge economy. Then follows the step of network building in which participants can be connected and create values. The final step is compassion that creates commitment through action [10]. The feeling of love connects knowledge with action.

This paper proposes a hybrid imaginative organism, a *catog*, though genetically this hybrid creature is impossible. This imaginary creature will be both more powerful and beneficial than a cat or a dog alone. Firmly based upon self-preservation, other-oriented emotional relationship can be established, as Adam Smith, David Hume, Baruh Spinoza, and Erich Fromm have pointed out. The evaluative litmus test of 21st century globalized education should be upgraded. Traditional emotional concerns of intercultural studies have been the establishment of mutual respect and trust, and the reduction of ethnocentrism, xenophilia, and xenophobia. Adapting the lifestyle of a different culture with ease, and having confidence in an unfamiliar cultural situation have been added in the focus lists. The foundation of globalized education in the 21st century should be concern for the other, whether it is named as care for the other, empathy, or love. Otherwise, higher education could turn into a jungle in which every creature fights to survive in the name of strategic advantage. Though we live in a highly competitive society, the final result of higher education should not be a competitive mad dog.

4. ENCOURAGING SYMPATHEIC ACTION AND EMERGENT KNOWLEDGE

How to turn knowledge into action, or the consistency between knowing and doing, is a crucial issue in establishing principles of global ethics. Talk frequently substitutes for action and fear prevents acting on knowledge. To surmount the knowing-doing gap, a reorganization of the decision making context should be studied. As Richard Thaler and Cass Susnstein have demonstrated, by harnessing the gap between the Automatic System and the Reflective System, nudging people to act can be realized in order to improve health, wealth, and happiness. The "Choice Architect in Action" proposed by these behavioral economists significantly reduces the knowledge-behavior gap and contributes to the implementation of global ethics, if properly appropriated [11].

Empathy has a behavioral aspect: empathic concern is related to emotional empathy, and lets a person sense not only how others feel but what they need. Empathic concern also means to manage our personal feeling when we feel the pain of others. Those who lack empathic concern may be distracted by anxiety about the other and fail to offer proper help. Empathic concern can be cultivated widely and affects the people one meets in life. By showing care for others, a person can build trust and loyalty, and thereby establish interactions in the workplace.

As givers are precious resources for any organization, encouraging the act of giving without burnout is a crucial ethical task. Adam Grant finds that the greatest achievers are givers, neither takers nor matchers − compromisers between giving and getting [12]. Some givers face inevitable burnout, totally exploited by takers, whereas other givers succeed and flourish, though they are more other-oriented than the others. Successful givers are eager to get power and achievement. They devote themselves to attaining individual excellence and obtaining personal recognition and influence. They are more other-oriented than others, and they are more ambitious than takers and matchers. Being other-oriented only can be impressive, yet giving only without considering self-preservation may not be effective in the long-term. By positioning *otherish* states, not selfish or selfless ones, we can revitalize ourselves instead of totally draining ourselves over good works. And well-organized action plans such as "The 100-hour rule" and "Embracing the Five-minute favor" are helpful to prevent compassion fatigue, an acute inability to empathize by stress and burnout. Providing a channel to reduce mental burden may diminish the discrepancy between knowledge and action.

It is noticeable that Western cultures are more concerned with Truth rather than Virtue. The quest for Truth has been the paramount academic goal in the West, whether it is empirical or metaphysical. In contrast, East Asian countries regard virtue, or good action, as the major tasks in life. Deng Xiaoping says "what does the color of the cat matter as long as it catches mice?" and global ethics should pay more attention to virtues. Some Western scholars attempt to reorient the relationship between knowledge and action including Karl Weick. His storytelling of being lost in the Swiss Alps suggests a new relationship between knowledge and behavior. A reconnaissance unit has gotten lost in the Alps during a military maneuver in a snowstorm. The unit had suffered and almost given up returning, until one member of the dispatched unit found a map in his pocket. They found their way back to civilization, and later it was pointed out that the map was of the Pyreness, not the Alps [13]. They could get out of the disaster with the wrong map, or false knowledge. It was not the knowledge but their actions that enabled them to get out of the disaster and to produce new possibilities. The traditional relationship between knowledge and action should be rearranged. This paper proposes to modify Weick's well-known passage from "How can I know what I think until I see what I say" to "How can I know what I think until I see what I *act*." To conform our action to our knowledge is still a sign of ethics. Yet knowledge can "emerge" in the course of action. In this context, behaviors which do not conform to our knowledge can be ethics as well, for they urge us get off the old treadmill, both in academic and real life settings.

5. UNLEARINING AND DREAMING EDUCATION

Higher education is designed to address contemporary issues. One of the best measures to cope with contemporary global problems is to establish a learning organization, and its cornerstone is systems thinking, the fifth discipline. Peter Senge sets up eleven laws of the fifth discipline, and the first one is "today's problems come from yesterday's solution" [14]. Senge's first rule here is relevant to developing an unlearning mindset and contextual intelligence. "Unlearning" implies to admit the limit of our knowledge and to get out of the fixed mindset, and "contextual intelligence" means an ability to catch the limits of our knowledge and to adapt the knowledge to an environment different from the environment in which it was developed [15]. Since the 1990s, as the data of non-OECD countries started to be widely incorporated, the widespread assumption − knowledge and strategies that work in advanced nations will work in developing countries as well − was dismantled. However, its implication here is not the necessity of grasping context, or localization, which contrasts sharply with the intention of the author of "contextual intelligence."

The underlying implication of contextual intelligence in academic education in the global era is humility, a kind of humbleness that certain collected data may not work in another context. This academic humility may produce the possibility of reconciliation instead of imposing a general rule upon the other. Authors who have a strong belief in their research based upon lots of data frequently disregard that the consequence of their study can be meaningless in the age of turbulence. This tendency can be strong when authors proclaim that their research is objective and can be scored and thus measured unambiguously in their intercultural studies like *Cultures and Organizations* and *Culture's Consequences*. Ironically the most widely-read books in intercultural studies do not say much about the future. Current research works may not have validity in the future, even though their exhaustive research may guarantee their reliability. Past-data based education does not meet the demands of contemporary society, and to regard cultural studies as the software of the mind may imply disregarding the presence of cultural agency, or the power to create new culture. In this regard, seemingly imperfect yet relevant data should not be ignored in order to reorient them for the future. Capturing imperfect yet relevant data requires higher education and training.

In addition, higher education in this global era requires academics to teach dreaming so as not to fall into a closed process of problem solving. This trap frequently starts from the problem awareness and problem definition steps, instead of desiring what we truly want. Dreaming has been more global than English and IT in human history across the world. Instead of finding facts and collecting cultural data, it is necessary to start higher education from imagining a desirable future, and it should be taught [16]. Imagination has two adjective forms: imaginary and imaginative. Whether it is fictional or factual, productive dreaming is imaginative.

Martin Luther King had a dream and delivered it through speech. Though he was an American male, his dream was global rather than local. Yet the point here is not the "globalnesss" of his dream but the globalness of his "dream." It is necessary to dream the future, and higher educational systems need to restore the power of dreaming the future for the current and future generation. The real progress of our civilization originates from dreaming, not from knowledge building. **Clearly Martin Luther King's global address was "I have a dream," not "I have information."**

Lechus, a hybrid form of Lethe and Bacchus, or of the goddess of oblivion and the god of fertility, could be put alongside logos, pathos, and ethos, as a key fundamental of higher education. To establish educational cornerstones across culture in the age of academic globalization, spirit as well as head, heart, and guts is needed. Through this hybrid imaginative term, Lechus, the creative power of imagination that breaks up outdated inert knowledge can be represented. In cultivating Logos, Pathos, Ethos, and Lechus, these tools can be adopted in education without depending upon English and IT under academic globalization settings, for sketching, field observation and ethnographic writing are as globally common as English and computers.

6. CONCLUSION

Overall, higher education across culture in the age of

academic globalization means to foster the capability to hold two opposing ideas in mind intellectually and emotionally so as to enrich our lives and create values through action. Through establishing a reconciliatory mindset and practicing *otherish* behaviors, higher education in the age of globalization can foster talents with hybrid forms of emotional intelligence.

To cope with global issues, this paper suggests a **"have one's cake and eat it too" mindset,** however illogical that might seem from traditional viewpoints. The contradictory **"can't have your cake and eat it too" mindset is** reasonable, controllable, and measurable, yet can be inhuman, over-dominating, and less-productive. Reconciling in head, heart, and action and establishing a connection economy ethos of "AND" hold the key of higher education across culture in the age of academic globalization. As Daniel Pink points out, 21st century talent needs not just argument but also story, not just logic but also empathy, not just seriousness but also play, and not just accumulation but also meaning [17]. To search globalization without McDonaldizing multiple voices is a challenging issue in higher education across cultures, which cannot be easily realized without harnessing the power of reconciliation.

Unlearning and dreaming education can be ignored in cybernetics and Informatics, especially in the current information systems and informing sciences in the name of inefficiency and unreliability. Yet in the whole process of knowledge generation and transference, especially in the early stages of it, wild dreams and unlearning can be beneficial in getting off the treadmill of tradition and committing to creating for the future. Higher education needs training to escape from our comfort zone. Glocalization is a likely barrier that limits meaningful innovation in higher education, for it provides the simplest approach to designing offerings for any emerging education field with some minor modifications. In this sense, a true globalization starts from curiosity and an unlearning attitude, rather than the acquisition of a dominant logic and established knowledge.

7. REFERENCES

[1] Philip G. Altbach, Globalization and the University: Myths and Realities in an Unequal World. **Tertiary Education and Management**. 10 (1), 2004, 3-25.

[2] Tim Sanders, **Love is the Kipper App: How to Win Business and Influence Friends.** New York: Three Rivers Press, 2002.

[3] Fons Trompenaars and Charles Hampden-Turner, **Riding the Waves of Culture: Understanding Diversity in Global Business**. New York: McGraw

Hill, 2012.

[4] Ibid.

[5] Bill Gates, **Creative Capitalism**. New York: Simon & Schuster, 2008.

[6] Daniel Lubetzky, **Do the Kind Thing**. New York: Ballentine Books, 2015.

[7] Richard H. Thaler and Cass Sunstein, **Nudge: Improving Decisions about Health, Wealth, and Happiness**. New York: Penguin Books, 2008.

[8] Daniel Goleman, **Emotional Intelligence: Why It can Matter more than IQ**. New York: Bantham Books, 1994.

[9] Herbert Simon, Designing Organizations for an Information-Rich World, in **The Economics of Communication and Information**. Cheltenham: Edward Elgar, 1997.

[10] Tim Sanders, **Love is the Kipper App: How to Win Business and Influence Friends**. New York: Three Rivers Press, 2002.

[11] Richard H. Thaler and Cass Sunstein, **Nudge: Improving Decisions about Health, Wealth, and Happiness.** New York: Penguin Books, 2008.

[12] Adam Grant, **Give and Take: A Revolutionary Approach to Success.** New York: Viking, 2013.

[13] Karl Weick, **Sensemaking in Organizations**. Thousand Oaks: Sage, 1995.

[14] Peter Senge, **The Fifth Discipline: The Art & Practice of the Learning Organization**. New York: Currency, 1990.

[15] Tarun Khanna, Contextual Intelligence, **Harvard Business Review.** 59 September, 2014, 59-68.

[16] Northrop Frye, **The Educated Imagination.** Bloomington: Indiana University Press, 1964.

[17] Daniel H. Pink, **A Whole New Mind: Why Right-Brainers will Rule the Future.** New York: Riverhead Books, 2005.

Does a Career in Information Security Appeal to Women?
An empirical analysis of job ads,
supplemented by job descriptions and narratives

Frauke Fuhrmann

Department Business, Computing, Law, Technical University of Applied Sciences (TUAS) Wildau
Wildau, Brandenburg 15745, Germany
frauke.fuhrmann@th-wildau.de

Margit Scholl

Department Business, Computing, Law, Technical University of Applied Sciences (TUAS) Wildau
Wildau, Brandenburg 15745, Germany
margit.scholl@th-wildau.de

ABSTRACT

Information security is a fast-growing, forward-looking career offering women good opportunities to assert their position and shape the development of the field and the future alike. However, worldwide the proportion of women in information security is very low. Increasing the number of women would help address the anticipated labor shortage and integrate diverse perspectives and experiences. In preparation for the development of a gender-sensitive job profile in information security, we analyzed existing ads in the field with regard to gender-sensitive images and language as well as the preferences of women (and men) for certain job characteristics and skill sets. The analysis was complemented by insights derived from job descriptions and interviews with female and male experts working in information security. Although the job ads highlight important issues for women, there is still room for improvement if more women (and men) are to be attracted to the field.

Keywords: STEM, gender, computing, information security, data protection, job ad analysis

1. INTRODUCTION

Information security (IS) is a future-oriented field that is still developing and is rich with opportunity. It has now started to specialize in different areas (e.g., cryptology, awareness trainings, fraud detection, and forensics). As information security becomes more and more important in private, business, and public life, being part of this development offers broad scope for influencing the direction in which the field is moving and shaping the future. With this in mind, information security provides a career for women with considerable prospects, as no established structures and programs of action exist. Thus, women are able to step in and claim their place in this development without being confronted by male decision makers holding influential positions, as is the case in other occupational fields, where men have occupied these positions for years. However, IS is a male dominated job area—increasing diversity in the field would have the beneficial effect of including different perspectives and experiences [17].

Lack of information about the specific jobs available in IT—e.g., security specialist—and how diverse and exciting they can be [16] makes it hard for pupils in school to be aware of information security as a career path: it is not part of the school curriculum, and so typically there is no opportunity for pupils to get a sense of the kind of work involved. As almost every pupil possesses a smartphone (in Germany, 97 percent of 12- to 19-year-olds) [13] and uses the possibilities they offer to connect and chat with friends, do online searches, play games, etc., information security should be an important topic in school. However, in a standardized, anonymous survey we conducted with 194 8th-grade students, 61 percent of them indicated that information security topics are not taught in school. To raise awareness of and interest in information security as a career—especially among female pupils—we launched the project "Gender-Sensitive Study and Vocational Orientation for the Occupation Security Specialist" (abbreviation: "Security"), which is being carried out in Germany and funded by the Federal Ministry of Education and Research.

In this paper we focus on the research work involved in the development of a gender-sensitive job profile. It consists of an analysis of existing job ads and descriptions on web-based career-guidance platforms, as well as interviews with female and male experts working in information security. The process was guided by the following research questions. The answers provide an indication of how we should formulate and design the job profile and what information we should present and mention in the job profile we are developing.

1) How appealing are existing job ads to women based on criteria derived from previous research findings?

2) Do existing job descriptions found on web-based career-guidance platforms show the diversity of the field?

3) In what respect do the narratives of people working in the field of information security complement the required attributes and skills mentioned in the job ads?

The paper proceeds as follows: section two gives an overview of relevant literature guiding the formulation of criteria for the analysis of existing job ads. In section three, we present our methodological procedure in analyzing existing job ads in information security. This is followed by our results in section four. At the end, in section five, we discuss the findings and limitations of our research and look ahead to the next steps in the project.

2. LITERATURE REVIEW: WHAT APPEALS TO WOMEN?

2.1. INTERESTS AND PREFERENCES OF FEMALES

Research indicates that job ads in computer sciences are often presented in a way that does not attract women or give them a sense of belonging to the field [11]. However, several studies and scientific projects investigate which job characteristics are important for women (and men) in order to answer the question of how to attract women to an occupational field in which they are so far underrepresented and of how to retain them thereafter. The findings of these research studies are also instructive in helping develop job ads and job descriptions.

Schuth, Brosi, and Welpe (2018) [17] examine which job characteristics galvanize female and male IT professionals to apply for an IT-related position. For both women and men, all of the five job characteristics investigated—work-family balance, salary and benefits, career advancement, challenging tasks, mentoring for women—had a significant, positive effect on the intention to apply. However, for both women and men work-family balance is the most important issue, while special programs for females, such as mentoring, are the least appealing attribute. In an article about how unconscious bias hurts men and the companies they work for, Kimmel (2015) [12] also concludes that female and male employees want the same things in life (e.g., being a good and involved parent) and value the same job characteristics, such as meaningful careers, making a lot of money in a successful career, and a supportive work environment. Thus, emphasizing the job characteristics that were identified as important has the benefit of attracting both women and men. In order to understand why women leave jobs in the technology industry twice as often as men, Holtzblatt (2017) [10] conducted interviews with women who did not drop out of technological jobs to identify key factors that motivate women to stay. These factors include a close-knit, cohesive team, projects and tasks that matter for the people themselves (e.g., learning, stimulation) or for others but need not necessarily be socially relevant, and nonjudgmental flexibility to balance work and private/family responsibilities. According to further studies, women are interested in group work, communication, practical problem-solving [16], and creative tasks [14] and want to interact with people [05]. Furthermore, they are interested in the interfaces the position has with other people, departments, and organizations [02].

2.2. LANGUAGE AND IMAGES

The language and images in a job ad or description can affect the extent to which women experience a feeling of belonging and a sense of fit in an occupational field. Thus, it is important to show both women and men, so that both sexes have the impression that they fit in the field [07, 09]. Gender-sensitive language is also expected to be a productive area [16]. In Germany, where the research is conducted, this means using not only gender-specific pronouns (she/he), but also paying attention to terms denoting

individuals. In the German language the ending of such a term can differ for males and females—for example, employee = *Mitarbeiter* (male) and *Mitarbeiterin* (female). In order to use gender-sensitive language, there is the option of using both female and male terms or of using words that are gender-neutral—for example, *Beschäftigte* (employee) or *Studierende* (students).

Based on gender stereotypes—"generalizations about the attributes of men and women" [08]—the attributes typically ascribed to females are communal attributes, while for males they are agentic. Using language that is both descriptive (what men and women are like) and prescriptive (how men and women should be) promotes gender bias [08] and often leads to misjudgments of the preferences of women and men [09]. As the literature cited above indicates, women and men value the same job attributes nowadays. However, research shows that job ads for positions with a high percentage of males tend to include more agentic than communal terms and that women feel less attracted to job ads with a higher number of agentic words. For men, the use of more agentic or more communal words has no impact [09]. Hentschel and Horvath (2015) [09] list typical agentic attributes (decisive, motivated to lead, career-oriented, competitive, assertive) and communal attributes (communicative, cooperative, team-building, diplomatic, motivating) used in job ads. Other authors conducting research in the same field also cite the words that appeal more to men (e.g., analytical) or to women (e.g., caring, reliable) [04].

2.3. STEREOTYPICAL IMAGE OF IT

Besides the pictures used in job ads, the image of IT and computer scientists is worth examining. Several studies suggest that women and girls still consider IT to be theoretical and boring and that it is all about coding. Furthermore, computer scientists are seen as male "geeks," sitting in front of their computers all day without any social contact [01, 14, 16]. However, the study of Brauner et al. 2018 [03] shows that while the majority of 99 school pupils who were asked to create a picture of a person working in the field of computer sciences drew a man (67.7 percent), 19.2 percent drew a woman. 13 percent were judged to be ambiguous. This is a promising result showing that the stereotypical image might be on the point of changing. This is what we are aiming for with our "Security" project. We want to depict the occupational field as it is: diverse, creative, communicative, and meaningful [16].

3. METHODOLOGICAL PROCEDURE

Based on the literature review in section two, we defined twenty-one criteria for the analysis of existing job ads in order to answer the first research question: the degree to which these ads appeal to women. The first thing we analyzed were the pictures. The next criterion was the use of gender-sensitive language. As we were analyzing job ads in German, this included the use of gender-specific terms to denote people. Based on the preferences of women and men, employee benefits (e.g., career advancement and promotion opportunities) and job attributes were the next two categories analyzed. We also checked the skill requirements to identify tasks women (and men) are interested in (e.g., communicative and communication skills). Finally, we looked at whether typical agentic or communal stereotypes are mentioned. The criteria were coded in binary

Table 1. Job ad analysis: criteria and results

Category	Criteria	Present in x of 57 job ads (%)
Images	only men	6 (10.53%)
	only women	7 (12.28%)
	men and women	24 (42.11%)
	image without people or no image	20 (35.09%)
Gender-sensitive language	male terms to denote individuals	39 (68.42%)
	male and female terms or neutral terms to denote individuals	12 (21.05%)
Employee benefits	special programs for women	0 (0%)
	work/family balance	25 (43.86%)
	salary and benefits	32 (56.14%)
	career advancement and promotion opportunities	33 (57.89%)
Job/Company description	challenging tasks	26 (45.61%)
	interface to other departments/institutions	50 (87.72%)
	impact of the job	22 (38.60%)
	working in a team	26 (45.61%)
Required skills	creativity	10 (17.54%)
	teamwork	26 (45.61%)
	communicative skills	36 (63.13%)
	language skills (German, English)	42 (73.68%)
	problem solving	8 (14.04%)
Agentic attributes	e.g., assertive, analytical thinking	18 (31.58%)
Communal attributes	e.g., friendly, cooperative	5 (8.77%)

form to indicate whether the factor was "present" or "not present" in the job ad. Table 1 summarizes the criteria we analyzed as well as the results of our analysis. Three people (2 females, 1 male) analyzed fifty-seven randomly selected job ads. In cases where their results differ, the coding of the majority was followed.

Besides the specific criteria we looked for to generate our research findings, the job ads also include further skills and company or job descriptions that cannot be directly assessed to determine how they appeal to women (and men)—e.g., leeway in decision-making. Furthermore, we did not analyze the tasks of the positions described except inasmuch as they served us as indications for the criteria we were examining. However, in order to gain insight into the diversity of the field of information security it would be worth analyzing these tasks in more detail.

In addition, we conducted searches on twenty German-speaking web-based career portals for descriptions of occupations in the field of information security to determine, in response to the second research question, whether the diversity of information security is depicted in the job descriptions.

To date, we have also conducted eight semi-structured interviews with male and female experts working in different areas of information security—e.g., service provider for training and sensitization measures; service provider for technical security measures and penetration tests; responsible person for IT security compliance and audits in a company or in public administration. The aim of these interviews is to identify different professional activities in the field of information security and their main and typical

tasks. We also explore which skills and attributes are required for these tasks in an attempt to identify similarities and differences between the various professional activities. The template for these interviews is based on the critical incident technique. In the context of our research, this involved us asking the interviewees to describe their core task and the typical duties of their daily working life and the skills and attributes that are crucial to carrying out their job successfully. By using this method, we wanted to make sure that only relevant abilities and attributes were identified rather than an endless list of desired attributes. We also wanted to ensure that they talked about tasks that pupils and non-experts can easily imagine. In this paper, we highlight the statements and insights from these interviews that relate to the results of our analysis of the job ads and descriptions.

4. RESULTS

The analysis of the job ads reveals that most of them use images that include both women and men, as is recommended. However, we did not quantify the degree to which men and women are equally presented: in most cases, the proportion was equal, but there were also examples with more men than women or with a man in the foreground and a woman in the background. With regard to gender-sensitive language, we determined that almost 70 percent of the ads use male terms or mainly male terms to denote individuals. Even if the visual language is more or less gender-sensitive in the ads we looked at, the phrasing in the descriptions of company employees or the people the prospective incumbent is expected to work with might create the impression that they are mostly men. One company explicitly encouraged women to apply for the position. Six companies highlighted the fact that they are an equal opportunity employer and would be pleased to receive applications irrespective of any specific group identification (e.g., sex, nationality).

With regard to employee benefits, it is striking that no job ad cited special programs for females. However, according to the study of Schuth et al. (2018) [17], these programs are valued by IT professionals. In terms of the other job characteristics Schuth et al. (2018) [17] investigated in their study, it is remarkable that over 55 percent of the employers miss the opportunity to attract both women and men by talking about the measures they have introduced to promote a work-family balance (e.g., flexible working hours, support for parents) for their employees. The majority of the ads analyzed address the issues of salary and benefits as well as career advancement and opportunities for promotion.

Based on the research findings presented above, the selected criteria specified in the job and company description are attributes female and male professionals like to see in a position. Bearing in mind that the question of whether or not a task is challenging is a highly subjective one and depends on a person's skills and abilities, we marked job ads which stated that the position includes challenging tasks or sole responsibility for a particular area. Almost half of the ads we analyzed mentioned something along these lines. The finding that almost 90 percent of the ads indicate who the prospective incumbent will work together with counteracts the stereotypical image of a computer scientist working alone in front of his computer. The occupational field information security could be characterized per se as meaningful as it is about identifying risks and implementing measures to ensure information security. However, we looked at if the job ads explicitly mentioned any special impact the job might have on their own organization (e.g., contributing to the company's success), their clients (e.g., successful customer projects), or society (e.g., improving people's lives, creating a safe future). As research states that women (and also men) attach importance to the impact of their work, employers are encouraged to highlight the meaningfulness of the jobs more precisely. Only 38.6 percent of those included in our analysis did that. Working in a close-knit, cohesive team is important for women. Based on this, we checked to see if job ads contain information about the position being part of a team. Less than half (45.61%) are currently doing this.

The next criterion covers the required skills that provide an insight into the job tasks women like to complete. Our results underline the internationality of this field, as a large majority (73.68 percent) of the employers require very good language skills in German and English. In close connection with this, communicative skills are essential, which in turn contradicts the stereotypical image of computer scientists. When it comes to information stating that the position is part of a team, the same number of ads (26) indicate that teamworking abilities are needed for the job. Creativity and problem-solving skills are seldom mentioned in these ads. However, according to the interviews we conducted with experts working in the field, these skills are extremely important (see below).

Although, a third of the job ads include agentic words such as assertive, these words are only sporadically used. We counted at most two typically agentic terms in the same ad. Hentschel and Horvath (2015) [09] found that high numbers of agentic words discourage women from applying for

the job. Thus, we cannot conclude that there is less encouragement for women to apply for the 31.58 percent job positions whose ads use agentic terms. Conversely, we only find communal attributes listed as required characteristics for the prospective incumbent in 8.77 percent of job ads.

With regard to our first research question—how appealing existing job ads in information security are to women—the majority of the job ads we analyzed include gender-sensitive visual language, salary and benefits, information about career advancement and promotion opportunities, the interfaces of the position, and communicative and language skills. However, existing job ads can improve their use of gender-sensitive language and their presentation of work-family balance, challenging tasks, the impact of the job, and how it relates to the team, as well as highlighting the required skills of creativity, teamworking, and problem solving. As there is a fairly even split between the number of criteria that are fulfilled by the majority of the ads and the number for which there is room for improvement, we conclude that existing job ads in information security do address women but can still increase their attractiveness in this respect.

To answer the second research question, first of all it is interesting to record that 14 (70 percent) of the web-based career-guidance portals we researched provide no information about the career field. The others offered information that was sometimes brief, but in most cases detailed—including the required skills and competencies, study courses, and vocational trainings—about the positions of IT security officer, ICT security expert or specialist, IT security coordinator, and IT security manager, as well as about more specialist jobs such as IT security consultant, evaluator of IT security products, fraud analyst, and cryptologist. One platform shows short videos of people working in some of these positions. The six career-guidance platforms that provide information about the broader jobs like IT security officer and about specialized areas such as cryptology show the diversity of the field, because they describe a variety of tasks. However, as most of the career-guidance platforms we researched did not present the field of information security at all, the second research question can be affirmed for only 30 percent of the platforms in our analysis, but not in general. This reveals the importance of developing and disseminating a job profile for the field of information security.

The third research question addresses what can be learned from female and male experts working in the field of information security with regard to the necessary skills and attributes. All eight interviewees stated that "creativity is extremely important in the field of information security." It became apparent that creativity is needed to achieve several different goals: for example, to find solutions for highly complex problems that are often currently unresolved; to develop different, customized solutions, to select the best solution out of a variety of possible measures, to look at problems and security issues from various aspects and perspectives, to explain security issues to people with different backgrounds, knowledge, and experience, to implement security measures, and to develop interesting training measures that keep information security in the minds of all (employees). Another important skill that was mentioned in all the interviews is the ability to communicate. For the experts, communicative competencies cover the ability to understand other people, empathize with them, and make complex information security issues comprehensible for everyone. Furthermore, for all those interviewed, communicative activities constitute a major part of their profession. Because information security is a fast-growing and important field, it is not surprising that the experts highlight the willingness to learn as an important attribute an information security specialist should possess. They also agreed that information security is a growing, forward-looking field with considerable prospects. It is thus not surprising that some of those interviewed advise young people to decide which area of information security they would like to specialize in. The interviews offer us a deeper and more vivid insight into the required skills and abilities than the job ads can provide.

5. DISCUSSION

Our analysis showed that typical agentic or communal words are very seldom used in the job ads we analyzed. Thus, from this point of view both women and men might feel attracted to the job ads. However, based on research findings regarding the use of gender-sensitive language and the preferences for certain job attributes, the organizations can improve in the following aspects in order to appeal more to both women and men. Although there are not many terms denoting people in the job ads, the title of the position and the way employees are mentioned in most cases reflect male terminology. Women might infer that it is mostly men working in this profession in the company and could be discouraged from applying for the job. Based on the research findings of Schuth et al (2018) [17], 56 percent of the organizations whose job ads we analyzed fail to attract both women and men by not mentioning any measures for creating work/life balance. In contrast to the interviews conducted with experts working in the field, both the job ads and the job descriptions fail to highlight the importance of creativity in information security—for example, as a means to find innovative, appropriate solutions to a given problem or to motivate and engage people to apply information security more rigorously via sensitization and training measures, or to conduct penetration tests to identify risks in the information management system of an institution.

However, in order to increase the proportion of women in computer science and information security, making job descriptions and ads appealing to women can only be the beginning. As statistics show that women also suffer from a gender pay gap in computer science and leave their IT jobs much more often than men, it is important to overcome these inequalities in order to retain women in their positions. The research project "Women in Tech" by Karen Holtzblatt [10] shows how this could be achieved.

Our research work also has limitations that can be overcome in future research. Although we analyzed the job ads based on different research findings, this analysis cannot be seen as representative or as a definitive result indicating the degree to which young women and girls feel attracted to the job ads because the ads were assessed by only three coders. However, for our purposes, to gain insights into how we should phrase and design a job profile for the field of information security, the coding based on criteria derived from research findings is sufficient, because we plan to have female students conduct an evaluation of the job profile we develop. Although we only coded the fulfilment of a criterion in a binary fashion, some job ads cited various measures (e.g., for work-family balance), while others mentioned only one (such as flexible working hours).

Thus, further studies that are interested in a deeper understanding of the gender-sensitive design of job ads in the field of information security could assess the criteria based on the extent to which they are fulfilled.

The next step in the development of a gender-sensitive job profile is the complete analysis of the interviews and a summary of the different professional specializations, including core and typical tasks as well as required skills and attributes, presented in a readable way that is easy for school pupils to process. Besides a more comprehensive description in a brochure, we are thinking about a video or simulation. This compilation will be guided by the results of our analysis of the job ads and descriptions. However, to overcome the limitations of subjectivity and the constraints of the coding cited above, we will have young females evaluate the job profile in focus groups and surveys.

6. REFERENCES

[01] C. Ashcraft, E. Eger & M. Friend, **Girls in IT: The Facts**, National Center for Women & Information Technology (NCWIT), 2012.

[02] C. Ashcraft, B. McLain & E. Eger, **Women in Tech: The Facts. 2016 Update // See what's changed and what hasn't**, National Center for Women & Information Technology (NCWIT), 2016.

[03] Brauner, P., M. Ziefle, U. Schroeder, T. Leonhardt, N. Bergner, and B. Ziegler, Gender Influences On School Students' Mental Models of Computer Sciences, *Proceedings of Gender & IT, Heilbronn, Germany, May 14–15, 2018 (GenderIT)*, pp. 113-122.

[04] Burel, S., 2018, "Gender Audit – zur sprachlichen Fassbarmachung von Geschlechterstereotypen in der Online-Kommunikation", *Proceedings of the 4th Gender&IT conference, Heilbronn, Germany (GenderIT'18)*, ACM, New York, NY, USA, pp. 59-61.

[05] Busch, A., "Die Geschlechtersegregation beim Berufseinstieg – Berufswerte und ihr Erklärungsbeitrag für die geschlechtstypische Berufswahl", *Berlin Journal für Soziologie*, Vol. 23, No. 2, 2013, pp. 145-179.

[06] Frost & Sullivan, **The 2017 Global Information Security Workforce Study: Women in Cybersecurity**, Frost & Sullivan, 2017.

[07] Gringer, J., "IT-Studium. Zeigt mehr Frauen!", *golem.de – IT-News für Profis*, March 5, 2018, 12:02 PM https://www.golem.de/news/it-studium-zeigt-mehr-frauen-1803-133014.html, accessed May 28, 2018.

[08] Heilman, M.E., "Gender stereotypes and workplace bias", *Research in Organizational Behavior*, Vol. 32, 2012, pp. 113-135.

[09] Hentschel, T., and L.K. Horvath, "Passende Talente ansprechen – Rekrutierung und Gestaltung von Stellenausschreibungen", In: C. Peus, S. Braun, T. Hentschel, and D. Frey (eds.), *Personalauswahl in der Wissenschaft. Evidenzbasierte Methoden und Impulse für die Praxis*, Springer-Verlag, Berlin, Heidelberg, 2015, pp. 65-82.

11

[10] Holtzblatt, K., *Women in Technology. Factors influencing work choices*, https://www.slideshare.net/Karen-Holtzblatt/women-in-high-tech-project-moving-from-discussion-to-action, 2017, accessed May 28, 2018.

[11] Kay, A., "How Job Ads Can Reinforce or Undermine the Status Quo", *NCWIT Summit*, https://www.ncwit.org/sites/default/files/a.kay_jobpostingbias_ncwitsummit12_0.pdf, 2012, accessed May 28, 2018.

[12] Kimmel, M., "How Unconscious Bias Hurts Men—and the Companies they Work for", In I.M. Welpe, P. Brosi, L. Ritzenhöfer, and T. Schwarzmüller (eds.), *Auswahl von Männern und Frauen als Führungskräfte Perspektiven aus Wirtschaft, Wissenschaft, Medien und Politik,* Springer Fachmedien, Wiesbaden, 2015, pp. 85-89.

[13] Medienpädagogischer Forschungsverbund Südwest (mpfs) (ed.), *JIM 2017. Jugend, Information, (Multi-) Media: Basisstudie zum Medienumgang 12- bis 19-Jähriger in Deutschland*, https://www.mpfs.de/fileadmin/files/Studien/JIM/2017/JIM_2017.pdf, 2017, accessed May 28, 2018.

[14] Microsoft, *Why Europe's girls aren't studying STEM, Region-wide research of 11,500 women reveals how we can get more young women into science, technology, engineering and math*, Whitepaper, https://na01.safelinks.protection.outlook.com/?url=http%3A%2F%2Ff3.hqlabs.de%2FHelper%2Fdownload_helper.aspx%3FmailingId%3D1840439%26key%3D43f36d961955f1ed094de0f8c645de704db9436f%26file%3D639489&data=02%7C01%7CIsabel.Richter%40microsoft.com%7Cef5bb2955a464ef-bbbef08d48bdde16c%7C72f988bf86f141af91ab2d7cd011db47%7C1%7C0%7C636287232465303550&sdata=7LOqHKZ2IsOF-HCgc1YnyoLS87qKHd2t6zGj%2FaFzMmlU%3D&reserved=0, 2017, accessed June 1, 2018.

[15] Morgan, S., "Cybersecurity labor crunch to hit 3.5 million unfilled jobs by 2021. The cyber crime epidemic is expected to triple the number of open positions over the next five years", *CSO*, June 8, 2017, 7:09 AM, https://www.csoonline.com/article/3200024/security/cybersecurity-labor-crunch-to-hit-35-million-unfilled-jobs-by-2021.html, accessed June 1, 2018.

[16] Paukstadt, U., K. Bergener, J. Becker, V. Dahl, C. Denz, and I. Zeisberg, "Design Recommendations for Web-based Career Guidance Platforms – Let Young Women Experience IT Careers!", *Proceedings of the 51st Hawaii International Conference on System Sciences*, 2018, pp. 5116-5125.

[17] M. Schuth, P. Brosi & I.M. Welpe, "Recruiting Women in IT: A Conjoint-Analysis Approach", **HICSS-51**, 2018.

7. ACKNOWLEDGMENT

The authors would like to thank research assistant Denis Edich and Franziska Klaus, a student from the research project, for their dedicated support in the study.

Solution-Focused Consultancy Work
Practice-Oriented Application of Distinction-Based Concepts Integrating Context Factors for Resilient Solutions

Tilia STINGL DE VASCONCELOS GUEDES, PhD
Management Consultant
2340 Mödling, Austria

Philipp BELCREDI
Systemic Management and Organizational Consultant
1030 Vienna, Austria

ABSTRACT[1]

For more than two decades now, systemic and systems-based approaches have been broadly applied in management consultancy. Numerous definitions attempt to describe the added value of a system-based consultancy—and they mostly emphasize a supposedly holistic view of problems and solutions. In Peter Senge's work *The Fifth Discipline*, for instance, the organizational learning approach or systems thinking offers perspectives, methods and ideas that are still en vogue.

However, as can be seen in the daily work of a systemic consultant, the greatest impact of this kind of work on leadership issues relies on the very basic concepts of distinction-based approaches as described by George Spencer-Brown or Niklas Luhmann. Being aware that any difference, even one that is perceived as small, may be *the* difference and then using this awareness as an impulse in the target direction is—as it can be shown in various empirical studies (cf. Steve de Shazer or Insoo Kim Berg)[1]—a very fast way for resilient solutions that include all relevant context factors. Working in organizations as communicating systems on the basis of differentiation/distinction rather than with content or interpretation offers us the possibility to make any goals of any type, even soft ones, manageable and controllable.

This paper uses data from an ongoing qualitative study that is part of Philipp Belcredi's[2] postgraduate work and analyses them from the point of view of theoretical concepts of distinction, second order cybernetics and social systems theory.

This theoretical analysis spots parameters in solution-focused leadership communication that produce more effective leadership outcomes, in terms of both communication and results, and that locate innovative possibilities for consultancy and leadership offered by aspects of second order observations.

Keywords: Systemic Consultancy, Second-Order Cybernetic, Theory of Distinction, Social Systems Theory, Solution Focused Work

1. INTRODUCTION

Using questions to collect relevant information is nothing new in both systemic and traditional management consultancy. Asking about the system that is looking for solutions, in order to distinguish and clarify the situation in terms of analysis, is a common approach: Issues can be ordered and prioritized, step by step. This process can be used to identify the root causes of issues, to set up an activity plan or to find solutions for current challenges.

The solution-focused systemic method works on the basis of useful differences (like resources—differences that make a difference—G. Bateson[2]), asking questions that focus on distinctions, which lead to a new perception of reality (first order observation). In terms of social systems theory: through solution-focused questions the system can be inspired to observe its environment in a slightly different way; during re-entry, it then integrates this difference into its own premises or codes. This enables fundamental changes and establishes reliable solutions.

In practice, the systemic solution-focused (also: 'comparative-systemic' or 'distinction-based') work shows an impressive capability to induce change in patterns of organizational communications. A few studies have already been made about this phenomenon, but the theoretical discussions about solution-focused work in organizations are still at the beginning, with major attempts at the topic only being made about ten years ago.[3] This paper aims to be a contribution to the scientific dialog centered on this topic and to open new paths to a solid development of this field.

---

1 For better readability the male form was chosen in the text. Nevertheless, all information in this paper refers to members of all genders on equal terms.

2 Philipp Belcredi is systemic consultant of many years' experience in the field.

Therefore, the present discussion will focus on the following questions, in particular on the systemic and systems-theoretical aspects:

1) How can second-order cybernetics add value in management issues?
2) What are the substantial differences between traditional, analytical consulting and distinctions/difference-based consulting?
3) Which types of situation are the ones in which comparative-systemic work can be most helpful to organizations?

2. SOLUTION-FOCUSED AND SYSTEMIC CONSULTANCY

Systemic approaches for the use in organizational and management consultancy are primarily rooted in constructivist ideas and methods of modern psychotherapy. That said, some of the concepts current in cybernetics and Social Systems Theory (e.g. Luhmann's ideas like the difference between system and environment), are fundamental parts of systemic work within organizations, together with autopoiesis and self-referentiality.[4]

The systemic idea also assumes that the behavior of people relies on the context. The belief that we have a primary personality determining our behavior cannot, therefore, fit with the systemic idea. Rather, systemic thought assumes that people behave according to the systems to which they belong. In the words of Insa Sparrer, "systemic approaches are characterized by the fact that they do not understand symptoms that occur in an individual person as a characteristic of that person, but as characteristics of relational structures of a system. These relationships are determined, among other things, by communication between the members or by communication processes."[5]

Today, systemic methods offer a possible answer to the Social-Systems Theory's assumption of operational closeness and autopoiesis. These assumptions tend to discourage any kind of interference in systems and to declare every intervention attempt ineffective. Furthermore, given Niklas Luhmann's consideration of human beings not as elements of a given social system but rather as part of the environment of that system, social systems theory at first glance seems to exclude any possibility for people to influence social systems. In fact, in our society there are notorious examples for this assumption. The legal system or religious institutions often illustrate this resistance to intervention: the 'world' changes, views are revised, but these changes arrive, say, in the church at best many years later. Even other, younger social systems show limits to their openness. Only messages that correspond to the actual codes of the system can be accepted. For example, if a business consultant explains that processes in a big profit business have to be changed because the Blessed Virgin Mary so desires, this information might be accepted as a joke but not, generally, as a basis for an implementable suggestion. Still, even with evidence of operational closure of social systems, there is a remaining link to interventions from the 'outside' world: communications.

The systemic consulting approach recognizes barriers for change and respects them, as they are also part of the system. Tensions within the system (see section *4. Tension Within Organizations*), however, can be used as the engine for expansion and/or development of the system as well as of individuals. Systemic methods try to work with (and not against) the 'templates of perception' of social systems in order to stimulate reflection and thus provide space for change. "It is true that intervention is a goal-oriented communication, but the outcome can only be realized by the targeted system. [...] However, [interventions] only achieve lasting effectiveness when they change structures."[6]

With a combination of systemic method and solution-focused approach, this 'goal-oriented communication' could be taken to a pinnacle of excellence. Especially in recent years, the number of attempts to enable productive supervision for solution-focused approaches has increased. Developed by Steve de Shazer, Insoo Kim Berg and other team members at the Brief Family Therapy Center (BFTC) in Milwaukee, the solution-focused approach is now being adapted especially for coaching and working with larger systems in organizational consulting, community work and regional development.[7]

Meanwhile, the efficacy of these methods has been examined in several studies; as a result, many consultants are changing their attitude and working methods and have begun to adopt systemic approaches both in theory and in practice. Instead of being agents of change, systemic consultants have become multipartial companions of change processes in organizations,[8] and the models and expertise used in counseling social systems such as families now offer a wealth of knowledge and hands-on experience for advising and supporting organizations.

3. THEORIES BASED ON DISTINCTION

"We take as given the idea of distinction and the idea of indication, and that we cannot make an indication without drawing a distinction."[9] The idea that cognition is based on distinctions is an old one, but in the late 1960s, Georg Spencer-Brown's approach embraced the concept of distinction. In his seminal work 'The Laws of Form' he proposed a theory that Luhmann would later use to explain essential events of human society.

Distinction-theories may be defined as those whose

referents are not explanations but rather 'agreement procedures' in the form of distinctions.[10] They are built around the assumption of an observer able to distinguish and denominate these differences and are counted among the theories based on constructivist ideas.

The comparative-systemic approach, which includes solution focused methods, understands that social behavior is not predetermined but rather adapted to social agreements and/or context situations. Working with differrences instead of definitions opens paths for innovative solutions, something that can be experienced every day working with patients. "One can know what is better without knowing what is good" is one of the favorite quotes attributed to Steve de Shazer.[11] In other words, it is easier to perceive something or a situation as better than another, than to recognize a thing/condition as *good*.

On this basis it is possible to work on enhancement using 'positive' differences while abandoning fruitless endeavors such as analyzing the past and searching for reasons and culprits; it even allows one to not know anything about the facts of a given situation.

Philipp Belcredi's ongoing qualitative study about tensions in organizations, performed in Austria with the cooperation of leaders of major companies, already demonstrates how a focus on useful differences puts new paths and solutions within reach.

4. TENSIONS WITHIN ORGANIZATIONS AND THE FOCUS ON SOLUTIONS

For people who consciously observe and experience, tensions are part of everyday life. Polar-opposite values or intentions, disappointed expectations and unfulfilled wishes are all well known. In organizations, tensions are sometimes created intentionally: Subdividing an organization into different departments helps it to consider contexts as broadly as possible, e.g., marketing observes opportunities on the market, while production is more interested in the feasibility of the products. The relationship between these two departments therefore has the potential to be charged with tension.

Belcredi's current scientific work is taking a closer look at these 'tensions.' After many years of distinction-based work with and within organizations, he is now running a qualitative study focused on 'tensions in organizations,' with the following research questions:[12]

> 1) To what extent do managers of organizations with more than 150 employees perceive tensions as such, without active hints or support in recognizing the polarity?
>
> 2) To what extent do managers of organizations with more than 150 employees welcome and use tensions as a driver to push the implementation of

further developments?

> 3) Do managers experience working with schemata from the distinction-based systemic work for the processing of tensions as useful assistance in finding valid solutions?

In the last six months six managers (one female, five male) have been interviewed on the topic of 'tensions,' and at least five more are expected to participate in the research. In order to better develop some aspects of the interpretation of these expert interviews, categories were created according to the rules of inductive category development.[13] In a first step, however, categories were set up based on previous theoretical analyses and assumptions that are now being reviewed during the study evaluation process (deductive category development).

Already in this first run-through, interesting aspects are emerging; they are good examples for how distinction-based systemic methods work and what kind of impact they can have in an organizational system. Therefore, in we would like to highlight some aspects of this still-ongoing study.

The study divides its categories in three main parts: (1) the manager's perception of tensions, (2) how they handle situations of tension, and (3) the differences managers can observe between handling tensions in their usual manner, that is, directly working on the content, and doing so with comparative systemic methods.

What makes these interviews differ from prior efforts are, above all, the types of questions that interviewees are asked to consider. They are systemic, solution-focused questions aiming at differences that make a difference and that usually open up new perspectives, assisting in looking at familiar situations in a more differentiated way. Systemic questions are known for stimulating the interviewee's imagination, thoughts and reflections, which in turn leads to new ideas for solutions.[14] The respondents are encouraged to focus on differences rather than content, culprits or causes; in so doing they are able to perceive new perspectives opening up before them and usually experience a positive—in terms of solution-focused—attitude. It is this change in attitude that makes it easier to finally step off the beaten track and to identify new paths and options, or rather that encourages interest in new paths and possibilities.

Well-known systemic and solution-focused question techniques are:[15]

- Circular questions (another perspective is raised, e.g., "What would your colleague say to that issue?").
- Scaling questions (e.g., "On a scale from 0 to 10, what would you …?").
- Hypothetical questions (e.g., "Assuming every-

thing that is bothering you today was solved, what would then be different?").

- Steve de Shazer's wonder question,[16]
- Paradoxical questions (e.g., "What can you do to make this even worse?"),
- Resource-oriented questions (e.g., "How did you solve a similar situation the last time?").

Scaling questions—one of the tools of the distinction-based approach—are used in the interviews in order to find differences that make a difference. For some questions interview partners are asked to answer on a scale from zero through ten. For example, "How much tension do you perceive in your daily working routine?" where zero represents no consciously perceived tension at all, while ten stands for 'all of my is work is managing tensions.' The questionnaire consciously works with subjective answers or valuations (and leaves open to the client what is relevant to him). Distinction-based questions raise chances to find relevant differences directly:

(a) The weighting of the contents of the answers is distinguished in 11 units. For example, if a person says that he is doing well today, we know more if the same person specifies that his well-being is a 6 on a scale of 0–10. 6 is not 8. Whatever 6 or 8 stand for, we still know that at 6 he is closer to half-way than to almost perfect. We know more than we would have learned just by the answer 'good.' We know a relationship in a context. We know there is more room for improvement than if the same person had stated that he felt like 8 that day.

(b) Results or insights do not depend on the contents of the answers in a narrow sense but rather use the insights about the relationships or differences—e.g. the relationship/differences between the current state and 'one step better.' There is also the relationship between 0 and the current state: The difference to 0 gives us information about already given resources. In order to learn if the interview was helpful it is sufficient to know whether the post-interview status is perceived as being the same, better or worse than before, without knowing how or why. 'Same, better or worse' after all are the most basic and relevant differences in order to gain insights about the success of a process in a living system. We can find out what the interview partner perceives as a state of 'better' without having to analyze the problem first.

(c) The distinction-based approach leads to more independence of different contexts, since working directly on useful differences we automatically include all relevant contexts into the most relevant difference: the facts which will let us know that now things are 'better' than they were.

By and large, the intermediate results of this study demonstrate the application and outcomes of distinction-based concepts such as comparative-systemic work. The managers' feedback, after being interviewed, offers a bird's-eye view of the effects of these methods. The interview guideline is mostly open and changeable, but the questions are all based on distinction-based systemic methods. At the end of the interview, all six managers express their positive surprise at the quality and depth of the outcomes of the conversation, and four out of six would like to talk again under those conditions.

5. TIME TO ACT 'AGILE'

Today, the new buzzword in the organizational context is 'agile:' agile organization, agile working, agile office etc. Agile working methods and agile frameworks ensure acceleration. Their proponents claim that agile methods map processes and correlations faster, that they are quicker in providing feedback to internal and external customers, and that they enable rapid prototyping in order to obtain the best and most useful result in the shortest time. Scrum, Design Thinking and Lean-Startup are just some of the terms the forefront of the agile wave.[17]

But as long as an organization's commitment to agile methods remains hollow, it will not fully enjoy their benefits; it must champion agility, supporting its values and culture. In particular, most agile concepts require very flat hierarchies, all project collaborators must be fully committed to the common goal, and everyone involved must willingly accept, indeed seek, responsibility for and ownership of the project. Creating such an environment is often difficult, as agile methods require advanced social skills, a high degree of self-motivation, and a strong sense of personal responsibility in order to work.[18]

Comparative-systemic approaches offer concrete tools to quickly deal with emergent situations—without having to change the overall organizational culture. These tools can be put into practice by any manager willing to do so, independently of the system in its entirety. This obviates the requirement for massive, all-at-once, structural changes but maintains the advantage of meaningfully impacting the organization, and paths can be built step by step from a multitude of local changes.

The 'speed-dating the boss' or 'agreement-and-decision-turbo'—a solution focused tool developed and used by Philipp Belcredi—offers a good example of how far these methods are able to improve communication within organizations. 'Speed-dating' is a compact and concise set of rules for any meeting aiming a decision. In order to bring an issue to a co-worker, the person seeking a decision has to prepare a small amount of information:

(a) He must be able, in two or three sentences at most, to explain the question for which he needs agreement, or the dilemma or problem requiring a decision.

(b) He has to prepare and offer two or three different potential solutions to the dilemma. Each of these must be explainable in just a few words.

(c) He is asked to argue in favor of one of the offered solutions, justifying the choice compared to the other potential solutions.

(d) The short ritual ends with the question: "Is there anything you would like to add?"

The result of this kind of speed-meeting ('speed-dating') usually is either a quick OK, and the decision is taken right on the spot (the topic was decided in the shortest possible time—the relevant 'differences that make a difference' have been discussed), or relevant yet overlooked issues can be raised quickly and in adequate detail. Most clients of Philipp Belcredi are successfully applying this technique.

But why is this approach counted among solution-focused tools? There are four aspects that stand out and which clearly make this tool a distinction-based, solution-focused method: (1) It is based on resources and feasibilities (instead of problems and analyses of the past). (2) The rules force the participants to stick to essential information (differences) for decision making. (3) Therefore, there is no room or time to look for culprits, to get worked up over past mistakes, or become lost in thought. (4) Last, the focus of 'speed-dating the boss' is and remains arriving at a decision.

At the end of the day, all that counts in organizations are the decisions that are taken. But we live in rapidly changing times, and many managers feel that decision-making is becoming ever more complex. About ninety percent of 150 German top managers (interviewed by Camelot Management Consultants for the study *Mastering Complexity*) feel that business life has become much more complicated in recent years. Five out of six surveyed managers are of the opinion that their companies have become far too complex.[19]

Many of today's efforts in management optimization aim to enhance the speed as well as the quality of decisions and processes. If deciders are able to filter relevant differences for their decisions, complexity (in terms of having to choose from an incalculable number of possibilities)[20] can be reduced drastically, generating a meaningful advantage.

6. DECISIONS THAT MAKE A DIFFERENCE

Organizations differ from other social systems mainly in the communication of decisions. This elementary operation 'communication of decisions' (also called basal unit) finds its utility in the absorption of uncertainty. By linking decisions, then, uncertainty is transformed into security. This serves as motivation for further decisions,

in their turn ensuring the survival of the system.[21]

Communication of decisions is therefore the operation that secures and continues the autopoiesis of the system. It generates the system/environment difference; consequently, each such operation forces a coupling of self-reference (reference to the network of one's own decisions) and foreign reference (in the sense of motivating decisions). This also means that the decision can only be communicated if the rejection of other possibilities is also communicated (what was decided against).

Each decision settles differences—between the organization before the decision was taken and the organization after the decision (past/future) and between the chosen alternative and all other possibilities. Awareness of this relationship also may open up new possibilities: "[D]istinction can be observed as form. It can be marked, and the processing of the mark may lead to forms of higher complexity."[22]

When an organization faces a challenge, it is still common for management to view it as a problem rather than as an opportunity to take decisions. The 'problem' paradigm works like this, more or less: First, the causes of the problem will be analyzed; second, solutions that worked in earlier, similar situations will be applied to this new challenge—even if the context may be different from back then. This approach represents the medical paradigm of 'diagnosis and treatment.'[23]

"Paradigms gain their status because they are more successful than their competitors in solving a few problems that the group of practitioners has come to recognize as acute. To be more successful is not, however, to be either completely successful with a single problem or notably successful with any large number."[24]

The need for paradigm changes is usually awakened by irritations from a system's environment. Traditional management concepts are not adequate for decisions in the complex context of many an organizational challenge. The search for alternatives is evident in the increasing supply and demand for innovative consulting methods.[25]

7. CONCLUSION

Heinz von Foerster's studies exploring the possibilities of second-order cybernetics concluded that, on the level of second-order observations "one has to observe not simple objects but observing systems—that is, to distinguish them in the first place. One has to know which distinctions guide the observations of the observed observer and to find out whether any stable objects emerge when these observations are recursively applied to their own results. Objects are therefore nothing but the *eigenbehaviours* of observing systems that result from using and reusing their previous distinctions."[26]

With the realization of what the results of second-order cybernetics work and all other distinction-based theories and methods mean for the relationship between human ad social systems, many other new possibilities emerge to understand, manage and lead social systems—especially organization systems. With the focus on distinctions, new forms of situations or systems can be observed and therefore more options to act or handle can be created.

In answer to the first research question, and as we demonstrated in the present paper, we may affirm that both distinction-based approaches (cf. section *4. Tensions Within Organizations*) and second-order cybernetics (cf. section *5. Time to Act 'Agile'*) contribute in many ways to management tools that are highly effective in complex situations.

Considering the second research question, about the substantial differences between analytical and distinction-based consulting methods, we have shown that the latter in particular show great potential for a paradigm shift. The questioning methods discussed above comprise the core of distinction-based interventions. The intent of these questions is to find meaningful differences based on resources, feasibility and solutions, as an alternative to analyses of the past or contents, as an important part of the substantial differences between these distinction-based and analytical consulting methods.

As for the third question, comparative-systemic work can be helpful whenever decisions have to be taken in a complex environment (cf. sections *3. Theories Based on Distinctions* and *6. Decisions That Make a Difference*). Of course, the methods don't necessarily need a consultant to be successful. Anyone willing to learn this way of thinking can use the tools and apply distinction-based methods to his daily challenges.

8. REFERENCES

[1] See e.g., Shazer, Steve, **Putting difference to work.** Norton, New York, 1991 or Shazer, Steve &. Berg Insoo Kim, **'What works'. Remarks on research aspects of solution-focused brief therapy.** In: Journal of Family Therapy 19, 1997

[2] G. Bateson, **Ökologie des Geistes.** Suhrkamp Taschenbuch Wissenschaft, 1981, p. 488.

[3] G. Lueger/ H.-P. Korn (eds.), **Solution-Focused Management.** Rainer Hampp Verlag München, 2006.

[4] R. Königswieser/A. Exnerm, **Systemische Intervention.** 3rd edition, Klett-Cotta, Stuttgart, 1999, p. 20 (loosely translated).

[5] I. Sparrer, **Systemische Strukturaufstellungen – Theorie und Praxis.** Carl-Auer-Systeme, Heidelberg, 2006, p. 3 (loosely translated).

[6] H. Kasper/W. Mayerhofer/M. Meyer, **Management aus systemtheoretischer Perspektive - eine Standortbestimmung.** In: D. Eckardstein: Management: Theorien – Führung – Veränderung. Schäfer Poeschel, Stuttgart, 1999, p. 190 (loosely translated).

[7] W. Gaiswinkler/M. Roessler, **Wunder, Skalen, Komplimente und ein anderer Blick – von den Klientinnen lernen.** 2004 http://www.netzwerk-ost.at/publikationen (last viewed April 15th, 2019).

[8] ibid.

[9] George Spencer-Brown: **Laws of Form.** Allen & Unwin, London 1969, S. 1.

[10] R. Todesco, **Differenztheorie.** https://www.hyperkommunikation.ch/lexikon/differenztheorie.htm (last viewed April 15th, 2019).

[11] M. Varga von Kibed, „**Systemisch" ist nicht systemisch – „Systemischer" ist systemischer.** Systemischer – Zeitschrift für Systemische Struktur-aufstellungen, Ferrari Media, Aachen, 1/2012, p. 7.

[12] Ph. Belcredi, **Spannende Gespräche.** 2019 In prepublication.

[13] Ph. Mayring, **Qualitative Inhaltsanalyse.** 7th edition, Weinheim: Deutscher Studien Verlag, 2000.

[14] R. Schuy, **Systemische Fragen: 6 Varianten & 71 Beispielfragen, die Sie unbedingt in Ihrem Repertoire haben sollten.** 2018 .https://clevermemo.com/blog/systemische-fragen/ (last viewed April 15th, 2019).

[15] ibid.

[16] See I. Sparrer, **Miracle, Solution and System.** Solution Books, Cheltenham, 2007, p.31ff.

[17] V. Nowotny, **Was ist eine agile Organisation?,** 2018 https://www.business-wissen.de/artikel/unternehmenskultur-was-ist-eine-agile-organisation/ (last viewed April 15th, 2019).

[18] ibid.

[19] Wirtschaftswoche, **Manager fürchten Komplexität,** 2012, https://www.wiwo.de/erfolg/management/studie-manager-fuerchten-komplexitaet/7388536.html (last viewed April 15th, 2019).

[20] T. Stingl de Vasconcelos, **Begehrtes Wissen.** Carl Auer Verlag, Heidelberg, 2012, p. 53.

[21] ibid.

[22] N. Luhmann, **Theories of Distinction.** Stanford University Press, 2002, p. 99.

[23] W. Gaiswinkler/M. Roessler, **Wunder, Skalen, Komplimente und ein anderer Blick – von den Klientinnen lernen.** 2004 http://www.netzwerk-ost.at/publikationen (last viewed April 15th, 2019).

[24] Th. Kuhn, **The structure of scientific revolutions.** 3rd edition, The University of Chicago, 1996, p. 23.

[25] T. Stingl de Vasconcelos, **Begehrtes Wissen.** Carl Auer Verlag, Heidelberg, 2012, p.267

[26] N. Luhmann, **Theories of Distinction.** Stanford University Press, 2002 p. 99.

A Case Study for HA Implementation of Selected Software Solution

Vedran BATOS and Ivona ZAKARIJA
University of Dubrovnik
Dubrovnik, 20000, Croatia

ABSTRACT

The purpose of this article is to present the case study for high availability (HA) implementation of selected software solution. The case study is based on developed software application that is running in real-time production environment where the measured response time is acquired. The measured values are analized and the simple HA solution is proposed to cover basic functionalities keeping expected application regular response time.

Keywords – high availability, software, replication, application server, database

1. INTRODUCTION

High availability (HA) of IT environment can be accomplished in many ways [1,2,5] using various technologies [8,11,12]. The aim of this paper is to monitor and acquire HA performance data of an implemented software application in real-time production environment, analyze results and propose simple solution achievable by many customers. Application module monitored in this process belongs to large Customer Relationship Management (CRM) project. Although various simple HA models [3,6,7] fit into one ore more of the following categories i.e.: replicated HW environment, replicated databases, and replicated software solution (including particular application processes) on single or distributed environment [4,9,10]), the target of this paper was to propose implementation of as simple as possible solution

with reasonable performances for the selected software solution.

2. HA ENVIRONMENT

Starting HA environment configurations consists of pairs of replicated application servers and database servers as shown below.

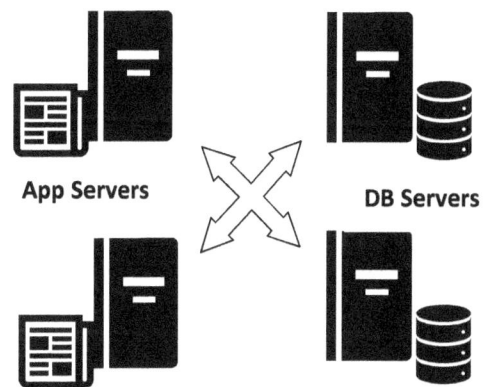

Figure 1. Initial HA environment

Simplified HA environment configuration consists of one pair of replicated application servers and single database server. Data consistency and availability at database server is ensured by internal replicated storage and software designed processes. Exposing that simple environment to Internet and adding basic HTTP server with FW (firewall) and load balancing process, leads to the initial simple configuration we used in our production process, as shown in Figure 2. As presented, the final pruduction High Availability solution served as the real-time test case consisting of two application servers running as a cluster along with an HTTP Server in front of them acting as a load balancer. The application DB requests are forwarded from application servers to DB server with implemented RDBMS (Relational Database Management System).

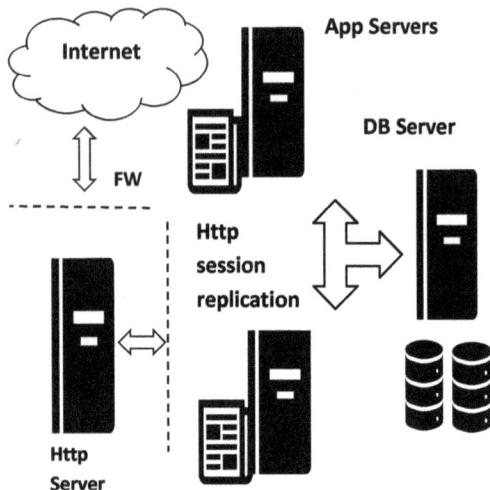

Figure 2. Final test HA

Particular IT environment systems may be installed and running at dedicated servers or within virtual machines. Testing tool allows hundreds of concurrent users to access implemented software solution. The initiated task becomes a part of test session as soon as the existing account signs in to the application and performs initial event driven actions. The session becomes closed one upon successful logout. Initial number of concurrent users is 50 with the user's considerations time of 1 second. Overall test was performed in periods of 600 seconds each with tentative usage load of 1 user per second, that leads to the number of 50 users reached within 50 seconds.

3. ANALYSIS OF THE RESULTS

Two basic options of the High Availability solution were tested. Both did utilize the same simplified architecture (load balancer + 2 application servers) but with different way of HTTP session handling. Failover mode would replicate the session across the cluster, while the other one would just perform load balancing task. To be able to compare the results with the option that did not include clustering, baseline tests were executed.

Application server instance that was implemented and tested had been installed over Linux operating system using Java based production application.

Baseline Tests

Application without clustering:
First tested case was the one with no load balancer and no cluster. This is the standard solution deployed on production servers at several locations. Application server was configured same way as the one that would be used in clustering. After the testing it was determined the average response time to be 0.96 seconds (with page elements 1.28 seconds). Equal test was executed with load balancer attached in front of the servers to determine if load balancer increases the average response time (and how much). The results were close to the tests without load balancer involved which means there is no significant slowdown caused by the load balancer itself.

Application without clustering with double assigned resources:
Second tested case was same as the first one (typical production situation), but with double assigned resources to the application server. As expected, this was leading to achievement of better results compared to simple cluster with two application server instances. The resulting average response time is 0.78s and 1.05s with page elements.

HA Tests

High Availability of application (no failover):
This HA case presented a highly available and scalable solution however it is not fault tolerant. In case of failure of one server, clients already logged into that server would get an error and then get redirected to the other working server. However, this kind of solution still did perform well and can accommodate large number of users. The results for concurrent 50 users are shown in the following Table 1.

Round	Succ. sessions	Succ. pages	Avrg resp. (s)	Avrg resp. with page elements (s)
1	1769	19805	0,76	0,94
2	1877	20830	0,7	0,87
3	1734	19536	0,76	0,96
4	1849	20495	0,7	0,89
5	1973	21892	0,66	0,8
Avrg	1840,4	20511,6	0,716	0,892

Table 1. Response time of the case with no replication (no failover)

Access toward the database is about 1MB/s per node, and from database to the application server about 800KB/s per node. Results show that by using a load balancer and two nodes, lower average response time can be achieved than by using a standard one application server instance solution. This is due to ability of application server itself to better utilize resources if it gets a smaller portion of resources (few GBs of memory per instance). Compared to the single application server solution this kind of High Availability solution is 25-33% faster than classic solution with 50% of the resources, or when same amount of resources is used, about 8-9% Results for higher number of concurrent users are shown as 2nd stage in Table 2.

No. of users	Succ. sessions	Succ. pages	Avrg resp.	Avrg resp. with page elements
50	1840,4	20511,6	0,716	0,892
100	2191	24678	1,26	1,81
200	2197	24931	2,75	4,03

Table 2. Response time of the case with no replication 2nd stage

High Availability of application (with failover):

Failover recovery for the implemented application is achieved by enabling session replication inside the application and letting application server to manage that. By enabling session replication it is possible to specify when, how often and how much of the session data should be replicated. Some of these combinations were tested and the results are below.

Replicating whole session immediately:
This case uses instant replication of the whole session. This is worst case scenario as it allows for replication to occur several times in one second (if the page is changed or refreshed) and because of the fact that the whole session gets replicated.

Round	Succ. sessions	Succ. pages	Avrg response	Avrg response with page elements
1	337	4007	6,28	6,42
2	294	3530	7,16	7,51
3	369	4381	5,73	5,86
4	352	4133	6,19	6,3
5	313	3800	6,55	6,68
Avrg	333	3970,2	6,382	6,554

Table 3. Instant and whole session replication

This leads to significant slowdown of the application, about seven time slower. It is recognized that the servers exchanged a significant amount of data, 1GB of data over 10 minutes, with average of 1.66 MB/s. Advantage of this kind of solution is that failover works almost always and if one server goes down, all of the users will have correct session data on the second server. Downside is expected slowdown of the system (these tests show about 7 times longer response times).

Replicating whole session at interval of 1000 miliseconds:
Second tested case was based on replication of the whole session but at an exact interval. Interval

chosen for this test was 1000 miliseconds This setting can be changed to reach better performance, i.e. longer interval will mean fewer replications and better performance. Even with replication occuring each 1000 miliseconds, results were quite acceptable. Presented slowdown was at the level of 20% slower. This kind of slowdown could be acceptable for failover.

Round	Succ. sessions	Success. pages	Average response	Average response with page elements
1	1645	18420	0,82	1,05
2	1559	17413	0,85	1,13
3	1652	18399	0,81	1,05
4	1670	18687	0,79	1,02
5	1650	18380	0,8	1,05
Avrg	1635,2	18259,8	0,814	1,06

Table 4. Replicating whole session at 1 second intervals

What can be seen here is that the amount of data exchanged between the servers is much lower than when replicating instantly. Total amount exchanged when replicating at an interval of 1 second is just 170MB for 10 minutes of 50 users. This makes an average of 290 KB/s. This lessened amount of data that is exchanged means that the servers are not slowed down as much. Amount of data that was exchanged can be further decreased by using higher values for interval, for example if using 4000 miliseconds interval (4 seconds), total amount of data exchanged between two nodes is just 70MBs. This setting can be fine tuned to get the best performance while maintaining failover capability. The further tests were run with 100 and 200 concurrent users. The results are shown as 2nd stage in Table 5.

No. of users	Succ. sessions	Succ. pages	Average response	Average response with page elements
50	1635,2	18259,8	0,814	1,06
100	1892	21172	1,55	2,18
200	1967	22392	3,06	4,53

Table 5. Results for 2nd stage replication at 1 second interval

Results observed with replicating at one second intervals are comparable to the results observer with no replication. The slowdown is about 20% at each level of certain number of users.

4. CONCLUSION

Two High Availability testing cases have proven that HA solution for selected implemente application is acceptable by proposed simple system configuration. Using HTTP Server as a load balancer in front of several application server instances is a simple and effective way of achieving scalability and high availability. Results of testing show that using two instances is slightly faster than one instance with double amount of the dedicated resources. Presented times of the solution are shown in Graph 1.

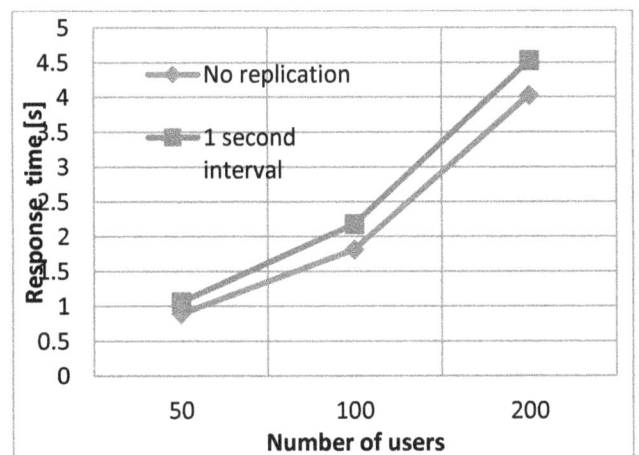

Graph 1. Comparison of no replication process against replicating at one second intervals

It is likely that increasing the amount of resources further and increasing number of instances would only increase the advantage of clustering over increasing resources. However when failover recovery is required, HA solutions must take care of performance limitations. For example if using instant session replication the resulting response time is about 7 times slower than without failover, however if session is replicated with one second intervals, this kind of slow down goes down to around just 20%. This kind of slowdown is low enough to warrant usage of this kind of reasonable HA solution. A note to be emphasized is the fact that replicating session with one second intervals is good enough from performance side, but it does not assure 100% of failover recovery. Acceptable HA solution is possible with a low effort and basic testing results could be used to improve production environment.

5. REFERENCES

[1] Ardagna D (2015), **Cloud and multi-cloud computing: current challenges and future applications**, 7th international workshop on principles of engineering service-oriented and cloud systems (PESOS) 2015. IEEE/ACM, Piscataway, pp 1–2

[2] Bielik N, Ahmad I (2012), **Cooperative game theoretical techniques for energy-aware task scheduling in cloud computing,** Proceedings of the 2012 IEEE 26th international parallel and distributed processing symposium workshops and Ph.D. forum. IEEE Computer Society, Piscataway

[3] C. Chi-Chung, Y. Man-Ching, A. Yip, **"Dynamic DNS for load balancing,"** Distributed Computing Systems Workshops, 2003, Proceedings. 23rd International Conference, pp. 962, 965, 19-22, May 2003

[4] A. Eu , Hassan, R. C. Holt, **"A Reference Architecture for Web Servers,"** Reverse Engineering, 2000. Proceedings. Seventh Working Conference, pp. 150-159, 2000

[5] M. McKeown, H. Kommalapati, J. Roth, **"Disaster Recovery and High Availability for Azure Applications"**, Microsoft Azure-MSDN, April 2014. Retrieved from http://msdn. microsoft. com/library/azure/dn251004. aspx

[6] Mell P, Grance T (2011), **The NIST definition of cloud computing**, Commun ACM 53(6):50

[7] Mesbahi M, Rahmani AM (2016), **Load balancing in cloud computing: a state of the art survey**, Int J Mod Educ Comput Sci 8(3):64

[8] P. Mvelase, N. Dlodlo, Q. Williams, M. Adigun, **"Custom-made Cloud Enterprise Architecture for Small and Micro Enterprises"**, 589-601, Grid and Cloud Computing, vol. 2, 2012

[9] National Institute of Standards and Technology, **"NIST Cloud Computing Standards Roadmap"**, NIST-US Department of Commerce, 2013

[10] Puthal D et al (2015), **Cloud computing features, issues, and challenges: a big picture. In: International conference on computational intelligence and networks (CINE)**, IEEE, Piscataway, pp 116–123

[11] I. Saha, D. Mukhopadhyay, S. Banerjee, **"Designing Reliable Architecture for State-ful Fault Tolerance"**, Proceedings of Seventh International Conference on Parallel and Distributed Computing, Applications and Technologies (PDCAT'06), pp. 545-551, 2006

[12] C. Weinhardt, A. Anandasivam, B. Blau, J. Stober, **"Business Models in the Service World"**, IEEE Computer, vol. 11, no. 2, pp. 28-33, 2009

A Case Study of Brand Management of We-Media

Yen-Fen Lo
Department of Business Administration, Shih Chien University
No.70, Dazhi St., Zhongshan Dist., Taipei City 104, Taiwan (R.O.C.)

Yen-Hsi Lo
Department of Business Administration, Shih Chien University
No.70, Dazhi St., Zhongshan Dist., Taipei City 104, Taiwan (R.O.C.)

Huang Shr-Shiuan
MBA, Shih Chien University
No.70, Dazhi St., Zhongshan Dist., Taipei City 104, Taiwan (R.O.C.)

Jung Hsiao
Material Analyst, SMS Infocomm Corporation
4051 TX-121 #100, Grapevine, TX 76051 (U.S.A)

ABSTRACT

With the Internet popularization and rapid development of we-media as well as new media industry, the chances of becoming famous overnight are significantly greater than before. Simply by using cellphones to document daily lives and promote products, ordinary people could become celebrities easily through the Internet. The purpose of this study is to understand how an ordinary person uses the Internet to operate an industry, to become a personalized new brand, and to manage a brand by utilizing we-media.

This study adopted qualitative research and interviewed five we-media operators using in-depth interview method. In addition, the five interviewees were observed by semi-structured interview method to understand the development process of their we-media brand. The interviewees were selected based on their popularity, size of audience, and field of expertise; the candidate's accessibility and willingness to participate were also decisive factors. The interview was designed with seven questions and presented in the form of verbatim manuscript, classification and summary. The results of the interview were further analyzed by brand management and media-related theories. The management implications and suggestions were proposed according to the results of the study.

The study found that media operators conform to three main characteristics: personalized we-media image, low entry threshold of the internet, and fast interactive connections with the audience. Along with the usage of pictures, text, and audio-visual tools, the we-media operators built relationships with their audience to further promote their brand and image. They utilized not only the visual tools but also related business management methods such as brand management, relationship marketing, and customer loyalty. The we-media operators often grow through the engagement with their audiences as they learn to adapt to common preferences. The profits for the we-media operators of managing their brand were expected to include more job opportunities, increased income, and other possible benefits.

Keywords: We-Media, Brand Management, Relationship Marketing, Customer Loyalty

INTRODUCTION

Research Motives and Aims

Engaged in the internet era, everyone has the chance to become an internet sensation; everyone can be we-media (Gillmor, 2004). According to the latest issue of the Global Digital Statshot, over 3.5 billion people use the internet on smartphones worldwide, and the internet usage on smartphones accounts for 54% of global internet data. In addition, 2.7 billion users access social media through mobile devices. The number of users of social media has reached 3 billion across the world and is still growing steadily. Facebook is the leading social media platform with 2 billion users, followed by Youtube with 1.5 billion (Business Next, 2017).

Based on the 2017 Taiwan Broadband Network Usage Survey conducted by The Taiwan Network Information Center (TWNIC), the number of internet users in Taiwan has reached 18.8 million. The Market Intelligence & Consulting Institute (MIC) conducted a research that targeted on local internet users in Taiwan. The research shows that 95% of the users are active on Facebook compared to 26% on Instagram and 33% on Google+. In addition, age is not a definite factor for the differentiation of users. About 97% of users that are 19 years old and younger uses Facebook, and the percentage only slightly decreases to 94% for users over 40 years old (Taiwan Business TOPICS, 2017).

"Internet celebrity" is a phrase originated in China that gained popularity in recent years, meaning a person or a group gained internet fame for their appearance, talent, or special events. They become celebrities through the promotion of other internet users, and watching the performance of internet celebrities is already a part of the daily lives of social media users (Yang and Kuo, 2017).

Most internet celebrities are we-media operators who successfully marketed their work through the internet, adding new values to their lives. The research motive is to understand the initiative of we-media brands and the methods used leading to the success of we-media. The aim of the research is to act as guidance for internet users to utilize the internet and become the best promotion media for themselves.

LITERATURE REVIEW

We-Media

Hsieh (2017) explained that every user is influential in the world of the Internet as everyone is equipped with the ability to spread and share information on social media platforms. Therefore, everyone represents an individual We-Media. Kao (2012) stated that We-Media is a form of social media, which is also called the Fourth Media. It can integrate words, pictures, and images to allow the consumers to feel as if they were at the scene. Lin (2016) stressed that We-Media is an important part of the new media as it allows the public to act as the media proactively whereas the public used to passively receive information from the old media. Hence, We-Media leads to the variety of information and resources on the social media platforms, and it allows more voices to be heard.

Bowman and Willis (2003) commissioned that We-Media as "a way to begin to understand how ordinary citizens, empowered by digital technologies that connect knowledge throughout the globe, are contributing to and participating in their own truths, their own kind of news." Gillmor (2004) compared We-Media with the old media in a way that it has the function of a traditional media but is not limited to the behaviors and structures of old media. Hsu (2015) listed the characteristics of We-Media as personalized media, extremely low entry threshold, and rapid connections and interactions.

Brands

The research conducted by Kolter (1991) indicated that a brand conveys information to consumers, and the information can be further divided into 6 categories: attributes, benefits, values, culture, personality, and user. Chu (2010) specified that a brand can also be interpreted as a form of affection, trust, and value. The brand is the soul of the enterprise as it is built through the years with complex factors such as image, development, promotion, service, and reputation.

Relationship Marketing

Berry (1991) defined relationship marketing as "a strategy of attract, maintain and develop relationship with customers." On the other hand, Shani and Chalasani (1992) specified that relationship marketing is "an integrated effort to identify, maintain, and build up a network with individual consumers and to continuously strengthen the network for the mutual benefit of both sides, through interactive, individualized and value-added contacts over a long period of time." Huang and Wang (2012) pointed out that the goal of relationship marketing is to establish customer loyalty and lifelong value through connecting and bonding with individual customers along with the aids of technology and data. Jan (2014) believed that the focus of relationship marketing is to strengthen the long term relationship between the company and the consumer in order to enhance customer satisfaction and loyalty, which will ultimately maximize the lifelong value of the customer. Hsu (2017) elaborated that utilizing relationship marketing can effectively attract new customers, maintain the loyalty of current customers, and create new value to the company.

Customer Loyalty

Sysoev and Neiman (2004) stated that loyal customers are satisfied customers, but satisfied customers are not always loyal. According to Molaee and Teimuori (2013), it is more beneficial to keep loyal customers as they tend to purchase more products than new customers. Oliver (1999) categorized customer loyalty into 4 stages: cognitive loyalty, affective loyalty, conative loyalty, and action loyalty. He also defined customer loyalty as "a deep commitment to rebuy or re-patronize a referred product or service consistently in the future, despite situational influences and marketing efforts having the potential to cause switching behavior."

RESEARCH DESIGN AND ANALYSIS

Research Methods

This research focuses on the We-Media operators' initiatives and motives of starting a business in the innovative industry. The survey is designed to understand the reason of choosing the career path of utilizing the internet to publish one's work, the degree of familiarity with the functions of social media platforms, the initial outline of brand marketing, the business module of interacting with other internet users, and the overall value of operating We-Media. Qualitative research is used for this study to analyze the survey results and to understand the development of the internet industry. The goal is to provide learning materials for newcomers in the industry.

Qualitative Research

According to Chen (2015), qualitative research is when the researcher gathers complete and abundant information through personal life, case studies, history backtracking, observation, interviews, and interactions in order to fully understand the behavior of the research target. Kuo (2012) stated that the purpose of qualitative research is to discover the concept of the original data, further analyze the data, and utilize the data in various fields.

In-depth Interview

In-depth interview, as defined by Taylor and Bogdan (1984), is to study the interaction between the interviewer and interviewee with the aim to understand the aspects and experiences of the interviewee; the participants can be a group or an individual.

A semi-structured interview is a method of collecting interview data that lies between unstructured interview and structured interview. The researcher designs the questions of the interview based on the purpose of the study beforehand, and guide the interviewee through the questions throughout the interview (Wong, 2016). This study chooses in-depth interview along with semi-structured interview so as to avoid limitations of the answers.

Research Target

The main focus of this study is to understand how We-Media operators manage their media platform as a brand. The 5 research targets chosen are We-Media operators who have their own channel on social media platforms – Love's Kitchen, BiBi, COMBOS, 100 Ideals, and Mom & Dad. In-depth interview is conducted and the contents are recorded and transcribed.

Research Question and Design

After the 5 research targets were chosen, the researcher conducted individual in-depth interview at either the interviewee's studio or home; the length of the interview was 1 hour. The 7 key interview questions are listed below:
1. What was the reason of becoming a We-Media? Could you talk about the current status and development of the internet industry?

2.   How did you find the direction for your company? Did you plan to manage your company by "brand positioning?"

3.   What is your management module? For instance, how often do you upload videos or interact with other users with photos or words?

4.   Which social media platform do you use the most? What thoughts do you have about this platform? Have you faced any challenges? What methods do you use to promote your brand?

5.   How do you interact with your fans? For instance, do you hold concerts, prize giveaways, live streams, or other events?

6.   How do you cultivate the uniqueness of your brand? What is the biggest difference between you and other internet celebrities?

7.   What is the greatest value of operating We-Media?

RESEARCH FINDINGS AND ANALYSIS

Based on the key interview questions designed solely for this study, the results of interviewing the 5 We-Media operators are summarized respectively. The summaries are further analyzed with theories related to We-Media, branding, internet marketing, relationship marketing, and customer loyalty.

- Summary 1: Echoing the 3 characteristics of We-Media - personalized media, extremely low entry threshold and rapid connections and interactions, the research targets choose to establish their brands on social media platforms after considering the financial costs of starting a new business.

- Summary 2: The 5 participants did not start the business with brand management; however, they realized the importance of brand marketing along the way. Many factors of branding are shown on the participants' channels, such as signs and logo designs. Moreover, the channels also expressed relations, trust, and value to the users. The We-Media operators cultivate their brand through image, development, advertisement, service, and reputation aiming to receive the profits of customer loyalty, brand recognition, perceptual quality, and brand association.

- Summary 3: All the participants utilize internet as the media, which corresponds to We-Media being a part of internet media that is also known as the Fourth Media. It can connect the users with the operator, allowing mutual interaction.

- Summary 4: Even though every We-Media operator uses different platforms and promotions, the common factor is that they all interact with their fans through messages on the channels. The interactions with fans can create word of the mouth effect which relates to relationship marketing theory. It is important to discover new customers, but it is more pivotal to keep the old ones and create value of the brand through the relationships.

- Summary 5: Replying the messages and engaging fans in discussions are necessary interactions. This corresponds to customer loyalty. The researcher believes if the customer loyalty is high, it means the customer is willing to repurchase the product, and this brings greater value to the company. Therefore, keeping old customers are pivotal as they are more willing to make promises of repurchase in the future. The We-Media operators should not only focus on publishing novel works on the channels,

but also take the fans' support as the motivation to create and innovate.

- Summary 6: Uniqueness is the public's first impression of the brand. The uniqueness can be shown through logos, names, or signature moves. The 6 categories of branding include attributes, benefits, values, culture, personality, and user. It is significant for We-Media operators to distinguish their brands from others in order to stay competitive in the industry.

- Summary 7: Every We-Media operator has a value they care the most that they earned through managing their own brand. Most We-Media operators have increased popularity and income; hence, it is concluded that managing We-Media on social media platforms is beneficial.

CONCLUSION AND IMPLEMENTATION

1. Brand Management in a Niche Era
    The 5 participants in the research did not start the business with any brand management, but gradually learned the importance of branding. Therefore, the researcher suggests for internet users that aim to be We-Media operators to make a short, mid, and long term business plan, including the name, logo, and slogan. Engaged in an information explosive niche era, it is important to cultivate uniqueness to capture the attention of users on social media platforms.

2. Providing Sincere Inputs and Interacting with Fans
    Huang and Wang (2012) pointed out that the goal of relationship marketing is to establish customer loyalty and lifelong value through connecting and bonding with individual customers along with the aids of technology and data. The internet users nowadays prefer sincere voices and opinions rather than data from We-Media channels. Therefore, it is important to provide new contents on the We-Media channels with personal input; it is also more efficient to encourage fans to share the contents to create word of mouth effect and increase credibility.

3. Brand Management of We-Media to Create Earning Value
    Oliver (1999) defined customer loyalty as "a deep commitment to rebuy or re-patronize a referred product or service consistently in the future, despite situational influences and marketing efforts having the potential to cause switching behavior." Hence, a popular internet celerity brand can be influential in the niche market. With increasing customer loyalty, the credibility of the brand is also established. The value created is not only limited to job opportunities and income, but also the relationship between people.

REFERENCE

1. Aaker, D. A. (1991), Managing Brand Equity. New York: The Free Press.
2. Armstrong, G. and Kotler, P. (2000), Marketing: An Introduction, (5th ed.). Prentice.
3. Berry, L. L. and Parasuraman, A. (1991), Marketing Service–Competing Through Quality, New York: The Free Press.
4. Berry, L.L.(1983), Relationship marketing, emerging perspectives on services marketing, Eds. Leonard L. Berry, G. Lynn Shostack, & Gregory Upah. Chicago.

5. Bowen, J. T., & Chen, S. L.(2001), the relationship between customer loyalty and customer satisfaction. International journal of contemporary hospitality management.

6. Bowman, S., & Willis, C. (2003). We Media - How audiences are shaping the future of news and information. Retrieved from http://www.hypergene.net/wemedia

7. Christopher, M., Payne, A. and Ballantyne, D. (1991), Relationship Bringing Quality, customer service and marketing together. Oxford: Butterworth-Heinemann.

8. Frederick, N.（2000）, Loyalty : Customer relationship management in the new era of internet marketing, McGraw. Hill.

9. Gillmor, D.(2004), We the media: Technology empowers a new grassroots Journalism, Santa Cruz, CA. Journal of Services Marketing, 6(4), pp.43-52.

10. Jones, T. O. and Sasser, W. E. Jr., (1995), "Why Satisfied Customer Defect",Harvard Business Review, 73(6), pp. 88-99.

11. Kotler, P., Lane Keller, K. (2010), Marketing Management, deessentie, 4nd editie. Amsterdam: Pearson Education Benelux.

12. Kotler,P.(1991), Marketing Management:Analysis,Planning,Implementation and Control ,7th edition, New Jersey: Prentice-Hall.

13. Molaee, M., Ansari, R., & Teimuori, H.(2013), Analyzing the Impact of Service Quality Dimensions on Customer Satisfaction and Loyalty on the Banking Industry of Iran. International Journal ofAcademic Research in Accounting, Finance and Management Sciences, 3(3),pp.1-9.

14. Morgan, R. P. (2000), A consumer-orientated framework of brand equity and loyalty. International Journal of Market Research, 42(1),pp. 65-78.

15. Moyo, L.(2011), Blogging down a dictatorship: Human rights, citizen journalists and the right to communicate in Zimbabwe. Journalism, 12(6), 745-760.

16. Oliver, R.L., Whence customer loyalty?, Journal of Marketing. 63(5) (1999) 33-44.

17. Philip Kotler, (2002), Marketing Management, eleventh edition, rentice Hall Inc: 184.

18. Raggio, R. D. & Leone, R. P. (2007), The theoretical separation of brand equity and brand value: Managerial implications for strategic planning. Journal of Brand Management, 14(5), pp.380-395.

19. Rapp,S.and Collins, T. (1990), The Great Marketing Turnaround. Prentice-Hall, Englewood Cliffs, NJ.

20. Reichheld, Fredrik F. & W. Earl Sasser (1974), Develping an image the store-loyal customer″ , Journal of retailing, 50(4), pp.73-84.

21. Shani, D.,and Chalasani, S.(1992), Exploiting niches using relationship marketing.

22. Sheth, J. N., and Parvatiyar, A.(1995), Relationship marketing in consumer markets: Antecedents and consequences, Journal of the Academy of Marketing Science, 23(4), pp.255-271.

23. Sysoev, S., Neiman,A.(2004), Love cannot be forced, or what is the customer loyalty, Maketer, 2 , pp.32-35.

24. Taylor.S.J. & Bogdan.R.(1984), Introduction to qualitative research methods: the search for meanings.New York: Wiley.

Designing digital learning environments

Phillip MIERSCH

Chair of Quality Science, Department of Machine Tools and Factory Management, Technical University of Berlin
Berlin, 10587, Germany

Prof Dr.-Ing. Roland JOCHEM

Chair of Quality Science, Department of Machine Tools and Factory Management, Technical University of Berlin
Berlin, 10587, Germany

ABSTRACT

The motivation and qualification of employees is a decisive success factor for companies. In addition, keeping pace in times of digitalization requires a constant build-up of skills, especially in small and medium-sized enterprises (SMEs) in the manufacturing sector. Such companies therefore often enter a market that offers external further trainings but in a not very transparent way. Often these offers are cost-intensive and often meet only a fraction of the actual expectations. The current technology makes it possible to transfer learning objects such as real production machines including their process flows into the virtual environment and to make them tangible. This offers great potential for digital education, as employees could acquire additional knowledge about processes or technologies in a cost-effective and flexible way. A recommendation algorithm should enable SMEs to identify their training needs and develop individual offers, especially with regard to the learning arrangement.

Keywords: Human resource development, Digital education, SMEs, Recommendation algorithm, Learning arrangement, Quality assurance.

1. INTRODUCTION

A promising factor for companies is the qualification of their employees. The age of digitalization also demands a constant build-up of skills [1]. At the same time, the latest technologies make it possible, for example, to simulate and construct virtual worlds and thus use new educational and learning formats. This promises a high benefit, especially in the area of production technology. For companies, faults in real operation often mean high follow-up costs. If employees have the opportunity to learn in advance in a simulated environment, the transfer of what they have learnt is ensured due to the closeness to reality and faults are avoided right from the onset. Due to the lack of know-how of those who are responsible for personnel development, companies often resort to external training courses [2, 3]. The selection for a further training offer has to be made among a large number of offers which are difficult to manage. These are usually expensive and do not meet the requirements of the companies and at the same time those of the individual learning styles. Expenditure on further training for employees of small and medium-sized enterprises (SMEs) in the manufacturing sector averaged € 1.517 per year [4]. Measured against a total employment figure of 5 million in the manufacturing industry, only about one third of the workforce was qualified via further training courses. An increase in this participation rate is achieved by using a company's own offer of learning content that is closely related to the work process and learning arrangements that are individually tailored to the learners. This saves costs. The primary task in supporting SMEs is therefore to provide interactive guidance on methodological design issues when setting up learning arrangements.

The creation of digital formats, such as virtual reality tutorials, is now easy to implement and can be carried out by almost everyone. Only a minimum of programming effort and a moderate use of technology are necessary. Using virtual production machines as learning objects, employees can be trained cost-effectively in technologies and processes. However, most SMEs lack suitable tools and a systematic approach, so that there are doubts about the use of technology and the design of digital learning environments in line with learning objectives is a big question mark. This is where the recommendation algorithm comes in, which uses the findings of cause-and-effect relationships and dependency analyses. This algorithm is provided on a platform for potential users.

At present, there is a multitude of systems on the market that either offer an infrastructure for the administration of existing content or represent individual solutions that concentrate only on one form of learning. However, these systems are not individually adaptable to the needs of the company and cannot be adapted to different learning contents and learning styles, so that a training program specifically tailored to the company cannot be created. The need to develop an infrastructure that "both provides knowledge and can be used as an instrument for the qualification of employees and for job changes" [5] was also cited by the Industry 4.0 Working Group. The project results of the research project of the Quality Science Department of the TU Berlin, "Virtual further training content in the application field of Quality 4.0", contribute to the development and creation of digital further training offers in SMEs without didactic previous training or extensive technical knowledge being required. Virtual content makes it possible to experience maintenance processes, simulate entire production processes and give learners a feeling for the dimensions of components [6, 7]. With realistic scenarios, the quality awareness of employees can be increased and faults can be avoided. The training process is controlled via a platform that enables the management and exchange of these training courses.

On the whole, the project results should support SMEs in solving crucial fundamental questions. In addition to the ability to create their own virtual content (e.g. videos, interactive trainings, serious games, and virtual reality tutorials), systematic description, storing and sharing will also play a central role. Finally, by publishing their own contributions, users will be able to access the content of other users via the platform. This basic idea of a self-regulating give-and-take platform does not only increase the development of courses and further training in SMEs, but also the number of users who become cost-effective access to content.

2. RECOMMENDATION ALGORITHM

The requirements for the algorithm are, on the one hand, the standardized description of the learning objective and the needs of the user via special characteristics, and, on the other hand, the corresponding characterization of the learning arrangement as the essential characteristic of the digital learning environment [8]. In the following the procedure can be represented on the basis of a simplified practical example, which is limited to the main characteristics: The aim is to design a further training offer with the learning objective "Application of quality testing for the classification of good and bad parts" for the target group "specialist" in a screw production. First the relevant information must be gathered from it in order to match with the characteristics describing the learning arrangement. Figure 1 shows the findings from a qualitative dependency analysis between the learning arrangement characteristics (e.g. learning format) and the learning needs characteristics (e.g. target group, learning objective). From this analysis it can be deduced for the present example that a Virtual Reality Tutorial can best meet the need, since only positive dependencies exist here (Figure 1).

001: Knowledge		+	+	...
002: Comprehension		+	o	...
003: Application		+	-	...
...		...	...	...
Learning objective / **Target group**	**Learning format**	010: Virtual Reality Tutorial	020: Serious Game	...
100: Skilled worker		+	-	...
200: Manager		o	+	...
300: Specialist		+	+	...
...		...	...	...

Symbols:

+	Postive dependency
o	Neutral
-	Negative dependency

Figure 1. Result of a qualitative dependency analysis in a T-matrix

The recommendation of the algorithm would therefore be: Representation of a virtual production in a Virtual Reality Tutorial, where good and bad parts occur and have to be recognized by the learner. On a virtual assembly line, the specialist should examine the produced parts and recognize reject parts that exhibit various possible defect patterns.

In real applications, however, the number of influencing factors is much higher, so that the dependencies assume complex dimensions. For example, the type of learner, the learning duration or the media experience can have a high influence. The current task is to identify all relevant characteristics and their dependencies. In addition, the dependencies are specifically quantified on the basis of current findings in educational science, which makes a more precise recommendation possible.

3. QUALITY ASSURANCE AND EVALUATION

A set of questions, which is tailored to the specific recommendation, helps to systematically identify user feedback and thus the learning success within the framework of an evaluation, to initiate continuous improvement and to derive targeted optimization measures. The evaluation is a building block in the quality assurance cycle.

The four-level model according to Kirckpatrick [9] is one the basic model for explaining the successive stages in the evaluation of educational processes. It distinguishes between the four levels of reaction, learning, behavior and results.

The first level, "reaction", reflects the satisfaction of the participants with the design of further training. Design characteristics concern, for example, the learning environment, the trainer or the learning method.

The second level "learning" comprises learning success. This describes the increase in knowledge of the participants in further training.

The transfer success characterizes the level "behavior". This is the ability to apply in the workplace what the learner has been learned.

On the fourth level, "results", extensive objective performance criteria and indicators can be used in the company to check whether certain organizational goals have been achieved through further training measures. Since it is often not possible to draw conclusions about a particular measure, the assessment at this level provides little information about the quality of further training. It was therefore not implemented in the project.

The evaluation process is carried out with the help of a dynamic questionnaire. Three of the four levels are addressed in Kirkpatrick's model. The users are questioned at three different points in time by specific questionnaires:

1. Satisfaction survey directly after the further training measure (reaction)
2. Learning success survey with short time interval (learning)
3. Transfer success survey with long time interval (behavior)

Immediately after the training, the user can access the first of a total of three questionnaires. This contains questions on the evaluation of satisfaction and the process of further training. Each question (item) is assigned to a specific quality characteristic.

The questionnaire is generated from a pool of 72 items, which are divided into two groups. The first group (up to 13 items) addresses a user's level of satisfaction with the training. The user evaluates the statements on a five-level scale from "strongly agree" to "strongly disagree". The second group refers to the process of further training. For this purpose, a pool of 59 items is used. All items are based on the German version of the Learning Transfer Systems Inventory (GLTSI) [10] and the "Maßnahmen-Erfolgs-Inventar" (MEI) [11].

The selection of items from the two groups is coordinated with the specific characteristics of further training. The questions from the second group are also selected individually on the basis of the results for the items in the first group. If, for example, a participant expresses dissatisfaction with the learning media (If you are satisfied with the learning media used. Answer: "strongly disagree"), specific questions are activated to determine the possible causes of this dissatisfaction (Figure 2). In this way, the evaluation can be carried out efficiently and the further training process can be analyzed as comprehensively as necessary at the same time. In this way, events in the further training process that have a negative influence on the overall assessment of the participant can be analyzed without confronting the participant with extensive questionnaires at the start.

Method of learning	strongly agree			strongly disagree
I was satisfied with the way the content was transferred.	☐ 4	☐ 3	☐ 2	✗ 1
				Enabled in this case
The learning methods were appropriate to the content and objectives of the training.	☐ 4	☐ 3	☐ 2	☐ 1
	☐ 4	☐ 3	☐ 2	☐ 1
The learning methods activated my abilities to absorb the contents.	☐ 4	☐ 3	☐ 2	☐ 1
...				

Description
Main question
Optional question

Figure 2. Questions for the characteristic "learning method"

The evaluation of the learning success is carried out via a questionnaire, whereby it is recommended to make this available to the participant at intervals of 1 to 7 days at the end of the continuing training measure. It comprises four items which enable the learner to assess success.

The transfer success can be evaluated via a third questionnaire. The corresponding questionnaire contains two items relating to the application of the training content in the everyday life of the user. Following the survey of the users, the evaluation takes place. In addition to an overall assessment, the developed evaluation tool also identifies causes for lack of learning and transfer success. The experiences of learners with different further training offers are expressed by a summary quality assessment with one to five stars.

4. CONCLUSION

In the course of the digitalization of work processes, occupational profiles will change increasingly, so that the development of employee skills is indispensable. Consequently, the goal must be a realistic and early preparation for innovations in the working environment. To this end, further training courses must be tailored to specific needs and used efficiently. The individualization of learning content supports the systematic acquisition of skills and can thus lead to significant efficiency gains in further training activities.

5. REFERENCES

[1] Haufe Akademie (2017): Digitaler Wandel braucht viele Lernkonzepte. [Zitat vom 06.11.2017] URL: https://www.haufe-akademie.de/blog/news/digitaler-wandel-braucht-viele-lern-konzepte/.

[2] Hormel, R. & Geldermann, B. (2009). Betriebliches Weiterbildungsmanagement für KMU. Beispiele aus der M+E-Industrie. Bielefeld: Bertelsmann. wbv.

[3] Kabst, R. & Wehner, M. C. (2010). Institutionalisierung der Personalentwicklung - Ist der Patient auf dem Weg der Besserung? In M. T. Meifert (Hrsg.), Strategische Personalentwicklung. Ein Programm in acht Etappen. Heidelberg, Neckar: Springer Berlin, S. 45-60.

[4] Statistisches Bundesamt (2015). Berufliche Weiterbildung in Unternehmen. Fünfte Europäische Erhebung über die berufliche Weiterbildung in Unternehmen (CVTS5).

[5] Kagermann, H.; Wahlster, W.; Helbig, J. (2013): Deutschlands Zukunft als Produktionsstandort sichern. Umsetzungsempfehlungen für das Zukunftsprojekt Industrie 4.0. Abschlussbericht des Arbeitskreises Industrie 4.0, S. 97.

[6] Menn, J. P.; Sieckmann, F.; Kohl, H.; Seliger, G. (2018): Learning process planning for special machinery assembly. In: Pro-cedia Manufacturing vol. 23, S.75-80.

[7] Mourtzis, D.; Zogopoulos, V.; Vlachou, E. (2018): Augmented Reality supported Product Design towards Industry 4.0. A teaching factory paradigm. In: Procedia Manufacturing vol. 23, S. 207-212.

[8] D.A. Kolb, **Experiential learning: Experience as the source of learning and development**, Upper Saddle River, NJ: Prentice Hall, 1984.

[9] D. L. Kirkpatrick, in: R. L. Craig & L. R. Bittel (Eds.), **Evaluation of training**, Training and Development Handbook; New York: McGraw Hill, 1967, pp. 87-112.

[10] S. Kauffeld, N. Lehmann-Willenbrock, in: W. Sarges, H. Wottawa & C. Roos (Eds.), **GLTSI. German Learning Transfer System Inventory - Das deutsche Lerntransfer-System-Inventar**, Handbuch wirtschaftspsychologischer Testverfahren, Band II: Organisationspsychologische Instrumente, Lengerich: Pabst, 2010, pp. 113-118.

[11] S. Kauffeld, J. Brennecke, M. Strack, in: S. Kauffeld, S. Grote und E. Frieling (Eds.), **Erfolge sichtbar machen: Das Massnahmen-Erfolgs-Inventar (MEI) zur Bewertung von Trainings**, Handbuch Kompetenzentwicklung. Stuttgart: Schäfer-Poeschel, 2009, pp.55-78.

Could the Development of On-line Services Contribute to Global Competitiveness?

Romel TINTIN
Government and Public Administration Department, Institute of Advanced National Studies (IAEN),
Quito, ZIP 170507, Ecuador.

Patricio ALTAMIRANO
Government and Public Administration Department, Institute of Advanced National Studies (IAEN),
Quito, ZIP 170507, Ecuador.

Carmen CHAVEZ
Government and Public Administration Department, Institute of Advanced National Studies (IAEN),
Quito, ZIP 170507, Ecuador.

Liliana TINTIN
International Studies Department, Chonbuk National University,
Chonbuk, ZIP 54896, Republic of Korea

ABSTRACT

The paper analyzes the United Nations (UN)'on-line services index (OSI), which is one of the components of their e-government development index (EGDI); and the World Economic Forum (WEF)'s global competitiveness index (GCI). Then, we identify whether or not a Pearson "r" correlation exists between these two indexes. To do so, we have analyzed indexes from the years 2005, 2008, 2010, 2012, 2014, 2016 and 2018. Our findings show that a high positive correlation does exist, and the respective conclusions and further work are drawn from our findings. They showed a general correlation average of 0.80 (high correlation) between the OSI and GCI indexes studied, therefore it would stand to reason that on-line services development does indeed contribute to the factors that would improve global competitiveness, making this analysis not a causality study.

Keywords: E-government, on-line services, competitiveness, United Nations' on-line services index, OSI, World Economic Forum's global competitiveness index, GCI, Pearson correlation coefficient.

1. INTRODUCTION

The aim is to make a comparative analysis on a global scale between the United Nations (UN)'s on-line services index (OSI) [1], and the World Economic Forum (WEF)'s global competitiveness index (GCI) [2]. The years analyzed in this study are 2005, 2008, 2010. 2012, 2014, 2016 and 2018. We also determined its Pearson "r" correlation coefficient [3] between the two mentioned indexes, their evolution and their tendencies during those years.

Since 2001, the United Nations Department of Economic and Social Affairs (UNDESA) has published its E-Government Survey. Following on their past editions, and looking at its current edition (tenth), we have observed that the Survey provides an in-depth analysis of progress concerning the usage of e-government. The Survey tracks the progress of e-government development via its E-Government Development Index (EGDI). The EGDI, which assesses e-government development at a national level, is a composite index based on the weighted average of three normalized indexes. One-third is derived from a Telecommunications Infrastructure Index (TII) which is based on data provided by the International Telecommunications Union (ITU); one-third is from a Human Capital Index (HCI) based on data provided by the United Nations Educational, Scientific and Cultural Organization (UNESCO) and one-third from the Online Service Index (OSI) based on data collected from an independent survey questionnaire which is conducted by UNDESA and assesses the national online presence of all 193 United Nations Member States

The focus of our study revolves more on the only usage of the OSI index taken from EGDI and the entire usage of GCI index. The reason why we didn't take all the components from the EGDI index on this research is because GCI contains the same two components that EGDI has. These two components are the Technological Infrastructure and Human Capital. These indexes are very similar to each other and if taken into account the data would be corrupted hence, we only took the OSI from EGDI and the rest from GCI.

Therefore, it is important to firstly define a few crucial terms like e-government, on-line services and competitiveness

1.1 Electronic Government

The United Nation's Public Administration Network (UNPAN) gives an overview of e-government as a conceptual framework embedded in the paradigm of human and social development. In that sense, e-Government encompasses the capacity and the willingness of the public sector to deploy ICT to improve knowledge and information for the service of citizens [4].

1.2 On-line Services

One of the components of e-government is online services and [5] defines it as follows:

It is possible to manage many government procedures through electronic sites, which lower the costs and times of citizens, because they are always available, without lines.

1.3 Competitiveness

Regarding the concept of competitiveness, the authors **[6, p. 7]** exposed the concept as follows:

For companies to be able to compete successfully, the economy of a country must be highly productive. Productivity depends, in many ways, on government actions on infrastructure, education and technological development, as well as public policies that promote or impede the growth of productivity, such as labor, fiscal and regulatory policies. In this way, while the productivity of the economy is reflected in the ability of companies to compete with one another, competitiveness depends on what these companies can do to compete fairly and successfully in the market.

2. PREVIOUS RELATED SYUDIES

To ensure uniformity of appearance for the Proceedings, your paper should conform to the following specifications. If your paper deviates significantly from these specifications, the printer may not be able to include your paper in the Proceedings.

Among the studies that analyze the relationship between the e-government Index, the on-line services index (OSI) and the Global Competitiveness Index (GCI), we can mention the followings:

On the [7] the importance of ICTs on the development of Competitiveness exists for exporting companies because in regard to the logistics of the companies, these can be carried out without having physical presence, making the services much faster, practical and efficient using technological means.

[8] identifies the influence of ICTs on European countries competitiveness by the fact that in the last 30 years the use of ICTs has increased. In his study, a regression panel analysis was previously performed. Data was collected from 5 periods going from 2007-2011. The data taken was from the Eurostat of Europe and from Global Competitiveness Report statistical bases. In his study it was found that ICTs have a high impact on the Global Competitiveness Index.

In other studies like [9], [10], [11], [12], [13], [14]; they too show the importance and correlation that e-government has with competitiveness.

Therefore, regarding our study, we could say we are one of the first to analyze the correlation between on-line services and competitiveness. Not to mention we have already done other studies involving how e-government corelates with other factors/variables like corruption. [15], [16].

In the case of our study, we want to base e-government and on-line services as a relevant tool for strategic issues globally with the intention to provide a service that can affect the improvement of the perception of corruption and competitiveness.

3. METHODOLOGY

To understand our methodology, we need to understand the inner workings of the two indexes we are studying.

Firstly, according to the UN reports of our studied years, we can appreciate the development of e-government through ratings that go from 0 to 1, with 1 being the most developed and those that are close to 0 are the ones with lesser development.

The e-government Development Index (EGDI) is made up of 3 components: quality and scope of online services, connectivity / telecommunications infrastructure and capacity / human capital. All these components go from 0 to 1 as well.

Secondly, the GCI analyzes 12 pillars / components: 1. Institutions, 2. Infrastructure, 3. Macroeconomic Environment, 4. Health, 5. Primary Education, 6. Higher Education and Training, 7. Efficiency in the goods market, 8. Efficiency in the labor market, 9. Development of the financial market, 10. Technological preparation, 11. Market size and 12. Business satisfaction and innovation. This GCI goes from 0 to 7.

We raised information from the databases of the UN and the World Economic Forum (WEF) for our studied years 2005, 2008, 2010, 2012, 2014, 2016 and 2018 and we determined the descriptive statistics and trends between OSI and GCI.

We proceeded to perform the correlational analysis to establish whether there was a correlation between the on-line services index (OSI) and the Global Competitiveness Index (GCI) on a global scale. A cross section analysis was considered for the years of 2005, 2008, 2010, 2012, 2014, 2016, and 2018 and once the type of correlation was determined among the countries worldwide we proceeded to determine their respective degree of linear correlation [17, p. 287].

The primary sources (data) used were the databases of the United Nations on-line services index (OSI) and the Global Competitiveness Index (GCI) of the World Economic Forum (WEF). To complement the analysis of the first data, secondary sources were reviewed in relation to similar works as to obtain insights on our findings on whether there was an existence of a correlation between the OSI and the GCI.

4. COMPARATIVE GLOBAL ANALYSIS OF OSI AND GCI TRENDS IN THE WORLD

4.1 Evolution of the OSI average (2005, 2008, 2010, 2012, 2014, 2016 and 2018)

Fig. 1

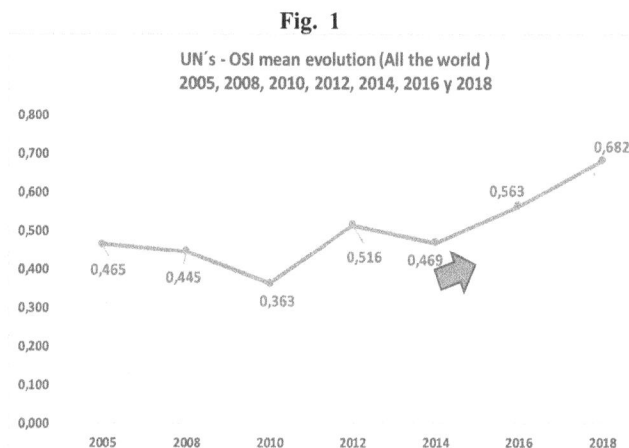

UN´s - OSI mean evolution (All the world)
2005, 2008, 2010, 2012, 2014, 2016 y 2018

Source: **[1]**
Preparation: **Authors**

Figure 1 shows the growth trend of the OSI from 2005 to 2018 in which the annual average in the world is 0.500 and it is noteworthy to mention that from 2016 to 2018 it has grown 21.12% in this period.

4.2 Evolution of the average of the GCI (2005, 2008, 2010, 2012, 2014, 2016 and 2018)

Figure 2 shows the GCI trend of growth especially from 2010 to 2018 in which the annual average for the world is 4,213 although between the period of 2016 to 2018 there is a decrease of -0, 3%.

Fig. 2

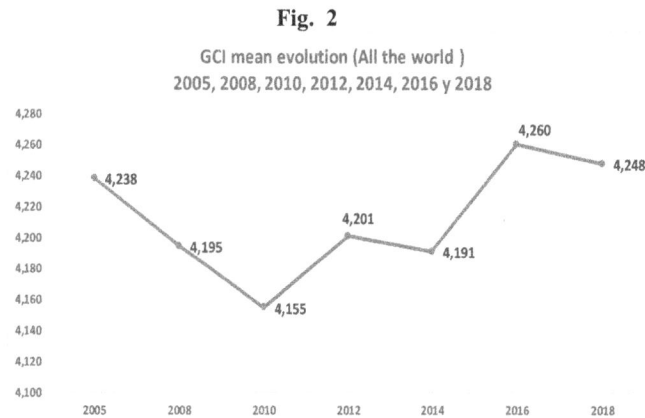

GCI mean evolution (All the world)
2005, 2008, 2010, 2012, 2014, 2016 y 2018

Source: [2]
Preparation: Authors

5. DISPERSION AND CORRELATION BETWEEN OSI´S AND GCI´S OF THE WORLD

5.1 OSI's and GCI's dispersion values of the world through the years of 2005 and 2018.-

Figures 3 and 4 show the dispersion between OSI and GCI indicators during 2005 and 2018.

Year 2005.-

Here, we can observe on figure 3 data that clearly reflect an important correlation with a value of 0,809. On this year 114 countries were analyzed.

Fig. 3

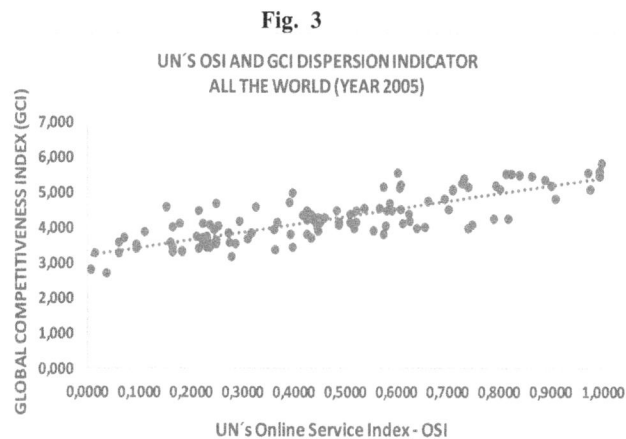

UN´S OSI AND GCI DISPERSION INDICATOR
ALL THE WORLD (YEAR 2005)

Source: [1], [2]
Preparation: Authors

Year 2018.-

On figure 4, the data reflects on this year a clear correlation with a value of 0,832. 133 countries were analyzed on this year

Fig. 4

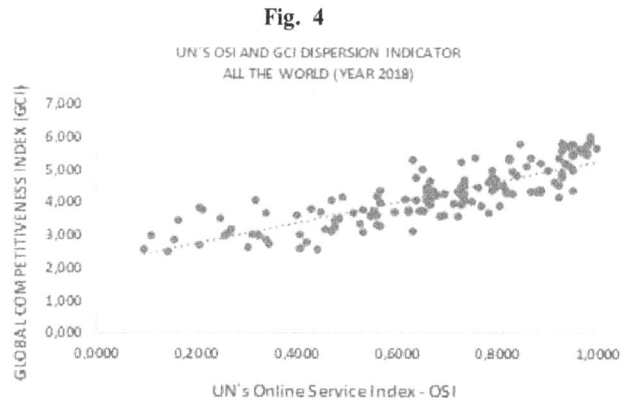

UN´S OSI AND GCI DISPERSION INDICATOR
ALL THE WORLD (YEAR 2018)

Source: [1], [2]
Preparation: Authors

In Figures 3 y 4 we can see that the dispersions of the OSI and GCI can result in positive Pearson "r" coefficients.

Dispersions for the years 2008, 2010, 2012, 2014 and 2016 can be seen in the Annex 1.

5.2 Pearson "r" correlation coefficient evolution between OSI and the GCI of the world (2005, 2008, 2010, 2012, 2014, 2016 and 2018).

Figure 5 shows the correlation evolution between OSI and GCI from 2005 to 2018.

Fig. 5

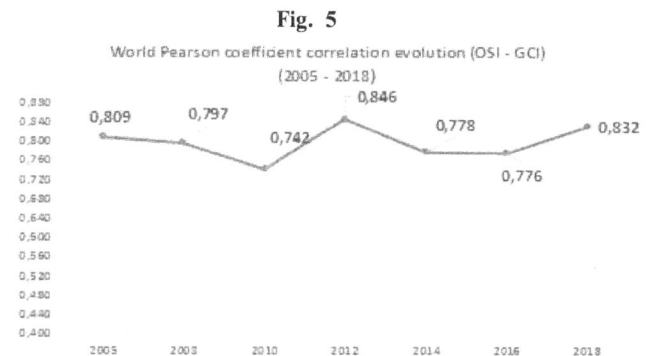

World Pearson coefficient correlation evolution (OSI - GCI)
(2005 - 2018)

Source: [1], [2]
Preparation: Authors

As we can see it can be highlighted that the Pearson "r" correlation of the world group has a positive upward trend and that it remains during the period 2010 to 2016 with a high correlation. It also portrays that for the year 2018 it increases to a good high correlation.

6. CONCLUSIONS AND FURTHER WORKS

6.1 Conclusions

1. There is a Pearson's "r" correlation between the OSI and the GCI and it is on average 0.80 which is high; this implies that

globally, e-government does indeed have an impact on the improvement of Competitiveness.

2. It is worth highlighting the efforts made by the countries that are developing their e-government and its Competitiveness especially the developed countries.

3. One of the countries that stands out in the South American region is Uruguay, currently it is the leader of e-government in the South American region. Since 2008, Uruguay has grown 22.1% of the OSI's highest score, which is 1 according to [[18] and has grown 5% of the highest score of the GCI, which is 7. Other countries that have made efforts to improve their OSI and its GCI are: The United Kingdom, New Zealand, Japan and Germany. These countries are countries that have enough resources to easily implement their e-government development.

4. We can reaffirm what mentions [19, p. 3]: "[...] e-Government services can actively contribute to increasing competitiveness".

6.2 Further Works

1. Carry out the current study but considering the grouping for example by the GDP per capita of each country, by quartiles or by country regions. Also, it should be taken into considerations further studies with e-government data that could be affected in the future by new technologies such as: Artificial Intelligence, Big Data, Cloud, Machine Learning, Block Chain, Robotics among others.

2. To propose new studies of correlations between e-government and other variables such as the existing institutionalism in the countries contemplated in the WEF (World Economic Forum).

3. We could also analyze new case studies such as Chile because it is the current leader in the region in competitiveness and e-government has influenced this situation. It would be interesting to analyze the program promoted on this country of Intelligent Industries and how it affects its competitiveness.

4. Expand new future studies that widely take data on productivity, Human Development, innovation, index of doing business or direct investments of the countries and correlate these variables with the variable of e-government.

5. In the future, on a more progressed study we could also consider developing a causal model to be tested with a multiple regression analysis.

6. Also we can consider the same analysis of this research considering different continents and see the trend from continent to continent.

7. ACKNOWLEDMENTS

This paper was partially elaborated thanks to the supporting research grants given by the Advanced National Studies Institute (in Spanish: Instituto de Altos Estudios Nacionales (IAEN)) from Quito – Ecuador, S.A. Also, we would like to thank all the professors and students of the IAEN who provided us with their valuable comments and ideas as we did this work.

8. REFERENCES

[1] NATIONS, UNITED, E-Goverment survey 2005 - 2018: E-Goverment in support of sustainable development, New York: Department of Economic and Social Affairs, 2005 - 2018.

[2] World Economic Forum, The Global Competitiveness Report 2006 - 2018, Genova, 2006 - 2018.

[3] E. W. Weisstein, ""Correlation Coefficient."," A Wolfram Web Resource, [Online]. Available: http://mathworld.wolfram.com/CorrelationCoefficient.html. [Accessed Julio 2017].

[4] United Nations Public Administration Network UNPAN, "A General Framework for E-Government: Definition - Maturity Challenges, Opportunities, and Success," [Online]. Available: http://www.unpan.org/Library/MajorPublications/UNEGovernmentSurvey/PublicEGovernanceSurveyintheNews/tabid/651/mctl/ArticleView/ModuleId/1555/articleId/20840/Default.aspx.

[5] A. Naser and G. Concha, *El gobierno electrónico en la gestión pública,* 2011, p. 11.

[6] L. Rubio and V. Baz, El poder de la Competitividad, Mexico: Centro de Investigación para el Desarrollo, s/f..

[7] J. J. G. Ochoa, J. D. D. León and J. P. Nuño, "Propuesta de un modelo de medición de la competitividad mediante análisis factorial," *Contaduría y Administración,* 2016.

[8] J. Zoroja, Fostering Competitiveness in European Countries with ICT: GCI Agenda, Croatia: International Journal of Engineering Business Management, 2015.

[9] R. L. Lizardo, *Estudio comparativo sobre la incidencia del Gobierno Electrónico en la percepción ciudadana sobre la corrupción en los países de Latinoamérica,* Caracas: CLAD, 2014.

[10] S. Srivastava and T. Teo, "The Relationship between E-Government and National Competitiveness: The Moderating Influence of Environmental Factors," *Communications of the Association for Information Systems,* 2008.

[11] M. Guerra, *El gobierno electrónico como herramienta para la competitividad.,* 2009.

[12] P. Belenyesi, Digital Competitiveness and Digital Evolution- Why Are Nordic Countries Ahead?, 2015 a..

[13] P. Belenyesi, Digital Competitiveness in Finland and its Driving Forces, 2016.

[14] J. Zhao, A. Truell, M. Alexander and R. Davis, "State E-Government service and economic competitiveness," *Issues in Information Systems,* vol. Volume VII, no. No. 2, 2006.

[15] R. Tintin, J. Altamirano, C. Chávez and L. Tintin, "Could e-government development contribute to reduce corruption globally?," Ambato, 2018.

[16] J. Altamirano, "Existe correlación entre el Indice de Gobierno electrónico de la ONU y el Indice de Percepción de la corrupción? Análisis en los países del mundo y otras regiones," 2018.

[17] J. Padúa, I. Ahman and C. Borsotti, Técnicas de investigación aplicadas a las ciencias sociales, México: Fondo de Cultura Económica, 2016.

[18] C. Chávez, *Porqué es líder en Sudamérica en Gobierno electrónico? : Caso Uruguay Tendencias, aciertos, desaciertos y buenas prácticas al 2016,* Repositorio IAEN, 2018.

[19] Red GEALC, OEA, BID, IDRC, "Boletín Red GEALC: E-Gobierno y Competitividad," 2015.

[20] A. Meier and L. Terán, EDemocracy & eGovernment. Etapas hacia la sociedad democrática del conocimiento., Quito Ecuador: Instituto de Altos Estudios Nacionales (IAEN), 2017.

ANNEX 1

DISPERSIONS FROM 2008 TO 2016:

Year 2008.-

Fig. 6

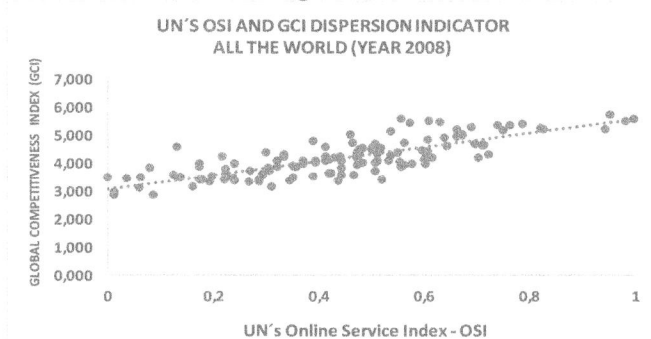

UN'S OSI AND GCI DISPERSION INDICATOR ALL THE WORLD (YEAR 2008)

Source: [1], [2]
Preparation: Authors

Year 2010.-

Fig. 7

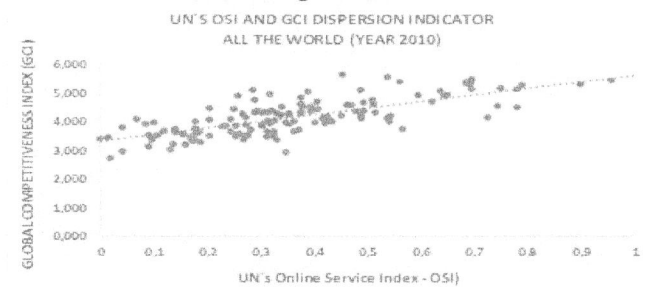

UN'S OSI AND GCI DISPERSION INDICATOR ALL THE WORLD (YEAR 2010)

Source: [1], [2]
Preparation: Authors

Year 2012

Fig. 8

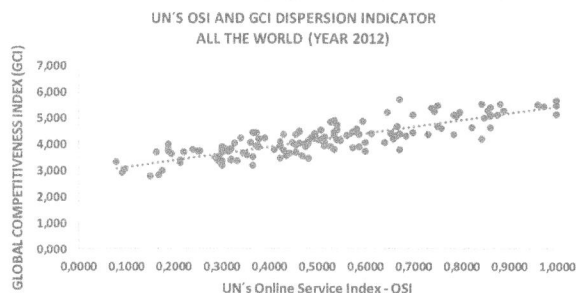

UN'S OSI AND GCI DISPERSION INDICATOR ALL THE WORLD (YEAR 2012)

Source: [1], [2]
Preparation: Authors

Year 2014.-

Fig. 9

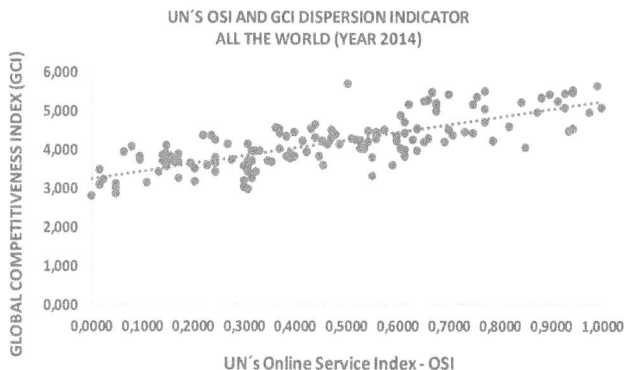

UN'S OSI AND GCI DISPERSION INDICATOR ALL THE WORLD (YEAR 2014)

Source: [1], [2]
Preparation: Authors

Year 2016.-

Fig. 10

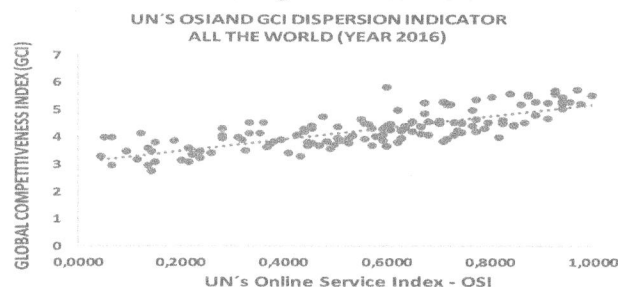

UN'S OSI AND GCI DISPERSION INDICATOR ALL THE WORLD (YEAR 2016)

Source: [1], [2]
Preparation: Authors

ANNEX 2

Abbreviation	Meaning
GCI	Global Competitiveness Index
OSI	Online Services
WEF	World Economic Forum
UN	United Nations
EGDI	E-Government development index
HCI	Human Capital Index
TII	Telecommunications Infrastructure Index

Infor's CSI / Mongoose in the Classroom: A Professor and Student Perspective

Brandon Barroca
CSI Intern
CPIS Student
Farmingdale State College

Dr. Jill O'Sullivan
Chair
Computer Systems Department
Farmingdale State College

ABSTRACT

Using industry products in the classroom are what makes a significant difference in student learning and preparation into the workforce. Students need skills sets that will differentiate them from other graduates when seeking employment.

The partnership with Infor allows students at Farmingdale State College to use the ERP CSI and Visual solutions prevalent in industry in the classroom. This partnership allows for a synergy between Education and Industry/Business that has resulted in many students obtaining jobs.

Infor and Farmingdale State College have a long-standing relationship from our use of their Visual ERP tool through their premier solution provider Synergy Resources to their new EAP program with CSI. The negotiated endowment for the CSI offering has been in the classroom successfully for a year now while the Visual tool has been in our class for more than nine years. Winning awards and accolades from companies who hire our students. Only through these very important Academic and Industry partnerships can we mutually succeed. These tools used in Dr. O'Sullivan's ERP classes at Farmingdale State College is where Brandon Barroca is the dedicated CSI Intern.

Keywords: Partnership, Education, Industry, Real world tools, ERP solutions.

1. INTRODUCTION

Information systems and software engineering are two very prominent aspects in today's business environment. The demand for knowledge in both areas is great. Although these two areas are different from one another, they do share a connection. A connection found in many businesses today.

Infor designs, implements, and deploys detailed ERP Cloud solutions that help companies deal with project management as well as other aspects of business like data processing. [1]

Students need access to these solutions in order to be best prepare for their future roles. Most companies use management information systems to deal with all functional areas of their organization. ERP systems governing the entire organization are crucial in assisting these companies to be efficient, effective and profitable.

Infor's Cloud Suite Industrial is an ERP system for businesses that allows for "predictive analytics, collaboration, lean production tools, and integration options".

Businesses are able to manage with the use of forms in the CSI tool; these represent many internal functions like scheduling, service management, metrics, and reports. Companies get the benefits of security and disaster recovery.

2. INTERNS PERSPECTIVE

From this CSI Intern student's perspective, the tool is easy to use as well as understand. From the user interface to filtering utility and the keyboard shortcuts, these are what makeup a proper and useful information system.

The well-designed interface allows users to be very efficient with the work that they have to perform. The interface offers a variety of functions, such as the ability to automatically open or pre-load specific forms that are needed for a specific user. Other functions are available in the toolbar, such as the ability to open forms and create new entries in a form.

The use of filters for forms and entries permits users to find information without looking through an entire list. These filters take input from specified fields and locates forms/entries with the similar or same exact information that matches what the user had inputted.

With the addition of keyboard shortcuts, there is now a quick solution of not having to find and click an option but instead, you just need press a key or two on your keyboard. This will allow users to get work done more efficiently.

Students using this tool are prepared with skills that have propelled their opportunities.

3. USING MONGOOSE

Infor's Mongoose program is an application builder that allows administrators to create their own custom applications with special functions.[2] Even though it might seem slightly more difficult to use, once you understand it better the program will become easier to navigate. Mongoose also provides various components and options when building forms like text fields, button, images, etc. With the high customizability of Mongoose, companies can cater this program to their needs, which is a great benefit to the companies using it.

4. STUDENT/FACULTY INTERACTION

Faculty-student interactions take on a more intense flavor in a tutorial-style classroom, or in a hands-on style ERP class as experienced in these classes at Farmingdale State College. Such close, intense, interactions seem to enhance student learning and intellectual stimulation, with both student and faculty valuing the opportunity.

This apprentice-type training, tutorial-style class setting mirrors industry required actions from their functional employees that make the company successful. This is what makes this class so successful. Students understanding the flow of the enterprise gives them an advantage compared to silo focused courses. Sitting with students in a faculty lead directive hands on application provides students with many opportunities to complete their assignments. Companies that visit the classroom or the many student lead manufacturers tours helps students convey the many process driven exercises they have to do. Having students see the same tools used in local companies gives them a great appreciation for what they are learning. Mirroring what businesses do in the classroom is clearly, what has enabled graduating students from Farmingdale State to be so successful. Having students learn in an apprentice style scenario allows for the closest training relevant to industry current and future ERP use.

5. CONCLUSION

Farmingdale State College, specifically, Dr. O'Sullivan, has recognized the need to bridge the gap from what is in business and what is taught in the classroom by providing students with the latest tools used by industry. Students who take this ERP course and use these tools for entry into the workforce can hit the ground running. Many ERP students employed claim that this is because of these skill sets learned in this class. [4] Using tools like CSI or Visual Infor products will be the cornerstone of keeping American industry vital into the far future.

The demand of qualified employees is absolute and the technology of ERP systems in the classroom that are up to date with industry timelines will improve our collaborations.

The continuous improvement of these relationships, techniques, and skills will net a solution for the current state. The necessary alignment between industry and academia will allow for meeting the needs of industry.

The widespread implementation of ERP systems has increased the demand for professionals with knowledge of ERP systems and their underlying integrated processes. Business as well as government organizations are investing significantly in ERP systems with the goal of streamlining their business operations and reducing information fragmentation.

The goal is to improve undergraduate education in systems and graduate a new generation of talent that will provide industries with the ability to secure, sustain, and grow their operations. Filling the skills shortage will stabilize a vulnerable technology environment before the problem reaches crisis proportions. Having a pipeline of prepared students for industry is what this collaboration is. From the initial Visual ERP tool from Synergy to this EAP INFOR CSI tool, together, we can improve and bridge that gap. Collaborating as an academic with industry to provide students with skills industry needs has improved student opportunities. This entire partnership contributes to the academic arena and benefits business and the industrial community.

Overall, information and ERP systems like Infor's are the ones that we need to be using in our classrooms to provide better learning experience with their innovative design and functionality. We need to continue partnerships with industry using real world tools to get closer to what they need in a prepared employee. The relationship has proven extremely successful. [3]

6. REFERENCES

1. https://www.infor.com/products/cloudsuite-industrial

2. https://www.infor.com/products/mongoose

3. J. O'Sullivan and G. Caiola, **Enterprise Resource Planning a Transitional Approach from the Classroom to the Business World**, The McGraw-Hill Companies, 2008.

Managing Information Security System Technology Changes across an Enterprise

Kevin E. Foltz and William R. Simpson
Institute for Defense Analyses
4850 Mark Center Drive, Alexandria, VA 22311
{kfoltz, rsimpson}@ida.org

ABSTRACT

The goal of information security systems in an enterprise is to make the right information available to the right entities at the right times and in the right formats while ensuring only authorized information flows occur. The standard approach is to purchase a new system to meet current needs. Patches, work-arounds, and added components satisfy the changing future needs while creating an increasingly complex system, and operational capability slowly degrades over time as complexity builds. The system is then rebuilt from the ground up, at great cost and inconvenience, and the cycle repeats. This paper describes an approach for constant change. Instead of building the best system possible based on today's needs, only to replace it in the future, the goal is a system that is capable of evolving toward a better future in a consistent and directed way. This prevents one-off fixes from lingering, and it keeps the distributed decision-making process aligned toward a common enterprise goal. Components not consistent with future goals are identified and scheduled for replacement. Current practices chosen for expedience are assigned expiration dates to prevent them from becoming solidified in the future architecture. The replacement cycle is applied to components of the system instead of the entire system. This stops the cycle of complete replacements by allowing constant change, which reduces overall cost and maintains a more consistent operational capability.

INTRODUCTION

Information security systems are complex. They are built using products with configurations, settings, and best practices that can be difficult to understand and implement. The products use protocols, which are instantiated in implementations that themselves have engineering trade-offs and configurations. These implementations build on underlying networking infrastructure, protocols, and configurations, and these rely on algorithms, mathematics, and physics to work. Just the simple act of loading a web page has built into it a vast array of technologies, configurations, settings, and other considerations developed over many years by thousands of individuals, companies, and other entities and refined by billions of users and trillions of interactions. This situation is only becoming more complex as new protocols, scientific research, products, and operational guidance are developed.

The first challenge for an enterprise is not just how to build a secure information-sharing system, but how to even define the goals in such a changing landscape. The goals must be set at the appropriate level. Too high, and they fail to guide real-world choices. Too low, and they become too rigid when new technologies emerge. With the right goals, the second challenge is to understand the past, present, and future. The past is all the

systems already purchased and operating. The present is the set of systems being put into place now. The future is the vision for upcoming systems, and the direction in which to move current systems. With this understanding of past, present, and future, the final challenge is to integrate and manage these in a cohesive way. As time progresses, the future becomes the present, the present becomes the past, and the past is retired. This cycle should be continuous in order to preserve a functioning system rather than thrash between new and shiny systems with great promise that quickly become frustrating old systems that no longer function.

CURRENT APPROACHES

Some current approaches to information security system management rely on the expert, the bureaucracy, or the vendor.

The Expert

With the expert approach, a single expert or small group owns the problem and the solution to all information system issues. They plan, coordinate, and direct computer-related activities in an organization; help determine the information technology goals of an organization; and are responsible for implementing computer systems to meet those goals. [1] Their competence enables the enterprise to rely on them for all its needs, and the expert is rarely questioned. This is partly because their competence allows them to make good choices, keep systems running, and respond quickly to requests, but also because no one else in the enterprise is qualified to ask the right questions to challenge them. This approach has the benefits of efficiency, consistency, and good alignment with enterprise goals. However, if the expert is a single person or a small group, this person may have their own hidden agenda or biases that drive their decisions. This would be difficult to stop or even discover. Also, an individual or small group may retire, take another job, or otherwise leave the enterprise scrambling for a replacement. Because the system was maintained by a single person, it may have idiosyncrasies that this person created and kept up with, but others coming into the job would not understand. Thus, changing experts requires a complete system overhaul, where a lot of the accumulated knowledge about the system, its users, and best practices is lost. Relying on these experts can be beneficial in the short term, but they may limit the growth and continuous improvement of the organization. [2]

The Bureaucracy

A bureaucracy can address some of the failings of the expert. It is a system for controlling or managing an organization that is operated by a large number of officials employed to follow rules carefully. [3] Instead of a single person who is largely unaccountable, a bureaucracy documents all of its procedures, processes, and decisions in detail. It often has oversight and periodic reviews as well. This allows the function of the bureaucracy to continue even as the people within it are constantly changing. However, bureaucracies often take a life of their own that can diverge from their original intent due to the tendency of the bureaucracy to try to survive through funding variances and changing political pressures. Also, bureaucracies are inefficient and slow to change, and they often make decisions based on who complains loudest or who has the most influence instead of who has the best ideas. They lack the accountability of a single person. [4] Where the expert can exercise good judgement on a case-by-case basis, bureaucracies are constrained by their own operating procedures, which do not always fit well with future problems that arise.

The Vendor

Vendors ultimately provide the products that are used to build information-sharing systems. They are current with technology, products, and best-practices. They anticipate future needs and work to meet them in their products. As a result, vendors often have better knowledge than a bureaucracy about how to build a system. Also, many vendors work as integrators to provide cohesive solutions for a related set of information-sharing problems. It is often tempting to go to vendors looking for solutions. However, the vendor goal is profit. Profit can be aligned with providing a good solution, but often in the long term it is not. In particular, vendors often strive to lock customers into their solutions by providing functionality that works well as part of their overall solution but does not integrate with other solutions. [5] When an organization is locked in, the vendor can increase prices until they are close to the significant cost to switch vendors. Comparing vendors or choosing a different vendor is not the solution, because the problem is inherent in the vendors' goals and the structure of the relationship.

THE VISION

A new approach is needed to address current problems. Our vision includes the following components:

- Describe design principles and goals
- Document the past, present, and future
- Trickle down from future to present to past
- Dedicate teams to continuously review and update documentation

The first part, where design principles and goals are described, forms the foundation for all later work. Current work on the Enterprise Level Security (ELS) security model starts with a set of tenets, a subset of which are shown in Figure 1. These are basic design principles that are used to build the ELS architecture.

Examples include simplicity, assuming malicious entities cannot be kept out of our system, extensibility, and accountability. These basic ideas and goals shape all detailed decisions for the system. Tied to these tenets are a set of key concepts for our system. These include important protocol decisions, the need to name all entities, and the need to authenticate all entities. Unlike the tenets, which could be applied to many different types of systems, the key concepts are related specifically to our information system. Tied to these concepts are a list of requirements. These include specific naming requirements, the requirement for unique identities, and the restriction against anonymity in communications. The requirements are still not particular to any product or service, but they apply generally across many products. These are high-level requirements for the entire information-sharing system. This basic security model, including the full sets of tenets, concepts, and requirements, is described in more detail in [6].

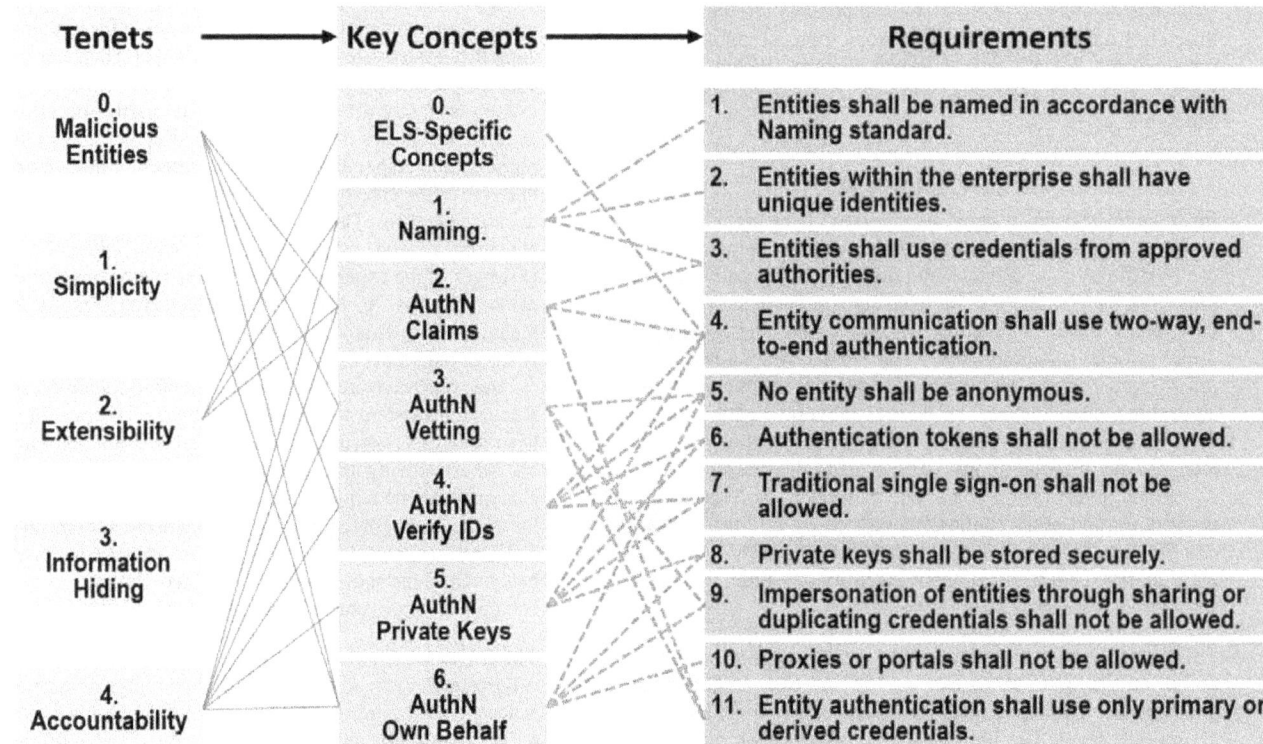

Figure 1. Mapping of Tenets to Concepts to Requirements

Beyond these tenets, principles, and goals are a set of documents that discuss specific technologies. These document the past, present, and future. The future is closely tied to the design principles and goals. This is the "Target Baseline," which consists of documents that describe the goal for the near future for different technologies. The first set of these documents consists of "Scenarios," which describe different enterprise needs and the questions they raise about how to use technology. The second part consists of "Technical Profiles," which describe how to use different technologies. These include authentication, access control, and other basic security functions. They also include mobile device management, databases, and operating systems, which rely on the basic security documentation and requirements. Scenarios are written as enterprise needs are identified. Technology profiles are written as the scenarios raise technology questions.

The scenarios and technology profiles describe the goal for the ideal future state. This is not constrained by current products or best practices. It seeks to apply the design principles and goals to particular technology problems by proposing technical solutions that are consistent with the design goals.

The present-looking documents are the "Implementation Baseline," which describe current products. Each document provides an assessment of how a currently available product compares against relevant Technical Profile requirements. "Capability Profile" documents bridge the gap between the Target Baseline and Implementation Baseline. These describe the capability a product implements and the relevant target baseline document requirements that apply.

A product with an Implementation Baseline document is not an approved product. It is simply a product that has been analyzed with respect to the goals for the security model and information sharing. With this analysis, it is possible to make informed decisions for risk management. The document identifies shortcomings in security and capability. It quantifies the security risks and provides forms of mitigation that may reduce risk.

The Implementation Baseline documents also include information about product vendor plans for the future, such as whether or when they plan to release an updated version that meets certain requirements or mitigates risks. For example, when setting up an encrypted communication path, a product may use several standard approaches. For many reasons, including vulnerabilities and compromises, the more current standards may be required as part of the baseline. The current release of a product may have implemented Transport Layer Security (TLS) version 1.0. This may not meet the baseline requirement of TLS 1.2 or subsequent. However, the developer may plan to provide TLS 1.2 in its next release. This future-looking assessment can be used to decide whether a product is more or less likely to meet future enterprise needs by comparing their plans to the future goals as stated in the Target Baseline. In some cases, the product will not be recommended if it is not on a path to satisfy the baseline.

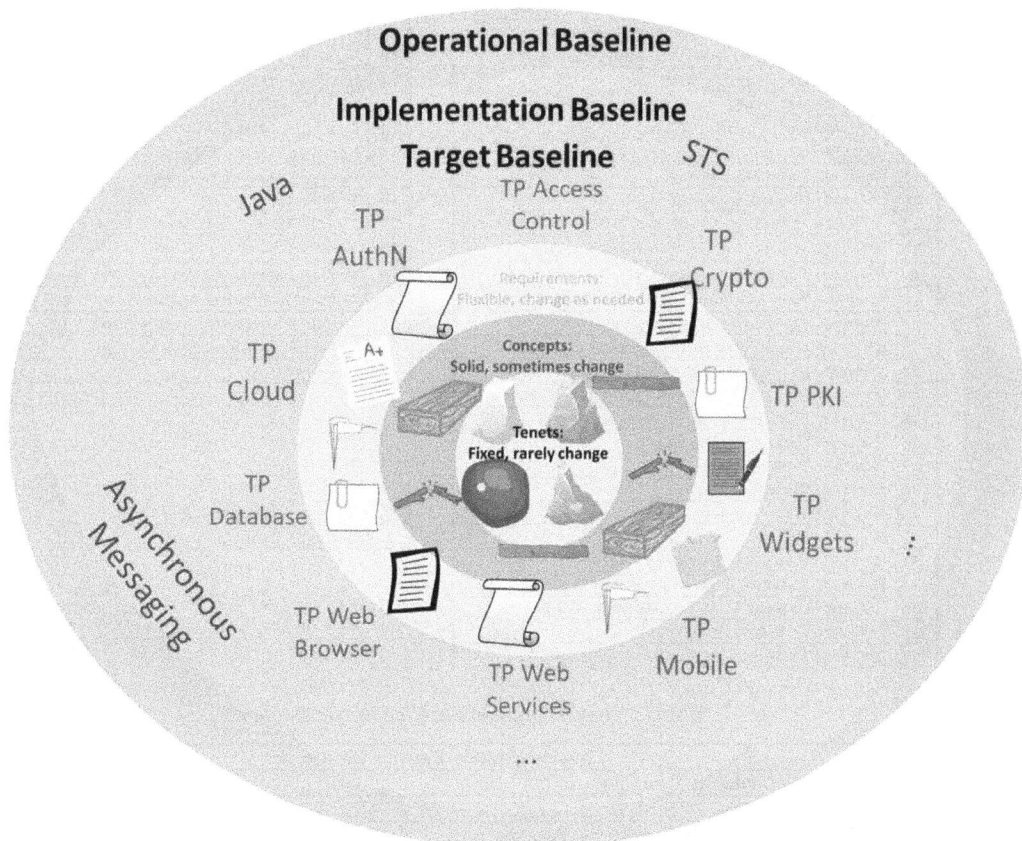

Figure 2. The Vision, from Tenets to Operational Baseline

The final set of documents is the "Operational Baseline," which looks to the past and describes the currently fielded products and their operational rules, configurations, and best practices. Like the implementation baseline, this operational baseline identifies shortcomings in security and capability. It quantifies the security risks and provides forms of mitigation that may reduce that risk. It can also provide an upgrade approach through the implementation baseline for current software that will bring it more in line with the target baseline. The operational baseline can be used to set budgets and provide support for vulnerability mitigation work. It is understood that these products probably do not meet the future goals, so the focus is on how these products are being used to best conform to the goals as described in the future-looking documents.

Figure 2 describes the overall vision. It starts at its core with the tenets, which are represented by solid rocks that are difficult to move or change. These are surrounded by concepts, which are represented by wood, which is still solid but more flexible than the tenets. The requirements are represented by formal documents, which can be changed easily but still have significant weight attached to them.

Beyond these central ideas are the three layers of documentation, the Target Baseline, the Implementation Baseline, and the Operational Baseline. Each layer is primarily related to and affected by the neighboring layers. The Target Baseline is directly driven by the Requirements, which are a practical expression of the higher-level Concepts and ultimately the Tenets. The Implementation Baseline products are evaluated directly against the Target Baseline's Technical Profile document requirements. In addition, as products are evaluated, there is a feedback process that can adjust the Target Baseline and the Technical Profile requirements to better align them with current technology. The Operational Baseline relates to the Implementation Baseline for currently fielded products that were not previously evaluated in the Implementation Baseline. These product configurations and operational practices are documented in the Operational Baseline, and any shortcomings with respect to Implementation Baseline documents for similar products are highlighted.

Table 1. Target Baseline Documentation

#	Technical Profiles		#	Scenarios
1	Application Security Guidelines		1	Access Management
2	Configure IDPS		2	Application Hosting
3	Manage Info - Provide Digital Policy with QoS		3	Application Performance Management
4	Provide Access Control		4	Data Management and Info. Exchange
5	Provide Access Control Annexes		5	Data on Human Users
6	Provide Authentication		6	Edge Information Management
7	Provide Automated Info Capture Services		7	Elasticity
8	Provide Cloud Services		8	Enterprise Info. Management
9	Provide Consolidated Storage Services		9	Ground Segment Telem. and Command
10	Provide Cryptographic Services		10	Incident Response
11	Provide Data Mining Services		11	Infrastructure and Application Defense
12	Provide Data/Info/Protocol Mediation Services		12	IT Service Management
13	Provide Database Services		13	Key Management
14	Provide Domain Name Services		14	Leverage Digital Signature
15	Provide Load Balancing		15	Leverage Infrastructure Services
16	Provide Messaging Services		16	Mobile Enterprise
17	Provide Metadata Tagging & Discovery Services		17	Mobile Enterprise Annex 1 AIDC
18	Provide Mobile Ad Hoc Network Services		18	Mobile Enterprise Annex 2 Loc. Services
19	Provide Monitoring Services		19	Mobile Enterprise Annex 3 Wireless
20	Provide Network and Application Defense		20	Mobile Enterprise Annex 4 Device Mgt
21	Provide Operating System Services		21	Mobile Enterprise Annex 5 IoT
22	Provide Public Key Infrastructure Services		22	Network and Precision Timing
23	Provide Presentation Services		23	Resiliency
24	Provide Service Desk Management Services			
25	Provide Streaming Media Services			
26	Provide Virtualization Services			
27	Provide Web Browsing			
28	Provide Web Hosting			
29	Provide Web Services		#	Capability Profiles
30	Provide Widget Services		1	Endpoint Management Service (CP)
31	Provide Ports and Protocol Policy			
32	Provide Satellite Communications			
33	Establish Space Time Information Correlation			
34	Provide Collaboration Services			
35	Provide Endpoint Device Management			

Table 2. Implementation Baseline Documentation

#	Implementation Baseline Document
1	Managed Platforms .NET Baseline
2	Application Services
3	Managed Platforms Database Server Baseline
4	Enterprise Level Security (ELS) Capability
5	Managed Platforms Enterprise Resource Planning (ERP) Systems
6	Managed Platforms Java Baseline

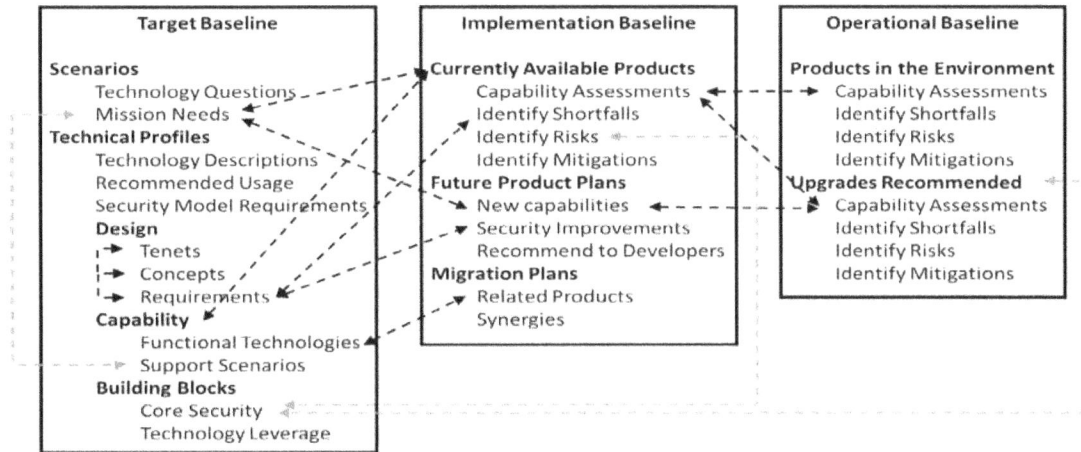

Figure 3. Documentation Hierarchy

Mitigations for vulnerabilities are also noted. Often, these are workarounds for missing capability that involve inefficiencies or security risks. By documenting these workarounds, the Implementation Baseline documents have better information about which shortcomings in current products have existing workarounds and which are fundamental problems that will require additional cost or effort. Ultimately, the Operational Baseline and the operational procedures should be driven by the Tenets, Concepts, and Requirements through this process, which keeps the entire enterprise consistent to the extent possible. Shortcomings are documented, workarounds noted, and expected compliance plans and dates are recorded.

REALIZING THE VISION

Scenarios include many different questions about how to perform different mission needs. The basic security model is documented in a special "Design Technical Profile" called "Application Security Guidelines." This describes the tenets, key concepts, and high-level requirements for building an ELS system. "Building Block Technical Profiles" include Authentication, Public Key Infrastructure, Access Control, and Monitoring. These apply across a large number of different capabilities and technologies. "Capability Technical Profiles" include the many technologies and capabilities that build on the core security functions to provide functionality for the enterprise.

"Capability Profiles" link the Target Baseline to the Implementation Baseline. An important question for these documents is what constitutes a capability versus a requirement. The capabilities in these documents must be described at a high enough level that they do not restrict a vendor's implementation. This allows for vendor creativity and inclusion of new technologies. However, the capabilities must be defined specifically enough that vendors cannot simply bypass key security requirements by using new and different approaches that are not proven or secure. Table 1 shows a sample list of Scenarios, Technical Profiles, and Capability Profiles.

The Implementation Baseline contains several documents. A potential set of these documents is listed in Table 2. It can be difficult to get enough information from vendors to assess their products against the fairly detailed security requirements in the Target Baseline Technical Profiles. It is tempting to simply ask the vendors if they meet all the requirements and happily accept a "Yes" answer to all such questions. However, the purpose of these documents is to provide reliable information about products, and vendors do not always provide such information freely, especially the information about requirements their products do not meet. Feedback to the groups producing target baseline documentation and education of the group writing the Implementation Baseline about current Target Baseline requirements will improve the overall evolution.

The process to perform full assessments is still under development. The need for full-time trained professionals in this area is great.

For the final component, the "Operational Baseline," the first step is to identify all current products in use. This is a considerable effort for a large enterprise, and results are often incomplete. Currently assigned personnel at the operational level do not have time to organize this aspect, and it may have to await staffing for this function. Essential feedback to both the target baseline and implementation baseline will improve the overall continuous improvement of the enterprise IT. It is expected that these documents will be very limited distribution.

Figure 3 shows the relationships between the different types of documentation. The Target Baseline also describes some of its internal structure.

The dashed lines indicate paths of influence between the document types. For example, mission needs identified in scenarios shape the Capability Technical Profiles, the products analyzed for the Implementation Baseline, and the assessment of vendors' future product plans. There is mutual feedback between the capability assessments of the Implementation Baseline and Operational Baseline. Upgrades for the Operational Baseline are influenced by, and can also influence, the core security requirements in the Building Block Technical Profiles. Many other interactions are possible. These help to keep all the documents more cohesive and relevant to each other and to current technology trends and products.

In addition to the influence between documents, the periodic discussions that follow these dashed lines help to inform owners of each document type about the other documents that are relevant. This helps to accomplish the following:

43

- Finding Target Baseline shortfalls in the Implementation Baseline and properly assessing associated risks.
- Finding, understanding, and assessing shortfalls, risks, and mitigations to the Operational Baseline.
- Adding necessary upgrades to the Operational Baseline, or replacing products if upgrades are not available or insufficient.
- Updating the Target Baseline to better align with current products and practices and avoid significant divergence from the commercial state-of-the-art.

FUTURE WORK

As the future becomes the present, we expect to see more products meeting the old requirements. The Implementation Baseline documents will be updated to reflect the current status of products with respect to the original Target Baseline. They will also be assessed against the updated Target Baseline as it evolves. For example, an Implementation Baseline document for a product may contain a history of relevant Target Baseline requirements and when they were first met. This provides information about a vendor's follow-through when promises are made to upgrade and become compliant with Target Baseline requirements.

As new products are purchased using the Implementation Baseline as guidance, these products will evolve toward the Operational Baseline as their configuration, use, and best practices are established.

Thus, with time, the Implementation Baseline and eventually the Operational Baseline will become more mature and populated with documentation. The process to track technology goals, products, and how we use them reduces the need to do a full assessment from scratch.

CONCLUSION

The ability to maintain a secure information system is a daunting task. We propose a systematic way to identify and document future goals, translate these to current actions, and track these over the lifetime of products in the system until they no longer meet operational needs. This requires a dedicated team to work on the future vision, another team to map this vision to currently available products, and a third to document operational procedures for current products. By maintaining these teams and fostering communication between them, it is possible to maintain the collective knowledge of an expert. The periodic review and documentation provides the stability of a bureaucracy. The mapping to current products in the Implementation Baseline and Operational Baseline ensures that these ideas track with current best practices of vendors. This approach is currently being developed and implemented, and it is evolving and maturing as more mission needs are raised, more technologies are analyzed, more products are reviewed, and the operational procedures for these products are matured and documented. This paper is part of a body of work for high-assurance enterprise computing using web services [7-13]

ACKNOWLEDGMENTS

This work was supported in part by the U.S. Secretary of the Air Force and The Institute for Defense Analyses (IDA). However, the publication of this paper does not indicate endorsement by any organization in the Department of Defense or IDA, nor should the contents be construed as reflecting the official or unofficial position of these organizations or their members.

REFERENCES

[1] United States Labor Department, Bureau of Vital Statistics, Occupational Outlook Handbook, Computer and Information Systems Managers, April, 2018, https://www.bls.gov/ooh/management/computer-and-information-systems-managers.htm , accessed on 11 October 2018.

[2] Gino, Francesca and Staats, Bradley, "Why Organizations Don't Learn," Harvard Business Review, November 2015. Available at https://hbr.org/2015/11/why-organizations-dont-learn .

[3] Cambridge University Press, Cambridge Dictionary, https://dictionary.cambridge.org/dictionary/english/bureaucracy , accessed on 11 October 2018.

[4] Johnson, Ronald N. and Libecap, Gary D., The Federal Civil Service System and The Problem of Bureaucracy, University of Chicago Press, January 1994. Available at http://www.nber.org/chapters/c8632.pdf .

[5] Opara-Martins et al., "Critical analysis of vendor lock-in and its impact on cloud computing migration: a business perspective," Journal of Cloud Computing: Advances, Systems and Applications (2016) 5:4. DOI 10.1186/s13677-016-0054-z

[6] Kevin E. Foltz and William R. Simpson, 2016. Proceedings of The 20th World Multi-Conference on Systemics, Cybernetics and Informatics: WMSCI, Enterprise Level Security – Basic Security Model, Volume I, WMSCI 2016, Orlando, Florida, 8–11 March 2016, pp. 56–61.

[7] William R. Simpson, and Kevin E. Foltz, 2017. Lecture Notes in Engineering and Computer Science, Assured Identity for Enterprise Level Security, Proceedings of the World Congress on Engineering, July 2017, Imperial College, London, pp. 440–445,

[8] William R. Simpson, and Kevin E. Foltz, 2017. Enterprise Level Security: Insider Threat Counter-Claims, Lecture Notes in Engineering and Computer Science: Proceedings of The World Congress on Engineering and Computer Science 2017, 25–27 October, 2017, San Francisco, USA, pp. 112–117.

[9] William R. Simpson and Kevin E. Foltz, 2017. Proceedings of the 22nd International Command and Control Research and Technology Symposium (ICCRTS), Escalation of Access and Privilege with Enterprise Level Security, Los Angeles, CA. September 2017, pp. TBD.

[10] William R. Simpson and Kevin E. Foltz, 2017. Proceedings of the 19th International Conference on Enterprise Information Systems (ICEIS 2017), Volume 1, pp. 177–184, Porto, Portugal, 25–30 April, 2017, Enterprise Level Security with Homomorphic Encryption, SCITEPRESS – Science and Technology Publications.

[11] Kevin Foltz, and William R Simpson, 2016. "Enterprise Considerations for Ports and Protocols, Lecture Notes in Engineering and Computer Science: Proceedings of The World Congress on Engineering and Computer Science 2016, 19–21 October, 2016, San Francisco, USA, pp.124–129.

[12] Simpson, William R., CRC Press, 2016. Enterprise Level Security – Securing Information Systems in an Uncertain World, by Auerbach Publications, ISBN 9781498764452, May 2016, 397 pp.

[13] Kevin E. Foltz and William R. Simpson, 2016. Wessex Institute, Proceedings of the International Conference on Big Data, BIG DATA 2016, Access and Privilege in Secure Big Data Analysis, 3–5 May 2016, Alicante, Spain, pp. 193–205.

Man-Machine Synergy in Systems for Critical Infrastructure Protection

Mario LA MANNA

Evoelectronics

Rome, Italy

ABSTRACT

The protection of critical infrastructures has to cope with increasing challenges, both in quality and in quantity. In order to provide effective measures against the pressure of new and sophisticated threats and to cover all security aspects, namely monitoring, detection and reaction, coupling of machine learning and human judgment is paramount. This paper proposes a novel methodology, based on a mixture of automated machine learning and human judgment and demonstrates that this joint approach is beneficial for the effective protection of critical infrastructures.

Keywords: Critical infrastructures, machine learning, situational awareness, environment monitoring, network security.

1. INTRODUCTION

An advanced security system for critical infrastructures (Fig. 1) is composed of the following subsystems: a) Sensor subsystem, whose function is to collect raw data coming from the environment; b) Data and Information Fusion subsystem, which has the function to merge data coming by the sensors and data and information coming from external intelligence sources; c) Human Agent in the Loop subsystem, which performs operations by means of a human operator in the decision loop; d) Intelligence subsystem, which gathers data coming from intelligence (mainly produced by human experts) and e) Core Processor, which combines all the information produced by the previous subsystems, performs machine learning and extracts real time outputs.

The system is based on an interdisciplinary (human/machine) approach, having to cope with the heterogeneity of the data produced by the system itself, those collected by the monitoring tools and secure information coming from different sources. Monitoring data are derived from different types of sensing units, while secure information comes from intelligent external sources, human in the loop agents and system intelligence. This paper focuses on a novel methodology, embedded in the system, which is based on the synergy between automated machine learning and human judgment and demonstrates that the application of this methodology is

beneficial for the effective protection of critical infrastructures.

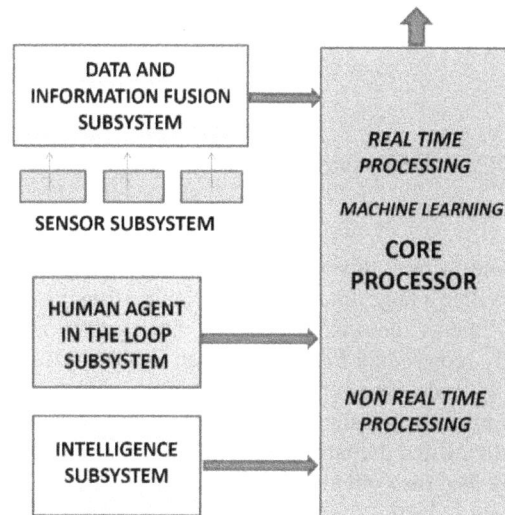

Fig. 1: Advanced Security System Architecture for the protection of Critical Infrastructures.

2. MACHINE LEARNING FOR CRITICAL INFRASTRUCTURE PROTECTION

The machine learning approach to the protection of critical infrastructures is based on artificial intelligence techniques (e.g. statistical modelling) and on computational intelligence techniques (e.g. nature inspired methodologies).

The techniques based on artificial intelligence are traditionally classified into supervised and unsupervised learning techniques. In the first category (supervised learning), the main solutions are: decision trees [7], rule learners [8], Bayesian networks [9], Naive Bayes approach [10], instance-based learners [11] and perceptron-based technique [12]. In the second category (unsupervised learning), the main techniques are: association rule learning [13], clustering techniques [14] and Markov chains [15].

The techniques based on computational intelligence are: genetic algorithms [16], artificial neural networks [17], fuzzy logic [18] and artificial immune systems [19].

3. THE ROLE OF HUMAN JUDGMENT

The previously listed machine learning techniques are derived from a high number of scientific fields, namely logics, statistics, optimization theory, etc.

Independently from the technique chosen for a specific case, the application of machine learning is structured in a number of steps, which constitute a process, typical of the protection chain. This process is composed of the following sub-processes (Fig.2).

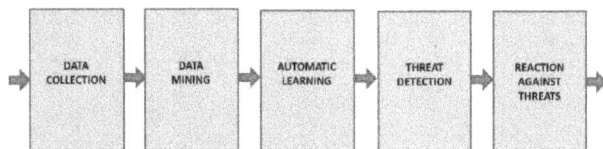

Fig. 2: Machine learning process for critical infrastructure protection.

1) Data collection: this sub-process consists of capturing and recording a huge amount of data coming from external sensors and/or communicated by intelligence actors (typically represented by human experts) for subsequent processing and training.

2) Data mining: this sub-process incudes pre-processing, standardizing and preparing the collected data, in order to correctly feed the system inputs inside the system.

3) Automatic learning: this sub-process implements three different steps, namely training, tuning and validating the previously prepared data. It allows to build internal intelligence and automatic capabilities, in order to respond to the incoming threats. Learning can be unsupervised (the system has not any knowledge about the learned variables) and supervised (there is knowledge about these variables).

4) Threat detection: this sub-process provides the crucial function of discovering threats and evaluating the relative risks for the system integrity and survival.

5) Reaction against threats: this sub-process has the function of defining appropriate actions to counteract the discovered threats and to minimize damages and risks for the whole system.

Independently from the technique adopted for machine learning during the whole process, from the experience gathered in real case studies, the synergy between man and machine is particularly important during Sub-process 3 (Automatic Learning) and Sub-process 5 (Reaction against threats). In particular, the most relevant aspects of the man-machine cooperation are; a) supervision in the machine learning prior to the training and b) human support to the reaction process.

We include the aforementioned aspects into a Man-Machine Sinergy Algorithm, which allows to provide the necessary intelligence and automatic capabilities, in order to neutralize rapidly and efficiently the incoming threats.

4. MAN-MACHINE SYNERGY ALGORITHM

The Man-machine Synergy Algorithm starts from the concept, derived from practical experience in real cases, that situation assessment (i.e. real time detailed information on what is happening on a determined scenario) is strongly dependent on the total amount of known significant characteristics of the environment. In particular, we observe that the main knowledge about these characteristics derives from human experience, more than from data coming from external sensors. This means that, in order to build a true model of the environment, the knowledge of a human expert is generally prevalent above the contribution given by an automated function. Moreover, a further contribution comes from the Human Agent in the Loop subsystem, which instructs the automated system to gather information contained in a certain amount of raw data. According to the above observation, the first section of the Man-Machine Synergy Algorithm has a direct impact on the automatic machine learning, In particular, independently from the adopted methodology for learning (supervised/unsupervised), a predefined knowledge scheme is introduced before the traditional automatic learning. This scheme is used to create a knowledge base, also with variables different from the ones involved in the automated sub-process. These variables come from the Intelligence and Human Agent in the Loop sub-systems.

The role of intelligence and human in the loop is to create a solid knowledge background, which can steadily improve the efficiency of the subsequent learning activity, mainly with respect to the known attacks and known attack strategies, but in most cases also regarding unknown attacks. From direct experience in real cases, the percentage of human information (coming from intelligence and human in the loop) vs. the total information gathered by a system can be described as a function of the system complexity, as reported in Fig. 3.

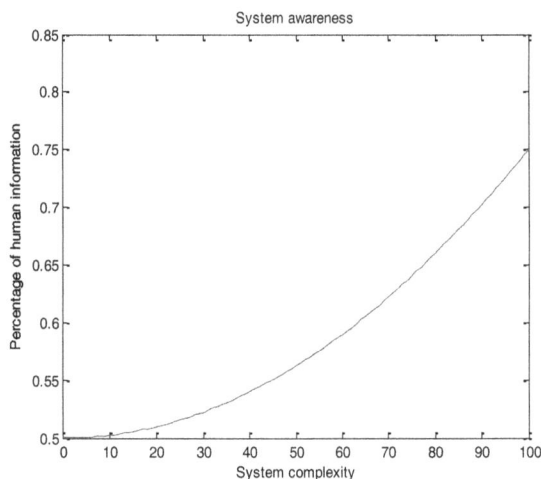

Fig. 3: Percentage of human information in system awareness as a function of system complexity.

The same Man-machine Synergy Algorithm has another impact on the reaction sub-process. According to its characteristics, the system reaction can be either passive or active. Passive reaction consists of raising an alarm or switching off the system. An active reaction means to counteract the threat, in order to avoid a system failure. This second type of reaction requires more judgment and deep knowledge coming from experience. For this reason, the a-priori knowledge base, created by intelligence and human in the loop, has the function to funnel the machine function to the most efficient actions. This part of the man-machine synergy algorithm can be described as an integrated recovery action. From direct experience, the percentage of human information (coming from intelligence and human in the loop) vs. the total information necessary for an efficient recovery as a function of the system complexity, can be approximated in the diagram reported in Fig. 4.

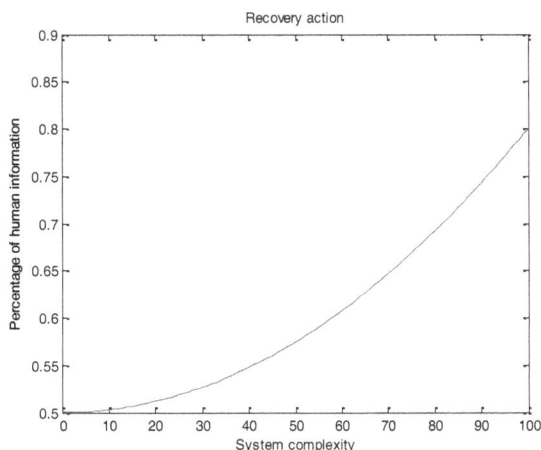

Fig. 4: Percentage of human information in a recovery action as a function of system complexity.

5. THE INTEGRATED SYNERGY PROCESS

This section has the goal to estimate quantitatively the benefit of the man-machine synergy algorithm with respect to system awareness. As discussed in the previous section, the knowledge base created by the operator, by means of the intelligence and human in the loop sub-systems has the function of improving the quality of the subsequent learning activity. In fact, the automation introduced by machine learning is quite useful when the tasks involved are intensive in computation or they occur when working conditions are extreme. On the other hand, human judgment results decisive to setup the system to a correct functioning in a determined context. Taking only into account the quantity of data that can be gathered by human operators, in order to be used by the learning process, as discussed in the previous section, the system

awareness is considerably enhanced by introducing the man-machine synergy algorithm. In particular, if we consider the system awareness of a typical system [6] and take into account the results reported previously (see Fig.3), we can derive the diagram of a typical system awareness as a function of system complexity, with and without man-machine synergy (Fig.5). From this diagram, we can observe that the synergy between man and machine can sensibly improve system awareness, starting from low complexity systems (starting from value 0) to very complex systems (up to value 100) .

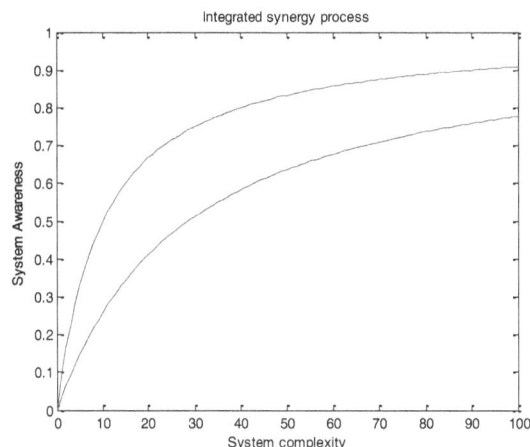

Fig. 5: System awareness as a function of system complexity, with (upper diagram) and without (lower diagram) man-machine synergy.

6. THE INTEGRATED RECOVERY ACTION

This section has the goal to estimate quantitatively the benefit of the man-machine synergy algorithm with respect to a recovery action. As discussed in Section 4, the knowledge base created by the operator, by means of the intelligence and human in the loop sub-systems, can also improve the effectiveness of the recovery action. If we take only into account the quantity of data that can be gathered by human operators, in order to be used by the recovery action, as discussed in the Section 4, the probability of recovery is considerably enhanced by introducing the man-machine synergy algorithm. In particular, if we consider the probability of recovery of a typical system [6] and take into account the results reported previously (see Fig.4), we can derive the typical probability of recovery as a function of system complexity, with and without man-machine synergy (Fig.6). From this last diagram, we can observe that the synergy between man and machine can sensibly improve the recovery action, in particular when the system complexity grows up and the number of environment characteristics tends to be high. In fact, the defensive action of the network has to be based on a suitable knowledge of the common vulnerabilities and exposures of the network, together with a deep understanding of the strategies of the possible attacker.

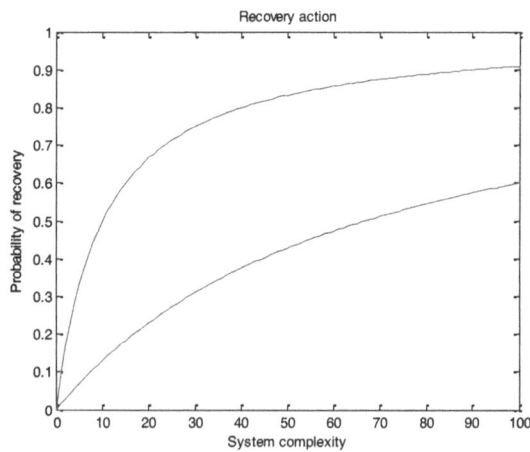

Fig. 6: Probability of recovery as a function of system complexity, with (upper diagram) and without (lower diagram) integrated recovery action.

7. CONCLUSIONS

This paper describes how to increase the effectiveness of the systems dedicated to the protection of critical infrastructures by building a synergy between human judgment and automated machine learning. In particular, we present a novel methodology, based on a mixture of automated machine learning and human judgment and demonstrate that this joint approach is beneficial for the effective protection of critical infrastructures. The advantages of our approach are measured quantitatively, taking into account two main critical aspects of the machine learning process, namely situation assessment and recovery action. Starting from data collected on the field in real applications, we show that both situation assessment and recovery action are considerably improved by merging machine learning and human judgment in a cooperative way.

8. REFERENCES

[1] M. LaManna "Urban Environment Monitoring: System and Technology Issues", IMCIC 2012, 25-28 March 2012, Orlando, FL.

[2] M. LaManna "Data Fusion of Heterogeneous Sensors in Urban Environment Monitoring" IMCIC 2013, 9-12 July 2013, Orlando, FL.

[3] M. LaManna "Cost-Benefit Analysis of Automated Systems for the Control of Urban Critical Infrastructures" WMSCI 2015, 12-15 July 2015, Orlando, FL.

[4] M. LaManna "Future Trends for Cyber Security for Critical Infrastructures" WMSCI 2016, 5-8 July 2016, Orlando, FL.

[5] M. LaManna "Technology Intercepts for Cyber Security applied to Critical Infrastructures" WMSCI 2017, 8-11 July 2017, Orlando, FL.

[6] M. LaManna "Multisensor Data Fusion for Cyber Security in Critical Infrastructures" WMSCI 2018, 8-11 July 2017, Orlando, FL.

[7] B. Kamiński, M. Jakubczyk, P. Szufel "A framework for sensitivity analysis of decision trees". Central European Journal of Operations Research, 2017.

[8] R.J. Urbanowicz, J.H.Moore "Learning Classifier Systems: A Complete Introduction, Review, and Roadmap". Journal of Artificial Evolution and Applications. 2009.

[9] N.Friedman, D. Geiger, M. Goldszmidt "Bayesian Network Classifiers". Machine Learning, Nov. 1997.

[10] H.Zhang "The Optimality of Naive Bayes", Florida Artificial Intelligence Research Society Conference, 2004.

[11] W. Daelemans, A. Van den Bosch, "Memory-Based Language Processing". Cambridge University Press, 2005.

[12] M. L. Minsky, S. A. Papert "Perceptrons, Expanded Edition". MIT Press, 1988.

[13] M.Hahsler "Introduction to arules, a computational environment for mining association rules and frequent item sets", Journal of Statistical Software, 2005.

[14] E. Achtert, C. Böhm, P. Kröger, A. Zimek "Mining Hierarchies of Correlation Clusters", International Conference on Scientific and Statistical Database Management, 2006.

[15] P.A.Gagniuc "Markov Chains: From Theory to Implementation and Experimentation", John Wiley & Sons, 2017.

[16] S.Skiena, "The Algorithm Design Manual", Springer Science and Business Media, 2010.

[17] S.Haykin "Neural networks : a comprehensive foundation", Prentice Hall, 1999.

[18] V. Novak, I. Perfilieva, J. Močkoř "Mathematical principles of fuzzy logic", Dordrecht: Kluwer Academic, 1999.

[19] L.N.de Castro, J. Timmis "Artificial Immune Systems: A New Computational Intelligence Approach". Springer, 2002.

Performance Comparison of HyperFileSQL and MySQL in WinDev applications for SMEs in Ecuador

Javier MUÑOZ

Information and Communications Division, General Contralory of the State,
Quito, Pichincha 170101, Ecuador

Silvia TRAVEZ

Software Development Division, ADS Software Cia. Ltda.
Latacunga, Cotopaxi 050101, Ecuador

Félix FERNÁNDEZ-PEÑA

Applied Informatics Research Group, Universidad Técnica de Ambato,
Ambato, Tungurahua 180103, Ecuador

ABSTRACT

Optimizing database operations can be translated into the reduction of both, the time required to develop a software system and the time spent carrying out management operations during software exploitation. This paper focuses on the study of the persistence layer of WinDev's applications. The results of the experiments that were carried out show that the performance when retrieving data using MySQL was increased 2.2 times. These results were statistically validated with a P-value less than 0.1 in a t-test. The use of MySQL in WinDev applications increases the performance of data management processes. These research results have a big impact on software industry in Ecuador if we take into consideration that WinDev is an IDE broadly used for the development of agile applications at SMEs in the country.

Keywords: database management, performance comparison, software development for a SME.

1. INTRODUCTION

The use of information technologies as a support to the business processes has had a huge growth in the last decades. Using the right tools in software industry has turned into a crucial element in order to generate a competitive advantage.

Due to the diversity of tools, it is necessary to evaluate, from a technical perspective, how to develop software for meeting organizations requirements whilst optimizing the use of resources.

In the context of software development for SMEs, WinDev brings a viable way for implementing desktop, web and mobile applications. WinDev is an integrated development environment that allows programmers to create applications based on the WinDev runtime engine. WinDev uses its own programming language --being the 5th generation of W-language-- which includes simple commands, similar to natural language, which make possible an easy and smooth learning curve.

This tool allows the easily writing of high visual content applications. With the use of natural language, PC SOFT manufacturer states that software development based on WinDev increases up to 10 times [1].

WinDev is considered as one of "the most productive languages" in nowadays market. It is used by over 150 000 professional developers around the world. Big european companies are using WinDev as their engine for enterprise solutions; some of them are Honda in France, Porche, Bristol Myers Squibb, Zambon Labs., Ferrero, WWF, Lafarge, among others. Likewise, some companies in North America have decided to use WinDev. Some of them are Property Boss Solutions, Soft Design Consulting LLC, Clean EZ Technologies, and more [2].

In Ecuador, it is possible to find solutions for different business models like the following: electronic documents management, sale point terminals, client relations management systems, loans, taxes, import management, scholastic integration systems, production control, water quality management systems, delivery control system, financial software, production cost management, human resources among many others.

WinDev, being a RAD (Rapid Application Development) environment, supports a native database engine called HyperFileSQL [3] among other kind of database servers. This way, the application programming keeps the same, regardless of the database used (as depicted in figure 1).

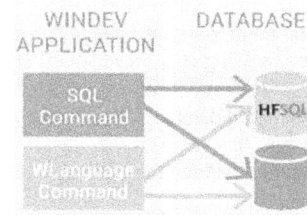

Fig 1. Communication between a WinDev applicaton and its native database or any other database.

When the applications are deployed using HyperFileSQL, the performance of the application decreases and running simple SQL queries takes too long (several seconds and even minutes to retrieve results).

This situation leads to look for an alternative to the native database, and to use another one with better performance and that could improve the software response time concerning queries made by WinDev applications. This is in correspondence with the criteria of experts that use this development environment, which is shown in table1.

TABLE I. CRITERIA OF EXPERTS THAT USE WINDEV APPLICATIONS.

Experts	Criteria
Senior Programmer (Software Architect)	HyperFileSQL should work very well with WinDev thus its integration is native.
Senior Programmer	Initially making projects with its HyperFileSQL, but the queries or transactions made with this database were too slow. Had problems with indexes and had to run and indexation process. Tables were damaged and there was loss of information. This caused client discomfort.
Senior Programmer	In general, HyperFileSQL database has no documentation on the database management. Besides, there is no info on connecting with applications in other languages.

MySQL is one of the open source databases more used worldwide. MySQL is very used in web applications, for example Facebook, Twitter, YouTube [4]. It has become in the main option for database due to:

- Performance and reliability.
- Low cost in computer requirements.
- It supports a great variety of operating systems.
- It has many configuration and installation advantages.

This paper is structured as follows. In section 2, related work is described. Then, the research problem is defined. The details of the experiment carried out are presented later, as well as the results. Finally, we arrive to conclusions.

2. RELATED WORK

The database management systems are nowadays part of management processes at SMEs around the world. Tongkaw et al. stated the necessity of studying the open source database management systems in OLTP processes (OnLine Transaction Processing). Once the study was finished, it was proven that the MySQL performance level was doubled to 1000 threads of OLTP-Simple with 4 workers of OLTP-Seats, while the resources use was similar in all cases, showing that MySQL has a highly better performance than MariaDB [5].

From a technical point of view, many authors have focused their efforts on showing the need of finding the optimal alternatives for improving software performance. From the comparison of relational databases and non-relational databases, it has been shown that MySQL is superior to MongoDB, concluding in some directions for offering a better performance level [6].

Under this criterion and due to the increase of bigger volumes of information, Neery and Baljit focused too on the comparative study between relational and non-relational databases. Contrary to the results of Gyorodi et al., comparing MySQL and CASSANDRA, Neery and Baljit concluded that the performance of non-relational databases can be better for working with column-oriented databases [7].

Other authors took as reference the importance of the communication management concerning mobility. They have evaluated the transactional model of mobile databases and how it can be manipulated if the consistency and data integrity is guaranteed [8].

Feraru and Zbancioc proposed the evaluation of the influence of the emotional state on the recognition rate of databases [9]. The emotional global acceptance percentage using the Rumanian database SROL and the German database EMO is 90% and 86% respectively [9].

With the rise of large and complex datasets, NoSQL databases have emerged. These databases have had a great acceptance due to their unexpected efficiency in managing information. Gupta and Rani carried out an assessment study on the performance of Elasticsearch and CouchDB (no-SQL databases). The study is based on doing operations like instancing, reading, updating and deleting in both databases. It was proven that CouchDB had better response times for inserting, updating and deleting operations while Elasticsearch showed a better performance on querying databases [10].

All these studies support our research methodology for looking for a viable candidate for replacing the use of HyperFileSQL as the database management system in WinDev applications. Our objective is to improve the response time when running queries against the database.

3. EXPERIMENT DESIGN

The research problem we faced is that the acceptance level of the WinDev native database does not meet the requirements of desktop applications development. So, the research question we defined was: can the response time, of data retrieval operations in the WinDev platform, be reduced when replacing the native database with MySQL? Our hypothesis was that data retrieval is faster using WinDev with MySQL than with its native database HyperFileSQL.

In the state of the art of comparing database servers, different kind of analysis have been made, such as: comparative studies between databases, parameters simulation, knowledge discovery processes in databases, response time measurement and evaluation of in-memory data performance [11-16].

This study follows the same research methodology applied by Tabares et. al. in their performance comparison of data retrieval [11]. Next, study's variables are formalized, and information is given about the participants, experiment materials and scenarios that were deployed for running the experiment.

Study's variables.
Independent variable: Kind of database.
Domain: MySQL, HyperFileSQL.

Dependent variable: Response time.
Domain: [0ms:15s]

Description of the participants in the experiment.
No users participate in the experiment. 50 rounds of data retrieval from 2 related tables deployed in both databases were carried out. This method is inspired in the strategy used in Tabares' experiment [11].

Scenario 1.
Server: Toshiba Laptop, with operative system Windows 10 Professional of 64 bits, file system NTFS, Intel processor Core i7 CPU 2.40GHz, RAM 8 GB, in which the two database servers were installed (MySQL and HyperFileSQL).

Client: Toshiba Laptop, with operative system Windows 10 Home of 64 bits, file system NTFS, Intel processor Core i7 CPU 2.40GHz, RAM 12 GB.

Scenario 2.
Client/Server: Toshiba Laptop, with operative system Windows 10 Home of 64 bits, file system NTFS, Intel processor Core i7 CPU 2.40GHz, RAM 8 GB, in which the 2 database engines are installed MySQL and HyperFileSQL, and the client application developed with WinDev.

Libraries.
libMySQL.dll was used for connecting the client-side app (implemented in WinDev) with the database engine deployed in a MySQL Server.

Experimental method.
Matched pairs design: A SQL query over two equivalent linked tables on HyperFileSQL and MySQL databases was run.

Experimental procedure.
The researcher run the desktop application developed in WinDev and sets the connection to one database (deployed on HyperFileSQL or MySQL). A panel with two tabs and a text control in each tab is part of the GUI that was implemented for carrying out the experiment (as shown in Figure 2). The text control allows to enter the SQL query. By clicking on the corresponding button, the SQL query is sent to the database and the resulting data are shown in the panel. Meanwhile, response time is automatically registered by the client application.

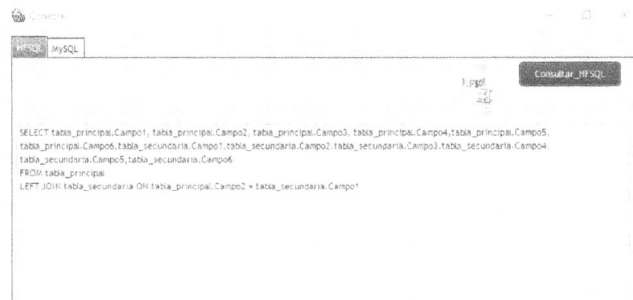

Fig 2. A window of a WinDev application, that connects to a Hyper FileSQL database for the experiment.

Response time was measured when retrieving data of both databases: HyperFileSQL and MySQL. Two scenarios were studied. The first scenario includes a connection between the client application and a remote server using TCP/IP. In the second scenario, the databases and the client application are physically in the same machine.
Equivalent MySQL and HyperFileSQL databases were created. Both contained the same number of tables, the same structure and the same data volume. MySQL 5.7.14 was used as database engine and InnoDB was the storage engine. HyperFileSQL ver. 20 was used as well.
In both databases, there is a master table with 1'587.889 records and 24 fields. A second table (a slave table) has 63 records with 37 fields. These tables are related as depicted in Figure 3.
The desktop application was implemented with WinDev version 20. The following functions were used: HExecuteSQLQuery allows to fill in a SQL query text and to send it to the database. HExecuteSQLQuery frees the memory resources and HReadFirst is used for retrieving the first record of the query.
TimeSys() returns the start time and final time of the query. Duration is a function that measures the time of the query. For showing the response time of queries on the interface, the function Trace was used.

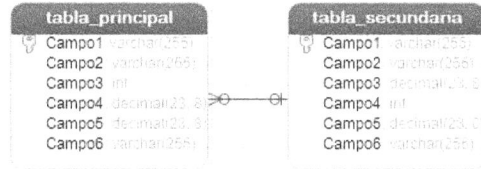

Fig 3. Tables used in the experiment. Due to rights of intellectual property, the names of the fields were obfuscated.

4. ANALYSIS OF RESULTS

The results of the experiment in the first scenario are influenced by negative factors of network traffic such as packages loss (this is the reason for worst response time measures). In this scenario, the average response time for HyperFile and MySQL databases showed up that SQL queries response time was reduced in at least 2.2 times when using MySQL instead of HyperFileSQL.

These results were statistically verified using a t-test. It was shown that the results are statistically significant with a certainty of almost 100% (P-value of 5x10-115). The standard deviation for each case was not significant. The statistical results are shown in table II.

TABLE II. EXPERIMENT'S RESULTS - FIRST SCENARIO.

Database	Average time (seconds)	Standard Deviation	P-Value
MySQL	58,274	1,985	5,3209 10E-115
HyperFileSQL	128,642	2,847	

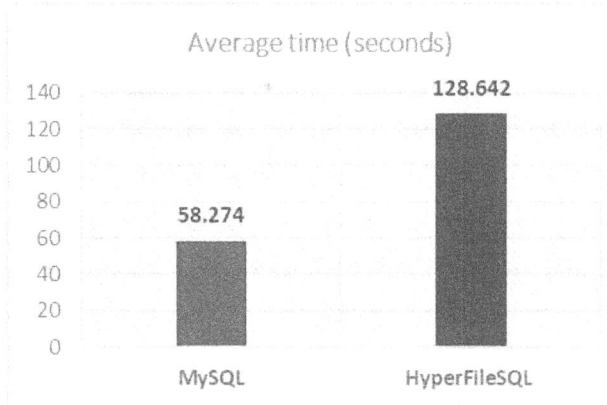

Fig 4. Average response time of MySQL and HyperFileSQL in scenario 1.

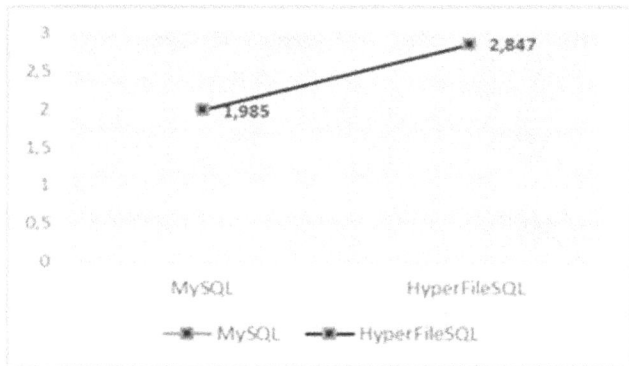

Fig 5. Standard deviation entre herramientas MySql e HyperFileSQL en escenario 1.

For the second scenario, the results were the following (table III):

TABLE III.   EXPERIMENT'S RESULTS – SECOND SCENARIO.

Database	Average time (seconds)	Standard Deviation	P-Value
MySQL	22,057	0,342	1,9006 10E-156
HyperFileSQL	72,195	0,883	

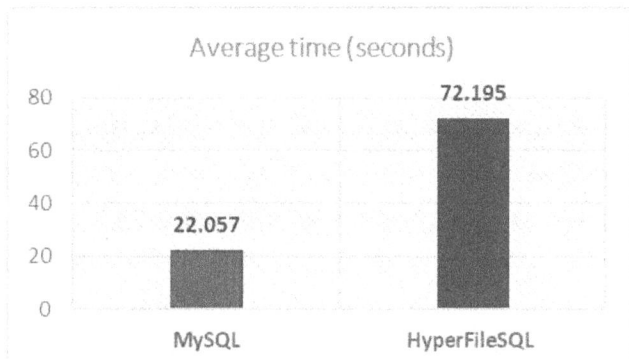

Fig 6. Average times of measurements for MySQL tools and HyperFile SQL in Scenario 1.

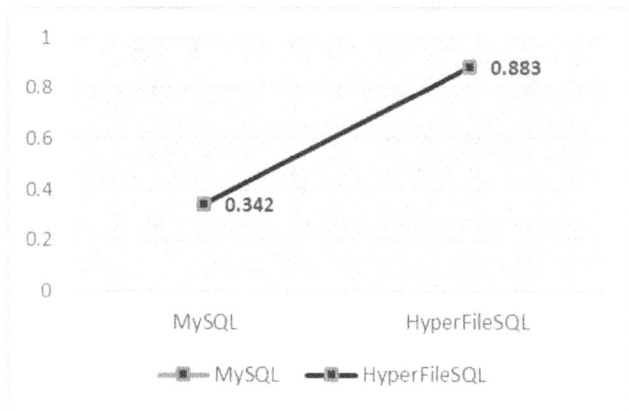

Fig 7. Standard Deviation between MySQL tools and HyperFile SQL in Scenario2.

With the statistical analysis of the results, it was confirmed that the response time (no matter of the scenario in which response time was measured) is significantly bigger when working with HyperFileSQL database and that the difference with the response time when using MySQL is statistically relevant according to the Student's t-test that was carried out.

5. CONCLUSIONS

Response time is fundamental in processes with high demand of data. The experiment carried out was designed taking into consideration actual needs of SMEs when using WinDev for the development of software.

It was soundly proved that MySQL is a better alternative for managing data in comparison to HyperFileSQL. Using MySQL in WinDev applications for SMEs increases the efficiency of data management processes.

The results were statistically verified using a Student's t-test. The obtained p-values of $1,9006 \times 10^{-156}$ and $5,3209 \times 10^{-115}$ prove that the results are highly trustworthy.

6. ACKNOWLEDGMENT

We would like to express very great appreciation to Universidad Técnica de Ambato, specifically to the Dirección de Investigación y Desarrollo (DIDE). Research results presented here were obtained with funding of the research project "Arquitectura de Servicios Web Semánticos para la Integración de Fuentes de Datos Estructuradas de Proyectos Urbanísticos" (Project number: PFICM19).

7. REFERENCES

[1]   WinDev, **Official website of WinDev** [Online], Available: http://www.WinDev.es/WinDev/index.html

[2]   WinDev, **Official Testimonials website of WinDev**. [Online], Available: https://www.windev-us.com/US/Testimonials.awp

[3]   Reis, R. O. S. A., "Framework for the Development of Educational Software", **WSEAS International Conference Proceedings, Mathematics and Computers in Science and Engineering**, No. 7, World Scientific and Engineering Academy and Society, Hangzhou, China, pp. 1-5, 2008.

[4]   MySQL , **Official web site of MySQL**, [Online], Available: https://www.mysql.com/why-mysql/

[5]   S. Tongkaw and A. Tongkaw, "A comparison of database performance of MariaDB and MySQL with OLTP workload", **IEEE Conference on Open Systems (ICOS)**, pp. 117–119, 2016.

[6]   C. Gyorodi, R. Gyorodi, G. Pecherle, and A. Olah, "A comparative study: MongoDB vs. MySQL", **13th International Conference on Engineering of Modern Electric Systems**, EMES 2015, pp. 0–5, 2015

[7]   Neeru and B. Kaur, "Cassandra vs MySQL: Modelling and querying format", **International Journal of Control Theory and Applications**, 9(11), pp. 5199–5206, 2016.

[8]   R. Haraty, "A comparative study of mobile database transaction models", **Proceedings - IEEE Symposium on Computers and Communications**, pp. 134–139, 2016.

[9]   S. Feraru and M. Dan Zbancioc, "Comparative analysis between SROL - Romanian database and Emo - German

database", **International Symposium on Signals, Circuits and Systems**, pp. 2–5, 2015.

[10] R. Rani and S. Gupta, "A Comparative Study of Elastic search and CouchDB Document Oriented Databases", **International Conference on Inventive Computation,** pp. 1-4, 2016.

[11] L. Tabares, F. Fernández, A.Leiva and J. Nummenmaa", An empirical performance evaluation of a semantic-based data retrieving process from RDBs & RDF data storages", **MASKANA Journal**, CEDIA, pp. 22-34, 2016.

[12] J. Zhu and F. Wu, "Study on the construction of the database of energy-saving building wall's thermal performance in Hangzhou", **Energy Procedia**, vol. 14, pp. 931–936, 2012.

[13] A. Sumoza-Toledo, M. Espinoza-Gabriel, and D. Montiel-Condado, "Evaluation of the TRPM2 channel as a biomarker in breast cancer using public databases analysis", **Boletin Médico del Hospital Infantil de Mexico**,
vol. 73(6), pp. 397–404, 2016.

[14] R. Osman, I. Awan, and M. Woodward, "Application of Queueing Network Models in the Performance Evaluation of Database Designs", **Electronic Notes in Theoretical Computer Science**, vol. 232 (C), pp. 101–124, 2009.

[15] P. Dehning, K. Lubinetzki, S. Thiede, and C. Herrmann, "Achieving Environmental Performance Goals - Evaluation of Impact Factors Using a Knowledge Discovery in Databases Approach", **Procedia CIRP**, vol 48, pp. 230–235, 2016.

[16] A. Kabakus and R. Kara, "A performance evaluation of in-memory databases", **Journal of King Saud University - Computer and Information Sciences**, pp. 6–11, 2016.

MOBILE APPLICATION BASED ON EXPERT SYSTEMS FOR DECISION MAKING OF MICROCREDIT REQUESTS. CASE STUDY

Jenny Alexandra Ortiz Zambrano,
Francisco Xavier Alvarez Solís,
Segundo Medina Medina Correa,
Jhoana Elisabeth Trejo Alarcón,
Eduardo Javier Reyna León
and
Carlos Samuel Yépez Suárez

Faculty of Mathematical and Physical Science
University of Guayaquil, Salvador Allende Av. Delta y Av. Kennedy
Guayaquil - Ecuador

{jenny. ortizz, francisco.alvarezs, segundo.medinac, johana.trejoa, eduardo.reynal, carlos.yepezs}@ug.edu.ec

ABSTRACT

The originality of this proyect is that it is the first bank that gives an immediate response to its clients that request micro-credits through the proposal of an application that helps decision-making based on expert systems in the requests of microcredits made by clients, thus reducing the waiting time that is normally four and up to six days, in addition to filling a endless documents that the client must submit as requirements in any bank and for the existing problem of not being able to evaluate a client creditily in the place of his micro business. The methodology that was used for the development was the agile SCRUM methodology, the same one that is attached to the project since each cycle is the functional delivery of a part of the project to the client. It was possible to reach the expectations set for the elaboration of the project: the mobile application satisfies the needs of the users, allowing to consult information online, which will be used for the analysis and evaluation of a microcredit application, taking into consideration that there is no tool in the area of microfinance that offers these services to the business advisor.

Keywords: request, microcredit, mobile application.

1. INTRODUCTION

The credit analysis process in Banco D-MIRO has been generated manually for years, as this was considered a strength due to the informality of microfinance. The little confidence in models generated for decision-making, added to everything that involves the analysis of a client's credit, for the approval of a credit operation. In addition, the need to document credit operations by taking as much documentation as possible is what has limited the development of microfinance.

The aspects that drive to generate this project are the problems that microentrepreneurs face when they have to close their business to go to a bank to apply for a loan, because that generates losses to it, in addition to the uncertainty of knowing if it qualifies or not and if the amount that the bank can deliver reaches to cover its investment needs.

Mobile applications are currently technological tools used to improve, facilitate and potentiate the activities that a person performs in their day to day, these are increasingly used by companies to generate added value to the service they provide, achieving a higher level of efficiency in its personnel offering fast and timely services, achieving with this the loyalty of its customers an important factor for the growth of a company [1], [2].

Mobile technology is a strategic ally for all companies, because it allows you to organize information quickly and have it available 24/7 (24 hours a day, 7 days a week). Likewise, mobile devices have become an essential part of our lives and allow to optimize and optimize response times [3], [4].

The objective of this research project is to develop a tool that allows to reduce response times, improve the level of productivity of a credit officer, improve customer retention by having more information at the time of the visit, which facilitates a credit operation is viable, helping in this way that Banco D-MIRO S.A. can optimize response times, customer satisfaction because it allows you to know immediately if the customer is subject to credit and improve the level of efficiency of a business adviser in the area.

2. PROBLEM APPROACH

2.1 LOCATION OF THE PROBLEM IN A CONTEXT

One of the biggest problems the bank faces when visiting a microcredit client is not having all the information necessary to carry out an efficient credit assessment and thus improve the response time and determine if a person is subject to credit or not. The uncertainty that can be generated in a client after the visit of the business advisor to not have at that time an answer on his request for microcredit is one of the factors that have generated the development of this research, since a microentrepreneur projects his investment and the growth of your business in this credit request added to this while currently delaying the response to the application submitted is what generates interest in the development of a mobile application to help solve this problem.

Response times for the approval of a microcredit proposal, can reach 4 working days which is currently a time that makes us lose competitiveness. The uncertainty of the client not knowing if he is subject to credit does not allow him to be free to apply in another institution if he does not qualify in BANCO D-MIRO, and he has to wait until he is given an answer within several days. See Fig. 1.

Knowing if the amount you are requesting is viable or if you qualify becomes vital since not meeting your need increases the loss of time in the client perceiving this as a bad service that can even generate losses of business opportunities for the client. To analyze the current problems, a survey was conducted to 51 credit counselors that make up the different agencies throughout the city that D'MIRO has, to consult the business department about the process they are currently carrying out to grant a microcredit to their clients.

3. OBJECTIVES

3.1 GENERAL OBJECTIVE

Develop a mobile application, with the use of open source tools that allow decision-making for micro-credit requests received in the area by business advisors, for the Banco D-MIRO S.A.

3.2 SPECIFIC OBJECTIVES

- Identify the problem through a survey of business personnel for the collection and analysis of information, as well as functional and non-functional requirements of the system.

- Design and develop a mobile application, which will allow obtaining the necessary credit information for the evaluation of microcredit applications taken in the area, by the business advisors for the Banco D-MIRO S.A.

- Demonstrate the functionality and operability of the system, through the approval of the proposal with the Zone Sub-Manager of Banco D-MIRO S.A.

4. METHODOLOGY

The SCRUM methodology [5] was applied for the development of the mobile application whose purpose is to make decisions according to the definition of expert systems since these are machines that think and reason as an expert would in a certain specialty or field [6] for requests for microloans received in the area by the business advisors for Banco D-MIRO SA, the roles involved in the methodology is the following: Scrum roles were designated for the designation of the activities that were carried out.

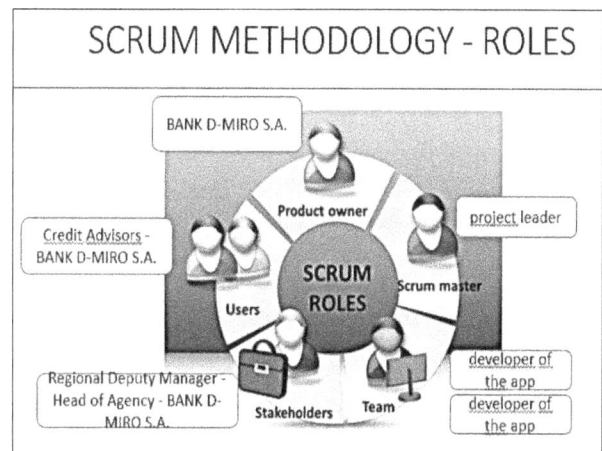

Fig. 1. SCRUM methodology of the project

Then the phases were established that had to be considered within the development stages of the application, which are:

- The design of the application allowed to consult if a client is a credit subject, by consulting diverse sources that include their recurring clients, in which the behavior of their payments is analyzed.
- Next, the client's data should be consulted online through a web service that connects to the Ministry of the Interior, to know if the client has a criminal record (the same as being positive, would be a reason for denial of the requested credit).

- Through the application, the client's credit situation was evaluated through the profit and loss statement where the client's payment capacity was calculated.
- The application had the capacity to suggest credit amounts through the analysis of the payment capacity and the quota that the client can cover.
- Through the application, the documents were stored digitally to the server when all the requirements were approved [7]. See Fig. 2.

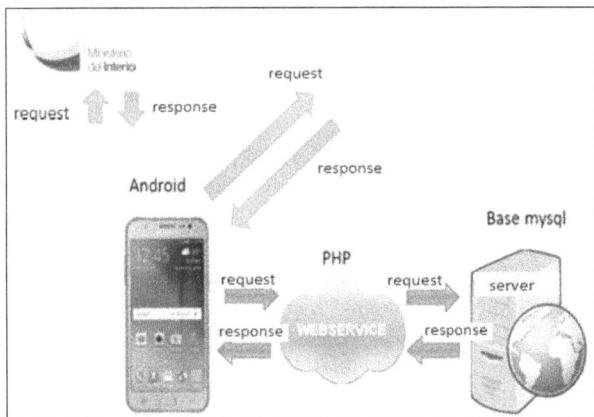

Fig. 2. Architecture of the mobile application

In the development of the proposal, other mobile proposals for SMEs were taken as reference [8], a development environment was presented that meets the technical specifications, the use of free software technologies that allow the coding of the application. The main tools used for development are:

- XAMPP
  - PHP 7.1.12
  - MariaDB 10.1.29
  - Apache/2.4.29
- Android Studio 3.0.1

See Fig. 3

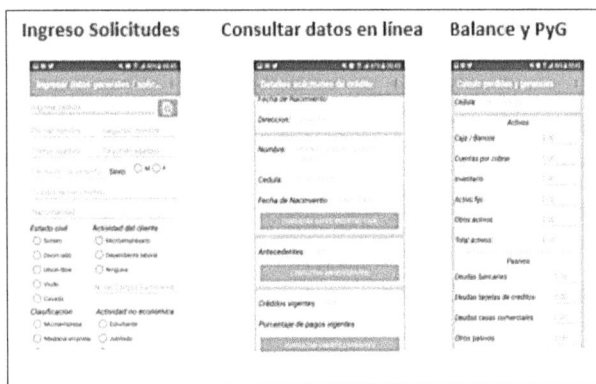

Fig. 3. Mobile application for bank loan request

Applying the validation method "JUDGMENT TO EXPERTS", the same that allows to obtain "an informed opinion of people with experience in the subject", a satisfaction survey was carried out so that the same is filled in by the Sub-Business Manager of Banco D- MIRO, whose objective among other things was that the application implements the basic considerations of usability that any software must take into account. See Fig. 4

Fig. 4. Expert Judgment Survey

5. RESULTS

- The application was developed with open source tools, for the mobile application we used the IDE of Android Studio development [9], [10], we also used the XAMPP package, which includes the Apache web server [11], the PHP language for the web Services and Mysql for the database, leaving the project fully functional.
- It was possible to reach the expectations set for the elaboration of the project: the mobile application satisfies the needs of the users, allowing to consult information online, which will be used for the analysis and evaluation of a microcredit application, being this of vital importance in the development of it, taking into consideration that there is no tool in the area of microfinance that offers these services to the business advisor.
- It was demonstrated that the mobile application is viable, because it allows users to make inquiries of recurring and new clients in real time, therefore, they can make decisions regarding the microcredit requests that are presented to them, while performing their work

in the zone, optimizing the response time and improving the client's perception of the quality of the service provided by Banco D-MIRO.

- Taking as a basis the surveys prior to the development of the project, carried out to the users, it was determined that the biggest problem they face when receiving a request for a microcredit in the area is the lack of information that allows them to make an affirmative or negative decisión which generates a loss of time for the business officer, since he must wait to reach the Bank to perform the client's consultation.
- The application allows the user to have access to the client's information, it will allow him to verify the identity of the user, his payment behavior in the Ecuadorian financial system, payment history in Banco D-MIRO, level of indebtedness, average quota that cancel at the time of the consultation and generate an Initial Balance with a statement of Losses and Profits that provide all the possible edges on the request for microcredit generating a high level of user confidence in the application.

6. CONCLUSIONS

Tests and validations were generated, prior to the acceptance of the application, which were satisfactory for the user. These were carried out in the presence of the Zonal Sub-Manager of Banco D-MIRO, who after the presentation was satisfied with the results obtained, being This is a solution to one of the biggest problems that a business advisor faces in Banco D-MIRO when this area, thus achieving compliance with the proposed objectives, the proposal being validated and accepted.

It is possible to conclude after the tests, that the project developed, managed to comply with all the proposed scope from the beginning, and that this application can be implemented in Banco D-MIRO, to provide greater support to daily activities that performs a business advisor, being this easy to use and understand.

7. RECOMMENDATIONS

- It is recommended that each business advisor should be assigned a mobile device or tablet to business advisors, which must have unlimited data packages for its proper functioning, the team must have at least 1 Gb of RAM or higher and a 2.4 ghz processor, for the correct functioning of the system the device must have the version of Android 6.0 and up.
- For a second phase in the implementation it is recommended that the web server domain support multiple simultaneous connections. With respect to the expectations raised, these were achieved, however, it is recommended to carry out quarterly reviews to identify new requirements by the user that help strengthen the

application and keep it updated, which will allow it to continue to be useful for the business advisors.
- Regarding the access or use of bandwidth the application works in 4G with a very good response time, it is recommended that it can be optimized for the use of widths of lower bands 3G or less.
- Regarding the viability of the application, in relation to the data query, it is important to recommend connection tests in sectors distant from the city, where the coverage of Banco D-MIRO as a credit zone arrives, in order to determine what will be the response time in these sectors and the challenges of working in distant urban areas, where perhaps the Internet connection is poor.
- Regarding the surveys carried out and taking into consideration the good acceptance that the project had, on the part of the business advisor in Banco D-MIRO, it is recommended to attach a space for online suggestions, this information may be used at any time to determine, if it is necessary to advance the process of maintenance and update of the application, achieving a better level of communication with the user.
- Regarding the access of information, it is recommended to generate users and passwords, for users as a method of verification and authentication of their data as they will have access to sensitive information.
- It is important to recommend to users that although the application provides all the facilities to offer a better service, this will depend on the customer's treatment of the customer, always being friendly and a smile will be the best way to reach a person and that this is willing to deliver all the information necessary for the evaluation of the credit application.
- Regarding the issue of connectivity in remote areas or low signal intensity, it is recommended the inclusion of off line mode which would allow the evaluation of a client despite not having access to the Internet and expect to have connection to perform the evaluation without having lost the opportunity to do business.
- Regarding the access or use of bandwidth the application works in 4G with a very good response time, it is recommended that this can be optimized for the use of widths of lower bands 3G or less, which allows it to cover peri-urban sectors without affect the response time.
- It is recommended to promote the application to other banking entities so that they can optimize the process they offer to their clients, thus avoiding the long wait that these types of processes take today.

8. REFERENCE

[1] J. Anchundia & J. Campoverde, Desarrollo de una aplicación móvil para cooperativas de taxis en general de la ciudad de Guayaquil mediante geolocalización., 2016.

[2] O. Guzmán & L.Jiménez, Desarrollo de aplicación móvil para automatizar las actividades académicas que realiza un docente en los niveles de educación básica y bachillerato., 2015.

[3]   D. Albán & J. Muñiz. Aplicación turística para el enlazamiento de la catedral metropolitana de Guayaquil para equipos bajo sistema operativo android, usando técnicas de realidad aumentada., 2015.

[4]   Mobile Market Association, g. d. (2011). Libro Blanco de Apps. Obtained from https://mmaspain.com/wp-content/uploads/2015/09/Libro-Blanco-Apps.pdf

[5]   SCRUM, M. T., Metodología Scrum. Universitat Oberta de Catalunya., 2012

[6]   E. Castillo, J. M. Gutiérrez, & A. S. Hadi, Sistemas expertos y modelos de redes probabilısticas. **Academia de Ingenierıa.**, 1997.

[7]   E. Williams, Propuesta para la digitalización del fondo documental del Dr. Belisario Porras. Universidad Internacional de Andalucía. Retrieved on January 14, 2018, of http://dspace.unia.es/bitstream/handle/10334/1789/0281_Williams.pdf?sequence=1, 2012.

[8]   MovilPyme. (2018). Retrieved on 10 of 01 of 2018, of http://www.movilpyme.com/microfm.html

[9]   Academia Android. (2013). Academia Android. Obtained from https://academiaandroid.com/android-studio-v1-caracteristicas-comparativa-eclipse/

[10]   Actualizar Android. (s.f.). Actualizar Android,. Obtained from https://actualizar-android.com/versiones/

[11]   Apache. (2017). XAMPP. Obtained from https://www.apachefriends.org/es/index.html

An Approach Towards a Native Voice Control System for the Web

Daniel TEBERNUM
Fraunhofer ISST, Emil-Figge-Strasse 91
Dortmund, 44227, Germany

Marcel ALTENDEITERING
Fraunhofer ISST, Emil-Figge-Strasse 91
Dortmund, 44227, Germany

Sergej ATAMANTSCHUK
Fraunhofer ISST, Emil-Figge-Strasse 91
Dortmund, 44227, Germany

ABSTRACT

Utilizing voice for human-computer interaction is becoming an increasingly popular topic in practice as well as academia. Users value the improved and more natural usability and for people, with certain disabilities, it can be the only way to take part in the modern web-based society. As a result, a solution is needed that enables a seamless interaction with web pages and can be deployed without great effort. Existing solutions do not sufficiently fulfill these requirements as they are often intended for distinctive usage scenarios or are limited in their support of web pages and web browsers. To overcome these disadvantages a novel voice control system for web pages is presented in this paper. The proposed JavaScript-based solution works natively in the web browser and automatically provides access by voice commands to web pages and web applications. In conclusion, possible future research directions and follow-up developments are discussed.

Keywords: human-computer interaction, voice control, voice browser, speech recognition, speech to text.

1. INTRODUCTION

The ability to speak is an important and efficient form of interaction and communication for humankind. The language, which is spoken, is used for communication and thus for the encoding and exchange of information [1]. The field of human-computer interaction aims to establish language, both in written and spoken form, as an interface between humans and computers. It is hoped that this will make interaction with computers easier. In recent years, the number of speech assistants and voice command systems has increased rapidly and more than 50% of smart phone users are already using their speech assistant [2]. Large companies such as Amazon and Google are also offering their own speech assistants with Alexa and Google Home, making this technology available to a broad range of users and developers. The trend towards more voice control can be explained by various advantages that users of voice control systems have. Randy Allen Harris describes that, depending on

the hardware, a voice control can be more comfortable and easier to use [3]. Smartwatches, for example, have a very small touch display, which makes user input difficult. With voice control, complex commands can be inserted in less time. Other reasons are situations in which devices, such as smartphones, may not be held in the hand. For instance, in many countries of the world smartphones must not be picked up while driving. You may only interact with the device via speakerphone and voice control. Voice control systems or speech assistants can also enable people with cognitive, sensory or physical disabilities to interact with computers.

Especially in the area of web pages and web applications, we see the necessity of a voice control mechanism to support users. This has mainly two reasons. The first reason is that the web benefits from accessibility, as it is the most important instrument for many people with disabilities to participate in social life [4]. The other reason is that more and more desktop and mobile applications are being developed using web technologies. For example, frameworks such as Electron for desktop applications or NativeScript for mobile applications are used to write applications using JavaScript. A voice control concept that automatically makes web pages voice controllable could be transferred to those desktop and mobile applications without great effort. In this paper, we present a voice control system, which runs natively in the web browser and makes web pages and web applications voice controllable with little effort. The solution presented is capable of automatically adding voice control to many web pages, so that no further adjustments by the operator of the web page or web application is necessary. The user of the voice control system only needs to learn a few commands to work with it. Click interactions are implemented in such a way that the user has a certain flexibility in his way of expressing himself. Due to the native implementation of our solution, there are only few dependencies on the user's hardware and software. Therefore, the responsibility to provide a barrier-free way of interaction is shifted towards the operator of the web page. For reasons of simplicity the proposed solutions currently only works with English web pages and utilizes voice commands in English. Supporting further languages can be part of future research.

In the remainder of this paper, we review existing works in this field and describe the methodological approach. Afterwards we present our solution and give an outlook on possible follow-up topics.

2. BACKGROUND

For identifying existing solutions in the area of voice controllable web browsers, we applied a combination of literature and market research. The research focused on finding existing solutions that allow for voice based, hands-free interaction with web browser. Other literature in this field with no regard to web browsing or in a business context were not taken into further consideration.

In literature, Christian et al. present in [5] an overview over a number of voice browsers for general or more distinctive purposes. In their definition, a voice browser is a web browser that can either "[...] render web pages in an audio format." or "[...] interpret spoken input for navigation". In the latter category, they present several systems, for example Conversa or PipeBeach. These work by issuing given short voice commands like *go back* or *follow link* possibly followed by an elements name. However, the presented solutions are no longer under maintenance or not publicly available any longer. The web browser Homer presented by Vesnicer et al. in [6] has met the same fate. They built a custom web browser for blind people that was based on the GTK web browser Dillo, but is no longer available. The web browser contained a screen reader as well as a speech to text component for issuing commands similar to the systems presented by Christian et al. More recently, Ghahari et al. in [7] and Corbett and Weber in [8] investigated solutions for controlling mobile devices with voice commands to enable hands-free communication and avoid possible distractions during other activities like walking or driving. In [7] the Dynamic Aural Web Navigation (DAWN) system is used to translate web pages into a voice controllable format. Afterwards a user can listen to the web content and use a small set of given commands such as *skip* or *back* to navigate through the content. Corbett and Weber in [8] introduced a system called VoiceNavigator that addresses challenges in learnability and discoverability of voice user interfaces. According to them, learning and understanding how to use a voice interface is often difficult for users. Therefore, their system works at the operating system layer and uses voice commands like *open* or *refresh* to interact with a web browser or any other application. Furthermore, they implemented several help commands to give more information about how to use voice commands and enable contextualized help. In addition to speaking an elements or applications name, VoiceNavigator also provides numerical labels that are superimposed to the icons and elements on the screen. This way a user might also select a displayed number for ease of use. Both papers also mention the possibility to use the built-in speech assistants. These, however, do not natively support browsing web pages but are mostly used for simple web search and issuing predefined commands.

In addition to the review of scientific literature, we conducted a review of existing solutions at the market. Towards this end, Groeben provides in [9] an overview of products supporting the use of voice commands in web browser and compares them regarding their performance on common features. According to

her the product portfolio Dragon of software-company Nuance is the best solution available followed by the products of Linguatec. Dragon Professional allows users to navigate a web page by making common elements like links, buttons, etc. accessible by speech. Therefore, a predefined voice command is used to access a certain element. For instance, in order to click a button, a user needs to say the command *click* followed by the elements name. In case there are multiple elements with the same name or the name is unknown (e.g. in case of text fields) the identified elements are marked with a numerical label similar to VoiceNavigator. To continue, the user can choose an element by speaking the *chose* command. Apart from controlling the web browser, the software can, just like VoiceNavigator, be used for executing commands in the operating system or other applications, especially in word processing applications. Dragon Professional is currently available for 399€ for Windows and Mac OS but only supports Internet Explorer and Chrome on Windows and Safari and Firefox on Mac OS [10]. Voice Pro 12 by Linguatec works similar to Dragon Professional but does not require predefined commands for accessing elements. For example, to click a button called submit the software does not require the command *click* but works solely with the elements name. Similar to Dragon Professional and VoiceNavigator the usage is not limited to web pages but can also be used in other applications. In contrast to Dragon Professional, Voice Pro is only available for Windows. A license costs 169€. Both tools come with very high speech recognition rates, which are achieved by a combination of individual user settings and continuous improvements based on the users' speech input. Due to the high recognition rates and compatibility with word processing software both tools are especially well suited for dictating texts or similar use cases [11].

All presented solutions are addressing the need for a voice augmented web browser that can be used hands-free. Most of them utilize voice commands in addition with numerical labels to interact with a web browser as well as other applications on a computer. However, the solutions also come with a number of disadvantages. Primarily, they do not provide a comprehensive solution that works in all environments. Since they are not build as native web applications that can be embedded into the HTML code of a web page, the support for operating systems, browser and web pages is often limited. Additionally, many solutions presented in literature are either no longer available (e.g. Conversa or Homer) or are intended for distinctive usage scenarios (e.g. VoiceNavigator). In order to address these downsides and realize a generic solution for voice control on web pages there is a need for a novel approach. The desired solution works natively in a web browser, supports common web pages and browsers and can be deployed without further costs or configuration.

3. METHODOLOGY

In the previous chapter, a literature review was conducted to get an overview of existing solutions in the area of voice controllable web browsers. Special attention was paid to solutions that can be used in the area of web interfaces or at least can be adapted to them. We applied the Webster and Watson methodology by defining a first set of search terms and then performing a forward and backward search [12]. As initial terms "web speech/voice control", "browser speech/voice control" and "web speech/voice selection" were chosen. For the research, the portals of Springerlink, DBLP Computer Science Bibliography, Elsevier and ScienceDirect were used. We only considered those works, which were available in English or German language and indicated a relationship with our subject in their abstracts.

Our own work is based on the methodological procedure of Design Science [13]. In this approach, the artifact to be considered, namely the voice control concept and the implemented library (see chapter 4), is iteratively improved through different phases. To prevent the artifact from specializing too much into a certain direction, we applied the Action Design Research (ADR) Methodology in particular [14]. This procedure lives from a close exchange of science and practice in order to optimize and generalize the artifact. ADR can be divided into the four phases "Problem Formulation", "Building, Intervention, and Evaluation", "Reflection and Learning" and "Formalization of Learning", whereby the first three phases can be passed through iteratively. Of the methods provided by ADR, literature research, focus group discussion and laboratory walkthroughs were used. Due to the limited space, available, individual iterations are not described in Chapter 4. The chapter directly describes our final solution approach.

4. PROPOSED SOLUTION

In this chapter, the concept of our voice control system for web pages and web applications as well as our evaluation will be described. The proposed system consists of two central components, namely the STT engine and the client library (see Fig. 1).

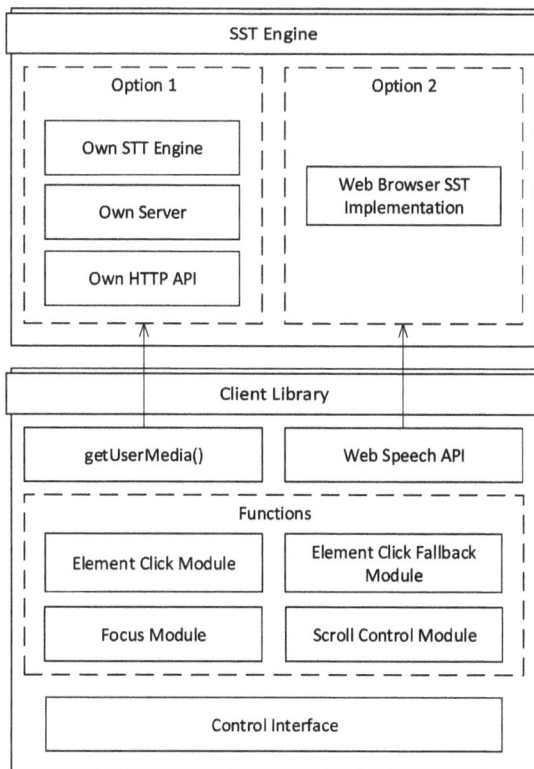

Fig. 1 Architecture of the voice control system

Speech to Text Engine

The first component is the speech to text (STT) engine that converts spoken words into a machine-readable string. The string received from the STT engine can be used by the second component to control the user interface. We did not develop a STT engine ourselves, as we wanted to offer the operators of web pages and web applications the greatest possible freedom. That is why we have designed our concept in a way that the STT engine is freely interchangeable. The hosts can provide their own speech to text engine on a server they own. This leads to a higher effort during the integration of our solution. However, this approach has the advantage that the voice recordings of the users do not necessarily have to be passed on to third parties, but are only exchanged between user and operator. This is particularly important with regard to data protection concerns. If you choose this solution, you need to provide the client side library of our voice control system the URL endpoint for the STT functionality. The library then automatically uses the browser's *getUserMedia()* API to record speech via the microphone. The recordings are transmitted to the specified endpoint and the engine returns a string with the spoken words. If no own STT engine is used, the Web Speech API provided by the browser is selected by the client library. Despite the specification of the API by the W3C, it is up to the browser manufacturers themselves how the speech recognition is implemented. In Google's browser Chrome, the audio recordings are sent to Google's server and will be processed there. In Firefox, the feature must first be activated and requires additional local software for the speech to text capability.

Client Library

The second central component is the client side library mentioned before. It is implemented in JavaScript and can therefore be executed natively in the web browser. The library offers four basic functionalities that are important for controlling the web page with speech (see Fig. 1 bottom). The first functionality focuses on the scrollability of web pages and is encapsulated in the so-called *Scroll Control Module*. To scroll the web page by speech, we have defined a set of four fixed commands: *scroll up*, *scroll down*, *scroll top* and *scroll bottom*. The commands *up* and *down* are used to scroll half pages up and down. The commands *top* and *bottom* are used to scroll to the top or the bottom of the page. The scroll functionality is not limited to the web page itself. In addition, dropdowns of select boxes can be scrolled the same way (see below).

The second functionality deals with the interaction on the web page. The interaction takes place primarily by clicking on elements. For this purpose, we have designed an interaction module, which converts speech input into click commands. We called it *Element Click Module*. The module is not dependent on fixed commands, but tries to identify the element intended by the user to be clicked, by approximation. The pseudocode in figure 2 shows our approach and will be described in further detail in the following.

```
audioCommand = record user voice input
sttResult = send audioCommand to STT engine
userWord[] = split sttResult in individual words
htmlElement[] = find clickable and viewable   elements

foreach htmlElement h
```

```
h.score = 0;
h.elementText = find corresponding viewable text
                of each viewable element;
h.elementWord[] = split elementText in individual
                words;
end

foreach htmlElement h
  foreach h.elementWord as e
    foreach userWord as u
      if e equals u -> h.score + 1
    end
  end
end

if htmlElement[] has winner with max score
  click winner element
else
  foreach htmlElement h
    foreach h.elementWord as e
      foreach userWord as u
        if e fuzzyEquals u -> h.score + 1
      end
    end
  end

  if htmlElement[] has winner with max score
    click element
  else
    goto FallbackMode
  end
end
```

Fig. 2 Element detection algorithm

If the user wants to interact with one of the visible and clickable elements via voice control, he can formulate a sentence that contains visible words that are assigned to the element. For example, there is a button with the text *show more*. The user can formulate a sentence like "Please show me more details". Another example would be clicking on an input field that displays *e-mail* as placeholder text. In this case, the user could see the field and say "I want to enter the mail". The spoken words are then send to the STT engine. After the conversion of the spoken user command to a string, the *Element Click Module* processes it further. In the first step, the individual words of the sentence are extracted and stored in a set that we call W_{user}. Then, the elements to be considered on the web page are determined. A web page usually consists of HTML elements A, of which only a subset allows user interaction I, where $I \subseteq A$. We have reduced the set I by looking only at the clickable elements C, where $C \subseteq I$ and thus $C \subseteq A$. We have not considered other ways of interacting with elements, such as by pressing key combinations, because clicking is the most common way to interact with web pages [15]. Sometimes HTML elements, which are not clickable due to their basic semantics, are made clickable by JavaScript. In this case, the owner of a web page can mark these elements clickable with the CSS class *clickable*. For example, clickable images can be made speech controllable. The CSS class extends the set C by the corresponding elements and we call it C'. We have further reduced the amount of elements considered by looking only at

the visible elements V. Similar to the interaction with the mouse, the user should only be able to click on the elements that are visible to him. Finally, in our module we will only look at the HTML elements of the set $X = C' \cap V$. For each of the elements from the set X, associated text shown on the web page is searched for. We are searching for text in the *placeholder* attribute, sibling elements of type *<label>* and inside the elements, if the HTML specification provides for this (e.g. the *<button>* element). The visible texts of each HTML element of set X is divided into individual words that we will call $W_{element_i}$ where i is an iterator for all elements in set X. Now, for each $W_{element_i}$ a word-by-word comparison with W_{user} is performed. We compare the resulting sets of the Cartesian product of $W_{element_i} \times W_{user}$.

In a first iteration it is checked, whether a spoken word of the user is equal to a word of the element. For the comparison, the string is sanitized by removing spaces and changing the letters to lower case. For each equal pair of words a score point of 1 is added to the element. If there is one element at the end of the iteration that has more points than all others do, that element is likely to be meant by the user and will be clicked. If there is no winner, a second iteration with word comparisons is performed. In this second iteration, the words are compared again, only this time with a fuzzy string comparison. The fuzzy string comparison is based on the *Bitap* algorithm [16], which performs an approximate string matching. As an indicator for approximate string matching the Levenshtein Distance [17] is used. If the fuzzy string comparison returns a hit, the element will be given a point just like during the first iteration. We defined a hit as a *Bitap*-Score of 0.2 or less. The item with the most points is clicked by the client library.

For web pages with many similar element names, we have integrated a *secure mode* into our concept. If it is activated, the element identified by the system is highlighted. The system then asks the user via a modal window whether the element should be clicked. The user can answer with *yes* or *no*.

There are situations in which the *Element Click Module* does not come to a result or the user does not know how to address an element due to missing visualized texts. For this case we have implemented a third functionality in the so called *Element Click Fallback Module*. If the *Element Click Module* comes to several equivalent solutions or no solution at all, the *Element Click Fallback Module* activates a visual layer, which superimposes a number over each possible element. The user can then say one of the numbers and the corresponding element is clicked. The user can also activate this mode manually by saying the command *show all*. Then the numbers will be displayed above all HTML elements of the set X. If the user is in this mode, he can leave it using the *stop* command.

As the last speech control relevant function we have integrated the so-called *Focus Module* into our concept. It regulates the functionalities when an element has been selected on the web page which requires further input. Here we have considered text input fields and select boxes. When the user has clicked on an input field using a voice command, our system switches to focus mode *text editing*. Everything the user says is forwarded to the STT engine and then written into the input field. We have added three commands to control the input. In order not to confuse the commands with the input in the text field, we decided to double the command word. With *stop stop* the system leaves the focus mode. With *delete delete* the last word in the text field is deleted. *clear clear* deletes all text in the text field. When the user has clicked on a select box, the system switches to the focus mode *select box*. The user can leave this mode similar to the *text editing* mode by saying *stop stop*. Selecting an element is done the same way as in the *Element Click Module*. The user can pronounce the entire displayed text of a possible option or parts of it. The system determines the most likely candidate. If none is found, numbers will be attached to the choices. If the list of options is too long for displaying, the user can scroll using the scroll commands from the *Scroll Control Module*.

To simplify the interaction with the system, a graphical user interface was implemented (see Fig. 3). The user can turn voice control on and off via the control panel. The panel also allows the *secure mode* to be switched on and off at runtime. Especially during the first attempts with the voice control, it can be of interest for the user to see how the STT engine converts the spoken word into a string. When the user says something, the result of the STT engine is displayed in the control panel. For example, it can be determined whether the selected STT engine can handle the accent of the user. The control panel also supports users in their first steps with the system by displaying instructions on how to use it.

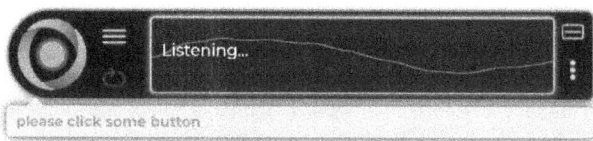

Fig. 3 Control panel is listening to user and is showing hints

Evaluation
The solution presented here was tested in an experimental setup with several participants. The native language of the participants is German. We carried out the evaluation with 4 computer scientists, 3 engineering students and a secretary from the administrative sector. First, the participants learned what we wanted to achieve with our work. Then we explained the existing voice commands. We did not demonstrated our solution in advance. We provided an action protocol that contained a number of tasks that the participants were asked to perform using a HTML5 test web page [18]. All forms of interaction described in this paper were queried. Table 1 shows in a summarized form the action protocol and the success ratio.

Nr.	Action	Success Ratio	Notes
1	scroll web page down	7/8	none
2	scroll web page up	7/8	none
3	jump to the bottom of the web page	5/8	users have forgotten command
4	Click *<input type=submit>* button	7/8	none
5	write random text into *textarea*	6/8	two users did not select the element but tried to write directly
6	delete last word in input	3/8	users forgot to double command
7	delete whole text	7/8	one user forgot *clear* command word
8	unfocus textarea	7/8	one user forgot *stop* command word
9	select radio button *Option 2*	4/8	fallback mode was activated, four users did not use the appearing numbers to select the element
10	jump to the top of the web page	7/8	none
11	click *Input fields* link	8/8	none
12	add checkmark to *Choice B* element	6/8	two users did not directly use the click command.
13	remove checkmark from *Choice A* element	8/8	none
14	open selectbox *Select*	8/8	none
15	select option *Option Three*	6/8	problems with pronunciation, as test persons have German as their mother tongue

Table 1 Action protocol for evaluating the voice command solution

A successful control of the web page elements was observed with input fields, select boxes, check boxes, radio buttons and buttons. Despite the success with the elements, there were often problems with the selection of the radio button with the text *Option 2*. Different STT engines sometimes translate the spoken input into *Option 2*, *Option two* or *Option too*. In the last two cases, the *Element Click Fallback Module* was activated and the users could click the radio button by saying the corresponding number. After the necessary commands had been memorized, the users could also enter text and scroll on the web page without problems. Overall, the users appreciated the possibility of being able to formulate their own sentences for clicking on elements that only have to contain parts of the elements description. The existing commands, which must be pronounced twice (e.g. *stop stop*), have attracted negative attention.

5. CONCLUSION

In this paper, we have presented a novel approach to navigate web pages using only voice commands. Therefore, a voice control system was designed and prototypically implemented that runs natively in the web browser and provides voice access to web pages and web applications with minimal effort. After integrating our proposed JavaScript library, the voice support is automatically added and no further adjustments are necessary. Evaluation was conducted by using solely voice to interact with an external test web page consisting of common HTML elements. Comparing to other solutions in literature and at the market our solution works natively in the web browser and is, thus, not limited to certain web browsers or usage scenarios.

Building on the research findings and overall experiences described this study has the following limitations that can be addressed in future research. Primarily, our solution requires further evaluation by testing its use in real-world scenarios. Therefore, its performance and usability on popular web pages could be compared and evaluated against other existing solutions. Technically, there is a need for further improvement of word recognition rates and reducing the amount of keywords in some use cases. The possible ways of interaction with web pages are currently limited to standard interaction methods such as clicking or typing. These could be extended to support more complex interaction methods like copying or inserting. Apart from extending the functionality, there is a need for further testing the system with different web browsers to ensure compatibility as well as technical correctness. Finally, in addition to English, it would be valuable to support further languages and make the proposed system available to a bigger audience.

ACKNOWLEDGMENT

This research was partly supported by the German Federal Ministry for Economic Affairs and Energy (BMWi).

REFERENCES

[1] Helmut Mangold. **Sprachliche Mensch-Maschine Kommunikation**, Volume 1. Oldenbourg R. Verlag GmbH, 1992.

[2] Niklas Veltkamp and Teresa Maria Tropf. **Sprachsteuerung setzt sich bei Smartphones durch**, 2018.

[3] Randy Allen Harris. **Voice interaction design: crafting the new conversational speech systems**. Elsevier, 2004.

[4] Helmut Vieritz. **Barrierefreiheit im virtuellen Raum: Benutzungszentrierte und modellgetriebene Entwicklung von Weboberflachen**, Springer-Verlag, 2015.

[5] Kevin Christian, Bill Kules, Ben Shneiderman, and Adel Youssef. „A comparison of voice controlled and mouse controlled web browsing", In **Proceedings of the fourth international ACM conference on Assistive technologies**, pp. 72–79. ACM, 2000.

[6] Bostjan Vesnicer, Janez Zibert, Simon Dobrisek, Nikola Pavesic, and France Mihelic. "A voice-driven web browser for blind people", In **Eighth European Conference on Speech Communication and Technology**, 2003.

[7] Romisa Rohani Ghahari, Jennifer George-Palilonis, Hossain Gahangir, Lindsay N. Kaser, and Davide Bolchini. **Semiaural interfaces: Investigating voice-controlled aural flows. Interacting with Computers**, 28(6), pp. 826–842, 2016.

[8] Eric Corbett and Astrid Weber. "What can i say?: Addressing user experience challenges of a mobile voice user interface for accessibility". In **Proceedings of the 18th International Conference on Human-Computer Interaction with Mobile Devices and Services**, pp. 72–82. ACM, 2016.

[9] L. Groeben. **Spracherkennungssoftware: Die besten Spracherkennungsprogramme im Vergleich**, https://www.netzsieger.de/k/ spracherkennungssoftware, 2018. Last accessed 16th August 2018.

[10] Nuance. **Installation and user guide**. http://supportcontent.nuance.com/dragon/12/ doc/DNS12UserGuide_e.pdf, 2018. Last accessed 23rd August 2018.

[11] Linguatec. **Voice Pro 12 Handbuch**. https://www.linguatec.de/wp-content/uploads/ 2015/05/vp12_manual.pdf, 2009. Last accessed 23rd August 2018.

[12] Jane Webster and Richard T Watson. **Analyzing the past to prepare for the future: Writing a literature review**. MIS quarterly, pages xiii–xxiii, 2002.

[13] Alan R Hevner, Salvatore T March, Jinsoo Park, and Sudha Ram. **Design science in information systems research**, MIS Quarterly, 28(1), 2008.

[14] Sein, M. K., Henfridsson, O., Purao, S., Rossi, M., & Lindgren, R. (2011). **Action design research**. MIS quarterly, 35(1), pp.37-56.

[15] Linda Tauscher and Saul Greenberg. **How people revisit web pages: empirical findings and implications for the design of history systems**, International Journal of Human-Computer Studies, 47(1):97–137, 1997.

[16] Sun Wu and Udi Manber. **Fast text searching with errors**, University of Arizona, Department of Computer Science Tucson, 1991.

[17] Vladimir I Levenshtein. **Binary codes capable of correcting deletions, insertions, and reversals**. In Soviet physics doklady, volume 10, pp. 707–710, 1966.

[18] Chris Bracco. **HTML5 Test Page**. https://github.com/cbracco/html5-test-page, 2018. Last accessed 13th September 2018.

Internet-of-Things Supply Chain Solution

Marco A. LARA GRACIA

Department of Engineering, University of Southern Indiana
Evansville, Indiana 47712, USA

ABSTRACT

Container terminals located all over the world are facing all kinds of challenges to achieve and maintain a competitive position in the multiple global supply chains they are part of. One of them is to maximize the efficiency and performance of container handling operations. This is the case, for instance, of the ports of Cartagena, Colombia and Savannah, Georgia, USA, which are now servicing Post-Panamax containerships pretty much in the same time interval they serve Panamax containerships. Post-Panamax containerships can carry 12,000+ TEUs (Twenty Equivalent Units) whereas Panamax containerships can carry up to 4,500 TEUs. A related issue is the need of deepening and widening the port's navigating channel and replacing existing Ship-To-Shore (STS) cranes with bigger STS cranes to accommodate Post-Panamax containerships. Other challenge is to electronically connect in real time with global supply chains comprised of multiple container terminals, shipping companies, custom brokers, port authorities, end customers, etc., which requires the digitalization of logistics and business processes. Related issues are secured sharing of data and effective and purposeful use of data analysis. Another important challenge faced by container terminals is to enforce port security. In this paper, an Internet-of-Things solution is introduced to provide container terminals and maritime ports technology-based means to maximize port security.

Keywords: Container Handling Equipment and Machinery, Internet-of-Things (IoT), and Smart Sensors, Artificial Intelligence (AI).

1. INTRODUCTION

1.1 Key definitions
- TEU or Twenty-Equivalent Unit: A 20' shipping container.
- Panamax containership: A vessel with dimensions (size) that fit the original locks of the Panama Canal. Carrying capacity 4,500 TEUs approx.
- Post-Panamax containership: A vessel with dimensions (size) that does not fit the original locks of the Panama Canal (too big to pass through the locks). Carrying capacity more than 12,000 TEUs.
- Ship-To-Shore crane (STS crane): Crane used at container terminals to load/unload shipping containers on/from containerships. See Figure 1.

Figure 1. STS crane.

1.2 Motivation of research project
Container terminals worldwide should be strategically integrated and fully connected to global supply chains as real time connectivity along global supply chains drives not only efficiency and performance but also collaboration, profitability, customer centricity, and port security, to name a few benefits. Around the world, however, there are container

terminals showing significant progress in terms of electronic connectivity to global supply chains but limited progress or no progress in terms of connectivity of equipment and machinery that operate at the lowest level of execution of the terminal's container handling operations, which results in a complete physical disconnection and electronic isolation of container handling equipment that leads to inefficiencies, underperformance due to disruption of terminal operations and supply chain processes, and eventually to a financial loss. Two cases are presented in this paper to illustrate how terminal operations and supply chain processes get disrupted due to lack of or limited connectivity of the equipment and machinery that operate at the lowest level of execution of the terminals' container handling operations.

Case 1 describes a situation in which an operator of container handling equipment working in the container terminal informs his/her supervisor using traditional communication tools (e.g. radio and telephone) or via an in-person conversation a mechanical failure of the equipment he/she is operating. This traditional method of communication between the operator of the container handling equipment in question and his/her supervisor can negatively impact the terminal operations and eventually result in a financial loss due to the time elapsed from the moment the equipment gets out of operation to the moment the supervisor becomes aware of the condition of the equipment and takes action to start the process to restore the operation of the equipment. The longer the time the higher the financial loss. Ideally, to minimize the time the equipment is out of service, maximize equipment's uptime, and most importantly to ensure the continuity of the terminal's operations, the equipment's operator should be equipped with a mobile device to be fully connected in real time with his/her supervisor and other key terminal's personnel to notify instantly any malfunctioning of the container handling equipment he/she is operating. Moreover, the container handling equipment itself should be equipped with electronic devices (e.g., antenas, receivers, transmiters, WiFi routers, etc.) to allow for the full, real time connectivity with key functional areas of the terminal, such as the operations and maintenance departments, in order to notify autonmously in real time any mechanical, electrical issues of the equipment as soon as they occur or they are about to occur. The full, real time connectivity of the container handling equipment with the operations and maintenance departments of the terminal also allows for the real time tracking and monitoring of the operation of the container handling equipment and the terminal's operations in general. Intelligent sensors are instrumental to achieve this advanced level of execution of the container handling operations of the container terminal.

Case 2 describes a situation in which a technician, who is remotely servicing a container handler which is out of order, communicates with the warehouse manager using traditional communication tools (e.g. radio and telephone) or in an in-person conversation to request the parts, materials, supplies, and even tools needed to repair the container handler. This case also refers to a situacion in which a warehouse operator cannot find in the warehouse the parts requested by the techician. Both cases result in a delay delivering the parts to the technician, which in turn increses the period of time the container handler is down. Such delay can impact negatively the terminal's operations and eventually result in a financial loss for the terminal. Ideally, to minimize the time the equipment is out of service, the technician should be equipped with a mobile device, which will allow him/her to be fully connected in real time with the terminal's warehouse management system to request online the parts required to restore the operation of the container handler in question. Moreover, the warehouse should be equipped with RFID technology, which will minimize the time locating parts in the warehouse. In addition to that, online access to service and parts manuals as well as to maintenance records of container hadling equipment will surely expedite the repair of equipment.

The cases described above are representative of many instances in the operation of container terminals in which terminal operations and supply chain processes get disrupted due to lack of or limited connectivity of the equipment and machinery that operate at the lowest level of execution of the terminals' container handling operations, which invariably result in operational inefficiences and eventually in a financial loss.

This paper is primarily focused on introducing an Internet-of-Things supply chain solution to enable a permanent, real time connectivity of electronic devices, intelligent sensors, and container handling equipment and machinery, which operate on a container terminal in order to ensure the timely, cost-effective execution of the terminal's container handling operations and supply chain processes.

1.3 Overview of operations of container terminal

The operation of a container terminal is extremely complex and is characterized by the utilization of expensive, highly specialized container handling equipment [1]. Five of the commonly used types of container handling equipment are [1]:

- Ship-To-Shore cranes (STS cranes), used at to load/unload shipping containers on/from containerships.
- Loaded Container Handlers (LCH), used to handle loaded shipping containers. It can stack up to 5 containers.
- Empty Container Handlers (ECH), used to handle, primarily stacking, empty shipping containers. It can stack up to 9 containers.
- Rubber Tyred Gantry (RTG), used to facilitate multiple container handling operations including but not limited to retrieval of containers from storage (high-density), placement of container in storage, transfer of containers from storage to trucks (flat beds) and from trucks to storage, and transfer of containers from storage to rail cars and vice versa.
- Terminal Tractors (TT), used to transport shipping containers mounted on container chassis; TTs haul container chassis.

Due to the relatively high cost of container handling equipment, one of the greatest challenges a director of a container port/terminal faces is to determine the optimal number of STS cranes, LCHs, ECHs, TTs, and RTG cranes in order to maximize the operating efficiency of the facility while minimizing both the total

investment in container handling equipment and the total operating cost [1].

For the most part, the logic of operation of a container terminal is similar to that of a distribution center. Shipping containers are unloaded from the containership and taken to the storage area. From there, containers are shipped to their next destinations inland. Outgoing shipping containers are taken from the storage area to a location next to the containership to be lifted and loaded on the containership. The type of container handling equipment involved in a move basically depends on the move itself and the type of container (i.e., loaded or empty) to move. For instance, if the move is to stack an empty container on top of a pile of 6 containers then an ECH is the type of container handling equipment to use. If the move is to unload a container from a containership then a STS crane is the equipment to use.

Traditional container terminals have limited electronic connectivity or no electronic connectivity with other companies or entities in the port or geographic area where they operate or with other parties in the global supply chains they belong to. In addition, they do not have container handling equipment equipped with electronic devices to facilitate tracking, tracing, or transmittal of any kind of data.

2. SMART PORTS

Ports are working towards a global network of ports and connectivity is the driving force behind the establishment of a global logistics network [2]. The logic is to electronically share data in a secure way to create synergies, make supply chain processes as efficient as possible and ultimately maximize customer centricity by adding value to supply chains.

Essentially, a smart or digital port is a connected port [2]. The decision to transform a traditional port to a smart or digital port is fundamentally a strategic decision. A strategic master plan is required to timely and systematically take the transformation process of the port through multiple phases.

The Port of Rotterdam introduced the Digital Maturity Model [2] that is based on four levels of "maturity", which are:

1) Digitalization of individual parties in the port.
2) Integrated systems in a port community
3) Logistics chains integrated with hinterland
4) Connected ports in the global logistics chain

Level 1 implies that all parties directly involve with the operation of a port such as container terminals, ocean carriers, port authority, stowage companies, customs authorities, third-party logistics providers, etc. digitize their supply chain processes to be able to work more efficiently individually and to prepare the basis for collaboration through information exchange. Digitalization of supply chain processes is the foundation of a Port Management System, which streamlines and automates most if not all the administrative and operative functions of the port.

Level 2 implies the development of a Port Community System (PCS), which is a platform that enables the port to work as a single entity through the secure exchange of digital information within the port community. The PCS supports most forms of business collaboration (i.e., B2B, B2G, etc,).

Level 3 implies the sharing of information available through the PCS with other businesses and logistics companies in the community, such as maintenance companies, container depots, trucking companies, etc. for them to better plan their operations and maximize the service they provide to the port.

Level 4 implies connecting the port or container terminal with other ports located anywhere in the word to facilitate digital interaction, which effectively creates the conditions that maximize efficiencies, performance, and customer centricity and minimizes waste and total cost throughout the network of ports. Studies show that emissions in international shipping could fall by 35% due to "just-in-time" shipping [2].

Determining which technologies, how to implement them and the way in which they can support the overall digital strategy of a port is a major challenge [3].

In order to become a data-commercialization company, the Port of Antwerp developed NxtPort, a computer-based, information sharing platform developed to collect and analyze data for companies from different industries [3].

NxtPort, is a key component of the Port of Antwerp's strategy for operational improvement. BASF, MSC, DP World, and PSA are some of the global companies using NxtPort [3].

The Port of Amsterdam has launched several apps. One of them, the I am Port app offers real time information on containerships locations and itineraries in the port and provides information on arrivals and departures [3].

3. INTERNET-OF-THINGS SOLUTION FOR CONTAINER TERMINALS

3.1 Definition of Internet-of-Things (IoT)

According to the Institute of Electrical and Electronics Engineers (IEEE), Internet-of-Things is a network of items including sensors and embedded systems which are connected to the Internet and enable physical objects to gather and exchange data [4].

In IoT platforms, sensors are primarily used to collect data. The types of sensors typically used in IoT platforms include motion sensors, inertial sensors, optical sensors, ultrasonic sensors, imaging sensors, and RFID readers.

3.2 Known IoT developments for ports

Over 9 million TEUs flow through the Port of Hamburg annually, which makes it the second busiest port in Europe. At some point in time, expansion of the port to handle more TEUs was not feasible as the port is located in an urban area of the City of Hamburg. The only option for the Port of Hamburg to be able to handle more TEUs efficiently was to operate "smarter", which led to the development of smartPort Logistics, one of the most innovative IoT platforms for maritime ports [5].

smartPort Logistics, which primarily helps keeping traffic flowing continuously and smoothly, was developed using the SAP HANA Cloud Platform to facilitate real time connectivity through a mobile cloud-based application. Users of smartPort Logistics include HPA, transportation companies, container terminals, ocean carriers, providers of port-related products and services, etc. Data analyzed by smartPort Logistics comes from people, processes, and "things" physically connected with the Port of Hamburg. smartPort Logistics' applications include but are not limited to various types of shipment schedules for transportation companies, truck traffic control and slot management, predictive and preventive maintenance schedules for port equipment, and vessel traffic services [5].

Ephlux Ports Terminal Asset & Operator Monitoring is an IoT platform, which uses different types of sensors to help container terminals and stevedoring companies monitor and track both equipment and equipment operators [6]. Ephlux develops customized IoT solutions using Oracle IoT Cloud AM.

3.3 IoT-based solution for port/container terminal security

Since 9/11, the US Department of Homeland Security has successfully implemented numerous security initiatives with a favorable outcome: No terror attack since September 11, 2001. However, studies show that maritime ports are highly vulnerable to terror attacks. A self-propelled semi-submersible, a small vessel, an improvised explosive device, and divers are examples of threats to maritime ports.

An IoT platform is a viable solution to enforce port security and protect maritime ports. Intelligent sensors and smart portable x-rays, scanners, and heat detectors can be attached to container handling equipment to detect radiation, illegal aliens, weapons, materials to build weapons of mass destruction, drugs, etc.

A spreader, which is shown in Figure 2, is a component of container handling equipment used to grab and release shipping containers.

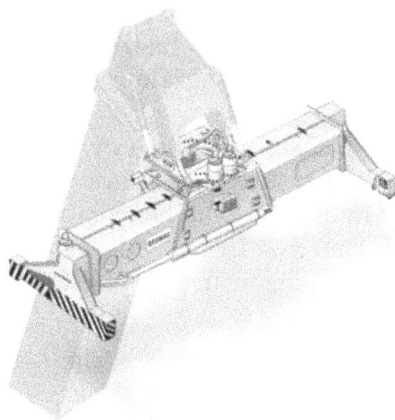

Figure 2. Spreader.

STS cranes, LCH, ECH, and RTG cranes are examples of container handling equipment that use a spreader to grab and release shipping containers. The yellow component of the RTG crane shown in Figure 3 is a spreader, which is holding a shipping container.

Figure 3. Spreader attached to a RTG crane.

Figure 4 shows a spreader attached to a STS crane loading/unloading a shipping container on/from a containership.

Figure 4. Spreader attached to a STS crane.

Intelligent sensors and smart portable x-rays, scanners, and heat detectors attached to container handling equipment autonomously notify in real time US law enforcement agencies about suspicious cargo detected in a shipping container and automatically stop the machine handling the shipping container in question.

The IoT platform to enforce port security and protect maritime ports can be expanded with intelligent sensors used to authenticate port personnel. In the case of operators of transport equipment, which enter the port to deliver or pick up a shipping container, intelligent sensors located at the gates of the container terminals, send electronic signals to the operator's TWIC card for authentication purposes. TWIC stands for Transportation Worker Identification Card. Sensors autonomously notify in real time US law enforcement agencies when the authentication process fails. A smart TWIC card should be integrated to the IoT solution for port security to prevent fraud and use of fake TWIC cards. In fact, to maximize port security, the biometrics of the operator in question should be fully embedded on the TWIC card.

Criminal organizations operating around the world open in-transit shipping containers to add illegal cargo or to illegally take cargo from the shipping container. The built-in weighting capabilities of container handling equipment can be effectively used to maintain the integrity of in-transit shipping containers. Moreover, the container handling equipment could be equipped with devices to electronically communicate, using wireless technology, with Port Police and law enforcement agencies to report in real time discrepancies between the documented and the actual weight of shipping containers. To enforce port security at the lowest level of operation, the twist locks of the spreader of container handling equipment should be automatically locked and its boom/mast should be automatically blocked to keep the shipping container off the ground in order to prevent that criminals take the shipping container away.

Drones equipped with intelligent sensors and AI-based vision systems can be used to patrol underwater, on the surface of the water, or in the air and to notify threats in real time.

4. CONCLUSIONS

This paper introduces an IoT solution to enforce port security at container terminals focused on the lowest level of execution of terminal's operations, which is container handling operations. The introduced IoT solution for container terminals can be expanded in different directions. One of them is to track and monitor performance of container handling equipment and for the equipment to autonomously notify in real time maintenance issues as soon as they occur or are about to occur.

As far as smart ports, it is important to keep in mind that becoming a smart port should part of the strategic plan of the port to effectively face current and future challenges and to materialize current and future opportunities.

The logic behind the development and implementation of IoT supply chain solutions is to support *Anytime – Anyhow – Anywhere – Anyone – Anything - Anyway* logistics operations, which will result in the timely, cost-effective, and lean execution of supply chain processes.

REFERENCES

[1] M.A. Lara Gracia, "Optimization of Container Port Operations Using Data Envelopment Analysis", **Proceedings of the 22nd World Multiconference on Systemics, Cybernetics and Informatics (WMSCI 2018)**, Volume I, pp. 82-87, Orlando, FL, July 2018.

[2] *Move Forward: Step by Step Towards a Digital Port*. Retrieved December 23, 2018 from https://www.portofrotterdam.com/en/port-forward/step-by-step-towards-a-digital-port.

[3] *Smart Ports*. Retrieved December 29, 2018 from https://www2.deloitte.com/content/dam/Deloitte/nl/Documents/energy-resources/deloitte-nl-er-port-services-smart-ports.pdf

[4] Y. Yang, M. Zhong, H. Yao, F. Yu, X. Fu, and O. Postolache, "Internet of Things for Smart Ports: Technologies and Challenges", **IEEE Instrumentation and Measurement Magazine**, February 2018, pp. 34-43.

[5] *The Hamburg Port Authority's Impressive IoT Project*. Retrieved January 6, 2018 from https:// www.forbes.com/sites/stevebanker/2016/04/01/ the-hamburg-port-authoritys-impressive-iot-project/# 8e16ed46c64c

[6] *Powering Ports & Terminal Operations Through IoT and Machine Learning*. Retrieved December 17, 2018 from http://www.ephlux.com/ports-terminal-stevedore-operations-using-iot-and-machine-learning

A pedagogical introduction to parametric modeling as a formal research tool

Sylvie JANCART
Faculty of Architecture, University of Liège
Liège, Belgium

Adeline STALS
Faculty of Architecture, University of Liège
Liège, Belgium

[sylvie.jancart@uliege.be, adeline.stals@uliege.be]

ABSTRACT

This paper starts with an overview of parametric modeling pedagogy in architectural design, notably with regards to mathematical perspective, and the inputs it generates in the design process. We focus on the pedagogical approach developed within the course "Digital Culture and Generative Processes of Form", part of the Master Program of the Faculty of Architecture (University of Liège, Belgium). We then develop the evaluation methodology applied in this context. Finally, we discuss the conduct of such a learning process.

Keywords: architecture, parametric modeling tools, formal research, pedagogical process.

1. INTRODUCTION

The course, "Digital Culture and Generative Processes of Form", is part of the Master Program of the Faculty of Architecture ULiège (Belgium). Our main objective in this course is to develop themes, related to formal and material research, within the architectural project approach. This perspective seems relevant as it combines, by digital means, the emergence of form, its control, and the media devoted to the materialization of designed objects. Based on parametric modeling, this relevance is reflected in the use of tools, whose performance in terms of design assistance, allows increased project control. The use of design tools has taken off in recent years, allowing increased methodological opportunities. We propose to address the concepts of geometry underlying the research of architects concerned with the genesis of architectural form and space. We introduce students to the use of programming language, specific to the selected modeling software, to generate complex 3D forms and to control them. Project-based learning enables students to develop their skills. Students learn through different means and information sources: theoretical contains, expert interventions (GH-Archicad© connection, Dynamo© connection, RElab Liège Fablab), exercises and tutorials.

This paper starts with an overview of parametric modeling pedagogy, notably with regards to mathematical perspective, and the inputs it generates in the design process. We then develop the evaluation methodology applied in this context and discuss the conduct of such a learning process.

2. PEDAGOGY OF PARAMETRIC MODELING IN ARCHITECTURAL DESIGN

On the one hand, Altet [1] defines pedagogy as the articulation between teaching and learning processes, involving knowledge and aims. Teaching refers to a process of transmission of knowledge by a teacher, learning refers to the process of acquiring knowledge by doing. On the other hand, as developed by Oxman [2], "any new framework for design pedagogy must be responsive to condition in which digital concepts are integrated as a unique body of knowledge consisting of the relationship between digital architectural design and digital design skills".

In her thesis, to answer the question « How to define the most relevant pedagogical positioning for parametric modeling in architectural design? » de Boissieu [3] highlighted several skills needed to be developed in parametric design: theoretical, know-how and soft skills. She identified two kinds of knowledge: one fundamental and stable, and the other evolving rapidly and according to the development of the tools necessary for numerical parametric modeling.

Theoretical skills' knowledge is given via a non-exhaustive list:
- knowledge specific to geometry and mathematics;
- knowledge related to computer science in general and programming in particular;
- digital knowledge in general;
- knowledge of mechanisms based on the propagation of parametric modeling;
- software specific knowledge;
- knowledge related to architecture and construction;
- and architectural design knowledge.

Concerning the know-how skill, de Boissieu mentions the pattern concepts developed by Woodbury [4], which consist of the division of a parametric modeling project into identifiable and understandable subsystems with simple interactions, which are then modeled using patterns. Finally, and still referring to Woodbury, the parametric design process is characterized by three principles according to which:
- designers develop rules and define their logical relationships while creating 3D visualization models;
- designers can modify their model at any time;
- and design alternatives can be developed in parallel at any stage of the process.

Finally, we can mention, without developing them, certain soft skills mentioned in the thesis [3]: abstraction, organization and anticipation, participation and maintenance of a network, curiosity and initiative.

Based on de Boissieu's work, we analyze retrospectively the content of our teachings going through the seven aforementioned skills' knowledge and others skills listed in this section.

3. PARAMETRIC MODELING EDUCATION METHOD AND MATHEMATICAL PERSPECTIVE

Connected to the skills' referential developed in the Faculty of Architecture of Liège, all teaching in the digital culture will enable students to develop specific skills. For our course, we identified two learning outcomes. The first one is **defining an architectural question**. The skills are developed by studying the various components of the theme and context (historical, landscape, economic, legal, technological, etc.). The second one is **drafting a spatial response** by:
- using verbal, written and graphic language as a means of designing, structuring, verifying and questioning thought;
- introducing experiments with implementation as a design parameter;
- and adjusting spatial resolutions through exploratory questioning (question-response-spatial validation and new cycle of questioning).

In our course, we encourage architectural practices such as non-standard architecture design or complex shape generation using parametric modeling. As developed by Gallas et al. [5], the proposed process is structured in three steps: analysis, implementation, and experimentation. This process associates digital design and fabrication tools to physical representation. As we know, mathematics plays an important role in the design and materialization processes that characterize non-standard architecture. This form of architectural expression uses a sequence of tools and devices embodying the concept of the digital continuum. We therefore refer to mathematical concepts to encourage students to use them in the early stages of design, either as a source of inspiration (cognitive engine of creation) or as a rationalization tool. We are mainly interested here by architectural geometry using constructability criteria directly linked to the mathematical characteristics of surfaces [6]. Kelly [7] defines parametric geometry modeling as a field studying algorithm that computes geometry. Modeling a free-form surface means more than fine-tuning control points. It is necessary to obtain a constructible result, which implies the understanding of mathematical concepts hidden behind these surfaces, and connect them to the material world. Among the options that allow us to design these surfaces, we retain the ruled and developable surfaces, curvatures (Gaussian, Mean) and polar, cylindrical, and spherical coordinates. Curved surfaces have mathematical (geometric) properties that directly influence these options and most CAD (Computer Aided Design) programs can visualize them. It is of course up to the designer to interpret them through color code and then decide to either change the result to meet the expected material, or find the material that will best correspond to the desired project [8]. Geometrical tools are then used to analyze the shape and relevance of a desired transformation, and thus avoid unwanted effects. To develop effective solutions, the properties of the shape and material must be known precisely in the 3D model, which implies that the mathematics behind the physical behavior must also be known. According to the project that the groups of students develop, we direct them towards the exploration of other mathematical concepts such as

Computational geometry (Voronoi diagram, A*Algorithm); Self-organized system (cellular automaton, swarm system); Rule-based system (L-system, shape grammar); and Optimization (genetic algorithm).

In parallel, we present examples of contemporary architecture such as the Lars Spuybroek Water Pavilion, the Toyo Ito Serpentine Gallery Pavilion, and the Norman Foster Great Court Roof of the British Museum. We describe their geometric process respectively: the beam structure as concatenation of circular segments; complex weave out of repeated nesting of rotated squares and extension into field of intersecting lines; algebraic overlay of three surfaces and shape optimization by method of relaxation [9]. These few examples allow us to share some digital culture on architecture, a culture poorly developed among our student community.

A brief overview of the integration of parametric modeling in Belgian architectural offices also helps to make students aware of the digital practices developed in their own country [10].

Digital culture, mathematics, and structural morphology are the three key themes in this teaching unit. We can summarize each one as follows:
- the influence of digital culture on architecture;
- the influence of mathematical sciences on the Fine Arts and architecture in particular, in the contemporary and modern periods; Mathematics and the genesis of form, non-Euclidian geometry, fractal design, and creation by iteration;
- and the contribution of structural morphology, free forms and controlled forms.

The integration of the mathematical theories during the analysis phase helps students to define the structure of the designed models, the project form, but also the process itself [5]. As geometric or positional numerical constraints are related to form a consistent set, they thus constitute a group of heterogeneous elements defining the parametric model [3].

These subjects taught in a frontal traditional way give some theoretical skills knowledge mentioned in the previous section.

It is important, at this point, to remind ourselves that to think complex geometry, appropriate tools, especially software, must be used to simulate these geometries, and especially to control their properties. The designer must then optimize both the form and the manufacturing processes for the benefit of visual printing [11].

In our course, pedagogy remains central to our teaching but we insist on the use of online learning resources to continue to deepen the learning of parametric modeling. This also allows students to stay up-to-date with rapidly evolving digital knowledge (as developed in the previous section). It is therefore necessary to teach students to learn, so that they can then learn by themselves by means of manipulation. The idea is to give the basic notions, basic explanations and what they provide. From the first session, exercises are proposed to the students. They allow them to get in direct contact with the software and the underlying programming. The exercises, which allow them a wide variability in their choice of design, quickly lead students to use tutorials to find explanations related to the programming itself. This way of proceeding enables them to discover the parametric programming community and other networks. Figure 1 shows different results from the first proposed exercise. As these columns are divided into three distinct but related parts, the exercise allows them to discover the notions of constraints and parameters. In particular, they become familiar with concepts such as project parameters, constants and variables.

Figure 1: Examples of columns design by students from the first proposed exercise.

With the continuous aim of developing their know-how, and some of the theoretical skills connected to software and programming, we offer students different design/architectural concepts (waffle, Voronoi, origami, curve, ...). We model some of them, and present the Grasshopper components to the students. For this step of learning, we assist students in class but we also advise them to refer to the AAD Algorithm-Aided Design book [12], as a reference to define the steps of their parametric approach. Beside this cognitive reflection, some students use 3D printing machines and digital fabrication devices, enhancing a digital continuum from digital file to physical object, as proposed by Marin and his colleagues [13]. The interest of 3D printing is introduced at the beginning of the teaching through the first exercise. The columns proposed by the students are then printed in 3D. This exercise allows students not only to familiarize themselves with the software but also to understand the benefits of the continuum design manufacturing. The visit of the RElab (Liège Fablab) and the opportunity to work in collaboration with it, encourage students to develop their project in the design-manufacturing continuum and to anticipate whether they will move towards 3D printing, laser cutting or CNC (Computer Numerical Control) machine.

In order to build software-specific knowledge, we invite experts to introduce GH-Archicad© connection, and Dynamo© connection. Students are then introduced to other software allowing parametric modeling. These sessions show them what this modeling can lead to, as the links to the BIM process are then presented.

Even if one difficulty lies in the transition from paper sketch to parametric structure [14], the defining characteristic of a parametric model is not the final project, but rather the construction and maintenance of relationships associated with the model. Rather than the formal product, it is the creation and the development of the process that is at the heart of the reflection involving and challenging some soft skills. The transition from sketch to logic model diagram, and the integration of material and structural constraints, will be the result of a computation process in which the user must manipulate geometric concepts through a visual representation program. The use of the parametric puzzle as a parametric design device can help students to create different levels of abstraction during the parametric modeling process. This device, experimented and developed during the digital modeling courses of the Faculty of Applied Sciences of the University of Liège is described in Gallas et al [5]. The parametric puzzle components can help to materialize defined modeling steps. Sketches are translated in graphical algorithms, integrating geometrical and logical entities as a middle-level abstraction step. Different ways of modeling are generated and the most pertinent can be selected. The last step of the modeling process integrates the translation of the graphical algorithm, using physical components, to a graphical algorithm, using Grasshopper components as a low-level abstraction activity.

4. STUDENT PROJECT EVALUATION

For the final work of this course, we ask students to carry out an exercise in which they present an architectural premise, including structural characteristics, so that the form is potentially feasible. This modeling work has to be done using the combination of the Rhinoceros© and Grasshopper© software and the results of their research are communicated in two forms: a poster and an oral presentation. In their visual communication, they are asked to detail the problems encountered, the solutions provided, and to evaluate if they have achieved their objective. This work does not entail carrying out yet another "project", but rather a methodological approach to formal and architectural research, on which the evaluation will be based.

The following example illustrates the project of a lamp modeled by two students: the anemone lamp. Figure 2 presents the evolution of their research and the final result the students have chosen to present. They mention that the lamp could be printed in plaster (gypsum) and is designed to be placed on a table, but it could just as easily be hung or placed on a stand.

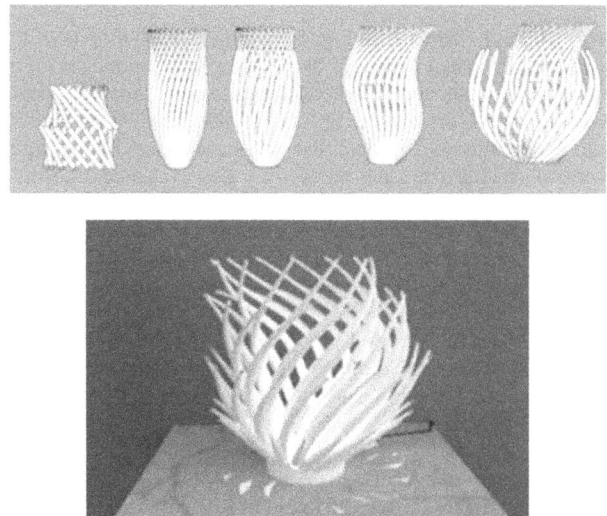

Figure 2: The evolution of transformation (on the left) and the final project (on the right): The anemone lamp.

Since the designer, in this case the students, decides which parameters to use and which range of variation is most relevant, the first criteria for assessing the final piece of work is the relevance of the choice of parameters, and how they impact upon the possibility of structuring form. Therefore, we evaluate the quality, method, and description of the approach (inventiveness, limits, solutions, etc.). They have to consider and present different possibilities (instances) by "playing" with the values of parameters. Figure 3 illustrates instances of the anemone lamp. The different results were obtained according to the position of the circle on the X axis, the scale of the circles, the numbers of rods or some shifts on the lists in Grasshopper respectively.

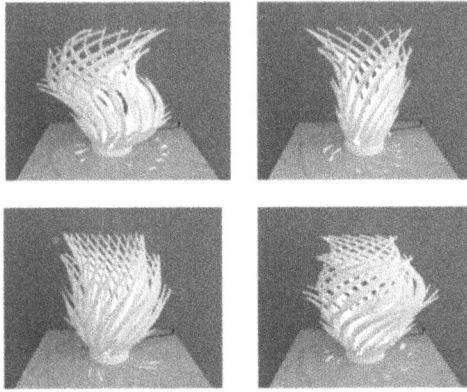

Figure 3: Different varieties of the anemone lamp, according to the position of the circle on the X axis, the scale of the circles, the numbers of rods, or some shifts on the lists in Grasshopper, from left to right respectively.

Finally, we ask students to illustrate their parametric design model, on the one hand, by the GH chain, and on the other hand, in a schematic conceptual representation (graphical IPO style). The construction, identification, and organization of the generative modules are taken into account.

5. STUDENT EVALUATION OF PROPOSED DEVICES

The different devices and information sources proposed to students have been evaluated by means of a questionnaire. We asked students about their interest in expert interventions to show GH-Archicad© connection, Dynamo© connection, and the visit and opportunity to work in collaboration with the RElab (Liège Fablab). Within the same survey, we also evaluated students' opinions of the main section structuring the course. The questions were mainly based on the interest of theoretical contains, the aim of a first exercise, the use of 3D printing and the importance of working in groups of two people.

The results of the survey show a great interest in visiting the RElab, both for the discovery of the machines, and their functionalities, but also because they allow a concrete and direct materialization of their project.

Although they did point out the lack of time allocated to the digital course (2ECTS) at the Faculty of Architecture of Liège, the students appreciated being confronted with several parameterization software, even though it presented a certain complexity. The intervention of an Archicad expert showing the link between this software and Grasshopper was also appreciated. It was of particular interest to them because of the functionalities it offers. Also, GH-Archicad© connection allows direct applications related to modeling and therefore a concretization of the latter.

The majority of students highlighted the interest in working on a small scale (here the modeling of a lamp). According to them, this scale allowed them to develop their creativity through parametric modeling, which offers several options. In addition, this scale allowed different tests to be carried out and materialized. Some have however deplored the lack of links between the course and the design studio.

According to them, collaborative work must be limited to two people given the difficulty of programming. However, it allows for a richer reflection: "Alone faster, two of us go further".

6. CONCLUSION

The course integrates a computational approach, both theoretical and practical, allowing the student to acquire a culture in contemporary architectural practices, knowledge and parametric modeling skills. It also enables experience in "design to manufacture continuum". To achieve this, the course is divided into three main steps: spread of digital culture; exercises to familiarize themselves with the software, and develop the ability to undertake a parametric approach; and a global project taking into account the architectural and material approach of a project.

Regarding our role, we consider ourselves to be facilitators, providing the tools and the opportunities to redirect students to the best sources of information for their own projects. With regards to our teaching and learning processes, we stimulate both the theoretical skills' knowledge, fundamental to parametric modeling, and skills evolving rapidly as defined by de Boissieu (2013). We stress to students the importance of developing the necessary skills in order not to become "magicians" who could lose control of the form.

This course provides students the basics they need to continue learning on their own and to develop a critical approach to learning.

9. REFERENCES

[1] M. Altet, **Les pédagogies de l'apprentissage,** 2e édition, Paris : Presses Universitaires de France, 2006.
[2] R. Oxman, **Digital architecture as a challenge for design pedagogy: theory, knowledge, models and medium**, Design Studies, No. 29, 2008, pp. 99-102.
[3] A. de Boissieu, **Modélisation paramétrique en conception architecturale**, Ph.D. Thesis, ENSA Paris la Villette, 2013.
[4] R. Woodbury, **Elements of parametric design**, Routledge, New York, 2010.
[5] M-A. Gallas, K. Jacquot, S. Jancart and F. Delvaux, **Parametric Modeling: An Advanced Design Process for Architectural Education,** Ecaade 33, 2015.
[6] H. Pottmann, A. Asperl, A. Hofer, and A. Kilian, **Architectural Geometry**, Bentley Institute Press, 2007.
[7] T. Kelly, **Unwritten Procedural Modeling with Skeletons**, Ph.D. Thesis, University of Glasgow, 2013.
[8] S. Jancart, A. Stals, and M-A. Gallas, **Mathématique et culture numérique : supports aux nouvelles formes d'expression architecturale**, Scan16, 2016.
[9] Hovestadt and Schaerer, **Algorithmic Extension of Architecture, algorithmic example**, ETHZ, Master of Advanced Studies in Architecture, Specialization in Computer Aided Architectural Design, consulted in July 2018.
[10] A. Stals, C. Elsen, and S. Jancart, **Practical Trajectories of Parametric Tools in Small and Medium Architectural Firms,** CAAD Futures, 2017.
[11] F. Scheuer and H. Stebling, **Lost in parameter space?** in Architectural Design, 2011.
[12] A. Tedeshi, **AAD-Algorithms-aided design**, édition le Penseur, 2014.

[13] P. Marin, J-C. Bignon and J-P. Wetzel, **From nature to manufacture.** International Symposium File to factory: The design and fabrication of innovative forms in a continuum, International Symposium File to factory, Chania, 2009.

[14] J-P. Couwenbergh, **L'approche computationnelle : un changement de paradigme en conception architecturale. Perspectives de recherches et d'enseignements.** Translated by M.A. Gallas, Journée de la Recherche et des Doctorants en LOCI [JDR+D_ - 2015], Université catholique de Louvain, Bruxelles, 2015.

The HTTP Error Response Extension Specification for the Emerging Self-served API-centric Architecture with AI based Self-healing Ability

Dr. Haoyue Bai
Technology & Operations, Royal Bank of Canada, 88 Queens Quay W
Toronto, ON M5J 0B8, Canada

Dr. Salah Sharieh
Technology & Operations, Royal Bank of Canada, 88 Queens Quay W
Toronto, ON M5J 0B8, Canada

Nebojsa Djosic
Technology & Operations, Royal Bank of Canada, 88 Queens Quay W
Toronto, ON M5J 0B8, Canada

Dinu Merca
Technology & Operations, Royal Bank of Canada, 88 Queens Quay W
Toronto, ON M5J 0B8, Canada

ABSTRACT

API-centric architecture using REST over HTTP is becoming more and more popular these days. Within modern enterprises, the API requests and responses often pass through a complex, nested layers of networking and software structures. Typically, these software structures consist of multiple layers of so called channel APIs, Business Domain middleware, and backend, Data Store applications. In between them there are typically multiple layers of network structures such as firewalls, switches, LTMs (Local Traffic Management), routers, load balancers, reverse proxies. An additional degree of complexity is introduced by adding messaging layers to the more traditional request-response solutions. This emerging trend is a result of splitting software development and operations work across smaller, independent teams. This gives businesses more flexibility and shorter release cycles. In this paper, we proposed an error response extension specification, which will overcome shortages of the current HTTP response status code standard, and various extensions, making it be easier for API consumers to trouble shoot issues by themselves, it will reduce support team workload, and keep the sensitive information leak to a minimum to satisfy the best security practices. AI error processing strategy is also included in the implementation of our specification.

Keywords: API, Response Status Code, Error Response, Cyber Security, Self-Serve, Error Logging, Artificial Intelligence

1. INTRODUCTION

APIs exposed over the HTTP have become a foundational technology for the development of robust and scalable enterprise applications. [11] Front-end apps are built using these APIs to deliver a rich user experience. APIs over HTTP are traditionally used to connect n-tier systems, front-middle-backend, both data and services, often referred to as North-South traffic. While this has remained, recent micro-service trend has introduced, so called, East-West traffic where micro-services use APIs over HTTP to connect other micro-services. Such complex interconnected "micro-services" structures using APIs over HTTP are called service mesh [12]. The widespread adoption of REST, JSON, and standards based access control, such as OAuth, OIDC using JWT, and the other similar conventions for API design, often delivered as frameworks such as Spring Boot means that developers can easily build and expose functionality using APIs over HTTP and/or use APIs in their applications with little overhead allowing them to focus on application functionality enabling fast delivery of features to end-users.

Within the space of the fast growing of API-centric architecture, some significant issues may arise. Diagnosing the issue according to the HTTP response status code and information returned by the first layer of middleware in a complex call sequence is a daunting task. We want to jumpstart the error resolution process early in order to make the error resolution a more self-serve process, which can free up humans from supporting this complex API calling flow. To achieve this, the more functional error responses are needed.

There are several companies or platforms which attempted to make the error response more functional. Microsoft IIS (Internet Information Services) 7 and later versions specify a set of extended HTTP status codes. [7] Here is one example:

- 400.1 - Invalid Destination Header.
- 400.2 - Invalid Depth Header.
- 400.3 - Invalid If Header.
- 400.4 - Invalid Overwrite Header.
- 400.5 - Invalid Translate Header.
- 400.6 - Invalid Request Body.
- 400.7 - Invalid Content Length.
- 400.8 - Invalid Timeout.
- 400.9 - Invalid Lock Token.

Google also owns patents [8,9] which define the Client extended error handling and Compounding of HTTP authoring protocol [3].

There's been a number of attempts to augment the HTTP standards [7,8]. However, we believe that to achieve the goal of building a more self-served API platforms, the limited amount of status codes offered by HTTP and various extensions cannot provide sufficient information to several classes of users to trouble shoot issues by themselves. In the emerging API platform complex structures the front-most support teams are typically under heaviest work load since they are the first point of contact and have to trace the request from the beginning to the failure point. On the other hand, it is against the best security practices to put detailed error information in the response body since it might expose sensitive information to malicious users. Based on the previous research and techniques [7,8,9], we propose here a new set of error response extension specification, that puts more focus on the enterprise application structure which contains multiple layers of HTTP calls between the end-user and backend services. The proposed specification provides more details for the end-users enabling them to attempt the error resolution by themselves if possible, or providing them with details where to look further for help. Since this technique could expose one more attack surface by providing social-engineering opportunity to lure users into clicking, calling, in general, following advice given in the user agent, the implementation of the specification will cover this concern as well as a security risks of exposing unnecessary but valuable details to malicious users.

2. PROBLEM STATEMENT

2.1 Waste of human resource time caused by insufficient information provided in the error response

Current status codes and non-standard error responses do not contain enough information and/or in a standard format that would allow systematic and/or programmatic approach to locating where the error occurred, and processing it further to resolution. As a result, in most cases it calls for humans reading log files and relying on past experience to determine the root cause. When teams get an error from the layer of middleware they are communicating with but not supporting, let us denote this layer as **M1**, the only way for this team to solve the issue is to contact the support team of **M1** if they cannot find the solution on their own. However, the error might have been caused by any other layer further downstream. The troubleshooting process could involve almost all the layers often unnecessarily as businesses proactively call teams to speed-up resolution resulting in a waste of time and effort.

2.2 Risk of exposing error details to malicious users

In order to include more information in the HTTP error response, the first straight forward idea is to put all available detailed information in the response body. However, this idea raises a serious problem: it is risky to put potentially sensitive information in the response body since malicious users can and will use this to attack API and/or end-users. Moreover, the error response sent to the end-users and the one sent to the business application users should be different, since the end users do not

need to troubleshoot and typically would have different access level and/or knowledge and permissions to do so. On the other hand, the business application users, like support teams, need more information to be able to help end-users or to do the troubleshooting to fix the broken systems.

3. ERROR RESPONSE EXTENSION SPECIFICATION

3.1 Error Schema

Our proposal focuses on the HTTP response payload rather than on extending the standard status code set. In particular we're proposing to standardize the HTTP response for error message payload for specific status codes. Given that a vast majority of HTTP (modern) traffic is REST over HTTP the response must be a JSON object of type error and the following fields should be included:

apiDomain - the domain the API belongs to
errorType - this is a short description of the error
errorCode - this is a numeric code that is unique within the apiDomain. It is an internal code used by RBC developers to get more details about an error
message - this is a human readable short message explaining the errorCode
referenceId -this is a unique ID for each error instance, that is used to track the error in the code

An error response should look like the following:

```
{
  "error": {
    "apiDomain":"com:acme:banking:personal:account:list",
    "errorType":"SystemError",
    "errorCode":"50001",
    "message":"Request timeout",
    "referenceId":"123e1dd7-2a7f-18fb-b8ed-ed78c3f92c2b",}}
```

To allow for extension of the system of record without impacts to the client, there should be a generic code for all the undefined errors, which will be a catch-all for all the undefined errors. Also, client code which is the business logic should gracefully handle error codes it does not understand.

There are two additional data elements that could, optionally, be returned in an error object:

- In case of an invalid input request passed in from the client: an ***inputValidation*** array
- In case the API calls other APIs downstream: an ***additionalDetails*** array
- The real content of the two data elements above may change according to the limitation of sensitive information in different enterprises.

Input Validation Errors

In case the data in the client request is not valid, optionally, the error object can also include an array of errors as follows:

- *inputValidation* - An array of individual issues with the input data

- *fieldName*: The name of the filed that has the error.
- *location*: Path to the field in the overall request object
- *issue*: The issue encountered. Include as much information as possible here. Note that this is a potentially sensitive in the case of login or similar data, but perfectly fine in case of postal code, dates, email address, phone, etc.

Errors in Nested Calls

In a more complex, also more realistic case, the initial HTTP request from end-user will pass through a series of service to service calls. Most if not all of these calls will also be over the HTTP. In some cases, for instance account balance aggregation, there will be more than one potential error, while the overall the API may respond with success, or error. For instance, mortgage and loans systems may be unavailable while other systems could be returning balances just fine. Similarly, there could be a case where orchestrator type service is returning an error because of another critical service failure. In such cases where one API calls another API downstream, and the error is due to one or more of the downstream API calls, optionally, the error object could also include an array of additional details as follows:

- *additionalDetails* - An array of error objects with the same format as described in this section representing errors caught during downstream calls.

An example of a nested error object may look something like the following example below, where imaginary Account Linking orchestrator couldn't proceed and complete all steps because it encountered an error returned from Account Status API, micro-service.

```
{
"error": {
"apiDomain":"com:acme:banking:personal:account:link",
"errorType":"BusinessError",
"errorCode":"50011",
"message":"Cannot link account to customer",
"referenceId":"644e1dd7-2a7f-18fb-b8ed-ed78c3f92c2b",
"additionalDetails":[
    {
     "apiDomain":"com:acme:banking:personal:account:status",
     "errorType":"BusinessError",
     "errorCode":"50021",
     "message":"Account is frozen",
     "referenceId":"644e1dd7-2a7f-18fb-b8ed-ed78c3f92c2b"}]}}
```

In the example above, notice that, Account Linker API, called from the front-end, as an orchestrator, wouldn't need to know details of business logic or implementation of a micro-service Account Status, or any other that it may need to call such as sending regulatory required confirmation. Nevertheless, it is still able to report full details of the error including root-cause. To fully understand the value proposition here, consider first receiving just the top-most error telling end-user, support team, the world, that account can't be linked to customer. The rest, the real reason, root cause, is buried somewhere in a log, the only option left to this end-user is to call support. When such call is made the call center agents would have to probably attempt to complete the action for the user and probably poke around various systems only to find out something that was available at the time of failure. Typically, some business application architects would build-in error processing in Account Linker orchestrator so that it can report root error cause. However, this

is might not be a good idea, since this might break the encapsulation and would tightly couple orchestrator with the implementation of otherwise independent service. In addition, this is probably not the only place where this will have to be done. Another response to this problem is building of custom frameworks that process errors. This is also inefficient since it introduces yet another layer that would now need to have intimate knowledge of error conditions and implementations from many micro-services. Here, we're proposing a standard that would allow any API to report error in a standard way without needing callers to know intimate details. This allows for collecting errors along the way from nested calls that many modern APIs, micro-services, will make.

3.2 Error Types and Examples

There are a few different types of errors:

3.2.1 End-User Input Validation error

This could be an array of errors, and should give the client as much information as possible, so that the client can change the request and try again.

If the JSON is well-formed, then the request can be checked against the JSON schema definition, and if there are input validation errors these will be returned as an array of items that the client can address. An example of the response can look like as below, please notice that the "*location*" content may not be necessary if it's considered as sensitive.

```
{
  "error": {
    "apiDomain":"com:acme:banking:personal:profile",
    "errorType":"InputValidationError",
    "errorCode":"40010",
    "message":"Invalid request format",
    "referenceId":"644e1dd7-2a7f-18fb-b8ed-ed78c3f92c2b",
    "inputValidation":[
       {
        "fieldName":"nickname",
        "issue":"Nickname must be between 8 and 14 characters long and
contain only letters and numbers",
        "location":"/profile/nickname "
       },
       {
        "fieldName":"phoneNumber",
        "issue":"At least one telephone number is mandatory",
        "location":"/profile/phoneNumber"}]}}
```

3.2.2 Server Business Error

This is the most common type of error for an API, microservice. The error payload may look like this:

```
{
  "error": {
    "apiDomain":"com:acme:banking:personal:transfer",
    "errorType":"InsufficientFundsError",
    "errorCode":"40004",
    "message":"The account balance is too low.",
    "referenceId":"644e1dd7-2a7f-18fb-b8ed-ed78c3f92c2b",}}
```

3.2.3 Server System Error

This is a critical error in the platform that runs the API. There are a few errors that would fall under the "Global" domain. For instance, the HTTP call from one API to another, failed to reach the other REST controller on the account of system running out of memory (something that auto-scaling should prevent, but nothing is perfect) at the time when servlet was about to process the request. In this case, there's no application code to handle and process error. This is where having an HTTP standard response payload for errors is really valuable since it would allow various frameworks, application servers, etc. to be able to respond with something that the receiving side can programmatically process. Interoperability is ensured and automation can be built on top to further reduce the human intervention. For instance, in this case, system could self-correct. In real-world examples, we have encountered high-business value APIs that run into problems and ops teams would have regex based log parsers to detect out-of-memory and then simply restart the specific server in the cluster. This, on the surface may look like a trivial task and a simple solution. However, in real-life scenario it is far from it. Often ops teams will use enterprise-grade monitoring applications, and in many cases more than one and the constant long-tailed cycle of migration takes long time to decommission legacy systems. Combined with different file locations, log collection, access permissions, and compounded with multitude of different, custom log messages, the task of monitoring logs for the purposes described here, along with all the rest of monitoring, is a continuous development effort to write and maintain many, custom log monitors, checking if they are running, giving them permissions, testing them, and so on. Since this is often neglected by the business and dreaded by developers, it is an ugly duckling of running API platforms. We expect the standard proposed here can be a potential for significantly improving the situation.

The error payload may look like this:

```
{
  "error": {
    "apiDomain":"com:acme:global",
    "errorType":"OutOfMemoryError",
    "errorCode":"50015",
    "message":"Process ran out of memory",
    "referenceId":"644e1dd7-2a7f-18fb-b8ed-ed78c3f92c2b",}}
```

3.3 Domain Error Catalogue

Our proposal for HTTP standard error response payload provides another benefit: Business Domain Error Catalogue. This is not a new idea. However, the major difference here is the existence of the standard response schema. Before error catalogues were custom, unique and specific to application or even an API. This, by definition, limits the usefulness of such a catalogue. The recent proliferation of B2B integrations using REST over HTTP making end-users ever more distant from the services they consume and making developers integrate with applications they have little to none intimate knowledge of. Having a standard HTTP error response would allow for better integration, but having an error catalogue to go with it would add a huge value to both the end-user and every contributor in the end-to-end API value chain. Each business domain would define files with data

structures that contain a collection of error specifications for that name space. Each error specification should include at least:

- description of the error with links to more information
- error code - this will be the top-level element
- the http status code returned by this error
- the error type - this is the same as the *errorType* returned in the error payload
- the message that is returned - this is the same as the message field returned in the error payload

An example of the error catalogue for an API domain may look like the example below:

```
---
40001:
  httpCode: 401
  errorType: InvalidAuthToken
  message: "Invalid Authorization Token"
  desc: "The API pass in a valid Client ID and Client Secret from PingF. This
error is returned when an invalid authorization token is passed in. The JWT is
invalid if any of the following is true: expired, signature validation failure, ..."

#
40000:
  httpCode: 400
  errorType: MessageParseError
  message: "Request invalid due to parse error: %s"
  desc: "An invalid input string has been passed in"
```

3.4 General Idea of the Implementation

Once we have the new error response extension specification, we will be able to send the error code from any API request/response communication. Figure 1 below gives a general idea of what would a logical diagram for a possible implementation look like.

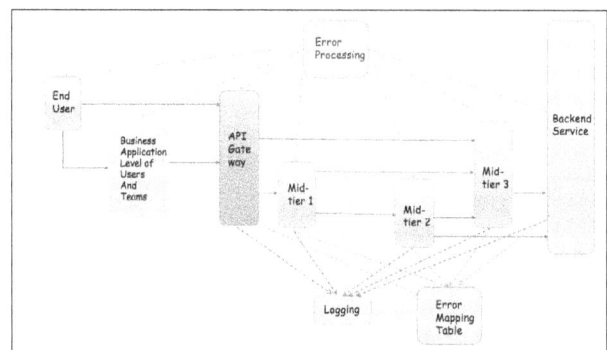

Figure 1. Structure with Multiple Layers of Middleware

In the Figure 1 HTTP requests from end-user flow either to the same-origin business application or be redirected to another business application with a different origin. The second flow is typical in popular industry standards and B2B integration, for instance OIDC (Open ID Connect). The API gateway layer shown is increasingly common and it is typically central focus of troubleshooting efforts when it comes to API integration and production problem investigation. The API gateway passes the API request to many layers of middleware behind the gateway. In some case the traffic flowing from one API to the next will also pass through some sort of API gateway or, more recently, in service mesh implementations using containers, so called side-car would play the role of the gateway. For the purposes of this examination we can think of it as a sort of distributed gateway.

The original request will eventually reach the backend application/service at which point the response traffic will traverse back the same way request came in. Notice that during this end-to-end request-response communication, there are several different paths each an API request could follow through the layers of middleware. We feed the central log aggregator from each layer. Logs from all components come all together into a single, highly available, distributed central logging service.

In one of our examples above, we used "out of memory" error to show what a response would look like. We already drew your attention to the fact that this error will need to appear differently, and it means different things to different user class. To a B2B app it may mean retry after some time, maybe the next request will hit different server and get through, to the support monitoring "bot" it may mean restart this instance, the end-user UI app may show, "we received your request, processing.." just to buy some time so that user doesn't think the front-end app is hanging. Here, we're drawing attention to what this error means to the development team. They will come after the fact and rely heavily on logs to further dig into the root cause and potentially find a fix other than "restart" or starting new container. Having a standard error payload, as proposed here, could jumpstart this process programmatically, even before the response reaches the end-user. An out-of-process error processor shown in Figure 1 could bit triggered to collect all relevant data and even start preprocessing. The logging service, in Figure 1, can consolidate all the logs according to the reference ID, and isolate only messages related to the flow that corresponds to a specific API request. This functionality exists already and is part of many frameworks. However, it's a patchwork of many components each promising quick-and-easy interoperability with anything one can imagine, but in real integration of any such system in many non and production environments in a large corporation will be costly, time and money consuming and far from easy. Our proposal for standard HTTP error response payload helps in this area as well. Having error payload standard schema, as proposed here, could offer a great help to both the logging service and error processing service. For instance, the domain element, in the error schema proposed, would uniquely identify the component where the specific log message, error in this case, came from. As a result, when an error occurs, logging and error services can locate the error catalogue easily and even enrich it by further checking the database or a look-up table for the error code specification. In this way, a properly implemented system could incorporate a human issue tracking system that's augmented by an AI feedback making it possible to build a self-healing API service mesh. Most importantly, at the very least, with the proposed error schema the logging and error services can map the domain and the error code in the proposed error schema to the detailed error root-cause and post-processing action information. This alone adds to the business value equation by increasing the return on investment of building such system.

Logging service built in this way can be highly valuable when used by the error processing service, which will serve all the classes of users and teams defined below. Enriched error processing service can present different amount of available error information depending on which level of access the user of error service has. For most of enterprises, there will be at least three dimensions corresponding to the class of users determining the level of access a user will be given when accessing the error processing system. Here, in Figure 2, we illustrated a general case for how to group the users of the error system.

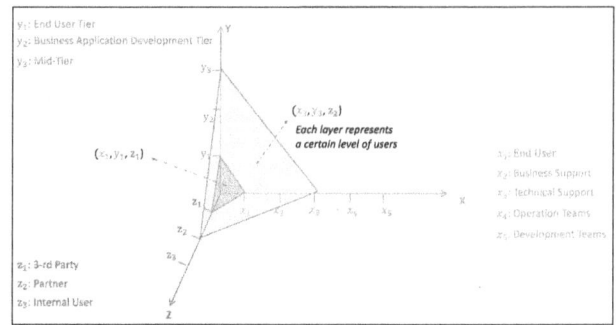

Figure 2. Three Dimension of the Levels of Users

In Figure 2, each of the three dimensions represents a different category which can be used to determine the level of user access, and then the final access level is determined as a position in the 3-D space. A set f_i with triple element (x_r, y_s, z_t) defines a level of access for users based on the position determined by x, y, z values, where

$$i = 1,2,3\dots,44,45;$$
$$r = 1,2,3,4,5;$$
$$s = 1,2,3;$$
$$t = 1,2,3;$$

Suppose two dimensions **X** and **Z** are fixed. We will examine a change in only one dimension **Y**, to explain how the proposed system will support different types of "Y" users. **Y** dimension would include front-end or UI development teams, and "real" end-users, the channel end-point application development teams, business-domain application development teams, the mid-tier teams, back-end or book-of-record developers, data modelling teams, and so on.

For end-users the error message will provide very little details. It will also provide different messages and details. On the one hand, the end-users do not need to troubleshoot the error if the error is not caused by their invalid input. On the other hand, the middle-tier APIs, the service receiving HTTP requests, have no absolute knowledge of the end-users and cannot fully trust them. In the other words, there is a potential for malicious users to take advantage of details exposed in the error response. Therefore, we do not want to expose too much in error messages, like information which contains structural details, to end-users.

In contrast to most end-users, business application users, next on the Y-axis, are usually development teams who are the consumer of backend B2B APIs. They use the error response from backend services as "input" in their own applications. As a result, when an error occurs, they need to handle the error programmatically, and also to troubleshoot the issue and thus need more functional details about the error. First, they will get the error message contained in the response body to program actions that their application will take when error happens. In some case they will also need to troubleshoot, investigate errors after the fact. Typically, the information provided in the response body at run-time will not be enough for troubleshooting. In that case, the business application team can send request to the error processing service to ask for more information about the error, after the fact, using a different API built for this purpose. The authentication and authorization mechanisms at this step would identify the error-service user and give it a **X, Y, Z** coordinates to determine the level of error details to share. The error processing service will provide more details about the error according to the authentication and authorization credentials user provided. What is more important is that, the error processing service is in fact a different channel from the API call channel. The process of consolidating the information using two independent channels makes the whole error processing process much more secured and flexible.

4. DRAWBACKS

With all of the advantages we mentioned above of our specification, we have to admit that there exist drawbacks. First thing is still about security. It should be carefully considered how detailed the error information should be, otherwise it might expose too much details in the error payload. On the other hand, the error response specification and its implementation are actually adding the total complexity of the whole architecture since it's one more layer of the current structure. Moreover, it involves each layer to add extra codes to generate and analyze the error payload. But for long-term consideration, we believe that our error response extension specification will benefit the whole API development and consumption.

5. FUTURE RESEARCH PLAN

We explained how we can improve error response using a standard schema carrying data which we use to find the reason for a failure when an error occurs. But sometimes, even with the detailed information, it's hard to identify the root cause. Even the error messages in the consolidated and aggregated logs are still not enough. In this case, we would like to introduce artificial intelligence to help us find the reason why error happened. Suppose we have sufficient number of "instances", where each instance consisted of a set of log messages representing errors, and this set of log entries leads to a specific cause of a failure. It would still be hard to find this specific cause of failure directly from this set of log messages. We could feed all these instances into a machine learning algorithm. We could further optimize the log entries using MapReduce techniques. The machine learning algorithm will learn by itself to generate a function $M(l_1, l_2, l_3, \dots) = r_i$, thus when we give the function M a set of simplified log entries $(l_1, l_2, l_3, \dots)$, it will output an error cause r_i. This is a general idea about how we plan to involve AI in the future implementation.

6. CONCLUSIONS

With increased usage of APIs over HTTP for both B2B communication and internal service reuse, and the increasing complexity of highly distributed systems, the sheer number of error response and processing problems is becoming a major impediment for further development and a major cost driver. Our error response extension specification is adding space complexity to reduce the time complexity. Within an enterprise application system with multiple layers of middleware, our new error response extension specification is obviously much better than relying on the standard HTTP response codes. Compared with the limited, non-standard, unstructured information that currently HTTP response with status code can provide, our error

response payload using standardized schema provides much more detailed information about the cause of the error, makes it much easier to locate the error, take actions to troubleshoot, and provide fine-grained access to different team on a need-to-know basis. This will save human involvement, cost and time. At the same time, the error response extension is flexible to provide either very detailed error information in the API response body or very limited amount, which lowers the risk of exposing structural details to malicious users. Moreover, our implementation plan provides a separate channel, "error processing service", which can retrieve the error logs, map the error code with the detailed information and provide different levels of error information depending on the level of the user access based on user types. This independent channel enhances the security of the error handling process. Future enhancement and implementation are under construction to involve AI into the error processing service to make the error response more useful and helpful for all users and teams that are involved in the API development and consumption.

7. REFERENCES

[1] R. Fielding, J. Reschke, Hypertext Transfer Protocol, HTTP/1.1: Semantics and Content, RFC 7231, IETF, 2017, rfc-editor.org

[2] T. Berners-Lee, R. Fielding and H. Frystyk, Hypertext Transfer Protocol, HTTP/1.0, RFC 1945, IETF, 1996, rfc-editor.org

[3] Y. Goland, E. Whitehead, A. Faizi, S. Carter and D. Jensen, HTTP Extensions for Distributed Authoring – WEBDAV, RFC 2518, IETF, 1999, rfc-editor.org

[4] R. Fielding, J. Gettys, J. Mogul, H. Frystyk, L. Masinter, P. Leach and T. Berners-Lee, Hypertext Transfer Protocol, HTTP/1.1, RFC 2616, IETF, 1999, rfc-editor.org

[5] J. Franks, P. Hallam-Baker, J. Hostetler, S. Lawrence, P. Leach, A. Luotonen and L. Stewart, HTTP Authentication: Basic and Digest Access Authentication, RFC 2617, 1999, rfc-editor.org

[6] M. Nottingham, E. Wilde, Problem Details for HTTP APIs, RFC 7807, 2016, rfc-editor.org

[7] IIS 7.0, IIS 7.5, and IIS 8.0, Internet Information Services, 2018, Microsoft

[8] D. Kruse, V. K. Chintalapati, S Watson, J. Paulus, D. Friesenhahn and A. Mohamed, Client extended error handling, Google Patent US8010850B2, 2005, Microsoft Technology Licensing LLC

[9] V.R. Chintalapati, D. Kruse, A. Mohamed, A. Watson, D. Fresenhahn, J. Paulus, S. Subbarayan, S. McAteer, Compounding of HTTP authoring protocol, Google Patent US7600030B2, August 2005, Microsoft Technology Licensing LLC

[10] B. Totty and D. Gourley, HTTP: The Definitive Guide, 2002, O'Reilly & Associates, Inc.

[11] E. Anuff APIs are Different than Integration, May 2014, Google, Apigee

[12] L. Calcote, The Enterprise Path to Service Mesh Architectures, August 08 2018, O'Reilly & Associates, Inc.

Reliability Modeling and Optimization of CMOS Standard Cells

Azam Beg
UAE University
Al-Ain, United Arab Emirates
abeg@uaeu.ac.ae

Rashad Ramzan
FAST National University
Islamabad, Pakistan
rashad.ramzan@nu.edu.pk

ABSTRACT

This paper presents a mathematical model-based method for calculating the reliability of nanometric CMOS standard logic cells. The models are useful in quickly identifying the supply voltages and MOS transistor sizes that would result in low unreliability while lowering the power and/or delay. By using the example of a medium-complexity cell, i.e., a full adder, we show how the reliability, power and delay can be considered simultaneously to achieve an optimal cell design. The presented method is scalable and is readily usable for other types of logic cells.

Keywords: CMOS standard cell, full adder, reliability, optimization, mathematical model, power, delay, performance.

1. INTRODUCTION

Many factors such as manufacturing processes, materials, and device structures, contribute to MOS transistor *unreliability* (Υ) [1]. The manufacturing-related causes of Υ include random dopant fluctuations, line-edge roughness, etc.

Redundancy is a well-known method for reducing Υ and enhancing fault tolerance. The common types of redundancy include *space, time*, or *information*. Logic circuits can utilize low or high-level redundancy, von Neumann multiplexing, or parallel restitution. Evidently, space redundancy incurs a heavy penalty in terms of power dissipation and area, especially as compared to the time and information-redundancy [2].

Standard logic cells range from simple gates (with a few transistors) to complex ones (with dozens of transistors), such as adders. The adders are essential cells used in a wide range of digital systems. An adder is required not only for addition but also for subtraction, division, multiplication, etc. Therefore, for years, the adders have been optimized for performance and power consumption [3–5].

Most of full adder designs of the past have been designed with area, power, delay, power-delay product as the targets. In the past few years, some attention has been to paid to designing reliable full adders, as in [6–9]. A few works focused on evaluating reliabilities of logic cells and circuits include [10–13]. Recently, some logic cells have been evaluated for reliability using mathematical models in [14]. However,

this paper is the first attempt to consider Υ in combination with power and delay for evaluating/optimizing the design of a CMOS full adder with the help of mathematical models and Spice simulations.

Section 2 provides some background information and Section 3 presents the proposed modeling method. Section 4 includes the details of experimental setup and simulations. Section 5 presents the results and discussion about the power, delay and Υ of a full adder. Section 6 contains the conclusions.

2. BACKGROUND INFORMATION

The primary factors that determine a MOS transistor's probabilistic behavior are: (a) the type (nMOS or pMOS), (b) the size (W and L), and (c) the input voltage [15]. The effect of randomness of doping levels on the transistor's *threshold voltage* (V_{th}) can be approximated by this equation [16]:

$$\sigma_{V_{th}} \approx 3.19 \times 10^{-8} \frac{t_{ox} \, N_{dep}^{0.4}}{\sqrt{L_{eff} \, W_{eff}}}, \qquad (1)$$

where L_{eff} and W_{eff} are the effective channel length and width, respectively. N_{dep} is the channel doping concentration at depletion edge for zero body bias.

In this paper, the Υ of a MOS transistor is represented by its *switching probability of failure*, and as is defined as a *probability density function* (PDF). The Υ/PDF is dependent upon $\mu_{V_{th}}$ and $\sigma_{V_{th}}$ as well as the gate voltage [17]:

$$\Upsilon = PDF(V_{GS}) = \frac{exp\left[-(V_{GS} - \mu_{V_{th}})^2 / 2\sigma_{V_{th}}^2\right]}{\sigma_{Vth}\sqrt{2\pi}} \tag{2}$$

3. MATHEMATICAL MODELS OF UNRELIABILITY

3.1 Basic Logic Cell Unreliability

If N transistors having $\Upsilon_{tr,i}$ are connected in *series*, the overall Υ would be [2]:

$$\Upsilon_{series} = 1 - \prod_{i=1}^{N}(1 - \Upsilon_{tr,i}), \tag{3}$$

and if the transistors are connected in *parallel*, their combined Υ would be [2]:

$$\Upsilon_{parallel} = \prod_{i=1}^{N} \Upsilon_{tr,i}. \qquad (4)$$

Now, we determine the Υ's of three common logic gates, namely, INV, NAND2 and NOR2 (Figure 1). As there are no parallel or series connections of transistors *per se*, the Υ of an INV is simply given by:

$$\Upsilon_{INV} = 1 - (1 - \Upsilon_{M0})(1 - \Upsilon_{M1}) \qquad (5)$$

For NAND2, the Υ for the P-stack (Υ_{sp}) is found by using Eq. 4 and the Υ for the N-stack (Υ_{sn}) by Eq. 3:

$$\Upsilon_{sp} = \Upsilon_{M0} \cdot \Upsilon_{M1} \qquad (6)$$
$$\Upsilon_{sn} = 1 - (1 - \Upsilon_{M2})(1 - \Upsilon_{M3}) \qquad (7)$$

and NAND2's overall Υ is calculated by:

$$\Upsilon_{NAND2} = 1 - (1 - \Upsilon_{sp})(1 - \Upsilon_{sn}) \qquad (8)$$

Similarly, for NOR2, the Υ_{sp} is found by using Eq. 3 and the Υ_{sn} by Eq. 4:

$$\Upsilon_{sp} = 1 - (1 - \Upsilon_{M0})(1 - \Upsilon_{M1}) \qquad (9)$$
$$\Upsilon_{sn} = \Upsilon_{M2} \cdot \Upsilon_{M3} \qquad (10)$$

and NOR2's overall Υ is determined by:

$$\Upsilon_{NOR2} = 1 - (1 - \Upsilon_{sp})(1 - \Upsilon_{sn}) \qquad (11)$$

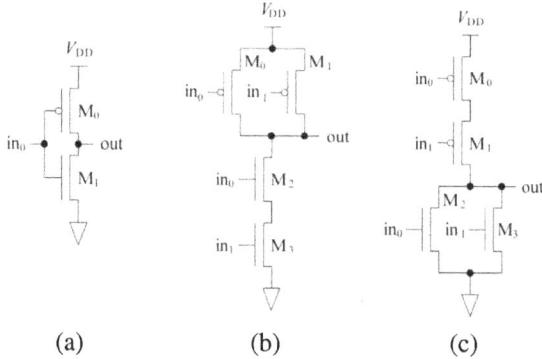

Figure 1: Gate schematics: (a) INV, (b) NAND2, (c) and NOR2.

3.2 A Full Adder's Unreliability

We have chosen a full adder as an example of a complex logic cell for Υ-modeling. To simplify the modeling process, we will find the equations for the full adder's P-stack and N-stack separately (using Eqs. 1–4), and then determine the full adder's (Figure 2) overall Υ; Υ_{pi} corresponds to the Υ of ith pMOS transistor p_i, and Υ_{nj} corresponds to the Υ of jth nMOS transistor n_j.

The Υ's for the *two* P-stacks, one for C_{out} and the other for *Sum*, are given by:

$$\Upsilon_{sp1} = 1 - \left[1 - \Upsilon_{p1} \Upsilon_{p2}\right] \times$$
$$\left[1 - (1 - (1 - \Upsilon_{p3})(1 - \Upsilon_{p4})) \Upsilon_{p5}\right] \qquad (12)$$
$$\Upsilon_{sp2} = 1 - \left[1 - \Upsilon_{p6} \Upsilon_{p7} \Upsilon_{p8}\right] \times$$
$$\left[1 - \Upsilon_{p9}\left(1 - (1 - \Upsilon_{p10}) \times \right.\right.$$
$$\left.\left. (1 - \Upsilon_{p11})(1 - \Upsilon_{p12})\right)\right] \qquad (13)$$

The Υ's for the *two* N-stacks, one for C_{out} and the other for *Sum*, are derived as follows:

$$\Upsilon_{sn1} = \left[1 - (1 - \Upsilon_{n1})(1 - \Upsilon_{n2}\Upsilon_{n3})\right] \times$$
$$\left[1 - (1 - \Upsilon_{n4})(1 - \Upsilon_{n5})\right] \qquad (14)$$
$$\Upsilon_{sn2} = \left[1 - (1 - \Upsilon_{n6})(1 - \Upsilon_{n7}\Upsilon_{n8}\Upsilon_{n9})\right] \times$$
$$\left[1 - (1 - \Upsilon_{n10})(1 - \Upsilon_{n11})(1 - \Upsilon_{n12})\right] \qquad (15)$$

The stack Υ's are combined in order to find the Υ of the carry-out (Υ_{cout}) and the sum (Υ_{sum}) outputs, which in turn give the full adder's Υ:

$$\Upsilon_{cout} = 1 - (1 - \Upsilon_{sp1})(1 - \Upsilon_{sn1}) \qquad (16)$$
$$\Upsilon_{sum_0} = 1 - (1 - \Upsilon_{sp2})(1 - \Upsilon_{sn2}) \qquad (17)$$
$$\Upsilon_{sum} = 1 - (1 - \Upsilon_{cout})(1 - \Upsilon_{sum_0}) \qquad (18)$$

4. EXPERIMENTAL SETUP AND SIMULATIONS

For the circuit simulations in this paper, we have used 22 nm PTM HP v2.1 (high-k/metal gate and stress effect) MOS transistor models [18] and BSIM4v4.7 level 54 model [19]. The V_{th}'s of the MOS transistors were determined using the equations given in the BSIM model. The nominal V_{th} for the nMOS transistors ($\mu_{V_{thn0}}$) is 0.503 V, and the nominal V_{th} for the pMOS transistors ($\mu_{V_{thp0}}$) is -0.461 V. The nominal V_{DD} is 0.8 V [18]. In our experiments, we fixed the transistor channel length as: $L = L_{min} = 22$ nm and nMOS widths $w_{ni} = 44$ nm. The pMOS widths w_{pi} ranged between 44 nm and 132 nm. The range of V_{DD} was from near-threshold value of 0.5 V to higher-than nominal value of 1.3 V. We arbitrarily chose the input-'noise margin' at 20% by setting the *low*-input $V_{in0} = 0.2 \times V_{DD} = 0.16$ V, and the *high*-input $V_{in1} = (1 - 0.2) \times V_{DD} = 0.64$ V. For all values of V_{DD}'s and W_p's, the Υ's for different input vectors (e.g., for the full adder: 000, 001, 010, ...) were calculated and then the *worst* Υ's were selected for reporting.

Eqs. 8 and 11 were used to determine the Υ's for NAND2 and NOR2, respectively. Eqs. 12–18 were used to calculate the Υ's for the full adder. As compared to the Monte Carlo simulations, the equation-based calculations of Υ's offered speedups of more

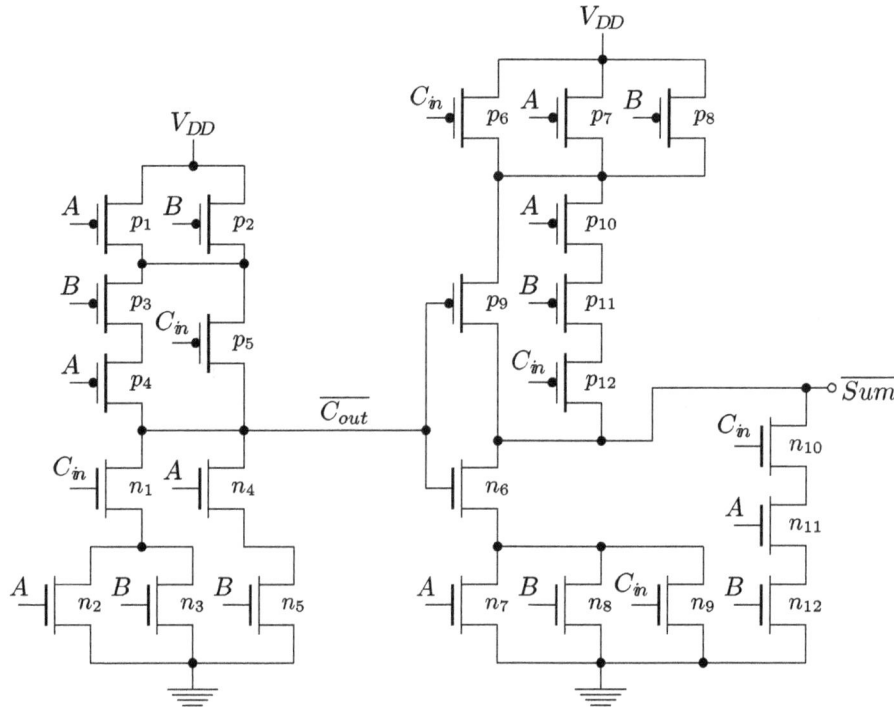

Figure 2: The schematic of a CMOS full-adder.

than 2000×, hence showing an advantages of the latter method.

5. OVERALL OPTIMIZATION A FULL ADDER

As alluded to earlier, the optimization of a logic cell entails reaching a trade-off among power, delay, area and (un)reliability. The simulation results (full adder's power and delay) from SPICE and the Υ's from the mathematical models are shown in different plots in Figure 3.

Figure 3(a) shows the results of a large number of simulations in order to measure the full adder's power. For the entire range of V_{DD} and W_p, we see the power consumption vary by an order of magnitude. The sensitivity of power to V_{DD} is not as prominent as to W_p. Overall, the minimum power is attained with near-threshold V_{DD} and with the lowest-sized pMOS transistors, i.e., $W_p = 44$ nm.

The plot in Figure 3(b) shows nearly 10% variation in delay as for the given ranges of V_{DD} and W_p. High performance can be achieved by operating near the nominal-V_{DD} and/or by lowering the W_p. Although not plotted here, the simulations show that the minimum energy (or power-delay-product) can be achieved with V_{DD}'s higher than the nominal operating voltage and with $W_p > 80$ nm.

Unlike the power and delay plots, the Υ plot in Figure 3(c) clearly shows a *valley* with the lowest values of Υ's, or the highest reliabilities. We observe that with $W_p \approx 3 \times L_{min} = 66$ nm, we are able to achieve the minimum Υ; somewhat uniform Υ's with the same W_p are available while V_{DD} stays above its nominal value of 0.8 V.

By having an overall look at all three plots, we can conclude that the full adder's reliability, power and performance are somewhat competing design targets. In other words, a W_p that gives the most *reliable* full adder may not be exhibit the lowest power dissipation or the lowest delay.

6. CONCLUSIONS

The proposed equation-based models can be used for sizing gate/cell-transistors for reliable operation.

V_{DD}'s from near-V_{th} to higher than the nominal voltage have been considered in the study. As an example, it has been shown that in order to limit the effect of V_{th} variations, the full adder has to be operated away from the lowest power consumption or the highest performance points.

In this work, we have incorporated manufacturing-related V_{th}-variations in the Υ calculations. The inclusion of other phenomenon, such as metal migration effects, temperature effects, etc. are under consideration.

7. ACKNOWLEDGMENT

This work is supported by the UAE University's UPAR 2016 Grant.

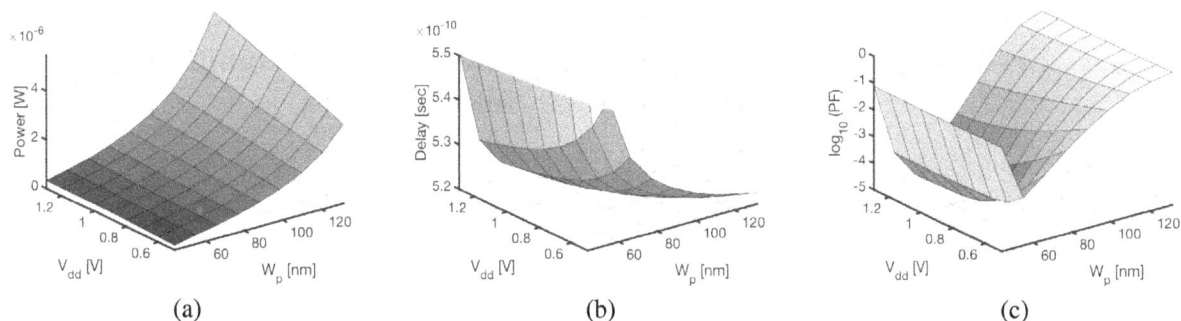

|(a)|(b)|(c)|

Figure 3: Full adder's characteristics as functions of V_{DD} and W_p: (a) power, (b) delay, and (c) Υ.

8. REFERENCES

[1] A. Beg and A. Elchouemi, "Enhancing static noise margin while reducing power consumption," in *2013 IEEE 56th Int. Midwest Symp. Circuits Syst.* Columbus, OH, USA: IEEE, aug 2013, pp. 348–351.

[2] E. Dubrova, *Fault-Tolerant Design.* New York, NY: Springer New York, 2013.

[3] B. Harish, K. Sivani, and M. S. S. Rukmini, "Performance comparison of various CMOS full adders," in *2017 Int. Conf. Energy, Commun. Data Anal. Soft Comput.*, Chennai, India, aug 2017, pp. 3789–3792.

[4] P. Agrawal, D. K. Raghuvanshi, and M. K. Gupta, "A low-power high-speed 16T 1-Bit hybrid full adder," in *2017 Int. Conf. Recent Innov. Signal Process. Embed. Syst.*, Bhopal, India, oct 2017, pp. 348–352.

[5] H. Naseri and S. Timarchi, "Low-Power and Fast Full Adder by Exploring New XOR and XNOR Gates," *IEEE Trans. Very Large Scale Integr. Syst.*, pp. 1–13, 2018.

[6] F. Kharbash and G. M. Chaudhry, "Reliable Binary Signed Digit Number Adder Design," in *IEEE Comput. Soc. Annu. Symp. VLSI (ISVLSI '07)*, Porto Alegre, Brazil, mar 2007, pp. 479–484.

[7] W. Ibrahim, A. Beg, and V. Beiu, "Highly reliable and low-power full adder cell," in *2011 11th IEEE Int. Conf. Nanotechnol.*, Portland, OR, USA, aug 2011, pp. 500–503.

[8] H. G. Mohammadi, P.-E. Gaillardon, J. Zhang, G. D. Micheli, E. Sanchez, and M. S. Reorda, "A Fault-Tolerant Ripple-Carry Adder with Controllable-Polarity Transistors," *J. Emerg. Technol. Comput. Syst.*, vol. 13, no. 2, pp. 16:1–16:13, dec 2016.

[9] S. Subramaniam, T. W. X. Wilson, A. K. Singh, and G. R. Murthy, "A proposed reliable and power efficient 14T full adder circuit design," in *TENCON 2017 - 2017 IEEE Reg. 10 Conf.*, Penang, Malaysia, nov 2017, pp. 45–48.

[10] A. Beg, "On pedagogy of nanometric circuit reliability," *J. Supercomput.*, vol. 59, no. 2, pp. 762–778, feb 2012.

[11] B. Srinivasu and K. Sridharan, "A Transistor-Level Probabilistic Approach for Reliability Analysis of Arithmetic Circuits With Applications to Emerging Technologies," *IEEE Trans. Reliab.*, vol. 66, no. 2, pp. 440–457, 2017.

[12] M. Kvassay, E. Zaitseva, V. Levashenko, and J. Kostolny, "Reliability analysis of multiple-outputs logic circuits based on structure function approach," *IEEE Trans. Comput. Des. Integr. Circuits Syst.*, vol. 36, no. 3, pp. 398–411, 2017.

[13] D. Celia, V. Vasudevan, and N. Chandrachoodan, "Optimizing power-accuracy trade-off in approximate adders," in *2018 Des. Autom. Test Eur. Conf. Exhib.*, Florence, Italy, mar 2018, pp. 1488–1491.

[14] A. Beg, "Modeling the Probabilities of Failures of 22 nm CMOS Logic Cells," in *2016 Third Int. Conf. Math. Comput. Sci. Ind.* Chania, Greece: IEEE, aug 2016, pp. 94–99.

[15] P. Gupta, A. B. Kahng, P. Sharma, and D. Sylvester, "Gate-length biasing for runtime-leakage control," *IEEE Trans. Comput. Des. Integr. Circuits Syst.*, vol. 25, no. 8, pp. 1475–1485, 2006.

[16] A. Asenov, A. R. Brown, J. H. Davies, S. Kaya, and G. Slavcheva, "Simulation of intrinsic parameter fluctuations in decananometer and nanometer-scale MOSFETs," *IEEE Trans. Electron Devices*, vol. 50, no. 9, pp. 1837–1852, 2003.

[17] V. Beiu, A. Beg, W. Ibrahim, F. Kharbash, and M. Alioto, "Enabling sizing for enhancing the static noise margins," in *Int. Symp. Qual. Electron. Des.*, Santa Clara, CA, USA, mar 2013, pp. 278–285.

[18] "Predictive Technology Model," 2016. [Online]. Available: http://ptm.asu.edu/.

[19] "Berkeley Short-channel IGFET Model," 2013. [Online]. Available: http://www-device.eecs.berkeley.edu/bsim/?page=BSIM4{_}LR

Erroneous Features in Freehand Sketching: Opportunities to Generate Visual Analogies

Eric LUCHIAN

Department of Visual and Performing Arts, Elizabeth City State University
Elizabeth City, NC 27909, USA

Corina SAS

School of Computing & Communications, Lancaster University
Lancaster, LA1 4WA, United Kingdom

ABSTRACT

The value of visual analogies in problem solving has been extensively researched, with most of the work focusing on their benefits [1, 2, 3]. This study explores the much less investigated research question of how visual analogies as cues for insight problem-solving are generated using freehand sketching. More specifically, we focused on the creative process of the first author who is a professional artist, to generate two sets of visual analogies to support solving the classic *8-coin* insight problem. First, a set of sketches was generated for analogies capturing the problem insights through static images, while the second set captured the problem insights through a dynamic, time-based media format. We employed an experiential research method consisting of the artist's reflections on his freehand sketching practice in his creative process. Inaccuracy of freehand sketches presents opportunities to generate new concepts for analogy. This study contributes to a deeper understanding of how visual cues can be generated, and what principles and tools, in particular freehand sketching, and what methods of practice can be used in research.

Keywords: Sketching, Creative Process, Generating Ideas, Visual Analogy, Reflection-On-Action Research.

1 INTRODUCTION

Sketching techniques facilitate reflection and provide a rich medium for discovery and communication of design ideas [4], in particular, in the early ideation and exploration stages [5]. These techniques are rich and diverse being used more as tools for exploring, thinking and discovery [6, 7] rather than for their aesthetic qualities. Leonardo da Vinci and the modern painter Carlo Carra used lines, shadows, arrows, dots, maps, and handwriting, all crowded on the same page in their sketchbooks [8]. Ideational sketching, both as process and artefact, offers a fluid space where thinking is presented in the immediacy of the thinking-act [9, 10]. Sketching content varies from simple to more elaborate drawings and develops over time as the project unfolds [8]. Sketching in both arts and design can be framed as a way of externalising thinking [11] through media (dry and wet), materials (pen/ink, charcoal, graphite pencil, pastel, chalk, marker) and techniques (scribbling, hatching, stippling). This paper focuses on sketching and its role in the creative process of ideation and the generation stages for visual analogies to support insight problem-solving.

2 GENERATING VISUAL ANALOGIES

Much previous work has shown that analogies are often employed by artists, architects and designers, particularly in the initial stages of planning, generating and visualising ideas [10, 12, 8, 11] for a concept.
Garner [13] suggested that freehand sketching in the design process may be a powerful catalyst in the generation process as the "inherent-imperfect" lines and shapes of sketches create *ambiguity* in visual representations, thus continuously stimulating reinterpretation. Suwa and Tversky [14] pointed out the value of developing computer-based design tools involving sketching capability to "enrich designers' perception", while

Purcell and Gero [15] considered sketching an "essential part of the process of thinking about a design problem and developing a design solution".
Clement [16] identified three methods of generating analogies: via a principle (abstract – often mathematical or verbal), via a transformation (changes) and via an association (a familiar situation to the unresolved problem). The first and the least used was the generation of analogy via a principle. Representations or relations based on a principle might sound like an analogy: "the cat's tail is like the steering wheel for the car" – suggesting the principle of navigation control. This method can be applied to generate analogies both within and across domains, i.e, near and far analogy. The second method of generating analogies is via transformation, when objects, situations or contexts are modified to obtain new objects, situations or contexts that still resemble the old ones while supporting new interpretations. Analogies generated via this method are often used within a field or domain. According to psychologists' views on the developmental curve [17], reasoning based on similarity in early childhood follows rule-based reasoning in adulthood; therefore, similarity relates to the figurative quality and is largely visual [18].
Although research in constructing visual analogy is limited, some studies suggest that contextual cueing [19] plays an important role in visual tasks and "is driven by incidentally learned associations between spatial configurations and target locations".

3 THE *8-COIN PROBLEM*

We generated the two sets of visual analogy (VA) concepts with the aim of developing and using visual analogies as an aide in the *8-coin* problem-solving process; the *8-coin problem* is notoriously difficult to solve. The success rate in solving the *8-coin problem* without external cues is between 4% and 8%, while providing participants with visual cues during the problem-solving (PS) process increases this rate to 42% [20, 19].
The *8-coin problem* requires the arrangement of an array of eight coins by moving only two of them to create a final array in which each coin touches exactly three others [20]. Like other similar visual insight problems [21, 22], its primary insights require a perceptual shift in terms of moving the elements of the problem in three rather than two dimensions [20].

Figure 1   Initial configuration for the 8-coin problem

The generation of the two sets of VAs was a lengthy process, involving several sketches of cues concepts and compositions that we thought would resemble the source (problem) and the target (solution).

The first set of generated concepts was intended for use in an experiment to test the effects of VAs capturing the problem insights in a static format (e.g., diagram, image) on participants in the PS process for the *8-coin problem*, and the second set of concepts for an experiment that was intended to test the effects of VAs when capturing the problem insights through a multimedia format (e.g., animation, video).

Figure 2 The configuration for the 8-coin problem solution

Both VA sets were intended to capture the problem's visual insights in appropriate formats to facilitate the incubation effect in the solving process of the *8-coin problem* leading to its correct solution (see Figure 2).

4 REFLECTION-ON-ACTION RESEARCH

Donald Schön's [23] influential work has inspired new approaches for exploring creative thinking and creative outcomes. The idea that a visual product gains richer meaning once is reflected upon is central to Schön's reflection-on-action approach. This suggests considering not only the outcome, but also the experience of the creator in the design process. The unexpected events during a creative process initiate two kinds of reflective practices: one that occurs immediately and one that occurs later. Reflection-in-action is the ability to develop artefacts or artistic events by applying professional competencies and reasoning to unfamiliar surprises at the same time, when they occur. In contrast, reflection-on-action is the process of thinking back to what happened during the creative act [24, 25]. The context of an occurred action and its relationship to the created artefact is equally important for a deeper understanding of the creative process and the tools used in such an act. The reflection-on-action method adds up to the research not only reflecting of the finished product but also the process that leads to its result.

5 METHOD

In this study, we employed a reflection-on-action method with the aim of observing sketching practices in the creative process of generating visual analogies to support insight problem-solving.

In order to capture this process, we employed a structured approach based on a self-observation template shown in Table 1. This template is based on Wallas' [26] model of the creative process and Schön's [23] guidance to a situation to reflect upon to capture the stages involved in the generation of each concept and its sketch. Schön defines reflection-on-action as reflecting on how practice can be developed, changed or improved after the event has occurred. The reason for employing the reflection-on-action approach rather than reflection-in-action [23] was to avoid the observed memory bias, and overshadowing effect [27] stating that when talking aloud, the perceptual information can interfere with the retrieval of that information from memory [28].

Traditional video recording footage used in studying the creative process has its benefits in exploring human behaviour; however, it is limited to only what is observable. The unspoken feelings and thoughts of a subject can only be guessed at or inferred [29], hence the need to employ a more introspective method. Some limitations of the chosen reflection-on-action approach include forgetting some thoughts and details about performed actions, or sources for analogy generation. In order to mitigate this, notes were taken right after each sketch was produced.

Understanding the challenge	1.	Understanding the task
	2.	Brief description of the goals
	3.	Promising opportunities to pursue
	4.	How am I going to do it?
Generating ideas	5.	How can the problem be stated differently?
	6.	What can be changed to achieve the set goals?
	7.	Explore the alternative possible solutions
	8.	Consider the possible solutions in a different context
Analyse, evaluate and refine promising solution	9.	Examine the most promising ideas
	10.	Analyse the possible best solutions for the task
	11.	Choose the best solution from the explored and state why it was chosen
	12.	Is there something to change in the chosen version?
Plan for support; appraising the task	13.	Analyse and examine the possible outcome of the created product
	14.	How can the chosen idea be strengthened?
	15.	Examine the actions and forms of implementing the idea
	16	Are you satisfied with the sketched idea?

Table 1 Reflection-on-action questionnaire

The strengths of such an experiential method of inquiry are in the data obtained from first-hand experience.

For data analysis, we used Hyper RESEARCH [30] software for coding and qualitative analysis.

Theoretical sampling was used to categorise the artist's reflective notes. Theoretical sampling is a technique that suits the need to obtain data to help the research in explaining its categories [31]. It enables the researcher to narrow down the emerging categories from the gathered data sets, and in particular, in analysing these two main sets of generated sketches for two experiments using static and dynamic analogies. By filling out the properties of a category, the researcher can create analytic definitions and rules for that category, describe and explain it, and specify the links and relationships between other categories and subcategories.

Several psychological [32, 33, 34], neurophysiological [35] and developmental [36] data on analogy-making [37] through a practice-based approach and reflection on practitioners' actions [23] support this research method.

5.1 Procedure

Twenty-two reflective notes were taken by the researcher during the developmental phase for analogies that were designed as cues for two experiments for a larger project to investigate the support of insight into the *8-coin problem*. The researcher used the reflection questionnaire (Table 1) to answer each question, for each sketched concept right after it was generated. The notes were gathered during the generation period for visual analogy development for the two experiments: the first using static and the second using dynamic analogies as aides in the solving process for the insight *8-coin problem*. In this article, we will refer to the generated set of VAs for Experiment 1 as the static set and for Experiment 2 as the dynamic set.

The gathered qualitative data from the notes was codified, categorised, and subcategorised for further qualitative analysis.

5.2 Coding Scheme

The primary data consisted of 22 reflection notes (10 for static and 12 for the dynamic set) and were completed with an overall number of 16 quotes (answers to each question from the template - Table 1) related to cues. During the coding process, we identified 34 emerging concepts (see Figure 3) that led to the development of categories grounded in the text and based on grounded theory approaches [38]. We employed the Glaser & Strauss approach, whereby the researcher does not have to force preconceived categories on the data, but allows the categories to emerge from the data [39] through a constant comparison of codes, subcategories, categories, and their properties. The following sentence is an example (an answer to question 15 from Table 1 on sketches - Appendix 1):

> "So, let me have a go: in the first frame will be shown (or not shown) a person with several buckets (probably 8 in total), aligned in 3 rows and seen from a frontal view; then the individual enters the scene and picks up a bucket from the centre and stacks it on the other 3 ones on the side".

This sentence was encoded into four codes. The first part of the sentence "So, let me have a go: in the first frame will be shown (or not shown) a person with several buckets" was encoded "Media" as the subject is pointing out the entrance frame for the animated cue. The second code was assigned to the part of the sentence where the artist mentioned the quantity of objects or order – "(probably 8 in total)" and "in 3 rows" and this was encoded "Number". The following segment: "aligned and seen from a frontal view" was coded as "Perspective", and the rest of the sentence "then the individual enters the scene and picks up a bucket from the centre and stacks it on other three ones on the side" was described as a "Transformational" indicator.

Codes including "Adding new things", "Break in", "Discarding things" and "Transform" trigger changes or transformations to be made in the sketch. "Character", "Composition", " Emphasis and focus" codes are describing aesthetic design principles, " Form", "Shape", "Line", "Perspective", "Media", "Number" and "Other sources" are related to the design elements and design tool groups. The ideation category included segments of the text describing thoughts, feelings and sources of inspiration in the generative process of VA and was coded as "Imagination", "Impression giving", "Thinking and inspiration", "Logic" and "Inspiration from real life". The last set of codes is composed of instances of evaluating and supporting cue development: "Promising ideas", "Satisfied", "Usable", "No good idea", "Too much" and "Unexpectedness" segments.

5.3 Categorisation

Categories and subcategories emerged from a constant comparison of data and codes.

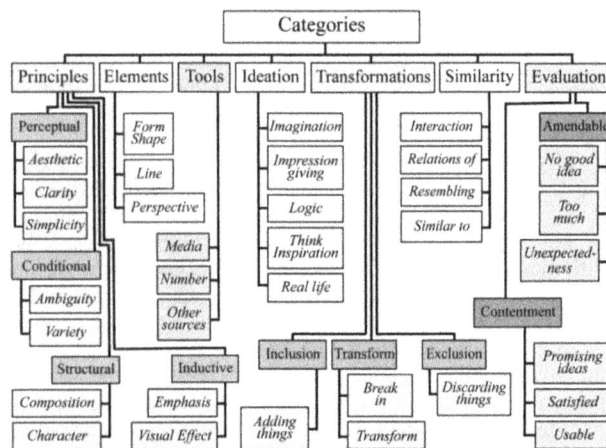

Figure 3 Emerging categories, subcategories, and codes

To gain a better understanding of how categories (1st level) and subcategories (2nd level) emerged, we assigned each code (3rd level) to a central category taking into account the structural aspect of objects and their properties mentioned by the artist, the relationship between them, instances, tools, inspiration sources and the evaluation of the sketch (see Figure 3).

The category "Principles" of the design was divided into the following subcategories:

1. "Perceptual" – including "Aesthetic" quality, "Clarity" and "Simplicity" codes describing the qualitative properties of perceived objects;
2. "Conditional" – such as "Ambiguity" (misleading insights in the sketch) and "Variety" (diversity of ideas in the concept) codes;
3. "Structural" – including "Composition" (harmony), and "Character" (object's quality) codes;
4. "Inductive" purpose – containing the "Emphasis" and "Visual Effect" codes.

The category of "Elements" of visual design included subcategories:

1. "Form and Shape" emerging from descriptions of surface(s) properties;
2. "Line" emerging from descriptions of lines characteristics (straight, curved, implying direction, etc.);
3. "Perspective" describing spatial structures of objects and their relationships.

The category of "Tools" consists of the instruments and mechanisms of communication to carry the *8-coin problem* insights and was divided into the following subcategories:

1. "Media" – codifying the text that describe discrete or continuous format of the future visual analogy in the sketch;
2. "Number" – describing the number of objects to be presented in the sketch; and
3. "Other sources" – describing other tools used in generating visual analogy (see example of a sketch for experiment using dynamic VAs - Appendix 3).

The category of "Ideation" includes a set of codes that divided it into subcategories:

1. "Imagination" – describing mental images, imagined things or situations;
2. "Impression giving" – describing the perceptual qualities of structures in the sketched concept;
3. "Logic" – containing text of analyses of objects and relations between them;
4. "Think and inspiration" – brainstorming for new analogy concepts;
5. "Real life" – descriptions of sources of inspiration (real life situations, art, etc.).

For example, the researcher writes in one of his notes: "Just sharpened my pencil to get ready, and there is a loaf of bread that's left from my breakfast", which points to the source of inspiration, and in this case, the segment was assigned to the inspiration from "Real life" subcategory and placed in the "Ideation" category. In the sentence, "The bread could be of a perfect cylindrical form and sliced into eight equal parts to match exactly the number and the forms of the units in the problem", the researcher uses his imagination and thoughts on how to connect that real-life situation (as inspiration) to come up with an analogy for a new cue (see Appendix 3) for the *8-coin problem*. In this note, he talks about forms, associations, number of units and structural components in common with the target problem, and fractured data were assigned to appropriate codes, subcategories, and categorised, respectively.

The category of "Transformations" emerged from the segments of text that describe changes to be made in sketches and was divided into three subcategories of instances:

1. "Inclusion" – describing adding things to the sketch ("Adding things" code);

2. "Transform" – describing changes such as break in or divide ("Break in" code) and transforming the imaginary object or visual sketch ("Transform" code);
3. "Exclusion" – discarding or abandoning things ("Discarding things" code).

The category "Similarity" is composed of four subcategories codified as:

1. "Interaction" – describing the interactivity of objects and their relationships;
2. "Relations of" – describing the connectivity of objects and relationships between objects;
3. "Resembling" – describing associations with other objects; and
4. "Similar to" – describing correspondences between objects, attributes, and their properties.

The last category, product "Evaluation", is divided into two subcategories:

1. "Contentment", which combines codes such as "Promising ideas", "Satisfied", and "Usable" as positive values; and
2. "Amendable", which includes "No good idea", "Too much" and "Unexpectedness" codes as a negative appraisal of the sketched analogy.

6 FINDINGS

Emerging categories are based on image making and theoretical frameworks for visual analogy. The four subcategories indicating the use of principles of design [40] in the analogy-making process [16] describe the perceptual, conditional, structural and inductive spatial arrangement aspect of objects in a scene [10]. Analysing the frequencies of the artist's statements between categories for the two sets of analogies, we noticed a significant increase in the dynamic set of the principles of design category (Figure 4). "Conditional" and "Inductive" subcategories (Figure 5) for this category show significant differences between static and dynamic sets. The "Conditional" subcategory consists of two codes: "Ambiguity" and "Variety" (Figure 6), which will be discussed later in more detail. Another two codes: "Emphasis" and "Visual Effect" from the "Inductive" subcategory of the "Principles" category will be detailed here, as well.

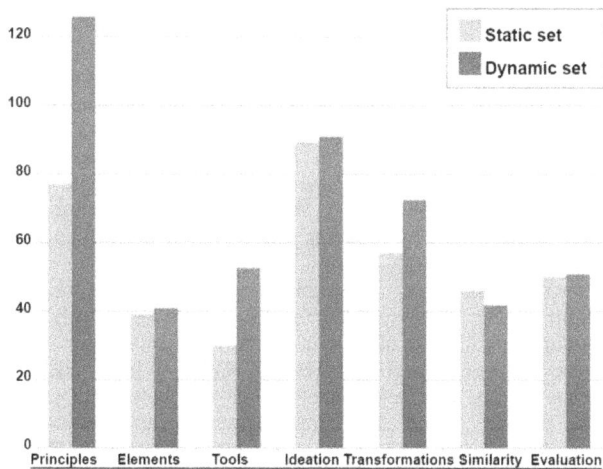

Figure 4…Between overall categories: static and dynamic

The statements about "Elements" of design in the researcher's reflective notes are aligned with the theoretical framework of elements identity [9] to represent forms and space [41]. In this category, no differences were observed between the static and dynamic sets of VA.

The "Tools" category also involves the intended media (static or dynamic) to fit the requirements [42] for the type of analogy and how the insight will be presented in the image [7]. Slight differences in statements between the two sets from this category were observed. The differences appear to be as a result of adding

the dynamic feature to the visual analogy intended to be used in the experiment with the dynamic analogy.

The "Similarity" category included segments of statements related to similarities, resemblances, relationships [43] and interaction between objects in context [19] and was based on Gentner's [44] structure mapping theory. There are no differences in this category between the statements of static and dynamic sets. The "Ideation" category includes segments of statements about mental images, inspiration, impressions, and logic that help the artist to come up with the concepts for analogy and are based on Clement's [16] methods to generate analogy and sources of inspiration for analogy [45, 46, 47]. The statements from this category were balanced in both sets of analogy.

The "Evaluation" category consists of two subcategories: "Amendable", where statements are negative, and "Contentment", where the artist is satisfied with the outcome of the sketched analogy. Overall, there are no differences between the two sets in this category. However, we noticed an opposite effect when comparing their subcategories: the "Amendable" and "Contentment" subcategories counteract each other. The more amendable the statements that are addressed during the process of development for an analogy concept, the less contentment is expressed and vice versa.

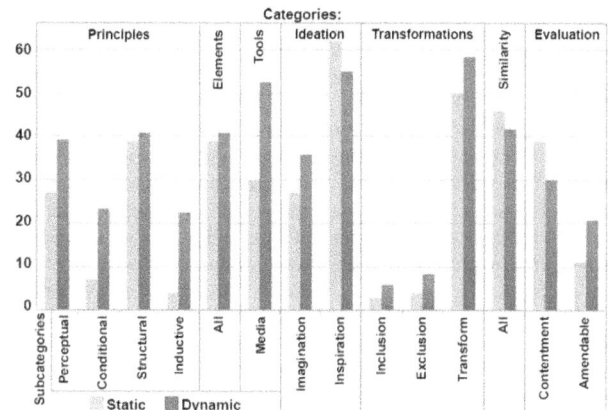

Figure 5   Between subcategories of static and dynamic sets

A careful examination and comparison between each code statement in both categorical and in-between sets of analogies revealed that the increase in the use of these means in the artist's reflective notes is due to the specific goals and tasks that each set of analogies required. In the first set, the term "Media" was used to clarify, appraise or evaluate a sketch (e.g., "…it will look good in 2D format"), while in the dynamic set of analogies, the term "Media" becomes dominant as the researcher takes into account the inclusion of time-based media and image schemata constraints needed for the dynamic capture of problem insights. The code "Number" from this category is equally used in both sets of sketches (e.g., "the second drawing to show them into two groups"), and the "Other sources" codes show the same ratio, as well. In the "Transformations" category, the increased need to use the terms for incorporated codes is due to the additional tasks requiring capture of the insights "in time" and using "gesture schema" required by dynamic analogy. Statements on "Adding things" and "Discarding things" in sketches that were coded and integrated into the same category are used significantly more in discussion for the same reason – for adapting a generated idea to the specifics of the experimental conditions of dynamic analogy. The second, a salient state with an inductive purpose subcategory of design principles, consists of two codes: "Visual Effect" and "Emphasis". It is worth investigating the combinatorial aspects of the relationships between these two codes in more detail. Here, during the analogy construction for the static set, both are mentioned twice, "Emphasis", in understanding the challenge and in the idea generation stages, and "Visual Effect", only in the evaluation stage. The notes on sketches for the dynamic set almost hold a perfect balance between the two state instances. During the process, the "Visual Effect" statements decrease at a constant rate, while the "Emphasis" statements increase at the same rate from understanding the challenge to idea generation to evaluation and the support stages (Figure 7).

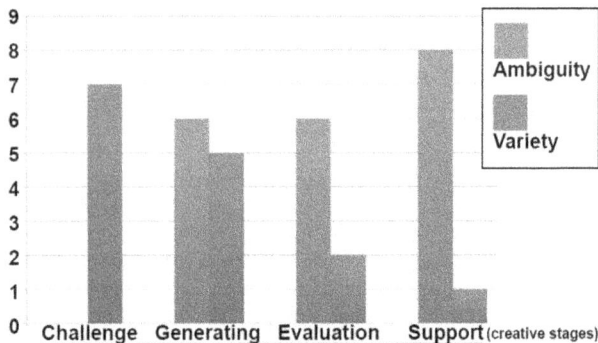

Figure 6…Overall Ambiguity/Variety statements

It is also worth further investigating the statements made for two subcategories of the "Evaluation" category in the generated analogy. The "Contentment" subcategory and "Amendable" subcategory rate is reversed in each set of analogies. The reflective notes for both sets were observed by the stages for their creative processes. Understanding the challenge stage is when the artist describes the goals, imagines potential scenes and looks for opportunities to scribble new ideas on paper. At this stage, the artist is more concerned with imagining and thinking about new ideas or situations along the principles of design and possible transformations to the mental image. As ideas are sought for implementation, a circular generating sketching stage begins and statements on principles of design and design transformations are more frequently mentioned. These increase at the same rate in both sets to their highest level in the evaluation stage and fall to their lowest rate in the plan for support, and the stage for appraising the tasks. It appears that statements on design tools and design element categories are constantly at the same rate, with a non-significant variation mentioned in the artist's notes during the entire creative cycle. The Similarity category, which includes "Interactions", "Relations of", "Resembling" and "Similar to" subcategory codes, is referenced at an increased ratio from the initial to the last stage of the sketching process.

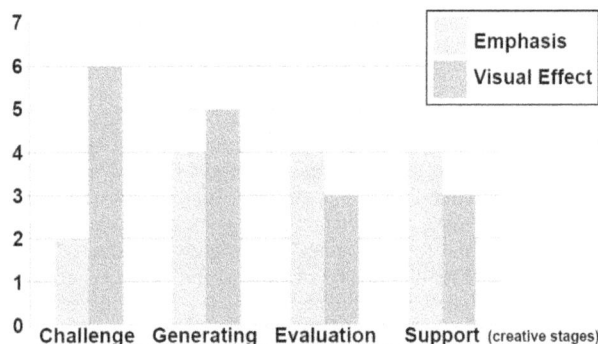

Figure 7   Overall Emphasis/Visual Effect statements

The notions of "Compositionality" and "Composition" appear in many reflective notes in the brief descriptions of the goals. "Simplicity", "Emphasis", "Focus of Attention", "Spatial Organisation", "Content", "Visual Effect" and "Meaning" are mentioned consistently in the artist's notes for all sketches. For example, in the "billiards game" note, the artist writes:

> "Primitive forms like spheres, which can be mobile and appear in focus would be an idea for now. A kind of game like ping-pong, or billiards? Yes, definitely, a billiards game could work if given a meaning to

it…there are enough balls and space on that table to think of a scenario."

The artist seeks inspiration for his sketches from different sources such as books, previous personal work, the work of other artists, and frequently, from nature. Doodling or sketching by playing with lines and shapes of objects, combining and transforming them helps him generate new ideas and, through modifications, create other new ones. Taking breaks and going out to watch movies refreshes his thoughts and "eliminates the details and sorts out the order of complex things in his head".

Thinking of scenes from real-life situations or structures, mediating and restating ideas, or the accidental discovery of scenes that are reminiscent of the problem at hand help him to adapt a concept to his tasks, and very often lead to him "working even backwards" (as the artist says in one of his notes). This is because a strategic plan is essential when thinking about many things and answering all kinds of questions related to a problem such as considering it from a different point of view and reassessing its meaning, breaking the whole into parts and bringing it back as a whole in a new configuration.

7 DISCUSSION

The artist's objectives for each concept varies depending on the type of analogy generated. He states that the information about the problem involves patterns, lines, shapes, forms, mental manipulations and transformations of imagined objects that can be selected, combined and refined in a continually dynamic way. As an analogy maker, he points out differences between the information he is attempting to convey while making analogies for the *8-coin problem* in a physical space by using physical objects and information about the created artefacts, which will be presented, on a fixed two-dimensional surface, either on a computer screen or a sheet of paper.

One of the major concerns in the challenges is the additional requirement for constructing an analogy specifically for each intended feature experiment, such as adding sequential and simultaneous delivery of insights, form and order of presentation and kinds of relations between problem insights.

So, the generation of cues is a constrained process of creativity. Once a mental image has been formed and the first line has been drawn on paper, sketching becomes structured thinking; this links back to sketching as a form of organising thinking [9, 11]. Transformations to the content are applied continuously and one idea leads to a different one [8]. These usually take place while thinking about the set problem and reaching its goals [48, 2].

Ambiguity in the freehand sketched concept is very important as it is not mentioned in analogy theory, and this is specific to cues. WordTree Design-by-Analogy Method [49] suggests using rich sources of adaptive mechanisms such as life form collections to overcome the fixation.

We speculate that designers are sensitive to visual inconsistencies; they create *ambiguities*, and these can conceive new opportunities for more ideas in the generative stage of the creative process. The role of freehand sketching in the creative process proved to be beneficial not only in collaborative practices [50], but also in individual practices serving as a method of "looking beyond" and reflecting on the visual qualities [23] of the artefact. In the *design principles* category, from the graph (Figure 5), we observed some differences between the statements of two sets in two subcategories: *conditional* and *inductive*. The *conditional* group combines two codes: "Ambiguity" – a condition of misleading, and "Variety" – a condition of unified diversity used in works of art. "Variety" is discussed more often in the dynamic set, but the frequency decreases towards the evaluation stage as opposed to "Ambiguity", which sees an increase in the supporting stage (Figure 6).

To generate new ideas, one needs ambiguity in sketches, as this ensures that sources of design symbols are unlimited. During visual analogy development processes, the artist had to take into consideration the similarities and differences of the goals between these analogy sets in order to fulfil the specifics for each experiment. Four main categories: "Elements", "Similarity", "Ideation" and "Evaluation" are discussed in reflective notes at the same rate in both studies. A slight increase in using such terms as media is observed in the "Tools" category in the artist's notes for a dynamic set of sketches.

8 CONCLUSIONS

Design theorists and practitioners have similar methods of analysis such as recording videos, documenting memos, using think-aloud strategies for protocols that provide access to a secret world of non-formal explanation of images as perceptions and actions, in opposition to scientists who use only the formal logic of mathematics. Reflecting on practices for generating ideas from the notes highlights the differences between a creative philosophy and traditional cognitive processes. An important aspect of sketching is that while trying to depict a mental image on a piece of paper, the inaccuracy of transfer or "ambiguity" in the created artefact generates new ideas and thoughts, inviting the practitioner to engage in the integration of cognitive and practical operations. Cheng & Lane-Cumming [51] investigated the drawing process using a digital pen that records graphic marks stroke-by-stroke. They focused more on the use of technology in service to design education and the gap between traditional and digital art issues, rather than on a deeper analytical examination of the cognitive processes associated with inaccuracies when dealing with such graphic marks.

Although the sketches that were reviewed for both experimental studies suggest that most of the analogies were generated by associations or similarities via structures, principles, actions or relationships between objects and inspired from real life situations, inaccuracy of sketches did play a role in the idea generation process for new analogies.

Discovery of an "inaccurate" line in a sketch leads the creator to make associations with other objects and create a new version of a visual analogy. Based on the results of a single study, and the recognition that the hypothesis records a preliminary solution, we propose to add an "ambiguity" mechanism to the existing models for the idea generation process, as it would enhance the quality and usability of analogies for problem solutions. Dealing with ambiguity, a subjective set of measures, leads to different behaviour while still sharing the main features, and this might give people a better understanding of the problem they face and help to generate new ideas to find solutions to the problem. It would also be worthwhile to investigate the effect of self-satisfaction and contentment/amendable procedures during a creative process on the quality and usability of the produced artefact as observations in this study suggest that the more balanced the contentment and amendable concerns are in a creative act, the more likely it is that the product will be of better quality and usability. It may be appealing to further investigate these observations, and particularly, the types of concerns related to the concept and such an investigation may offer surprising results.

9 REFERENCES

[1] G. Goldschmidt and M. Smolkov, "Variances in the impact of visual stimuli on design problem solving performance," *Design Studies,* vol. 27, no. 5, pp. 549-569, 2006.

[2] S. M. Smith and S. E. Blankenship, "Incubation and the persistence of fixation in problem solving," *The American Journal of Psychology,* vol. 104, no. 1, pp. 61-87, Spring 1991.

[3] K. N. Dundar, "How scientists really reason: Scientific reasoning in real-world laboratories," in *Mechanisms of insight*, R. J. Sternberg and J. Davidson, Eds., Cambridge, MA: MIT Press, 1995, pp. 365-395.

[4] M. Tohidi, W. Buxton, R. Baecker and A. Sellen, "User sketches: a quick, inexpensive, and effective way to elicit more reflective user feedback," in *Proceedings of the 4th Nordic conference on Human-computer interaction: changing roles*, New York, USA, 2006.

[5] P. A. Rogers, G. Green and A. McGown, "Using concepts sketches to track design progress," *Design Studies,* vol. 21, no. 5, pp. 451-464, 2000.

[6] M. Suwa and B. Tversky, "What architects see in their sketches: Implications for design tools," in *Conference companion on Human factors in computing systems: common ground*, Vancouver, 1996.

[7] G. Goldschmidt, "The dialectics of sketching," *Creativity Research Journal,* vol. 4, no. 2, pp. 123-143, 1991.

[8] D. Patherbridge, The primacy of drawing: histories and theories of practice, New Haven, CT: Yale University Press, 2010, p. 521.

[9] T. Rosenberg, "New Beginnings and Monstrous Births: Notes Towards an Appreciation of Ideational Drawing," in *Writing on Drawing: Essays on Drawing Practice and Research*, S. Garner, Ed., Bristol, Intellect Books, 2008, pp. 109-124.

[10] E. Y.-L. Do and M. D. Gross, "Drawing as a means to design reasoning," *AI and Design,* 1996.

[11] B. Tversky, "What Does Drawing Reveal about Thinking?," in *Visual and Spatial Reasoning in Design*, J. S. Gero and B. Tversky, Eds., Sydney, Key Centre of Design Computing and Cognition, 1999, pp. 93-101.

[12] W. Kandinsky, Point and line to plane, Mineola, NY: Dover Publications, 1979.

[13] S. Garner, "Comparing graphic actions between remote and proximal design teams," *Design Studies,* vol. 22, no. 4, pp. 365-376, 2001.

[14] M. Suwa and B. Tversky, "What do architects and students perceive in their design sketches? A protocol analysis," *Design Studies,* vol. 18, no. 4, pp. 385-403, 1997.

[15] A. T. Purcell and J. S. Gero, "Drawings and the design process: A review of protocol studies in design and other disciplines and related research in cognitive psychology," *Design Studies,* vol. 19, no. 4, pp. 389-430, Oct 1998.

[16] J. J. Clement, Creative Model Construction in Scientists and Students: The Role of Imagery, Analogy, and Mental Simulation, Amherst, MA: Springer, 2008, pp. 33-34.

[17] W. C. Crain, Theories of Development: Concepts and Applications, 6 ed., New York, NY: Prentice Hall, 2010, p. 432.

[18] D. Gentner and M. J. Rattermann, "Language and the career of similarity," in *Perspectives on language and thought: Interrelations in development*, S. A. Gelman and J. P. Byrnes, Eds., London, Cambridge University Press, 1991, pp. 225-277.

[19] M. M. Chun and Y. Jiang, "Contextual Cueing: Implicit Learning and Memory of Visual Context Guides Spatial Attention," *Cognitive Psychology,* vol. 36, pp. 28-71, 1998.

[20] T. Ormerod, J. MacGregor and E. Chronicle, "Dynamics and constraints in insight problem solving," *Journal of Experimental Psychology: Learning, Memory, and Cognition,* vol. 28, no. 4, pp. 791-799, 2002.

[21] J. Metcalfe, "Feeling of knowing in memory and problem solving," *Journal of Experimental Psychology: Learning, Memory, and Cognition,* vol. 12, no. 2, pp. 288-294, 1986.

[22] M. Scheerer, "Problem solving," *Sci Am,* vol. 208, pp. 118-128, 1963.

[23] D. A. Schön, The Reflective Practitioner: How Professionals Think in Action, New York, NY: Basic Books, 1983.

[24] S. Burns and C. Bulman, Reflective Practice in Nursing: The Growth of the Professional Practitioner, Oxford: Blackwell Science, 2000, p. 199.

[25] R. Hughes, "The poetics of practice-based research writing," *The Journal of Architecture,* vol. 11, no. 3, pp. 283-301, 21 Nov 2006.

[26] G. Wallas, The Art of Thought, Tunbridge Wells, England: Solis Press, 2014, p. 202.

[27] J. W. Schooler, S. Ohlsson and K. Brooks, "Thoughts beyond words: When language overshadows insight," *Journal of experimental psychology: General,* vol. 122, no. 2, p. 166, 1993.

[28] J. W. Schooler, S. M. Fiore and M. A. Brandimonte, "At a loss from words: Verbal overshadowing of perceptual memories," in *The Psychology of Learning and Motivation,* vol. 37, D. L. Medin, Ed., San Diego, CA: Academic Press Inc., 1997, pp. 291-340.

[29] M. A. DuFon, "Video Recording in Ethnographic SLA Research: Some Issues of Validity in Data Collection," *Language Learning & Technology,* vol. 6, no. 1, pp. 40-59, Jan 2002.

[30] ResearchWare, Inc., "HyperRESEARCH," ResearchWare, Inc. - Randolph, MA 02368, USA, 1997-2012. [Online]. Available: http://www.researchware.com/products/hyperresearch.html. [Accessed 14 June 2012].

[31] K. Charmaz, Constructing Grounded Theory A Practical Guide Through Qualitative Analysis, London: SAGE Publications Ltd, 2006.

[32] L. J. Ball, T. C. Ormerod and N. J. Morley, "Spontaneous Analogising in Engineering Design: A Comparative Analysis of Experts and Novices," *Design Studies,* vol. 25, pp. 495-508, 2004.

[33] J. H. Larkin and H. A. Simon, "Why a diagram is (sometimes) worth ten thousand words," *Cognitive science,* vol. 11, no. 1, pp. 65-100, 1987.

[34] S. Vosniadou, "Analogical reasoning as a mechanism in knowledge acquisition: A developmental perspective," in *Similarity and Analogical Reasoning,* S. Vosniadou and A. Ortony, Eds., New York, NY: Cambridge University Press, 1989, pp. 413-437.

[35] C. M. Wharton, J. G. Grafman, S. K. Flitman, E. K. Hansen, J. Brauner, A. R. Marks and M. Honda, "The neuroanatomy of analogical reasoning," in *Advances in analogy research: integration of theory and data from the cognitive, computational, and neural sciences,* K. J. Holyoak, D. Gentner and B. Kokinov, Eds., Sofia, 1998, pp. 260-269.

[36] U. Goswami, Cognition in children, 1 ed., P. Bryant and G. Butterworth, Eds., Hove: Psychology Press/Erlbaum, 1998, pp. xxii-328.

[37] D. C. Kowaltowski, G. Bianchi and V. T. de Paiva, "Methods that may stimulate creativity and their use in architectural design education," *International Journal of Technology and Design Education,* vol. 20, no. 4, pp. 453-476, 2010.

[38] U. Kelle, "The development of categories: Different Approaches in Grounded Theory," in *The Sage handbook of grounded theory,* A. Bryant and K. Charmaz, Eds., London, SAGE Publications Ltd, 2007, pp. 191-213.

[39] B. G. Glaser and A. L. Strauss, The discovery of grounded theory: Startegies for qualitative research, Hawthorne, NY: Aldine de Gruyter, 1967, pp. 104-106.

[40] W. Lidwell, K. Holden and J. Butler, Universal Principles of Design, Revised and Updated: 125 Ways to Enhance Usability, Influence Perception, Increase Appeal, Make Better Design Decisions, and Teach through Design, 2 ed., Beverly, MA: Rockport Publishers, 2010.

[41] T. Samara, Design Elements: A graphic Style Manual, Gloucester, MA: Rockport Publishers, 2007.

[42] B. B. De Koning, H. K. Tabbers, M. J. R. Rikers and F. Pass, "Attention Cueing as a Means to Enhance Learning from an Animation," *Applied Cognitive Psychology,* vol. 21, pp. 731-746, 2007.

[43] R. L. Goldstone, D. Gentner and D. L. Medin, "Relations relating relations," in *Proceedings of the 11th annual Conference of the Cognitive Science Society,* 1989.

[44] D. Gentner, "Structure-mapping: A theoretical framework for analogy," *Cognitive Science,* vol. 7, no. 2, pp. 155-170, 1983.

[45] J. M. Benyus, Biomimicry: Innovation inspired by nature, New York, NY: William Morrow, 1997.

[46] S. Eryildiz and L. Mezini, "Bioarchitecture - Inspirations From Nature," *Gazi University Journal of Science,* vol. 25, no. 1, 2012.

[47] B. T. Christensen and C. D. Schunn, ""Putting blinkers on a blind man" Providing Cognitive Support for Creative Processes with Environmental Cues," in *Tools for Innovation - The science behind the practical methods that drive new ideas,* A. B. Markman and K. L. Wood, Eds., New York, Oxford University Press, Inc, 2009, pp. 48-74.

[48] R. L. Dominowski and P. Dallob, "Insight and problem solving," in *The nature of insight,* R. J. Sternberg and J. E. Davidson, Eds., Cambridge, MA: MIT Press, 1995, pp. 33-62.

[49] J. Linsey, K. Wood and A. Markman, "Increasing innovation: presentation and evaluation of the wordtree design-by-analogy method," in *Proceedings of the ASME IDETC Design Theory and Methodology Conference,* Brooklyn, 2008.

[50] L. Mamykina, L. Candy and E. Edmonds, "Collaborative creativity," *Communications of the ACM,* vol. 45, no. 10, pp. 96-99, Oct 2002.

[51] N. Y.-w. Cheng and S. Lane-Cumming, "Teaching with digital sketches," in *Design Communication Association's 11th Biannual Conference,* San Luis Obisbo, CA, 2004.

[52] R. A. Finke, Creative imagery: Discoveries and inventions in visualization, Hillsdale, NJ: Erlbaum, 1990.

[53] E. M. Eisenberg, "Ambiguity as Strategy in Organizational Communication," *Communication Monographs,* vol. 51, no. 3, pp. 227-242, Sept 1984.

[54] J. D. Landau and D. P. Lehr, "Conformity to Experimenter-Provided Examples: Will People use an Unusual Feature?," *The Journal of Creative Behavior,* vol. 38, no. 3, pp. 180-191, Sept 2004.

10 APPENDICES

Appendix 1 Stacking buckets

Appendix 2 Photography session (V 1)

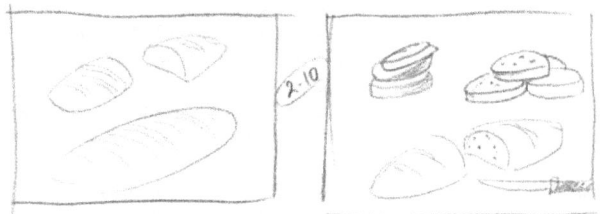

Appendix 3 Bread loaves

An Empirical Analysis of the Influence of Seismic Data Modeling for Estimating Velocity Models with Fully Convolutional Networks

Luan Rios Campos
Manufacturing and Technology Integrated Campus – SENAI CIMATEC
Salvador, Bahia 41650-010, Brazil

Peterson Nogueira
Manufacturing and Technology Integrated Campus – SENAI CIMATEC
National Institute of Science and Technology for Geophysics of Petroleum - UFBA
Salvador, Bahia 41650-010, Brazil

Davidson Moreira
Manufacturing and Technology Integrated Campus – SENAI CIMATEC
Salvador, Bahia 41650-010, Brazil

Erick Giovani Sperandio Nascimento
Manufacturing and Technology Integrated Campus – SENAI CIMATEC
Salvador, Bahia 41650-010, Brazil

ABSTRACT

Seismic modeling is the process of simulating wave propagations in a medium to represent underlying structures of a subsurface area of the earth. This modeling is based upon a wave equation and it depends on a set of parameters of the subsurface. Recent studies have demonstrated that deep learning methods can be trained with seismic data to estimate velocity models that give a representation of the subsurface where the seismic data was generated. Thus, an analysis is made on the impact that different sets of parameters have on the estimation of velocity models by a fully convolutional network (FCN). The experiments varied the number of sources among four options (1, 10, 25 or 50 shots) and used three different ranges of peak frequencies: 4, 8 and 16 Hz. The results demonstrated that, although the number of sources have more influence on the computational time needed to train the FCN than the peak frequency, both changes have significant impact on the quality of the estimation. The best estimations were obtained with the experiment of 25 sources with 4 Hz and increasing the peak frequency to 8 Hz improved even more the results, especially regarding the FCN's loss function.

Keywords: Deep Learning, Geophysics, Velocity Model Estimation, Seismic Data Analysis, Fully Convolutional Networks.

1. INTRODUCTION

The exploration of subsurfaces of the earth is an expensive process. The first step is to place sources and receivers along a certain area and then propagate waves from one equipment to be recorded by the other. This process generates seismograms that have much information of the structures underneath the region where the acquisition was made and it may lead oil and gas companies to drill an area that may contain, for example, petroleum. However, two problems arise: the raw data by itself does not provide such kind of detailed information and they are too big and complex to be analyzed by humans.

In this scenario, seismic data modeling is done so certain methods, such as the Reverse Time Migration (RTM) or Full-Waveform Inversion (FWI), can be used. The RTM is a method that outputs an image where it is possible to identify the underlying structures of a subsurface, whilst the FWI is an iterative method that tries to solve a nonlinear inversion problem to output a high-resolution model of velocities of the subsurface. The latter complements the former, since its output is an input for the other, and both methods require seismic data and a velocity model to operate.

In the geophysics literature there are methods that help the production of initial velocity models. Authors such as [2] and [3] have, respectively, studied the use of reflection tomography and migration-based velocity analysis for such tasks. There are also approaches that consider the use of genetic algorithms [4] and simulated annealing [5]. However, the first two methods are high time-consuming tasks and the last two demand more computational resources as the subsurface being analyzed increases in size, since they will require more modeling steps to carry the search on. More recently, researchers have been experimenting the use of deep learning techniques to solve geophysics problems [6], including seismic inversion [7] [8] [9] [10]. As far as it is of our concern, the first use of a fully convolutional network (FCN) for the velocity model estimation problem was addressed by [11], on which the FCN is trained with the seismic data as its input. The seismic data was generated with sources and receivers placed on both the top and the bottom layers of the subsurface. None of the works previously mentioned address the consequences of changing the number of sources or the peak frequency when training a deep learning method, except for [11], which compares only the case of seismic data with 1 and 10 shots.

The goal of this study is to empirically analyze how the seismic data generated from synthesized velocity models can influence the estimation of such models using an FCN. This can contribute to the oil and gas industry by either demonstrating that deep learning methods may not necessarily require a high number of seismic shots, as it happens with other techniques, in order to be

93

able to estimate a comprehensible velocity model, which can lead to reduce the expense to simulate, store and process non-synthetic seismic data, or offering a technique that perhaps is less sensitive to higher frequencies.

The experiments discussed here consider a finite-differences approach for the seismic modeling and alterations on some of its parameters, such as the number of sources and peak frequency, with the former varying from one central shot to 10, 25 and 50 equally spaced shots and the latter varying from 4 to 8 and 16 Hz. The seismic data is generated with basis on the same dataset of velocity models independently of changes on the modeling parameters, which consequently yields the same training and testing dataset throughout the entire analysis with modifications only on the resolution of the seismic data due to the differences of parameters.

The analysis is twofold: to compare the graphical results of the estimated velocity models of each experiment made as well as their metrics obtained after the FCN is completely trained. Analyzing the metrics can offer a statistical and more precise evaluation of the FCN results, since only a graphical analysis can mislead the interpretation of how changing the modeling parameters effects on the neural network training.

This study is organized as follows: the following section presents the mathematical and physical theory behind the seismic modeling; section three briefly presents the importance of velocity models; section four overviews fully convolutional networks applications and theory; section five describes the methodology and experiments; in section six a discussion of the results obtained with the experiments is made; and section seven concludes this work and points new directions of research based on the results obtained.

2. SEISMIC MODELING

Seismic modeling simulates the process of propagating waves on a subsurface area. This is done so researches can advance on processes that aid the understanding of subsurface areas prior to going into expeditions to them. This section is dedicated to briefly present some of the equations considering the modeling via the acoustic wave equation.

$$\frac{1}{v(x)^2}\frac{\partial^2 P_s(x,t)}{\partial t^2} - \nabla^2 P_s(x,t) = s(x,t) \tag{1}$$

The acoustic wave equation [12] [13] is described by Eq. (1), of which $x = (x', z')$ is the position on the subsurface for a 2D representation, $v(x)$ is the velocity at a given position, $P_s(x,t)$ is the source wavefield and $s(x,t)$ defines the seismic source of the acoustic wave. Eq. (2) denotes the second spatial derivatives, i.e., the Laplacian operator (∇^2), for the two-dimensional case as:

$$\nabla^2 = \frac{\partial^2}{\partial x'^2} + \frac{\partial^2}{\partial z'^2} \tag{2}$$

One way to perform the seismic modeling is with the finite-differences method [13], which can be discretized by the Taylor [14]. Both Eq. (1) and Eq. (2) can be expanded by a Taylor series, but some conditions must be met in order to avoid the numerical dispersion and instability that may arise when discretizing a continuous-time equation [14].

On one hand, Eq. (3) [14] denotes the conditions to avoid the numerical instability of a 2D model, on which Δt is the time sampling interval, $max(v)$ is the maximum velocity of the model, $\Delta x'$ and $\Delta z'$ are the spatial sampling interval respectively on the x and z axes.

$$\Delta t \leq \frac{1}{max(v)\sqrt{\frac{1}{\Delta x'^2}+\frac{1}{\Delta z'^2}}} \tag{3}$$

On the other hand, Eq. (4) [14] illustrates the conditions to avoid the numerical dispersion problem of a bidimensional model: f_{max} is the maximum value of frequency allowed so the dispersion does not occur considering a given model, i.e., its maximum spatial sampling interval ($max(\Delta x', \Delta z')$) and its minimum velocity ($min(v)$). The parameter F is constant according to the order used for the Taylor series and it decreases as the order increases.

$$f_{max} = \frac{1}{F}\frac{min(v)}{max(\Delta x', \Delta z')} \tag{4}$$

The peak frequency (f_{peak}) is defined as approximately half of the max frequency (Eq. (5)) and represent the point of the spectrum of frequency with maximum amplitude.

$$f_{peak} = \frac{f_{max}}{2.3} \tag{5}$$

The information generated by the simulation of the wave propagation is translated into the seismic data, which corresponds to the values of transit time of the wave, the amplitudes and the phase of the events. The seismic data varies and respects undulation phenomes such as reflection, refraction and transmission

3. VELOCITY MODEL

A velocity model offers a representation of the structures present in a subsurface based on the velocity of propagation of the waves emitted from the sources and recorded by the receivers that are placed on the surface when the seismic data is being modeled. This is because the velocity of propagation directly depends on the type of medium through which a wave travels. Therefore, it is possible to determine a structure, i.e., rock, water, salt body, etc., according to its velocity.

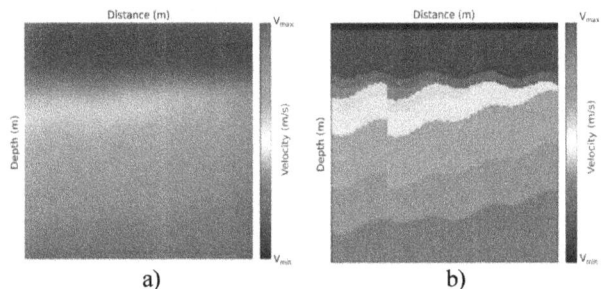

Figure 1 - An example of velocity model in its a) smoothed and b) ground-truth versions

As said before, there are different approaches to handle the initial velocity model problem in the geophysics literature and an optimal model can help when applying the full-waveform inversion. These models, however, are said to be smoothed

(Figure 1a) and, although they can display an initial guess of the velocities of the subsurface, they lack details on its structural composition. In that sense, estimated models that have their structures clearly identified by their velocity values and are highly correlated to their ground-truth (Figure 1b) counterpart are known as high resolution models.

4. FULLY CONVOLUTIONAL NETWORKS

Convolutional Neural Networks (CNN) were firstly introduced by [15] as an option for recognizing handwritten digits from the U.S. Postal Service. Later it was proved that CNNs can handle, besides images, speech and time-series problems [16]. In the recent years, deep learning has gained even more importance, especially after the ImagetNet contest in 2012 and the development of AlexNet [17]. Since then, different proposals of deep learning methods with CNNs have been made, including the fully convolutional networks (FCNs).

The first proposition of use of an FCN was for handling semantic segmentation problems [18], which is the task of segmenting an image into parts and classifying those parts into one of the predetermined classes.

Eq. (6) demonstrates the operation of the basic components of CNNs as [18] point out. In this case, x_{ij} is the data vector, y_{ij} is the next layer, k is the size of the kernel, s the subsampling factor and f_{ks} defines the type of the layer (convolution, pooling or activation function). Therefore, [18] nominate CNNs that contain only layers ruled by Eq. (6) as fully convolutional or deep filter, since, differently from conventional approaches that use CNNs, the FCN does not contain fully connected (dense) layers, producing with its operations a nonlinear filter instead of a nonlinear function and reducing the number of parameters, computational time and dependency of the size of the image.

$$y_{ij} = f_{ks}(\{x_{si+\Delta i, sj+\Delta j}\}_{0 \leq \Delta i, \Delta j \leq k}) \qquad (6)$$

5. METHODOLOGY AND EXPERIMENTS

The velocity models and seismic data are both synthetic and they are built in different occasions. Firstly, the velocity models are randomly generated and then the seismic modeling is applied on each recently-created velocity model to create its corresponding seismic data.

The subsurface area being represented by the synthetic velocity models is a marine region of 3000 m in length by 3000 m in depth. The models are two-dimensional grids of 150 samples on both x (nx') and z (nz') axes and their number of layers vary from 8 to 12 layers, of which the first layer represents a water blade of 100 m deep and velocity of 1500 m/s. Subsequent layers have their depth randomly defined and their velocity incrementation (V_{incr}) occurs in a crescent order, beginning from the first layer velocity, depending on how many layers the model has (n) and what it is the maximum ($V_{max} = 3500\,m/s$) and minimum ($V_{min} = 1500\,m/s$) velocities (Eq. 7), e.g., if the model has 12 layers, then the velocity will be incremented in 166,66 m/s at each layer. Furthermore, the models can have their layers inclined, undulated or containing fault structures. Figure 2 displays an example of such model.

$$V_{incr} = \frac{V_{max} - V_{min}}{n} \qquad (7)$$

The seismic modeling is conducted on two fronts. The first front is to make different modeling changing only the number of sources and fixing a low frequency of 4 Hz. Since the sources are positioned on points (x', z') of the subsurface, to decrease their quantity may inflict on the acquisition of information belonging to some parts of the ground region. Hence, the goal is to analyze how the changes on the number of sources will affect and how much of the velocity model the FCN can estimate.

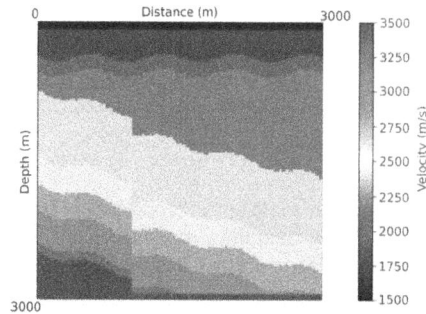

Figure 2 - A synthetic velocity model containing 10 layers, undulations, inclinations and fault structures

The experiments of the second front consider modifications of the frequency using three different bands: 4 Hz, 8 Hz and 16 Hz. As said before, the frequency is important to avoid the numerical dispersion that may occur when calculating the acoustic wave equation through the Taylor series. The frequency of 16 Hz is the frequency of peak obtained from Eq. (5) after calculating the maximum frequency needed to avoid numeral dispersion by applying the parameters depicted in Table 1 to Eq. (4) with $F = 2$ as a 32-order finite-differences was applied. It is safe to say that any value below this threshold does not disperse the wave equation modeling, whereas frequencies above it disperse.

The frequency influences on how much of detail of the structures the modeling will be able to capture. It is expected that by lowering the frequency the seismic data becomes smoother and consequently the non-linearity of the problem is decreased. Hence, the values picked for the experiments represent low-band (4 Hz), medium-band (8 Hz) and high-band (16 Hz) frequencies and aim to aid the understanding of how different bands can determine the level of details of the estimated models.

The FCN implementation takes the seismic data previously described as input and tries to estimate the velocity model corresponding to the input by minimizing the error between the estimated model and the ground-truth that generated the seismic data.

The work of [11] proposes the use of a U-Net [19] to perform the inversion of seismic data into velocity models. This FCN consists of two parts: an encoder, composed of convolution and max-pooling layers, which gradually reduces the size of the image at the same time it determines what are the features of the input data; and a decoder that also has convolution layers, but the max-pooling are replaced by up sampling layers. This results in an increasing of the image size, to match the original image, and consequent localization of the features identified during encoding.

Table 1 - Fixed parameters considered when modeling the synthetic velocity models

Parameter	Value
nx'	150 samples
$\Delta x'$	20 m
nz'	150 samples
$\Delta z'$	20 m
nt	1500 samples
Δt	0.002 s

This study relies on the same U-Net proposed by [11], having the same quantity of layers and the same number of filters on each convolutional layer. However, two major changes were made in order to improve the results. Firstly, the stochastic gradient descent (SGD) optimization function was replaced by Adamax [20], which computes adaptive learning rates for each parameter and offers a more robust solution than the SGD's fixed learning rate when training a neural network model. Secondly, the rectified linear unit (ReLU) activation function was replaced by the parametric rectified linear unit (PReLU). The PReLU is an alternative to avoid the ReLU's vanishing gradient problem, as it learns to parameterize negative inputs to the neurons instead of assigning zeros to them as ReLU does (Figure 3).

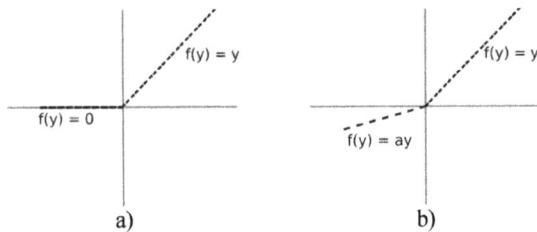

Figure 3 - Plot showing how the a) ReLU and b) PReLU activation functions work

The FCN is trained for 200 epochs with a batch size of 2 on 80% of the total of seismic data generated, saving 20% for the testing stage. The testing dataset is a portion of the original dataset that has never been presented to the FCN during the training phase, so it can offer an unbiased analysis of the model's performance. The batch size is small due to the size of the input and it was kept unchanged throughout all experiments.

The evaluation of the FCN is made based on five different metrics with respect to the testing dataset: mean squared error (MSE), which is also the loss function, mean absolute error (MAE), coefficient of determination (R²), Pearson's coefficient of correlation (r) and factor of two (fac2).

In this context, the MSE (Eq. (8)) measures how far an estimated model is from its respective ground-truth model. The bigger the differences between one output and its corresponding target, the greater the penalization and, consequently, the associated error. The MAE (Eq. (9)) have lower values when compared to MSE's

and indicates how much the difference of velocities between an estimated and its ground-truth model vary, i.e., if the MAE is of, say, 100, it means the output have 100 m/s of average error compared to the target.

$$MSE = \frac{1}{N}\sum_{k=1}^{N}(y_k - \hat{y}_k)^2 \qquad (8)$$

$$MAE = \frac{1}{N}\sum_{k=1}^{N}|y_k - \hat{y}_k| \qquad (9)$$

The coefficient of determination (Eq. (10)) indicates how better the estimation is when compared to a baseline model - either $\overline{y}$ or $\overline{\hat{y}}$ variables of Eq. (10). The Pearson's coefficient (Eq. (11)) quantifies the linear relationship between an estimated model and its ground-truth counterpart, of which the value of -1 means opposite correlations, 0 means no correlation at all and 1 means total correlation. The factor of two (Eq. (12)) determines how much of the estimation can be considered an outlier.

$$R^2 = \frac{\left[\sum_{k=1}^{N}\left(\hat{y}_k - \overline{\hat{y}}\right)y_k\right]^2}{\sum_{k=1}^{N}\left(\hat{y}_k - \overline{\hat{y}}\right)^2 \sum_{k=1}^{N}(y_k - \overline{y})^2} \qquad (10)$$

$$r_{y\hat{y}} = \frac{\sum_{k=1}^{N}(y_k - \overline{y})\left(\hat{y}_k - \overline{\hat{y}}\right)}{\sqrt{\sum_{k=1}^{N}(y_k - \overline{y})^2}\sqrt{\sum_{k=1}^{N}\left(\hat{y}_k - \overline{\hat{y}}\right)^2}} \qquad (11)$$

$$fac2 = 0.5 \leq \frac{\hat{y}_k}{y_k} \leq 2 \qquad (12)$$

The parameters from Eq. (8) to Eq. (12) are as follows: N is the size of the velocity model grid, y_k is the $k\underline{th}$ velocity of the ground-truth model (target), $\hat{y}_k$ is the $k\underline{th}$ velocity of the FCN's model (estimated output), $\overline{y}$ is the mean of velocities of the target output and $\overline{\hat{y}}$ is the mean of velocities of the estimated output.

6. RESULTS

The analysis of the results is made both graphical and statistically. The statistical comparison is to give a more reliable analysis, since considering only the estimated image of the velocity model can mislead the interpretation of the results. In this case, the goal is to minimize both the loss (MSE) and MAE metrics at the same time it maximizes R^2, r and $fac2$ to values as close to 1 as possible. Besides the metrics, the time (in hours) taken to train the model also composes the analysis.

The graphical results of the estimation of one ground-truth model from the testing dataset can be seen in Figure 3. The ground-truth model contains undulated and inclined layers, and a simple fault structure that is identified by the yellow ellipsis in Figure 4a. Analyzing only the images leads to pointing out that Figure 4c, Figure 4f and Figure 4g obtained the best representation of the ground-truth model because they contain not only well-positioned layers, with identification of their undulation and inclination, and a high precision of the velocities on each layer, as the other estimations do, but also a fair depiction of the fault structures.

On one hand, this analysis is made upon a single example of the testing dataset and it may indeed be a case where the FCN models estimated an optimal velocity model from the seismic data they were trained by, but there may also exist cases that the estimations greatly differ from their ground-truth models. On the other hand, this analysis indeed validates the use of FCNs to produce velocity models from unknown seismic data.

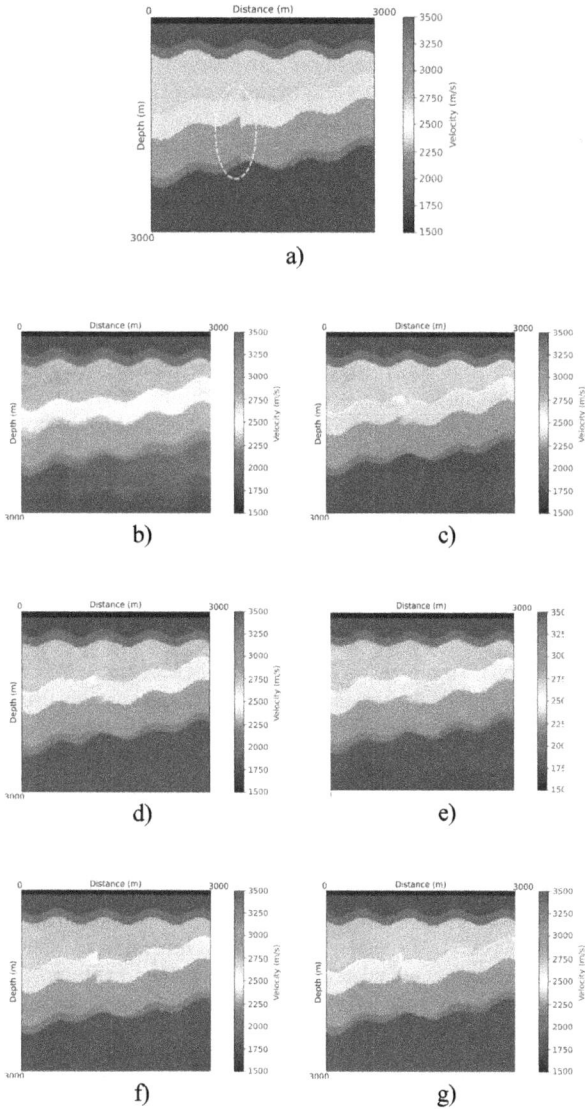

a)

b)   c)

d)   e)

f)   g)

Figure 4 - a) Ground-truth velocity model and graphical results obtained with the experiments of b) 1 source, c) 10 sources, d) 25 sources and e) 50 sources all modeled with $f_{peak} = 4$ Hz and f) 8 Hz and g) 16 Hz both having 25 shots

Once the graphical investigation of many examples is imprecise and impractical, a quantitative evaluation of the statistical indicators belonging to each one of the experiments is conducted. These metrics are measured after the training phase using the entire testing dataset. Table 2 displays the metrics, the corresponding time it took for the models to be trained and the peak frequency for each experiment.

Before venturing into the comparison of the metrics, an association between the experiments and the computational time is conducted. It is possible to see from Table 2 that as the number of shots increases, so it increases the computational time taken to train the FCN. This happens because the number of shots have a direct influence on the size of the seismic data as additional shots mean adding matrices of size $nt \times nx'$ to the seismic data.

Nonetheless, the peak frequency does not seem to have much importance to the computational time. Considering the experiment of 25 shots in Table 2, since the modeling had a peak frequency of 4 Hz, and comparing it with the time of the experiments of 8 Hz and 16 Hz, as both have 25 shots, there is no clear relation of computational time and higher or lower frequencies. In fact, the result that achieved the lowest time is the one with the highest frequency and the experiment with medium frequency took the longest to train.

Table 2 - Results of the evaluation metrics and the time for training (in hours) for each one of the experiments with changes on the number of sources (shots) with fixed peak frequency of 4 Hz and on the frequency with a fixed 25 number of shots

	1 shot	10 shots	25 shots	25 shots	25 shots	50 shots
f_{peak} (Hz)	4	4	4	8	16	4
Time (h)	7.19	7.43	8.10	8.14	8.09	9.07
MSE	14172	7313	6837	6126	7578	7207
MAE	75.39	45.41	44.19	46.79	54.69	49.72
R²	0.954	0.975	0.977	0.980	0.974	0.976
R	0.983	0.989	0.990	0.991	0.990	0.990
fac2	0.999	1.0	1.0	0.999	1.0	0.999

The evaluation metrics of each experiment, in general, demonstrated close values, but it is possible to notice that training the FCN with seismic data that have more shots does not necessarily indicate a better estimation. Even though the experiment with 50 shots demonstrates valuable results, i.e., it accomplished values close to 1 for the r, R^2 and $fac2$, and relatively low values for MAE and MSE, other experiments were able to surpass it. In this case, both experiments with 10 and 25 shots obtained better values in all metrics, of which the latter bested the former. Moreover, the experiment with 25 shots could be further improved when the modeling was made with 8 Hz, reaching the lowest value with the loss function (MSE) and the highest with R^2 and r metrics for all experiments. This, however, happened at the expense of slightly decreasing the MAE and $fac2$ metrics to values below the experiment of 25 shots and 4 Hz.

On the other hand, neither reducing much the number of shots nor increasing even more the peak frequency mean improvement on the estimation either. The worst results belong to the experiment with the central shot. In this case, the values of R^2, r and $fac2$, though show little differences from the same metrics of the other experiments, were the lowest and the MSE and MAE were the highest amongst all. Moreover, the experiment with 16 Hz resulted in worst metrics than the one with 50 shots.

Although having the worst metrics, the FCN successfully inverted a seismogram of one shot into a velocity model. This possibly happened due to the size of the subsurface and the velocity model, which are considered small from a geophysics perspective, but this cannot be confirmed to happen as the subsurface becomes larger considering only the analysis made in this work.

Hence, considering the extent of the experiments conducted in this work, it is possible to conclude that the FCN not only can produce velocity models from unknown seismic data, but it can also deliver high-resolution models. Furthermore, the parameters used to generate the seismic data, combined with the size of the subsurface area and the size of its velocity model representation, play an important role in determining how high the model's resolution is going to be.

7. CONCLUSIONS

This work demonstrated how changing the number of sources and peak frequency of the seismic modeling can affect the training and evaluation of an FCN model that takes seismic data as input to estimate 2D velocity models.

The experiments were conducted with variations on the peak frequency and the number of shots. The best metrics for the FCN were obtained with the experiments of 10 and 25 sources and increasing the peak frequency from 4 to 8 Hz improved even more the latter's estimation, especially regarding the FCN's loss. When the peak frequency was increased once again, the FCN reached lower metrics than the experiment with 50 shots. Nevertheless, the worst results amongst all were obtained with the seismic data produced by a single central shot.

Initial conclusions for the experiments addressed in this work indicate that, depending on the size of the subsurface, training the FCN with seismic data that have few shots is enough to estimate a velocity model. However, as the size of the model and subsurface increases, more shots may give a better representation of the area. Furthermore, the results imply that the FCN is, up to a certain point, less sensitive to higher peak frequencies as the results improved when the modeling was changed from 4 to 8 Hz, but they worsened when 16 Hz was considered.

The results demonstrated to be valuable, since they show the possibility of estimating optimal velocity models from different seismic data. Further studies point to the need of analysing whether few shots are indeed enough to estimate velocity models of larger and more complex subsurfaces. Furthermore, improvements on the training stage, such as mixing the dataset with low, medium and high frequencies or substituting the max-pooling layers for convolutional layers, can be made, and other deep learning methods, such as generative adversarial networks (GAN), may be studied to determine whether they behave differently from the FCN for the seismic inversion problem.

8. REFERENCES

[1] CARCIONE, Jose M.; HERMAN, Gérard C.; TEN KROODE, A. P. E. Seismic modeling. **Geophysics**, Vol. 67, No. 4, 2002, pp. 1304-1325.

[2] STORK, Christof. Reflection tomography in the postmigrated domain. **Geophysics**, Vol. 57, No. 5, 1992, pp. 680-692.

[3] AL-YAHYA, Kamal. Velocity analysis by iterative profile migration. **Geophysics**, Vol. 54, No. 6, 1989, pp. 718-729.

[4] SAJEVA, Angelo et al. Estimation of acoustic macro models using a genetic full-waveform inversion: Applications to the Marmousi model Genetic FWI for acoustic macro models. **Geophysics**, Vol. 81, No. 4, 2016, pp. R173-R184.

[5] DATTA, Debanjan; SEN, Mrinal K. Estimating a starting model for full-waveform inversion using a global optimization method. **Geophysics**, Vol. 81, No. 4, 2016, pp. R211-R223.

[6] WANG, Wenlong; YANG, Fangshu; MA, Jianwei Automatic salt detection with machine learning. In: **80th EAGE Conference and Exhibition 2018**. European Association of Geoscientists and Engineers, 2018.

[7] RÖTH, Gunter; TARANTOLA, Albert. Neural networks and inversion of seismic data. **Journal of Geophysical Research: Solid Earth**, Vol. 99, No. B4, 1994, pp. 6753-6768.

[8] LEWIS, Winston; VIGH, Denes. Deep learning prior models from seismic images for full-waveform inversion. In: **SEG Technical Program Expanded Abstracts 2017**. Society of Exploration Geophysicists, 2017, pp. 1512-1517.

[9] ARAYA-POLO, Mauricio et al. Deep-learning tomography. **The Leading Edge**, Vol. 37, No. 1, 2018, pp. 58-66.

[10] WU, Yue; LIN, Youzuo; ZHOU, Zheng. InversionNet: Accurate and efficient seismic waveform inversion with convolutional neural networks. In: **SEG Technical Program Expanded Abstracts 2018**. Society of Exploration Geophysicists, 2018, pp. 2096-2100.

[11] WANG, Wenlong; YANG, Fangshu; MA, Jianwei. Velocity model building with a modified fully convolutional network. In: **SEG Technical Program Expanded Abstracts 2018**. Society of Exploration Geophysicists, 2018, pp. 2086-2090.

[12] ALFORD, R. M.; KELLY, K. R.; BOORE, D. Mt. Accuracy of finite-difference modeling of the acoustic wave equation. **Geophysics**, Vol. 39, No. 6, 1974, pp. 834-842.

[13] BAYSAL, Edip; KOSLOFF, Dan D.; SHERWOOD, John WC. Reverse time migration. **Geophysics**, Vol. 48, No. 11, 1983, pp. 1514-1524.

[14] DOS SANTOS, A. W. G. **Waveform inversion applied to the analysis of seismic velocities using a multi-scale approach**. Master's thesis, Universidade Federal da Bahia, 2013

[15] LECUN, Yann et al. Handwritten digit recognition with a back-propagation network. In: **Advances in neural information processing systems**, 1990, pp. 396-404.

[16] LECUN, Yann et al. Convolutional networks for images, speech, and time series. **The handbook of brain theory and neural networks**, Vol. 3361, No. 10, 1995, pp. 1995.

[17] KRIZHEVSKY, Alex; SUTSKEVER, Ilya; HINTON, Geoffrey E. Imagenet classification with deep convolutional neural networks. In: **Advances in neural information processing systems**, 2012, pp. 1097-1105.

[18] LONG, Jonathan; SHELHAMER, Evan; DARRELL, Trevor. Fully convolutional networks for semantic segmentation. In: **Proceedings of the IEEE conference on computer vision and pattern recognition**, 2015, pp. 3431-3440.

[19] RONNEBERGER, Olaf; FISCHER, Philipp; BROX, Thomas. U-net: Convolutional networks for biomedical image segmentation. In: **International Conference on Medical image computing and computer-assisted intervention**. Springer, Cham, 2015, pp. 234-241.

[20] KINGMA, Diederik; BA, Jimmy. Adam: A Method for Stochastic Optimization. **International Conference on Learning Representations**, 2014.

Unsupervised Topic Labeling of Text based on Wikipedia Categorization

Tetyana LOSKUTOVA

Wits Business School, University of the Witwatersrand

Johannesburg, Gauteng, South Africa

ABSTRACT

Defining text topicality is often an expensive problem that requires significant resources for text labeling. Though many packages already exist that provide dictionaries of labeled text, synonyms, and Part-of-Speech tagging, the problem is ongoing as language develops and new meanings of words and phrases emerge. This paper proposes a cheap in human labor solution to topic labeling of any text in the majority of languages. The methodology uses links to the naturally emerging corpus of labeled text – the Wikipedia. Wikipedia categories are processed to extract a weighted set of topic labels for the analyzed text. The approach is evaluated by processing categorized texts and comparing the similarity of the top ranks of topic labels to the text category. The topic labels extracted using this methodology can be used for comparing similarity of texts, for the assessment of the completeness of topic coverage in automated marking of essays, and for coding in qualitative text analysis. The paper contributes to the field of NLP by offering a cheap and organically developing method of topical text labeling. The paper contributes to the work of qualitative analysts by offering a methodology for the analysis of interview transcripts and other unstructured text.

Keywords: Unsupervised Topic Labeling, Context Recognition, Abstractive Labeling.

1. INTRODUCTION

The development of the Internet has made large amounts of text data available for analysis, thus setting in motion significant advances in Natural Language Processing (NLP). Large amounts of text are difficult to analyse due to the hardware memory requirements and the difficulty of comparing texts: very different in word representation texts may mean the same and the meaning is often dependent on the questions of the analysis. The task of recognizing the topic of the text and finding a suitable representation for it, such as labels, is becoming more important as it allows crunching a large body of text into a smaller representation without the loss of meaning. This smaller representation can be for human consumption (summarization) or for computer analysis and comparison (topic labeling). While earlier approaches to text analysis were based on quantitative measures, such as frequency [1], such approaches often failed to preserve the meaning. Later approached attempted to fix the problem by applying predefined context rules, such as removing most commonly used words in a language, assigning different weights to the words based on their location in text, and adjusting for the similarity to the title [2]. These approaches, despite being successful in certain applications lack the ability to define the topic of a random text without prior knowledge of the context. Language has words that have different meaning in different contexts (homonyms) and same phrases can mean different things depending on whether they are used literally, sarcastically, or metaphorically.

Additionally, different syntactical structure of texts in different languages prevents from applying same rules across languages. Allahyari et al. [3] pointed that commonly used approaches take context and type of text as inputs in order to produce meaningful outputs.

Despite the significant recent advances in text classification, translation, and text generation, current methods of topic identification depend on the prior knowledge of the higher-level context, labeled, tagged, and classified data, and context-dependent rules. The goal of this paper is to propose and evaluate a methodology for unsupervised topic labeling of text without prior filtering on the text structure or context.

2. LITERATURE REVIEW

Topic labeling is defined as the task of generating a set of words and phrases that capture the topics and subtopics discussed in text. Topic labeling task pursued in this paper is similar to both the tasks of summarization and keyword extraction. The difference from summarization is that topic labeling does not intend to capture the overall meaning expressed in text but rather selects the main topics being discussed. Allahyari et al. [3] suggested using the terms extraction and abstraction to explain how text summaries can be created: extractive summarization is the approach of building summaries from the phrases already used in text while abstractive summarization attempts to create a completely new text that captures the meaning of the text under study. These terms help understanding the difference between keyword extraction and topic labeling: although keywords and topic labels generally aim to capture the main topics, keywords extraction is an extractive method (limited to the words used in text) while topic labeling is an abstractive method that can use completely different words. Topic labeling accomplishes an important task of re-phrasing. The approach is different from classification as text is expected to cover several topics – one main topic and several topics supporting the main point [4] – and topic labels need to capture these topics instead of giving probability of text belonging to a particular class.

Existing methods of unsupervised summarization and keyword extraction are mostly extractive. Among the extractive methods, Latent Semantic Analysis (LSA) has been proposed to produce high-quality summaries from existing sentences. Gong and Liu [4] proposed an iterative approach where the most relevant sentence is selected first, then the terms from the most relevant sentence are eliminated from the text, and the approach is repeated until a desired number of sentences is selected. In this approach, the sentences are ranked by their importance and the most different sentences are extracted. Gong and Liu applied Singular Value Decomposition (SVD) as a solution for sentence ranking. In semantic sense the application of SVD allows assigning of close ranks to semantically similar sentences; those ranks are represented by singular values in the method's matrix.

While Gong and Liu made provision for the use of any suitable function for getting the importance score [4], in the most basic version, term frequency in the general corpora and the term frequency in the text are used for summarization using SVD.

The LSA SVD approach was improved by Steinberger and Jezek [5] who proposed a salience score for summarization based on the length of each sentence's vector adjusted for its corresponding singular value (singular value is used for ranking in the basic approach). Dokun and Celebi [6] proposed yet another modification of the initial ranking algorithm: in their approach summarization is created from sentences whose term-ranking is average.

As an alternative to LSA approach, Han et al. [7] proposed a Sentence-Level Semantic Graph Model where sentences are vertices in the graph and the relations between the sentences are graph edges. The graph is evaluated using sentences' importance values calculated using PageRank and the values of edges' importance derived using semantic analysis. Several other modifications of the above methods and other methods based on frequencies and rules exist for extractive summarization [3].

Abstractive methods are more difficult because the meaning of the topic needs to be reconstructed anew [3]. Ganesan, Zhai, and Han [8] suggested separating two types of abstractive methods: the first uses preexisting knowledge and the second uses natural language generation. The first approach is generally template-based and abstraction can be perceived as filling in a template or a form. The second approach generates text that is domain dependent [3]. Both these approaches are not useful for achieving unsupervised topic-labeling of unknown domain text.

More relevant approach is Opinosis method [8], which intends to summarize text of unknown domain using abstraction. Opinosis's approach is based on (1) generating graphs of text, (2) evaluating the paths of the graph using the measures of valid paths, redundant paths, and collapsed paths, and (3) using a special algorithm to stitch parts of paths into a valid sentence. While this algorithm allowed achieving reasonable performance on highly-redundant opinion polls (spoken language on a particular topic) [8], its application for an unspecified text structure and other than English languages may require significant additional work.

Other relevant abstractive methods are based on Neural Networks and benefit from the achievements in machine translation. Attention-Based Summarization (ABS) [9] has proven to be effective on paraphrasing short texts, however the outputs bear high similarity with the initial text and are not capable of labeling related subtopics. ABS model also tends to pick correct names and places from keywords while showing lesser accuracy in getting the meaning of the text. A Deep Reinforced Model for abstractive summarization [10] is also based on a neural network and uses a hybrid learning objective to account for the deficiencies of the previous methods; this model demonstrates higher performance of larger texts. Both models require large computational resources and the creation of training sets. Compared to the goal of the current paper, all summarization approaches, including those with paraphrasing ability, are not able to extract related subtopics from text.

Overall, the limitations of the existing methods for text topic labeling include the lack of abstractive methods, the lack of unsupervised methods, the dependence of the existing methods on context-dependent rules, and the lack of language-independent methods.

3. METHODOLOGY

The goal of this paper was to propose and evaluate a methodology for unsupervised topic labeling of text without prior filtering of the text based on structure or context. The following methodology was applied to achieve this goal:

Step 1: Data pre-processing: the extraction of nouns from text.
Step 2: Wikipedia search for topics based on nouns.
Step 3: Extraction of Wikipedia categories and ranking of the categories by the number of appearances in the results.
Step 4: Selection of the top 6 categories or top 3 ranks (the actual number was dependent on the number of categories in a rank). These categories were considered topic labels.

The methodology was evaluated using quantitative and qualitative approaches. The quantitative evaluation was done using Wu-Palmer similarity index to compare the topic labels with the category of the sample. Wu-Palmer similarity index is a measure that defines the similarity of words by comparing their positions in the hierarchy of concepts that define them [11]. The qualitative evaluation was performed on a 10% sample and included reading the text of the article and dividing the generated topic labels into 3 groups: "Topic of text", "Related topic", "Unrelated label".

The details of each step and the evaluation are discussed further.

Implementation

Three sets of data were downloaded from webhose.io: Set 1 was archived articles categorized as "business", Set 2 was archived news articles and news highlights (2-line extract from a news article) categorized as "politics", Set 3 was generated using search term "coffee or tea" and consisted of recent news articles. Out of these datasets, 100 texts were selected randomly for further processing. The texts were minimally processed using Natural Language Toolkit: NLTK 3.4.1. The NLTK processing removed the common stopwords and names using and selected nouns from each sentence, which were then used to search Wikipedia articles. Python package wikipediaapi was used to do the search. If a correspondent page was found (wikipedia page was found for all texts in Set 1 and 3 and for 86% of texts in Set 2), the page categories were added to the list of labels for the text. A list of "stop-labels" was created to remove categorization specific to Wikipedia, such as "pages using dmy dates", "pages using American English", "pages needing attention", and so on. Additionally, nouns related to the time of events described in the text were removed.

The quantitative evaluation of the relevance of the extracted labels consisted of the following steps:

Step 1. The categories extracted from the Wikipedia were ranked by the number of appearances in a text with the aim of extracting top 3 ranks or top 6+ categories. The following algorithm was used for the selection: (a) categories from the first rank were selected; (b) if the selection resulted in 6 or more categories, the process was completed and the categories from rank 1 were used as topic labels; if not, the next rank was selected. The process was repeated until at least 6 categories or

3 ranks were selected. The extracted categories were considered topic labels and were used for comparison with the initial dataset category

Step 2. NLTK synonyms (synsets) were collected for each of the labels: *allsyns_labels*. NLTK synsets are based on WordNet database where synsets are defined as hierarchies of words connected by their lexical and conceptual-semantic relationships [12].

Step 3. NLTK synonyms were collected for the initial categories: *allsyns_categories*.

Step 4. Wu-Palmer Similarity score was computed between *allsyns_labels* and *allsyns_categories*. WordNet's Wu-Palmer similarity implementation was used. In this particular implementation, Wu-Palmer similarity is a measure between 0 (not similar at all) and 1 (the same) of two words based on their hierarchical position in WordNet's synsets.

The qualitative assessment was performed on 10% of the texts in all analyzed datasets to determine the goodness of fit of all the top labels.

4. RESULTS

The results for all three sets of data are presented separately and then summarized below.

Set 1 – Business news: Total articles: 14794, sample 100. The quantitative assessment showed average best similarity of synonymous terms 0.78 and the worst of 0.14.

An example of the analyzed text (for readability, special symbols are replaced with spaces):

Cameroon: Crime Prevention - UN Discusses Social, Economic Challenges. BRICS countries hold 40 per cent of the world's population and a quarter of all economic output. The development bank is expected to be operational by the end of the year from its headquarters in Shanghai and predicts it will have up to 100 billion dollars in capital to finance infrastructure projects in developing countries. Dumisani Hlophe, the Director of the Kunjalo Centre for Development Research in Johannesburg, told RFI that the new bank may be met with suspicion from South Africans. He is sceptical that South Africa needs to belong to another foreign development investment bank. "What remains to be seen is whether it is going to remain one of those diplomatic points that the country scores without necessarily speaking to the needs of society," he said. For President Putin, hosting of the seventh BRICS summit comes at a great time. The sanctions imposed by the European Union and the United States over the country's involvement in the conflict in Ukraine continue to bite, and Russia is looking to strengthen its economic ties elsewhere. Andrew Foxall, the director of the Russia Studies Centre at London-based thinktank the Henry Jackson Society, believes Putin is using the opportunity to show the West that the country isn't isolated economically. Foxall told RFI that "the dynamics within the BRICS has changed a lot" over the period that the bloc has been in existence, and the "shining star" of Russia has been waning. The summit runs Thursday and Friday. South Africa

The text above received the following topic labels:
'Countries'
'Human geography'
'Banking'
'Banks'
'Economic history of Italy'
'Italian inventions'
'Legal entities'

The results show that topic capture the context better than the original category 'business' as the article is concerned with countries, geopolitics ('human geography'), and banking. The labels 'Economic history of Italy' and 'Italian inventions' are less clearly related to the topic of the article and their presence is explained by the fact that banking in its modern form (deposit banking) is considered to be an Italian invention and an important event in Italian economic history. While first 4 labels and the last label capture the topic of the article, the 5th and 6th represent related topics.

Set 2 – Political news and highlights: Total articles: 87156, sample 100, out of which 86 got labeled. The quantitative assessment showed average best similarity of synonymous terms 0.68 and the worst of 0.12.

An example of the analyzed text:

Privacy Policy. More Newsletters AP FILE - In this Aug. 24, 2015, file photo, former Arkansas Governor and Republican presidential candidate Mike Huckabee speaks to reporters in Little Rock, Ark. Republican presidential candidate Mike Huckabee came under fire for a tweet he sent while the Democratic candidates took to the debate stage in Las Vegas, Nevada, on Tuesday, NBC News reported. The former Arkansas governor likened his trust of Vermont senator Bernie Sanders to "a North Korean chef with my labrador!" I trust @BernieSanders with my tax dollars like I trust a North Korean chef with my labrador! #DemDebate — Gov. Mike Huckabee (@GovMikeHuckabee) October 14, 2015 The response on Twitter to Huckabee was swift with many calling his comments racist. Huckabee followed up his tweet hours later, writing, "Poor liberals think it's racist to deplore a brutal dictatorship."

The text above received the following topic labels:
'Elections'
'Chefs'
'Culinary terminology'
'Occupations'
'Restaurant staff'
'Restaurant terminology'
'Skills'
'Internal territorial disputes of Canada'
'Labrador'
'Discrimination'
'Hatred'

'Politics and race'
'Racism'

The results show lesser accuracy than with Set 1, which is likely explained by the prevalence of shorter texts with incomplete sentences. Potentially, improvement may be achieved by considering other than nouns parts of speech, stable phrases and colloquialisms, and supplementing the Wikipedia with dictionaries or other encyclopedias to account for terms unavailable in the Wikipedia.

Set 3 – 'Coffee or tea' news: Total: 100 automatically sampled from webhose.io (537 total). The quantitative assessment showed average best similarity of synonymous terms 0.80 and the worst of 0.21.

An example of the analyzed text:

(Extract) World Coffee Producers Forum declares need for action on coffee price Posted on Wednesday 27th, March 2019. Share World Coffee Producers Forum organisers have released an official declaration calling for serious and immediate action to be taken on the historically low international coffee price. Thirteen coffee producers' groups, including the Federación Nacional de Cafeteros de Colombia (FNC), are listed on the declaration....Producers who stay in coffee will not be able to afford the proper care of their farms and their coffee which leads to improper fertilization and care of the trees, affects quality and deprives consumers the diversity that they enjoy today. Adaptation and mitigation of the effects of climate change are other burdens that falls on the shoulders of producers.

The text above received the following topic labels:

'Crops'
'Coffee'
'Herbal and fungal stimulants'
'Hot drinks'
'Non-alcoholic drinks'
'Turkish words and phrases'
'Pricing'

This category was much better defined than the previous two. This clarity also resulted in better results. The quantitative assessment showed best results of 0.80 and the worst of 0.21. For comparison the results of Wu-Palmer similarity for clearly related words 'dog' and 'animal' are: best=0.88, worst=0.27.

Qualitative evaluation: The Wu-Palmer similarity score gives a very rough estimate of the appropriateness of the topic labeling. Qualitative assessment is a much better evaluation method for the goal of the topic labeling method. In this first version of the method, to complement the results of the quantitative (Wu-Palmer similarity) assessment, a qualitative assessment was performed on 10% of texts in all three sets. The results are presented in Table 1.

Table 1. Qualitative evaluation of topic labels.

Data set	Topic of the text, %	Related topic, %	Unrelated label, %
Set 1	65,9	30,8	3,3
Set 2	75	22,2	1,4
Set 3	60	22,9	17,1

Overall, the short twitter-type texts in Set 2 showed the lowest labeling performance, which can be explained by the lack of information that the method receives to evaluate the relevance of a particular topic. This problem can be addressed using additional topic filtering methods, for example, measuring the similarity between the selected labels and the analyzed text.

5. CONCLUSIONS

The method proposed in this paper performs unsupervised topic labeling of texts of unknown context and structure. This functionality is similar to finding synonyms, however synonyms of the whole text as opposed to the synonyms of a word. The method is useful for generating short representation of text that can be used in text comparisons. The topic labels give a good sense of the range of the topics discussed, which can be used practically for essay scoring to ensure the completeness of the topic coverage.

The method is potentially language independent and can be applied to any language that is used in the Wikipedia and can be tagged by parts of speech.

Future development of the method should focus on the improvement of the labeling ability of the method for shorter texts. Another important development is the ability to distinguish the main topic label, subtopic labels, and related topic labels. To improve the reliability of the qualitative assessment of the method, the topic extraction ability of the method should be verified using human-coding of the same texts.

6. REFERENCES

[1]   H. P. Luhn, "The automatic creation of literature abstracts," *IBM Journal of research and development*, vol. 2, no. 2, pp. 159–165, 1958.

[2]   H. P. Edmundson, "New methods in automatic extracting," *Journal of the ACM (JACM)*, vol. 16, no. 2, pp. 264–285, 1969.

[3]   M. Allahyari *et al.*, "Text summarization techniques: a brief survey," *arXiv preprint arXiv:1707.02268*, 2017.

[4]   Y. Gong and X. Liu, *Test summarization using relevance measures and latent semantic analysis*. Google Patents, 2009.

[5]   J. Steinberger and K. Jezek, "Using latent semantic analysis in text summarization and summary evaluation," *Proc. ISIM*, vol. 4, pp. 93–100, 2004.

[6]   O. Dokun and E. Celebi, "Single-Document summarization using Latent Semantic Analysis," *International Journal of Scientific Research in*

Information Systems and Engineering (IJSRISE), vol. 1, no. 2, pp. 57–64, 2015.

[7]   X. Han, T. Lv, Q. Jiang, X. Wang, and C. Wang, "Text summarization using sentence-level semantic graph model," in *2016 4th International Conference on Cloud Computing and Intelligence Systems (CCIS)*, 2016, pp. 171–176.

[8]   K. Ganesan, C. Zhai, and J. Han, "Opinosis: A graph based approach to abstractive summarization of highly redundant opinions," in *Proceedings of the 23rd International Conference on Computational Linguistics (Coling 2010)*, 2010, pp. 340–348.

[9]   A. M. Rush, S. Chopra, and J. Weston, "A neural attention model for abstractive sentence summarization," *arXiv preprint arXiv:1509.00685*, 2015.

[10]   R. Paulus, C. Xiong, and R. Socher, "A deep reinforced model for abstractive summarization," *arXiv preprint arXiv:1705.04304*, 2017.

[11]   Z. Wu and M. Palmer, "Verbs semantics and lexical selection," in *Proceedings of the 32nd annual meeting on Association for Computational Linguistics*, 1994, pp. 133–138.

[12]   Princeton University, "WordNet. A lexical database for English," *Princeton University*, 01-Jun-2019. [Online]. Available: https://wordnet.princeton.edu/

Short-range wind speed predictions in subtropical region using Artificial Intelligence

Pedro Junior ZUCATELLI
Technological Center, Federal University of Espírito Santo – UFES
Vitória, Espírito Santo, Brazil

Erick Giovani Sperandio NASCIMENTO
Manufacturing and Technology Integrated Campus – SENAI CIMATEC
Salvador, Bahia, Brazil

Alejandro Mauricio Gutiérrez ARCE
Universidad de la República – UDELAR
Montevideo, Uruguay

Davidson Martins MOREIRA
Manufacturing and Technology Integrated Campus – SENAI CIMATEC
Salvador, Bahia, Brazil

ABSTRACT

Short-range wind speed predictions for subtropical region is performed by applying Artificial Neural Network (ANN) technique to the hourly time series representative of the site. To train the ANN and validate the technique, data for one year are collected by one tower, with anemometers installed at heights of 101.8, 81.8, 25.7, and 10.0 m. Different ANN configurations to Multilayer Perceptron (MLP), Recurrent Neural Network (RNN), Gated Recurrent Unit (GRU) and Long Short-Term Memory (LSTM), a deep learning algorithm based method, are applied for each site and height. A quantitative analysis is conducted and the statistical results are evaluated to select the configuration that best predicts the real data. These methods have lower computational costs than other techniques, such as numerical modelling. The proposed method is an important scientific contribution for reliable large-scale wind power forecasting and integration into existing grid systems in Uruguay. The best results of the short-term wind speed forecasting was for MLP, which performed the forecasts using a hybrid method based on recursive inference, followed by LSTM, at all the anemometer heights tested, suggesting that this method is a powerful tool that can help the *Administración Nacional de Usinas y Transmissiones Eléctricas* manage the national energy supply.

Keywords: Computational Intelligence, Artificial Neural Networks, Wind Energy, Wind Speed Forecasting, Computational Modelling.

1. INTRODUCTION

The integrity of natural systems is already a risk because of climate change caused by the intense emissions of greenhouse gases in the atmosphere. Currently, environmental pollution is a global issue that is receiving considerable attention, and alternative renewable resources to reduce pollution must be developed [1]. As a burgeoning type of renewable energy, wind energy has developed rapidly in the past decade [2,3]. [4] reported that wind power has the largest market share among renewable energy sources and is expected to maintain its rapid growth in the coming years. The country of Uruguay, which is in Latin America, surprisingly obtains 94% of its electricity from renewable sources [5]. Among the countries of the world, Uruguay ranks 4th in the generation of wind energy, according to

the Renewables 2017 Global Status Report [6]. Wind speed forecasting is fundamental in the planning, controlling, and monitoring of intelligent wind power systems. However, owing to the stochastic and intermittent nature of wind, it is difficult to make satisfactory predictions [7]. Accurate short-term wind speed forecasting (1 to 12 h ahead) plays a substantial role in addressing this challenge. A correct forecast of the wind speed can reduce the risk of wind energy breaking in hybrid energy systems.

Regarding wind energy, the variability of the wind direction and speed throughout the day makes it difficult to decide whether to drive wind turbines, because in practice, wind exhibits temporal variations of several orders of magnitude, e.g. annual variations (owing to climatic changes), seasonal variations, daily variations (owing to the local microclimate), hourly variations (owing to land and sea breezes), and short-duration variations (bursts). Computational methods have been used to evaluate the wind behaviour and thus obtain valuable information for the electro-energy sector in several parts of the world and computational models can be useful for the identification of locations with high wind potential and, when used operationally in daily integrations, short-term energy generation forecasting [8]. The use of wind power generation for fuelling society and industries is very challenging for current power system operations. One reason for this is that wind power is an intermittent energy source with a high degree of randomness and instability [9]. ANN are among the most important soft computing methods, widely used for a great range of applications spanning across various scientific fields. In [22], the short-term wind speed forecasting for Colonia Eulacio, Soriano Department, Uruguay, is performed by applying ANN technique to the hourly time series representative of the site. The ANN MLP was trained to perform the forecasting of 1 hour ahead and then, using it, the trained network was applied to recursively infer the forecasting for the next hours of the wind speed.

Therefore, the objective of this study was to identify the most efficient ANN configurations applying fully-connected RNN, GRU, and LSTM with Adam optimizer training algorithm for wind speed forecasting 1 hour ahead, and do a comparison with ANN MLP researched and developed in [22]. The Adam optimization algorithm is an extension to Stochastic Gradient Descent (SGD) that has recently seen broader adoption for deep learning applications in computer vision and natural language processing [23]. The algorithm was also applied for 3, 6, 9, and 12 h forecasts by using observational data collected from one tower, which was located in Colonia Eulacio, Soriano Department, Uruguay, as a reference. Anemometers were installed at heights of 101.8, 81.8, 25.7, and 10.0 m, during the period between August 08, 2014 and August 07, 2015. In the literature, there are no published short-term forecasts of the wind speed for 1, 3, 6, 9, and 12 h at four different anemometric heights in subtropical regions (south temperate zone), such as Uruguay, using and comparing the results of MLP [22], RNN, GRU and LSTM. Therefore, this study is a novel investigation related to the operation of wind power plants for Colonia Eulacio in Soriano Department. The main contributions of the study are as follows:

i) Another innovative aspect of this work is that it uses an approach to train the model for the next hour forecasting, then recursively inferring the forecasting for the following hours, in addition to applying this artificial intelligence method targeting short-range wind speed forecasting for this height using RNN, LSTM and GRU.

ii) The proposed models elucidate the behaviour of the wind speed and allows accurate wind speed prediction at different anemometric heights, e.g. 101.8, 81.8, 25.7, and 10.0 m. The model can be used to identify optimal locations of wind turbines and forecast irregular wind energy, for different anemometric heights. Short-term wind energy forecasting can be improved using this model to enhance the wind power quality 12 h ahead.

iii) No previous studies applied artificial neural networks, as RNN, LSTM, GRU, and did a comparison with a classical type of neural network (MLP) for short-term wind speed forecasting for such heights in Uruguay, which is a humid subtropical climate region. Therefore, the results constitute a significant contribution to the scientific community.

iv) The short-term wind speed forecasting model is an important contribution for reliable large-scale wind power forecasting and integration in Uruguay.

This work is organised as follows: Section 2 presents the methodology, Section 3 presents the numerical results and discussions, and Section 4 presents the conclusions.

2. METHODOLOGY

Regarding the computational procedure, was adopted an artificial-intelligence model using a Multilayer Perceptron, Fully-connected Recurrent Neural Network, Gated Recurrent Unit and Long Short-Term Memory ANN with Levenberg–Marquardt Backpropagation to MLP and Adam optimizer [23] to RNN, GRU and LSTM and a training algorithm for short-term wind speed forecasting (1, 3, 6, 9, and 12 h) in Colonia Eulacio, Soriano Department, Uruguay. The mean wind diurnal cycle in different seasons for this location was described by de [10], whose analysis employed the same data used in the present study. ANN models are implemented through layers of interconnected nodes, which are called neurons, and the definition of the number of layers is variable, depending on the characteristics of the problem. At least three layers are required: an input layer, a hidden layer, and an output layer [11].

Validation employs a set of data used to calculate the error during training, for monitoring the fit level of the ANN to the training data. Generalisation is the ability of the network to respond correctly to conditions never experienced before, that is, the testing dataset. According to [12], there are different possibilities for structuring an ANN, because it is necessary to select the type of neuron, the number of input parameters, the number of hidden layers, the type of training, and the architecture configurations. To develop an ANN model, a set of input parameters and a set of output parameters are necessary. These sets are subdivided for use in two different steps: network training and validation of the

produced estimates. The correct selection of the predictors is fundamental for a satisfactory performance of the model [13]. The advancement of wind energy technology has allowed for the installation of turbines at high altitudes; thus, knowledge of the wind potential at these heights is required. To validate the estimates and increase the number of wind farms installed in Soriano Department, anemometric towers with a height of 100.8 m were installed at locations with promising winds in Colonia Eulacio, which is the region considered in this study (Figure 1).

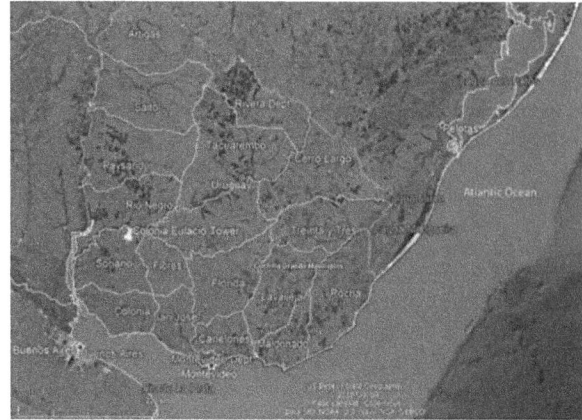

Figure 1. Location of the Colonia Eulacio Tower in Soriano Department, Uruguay [22].

As previously mentioned, the measuring station used for this study is located in the southwestern region of Uruguay (Colonia Eulacio, Soriano Department) and is composed of a triangular tower 100.8 m in height and 0.45 m wide. According to Datum WGS84, it is located at 33° 16 'S, 57° 31 'W [10]. The altitude of the installation location is approximately 100 m, and the location is surrounded by fields with plains; thus, it is characterised by non-complex terrain. The station is owned by the *Administración Nacional de Usinas y Transmissiones Eléctricas* (UTE), which is a state-owned company in Uruguay that is responsible for the generation, distribution, and commercialisation of electrical energy in the country. The software used to program and perform this computational procedure was *MATLAB* version 7.10.0 2010, together with the NNTool (Neural Network Toolbox) graphical interface and *Pyhton* with Google Colab, Google's free cloud service for Artificial Intelligence (AI) developers, using *Keras*. The proposed ANN configurations to be analysed to MLP, RNN, GRU and LSTM are as follows (Table 1). In this study, was applied a fully-connected network structure for RNN, GRU and LSTM. Fully connected layers were defined using the Dense class.

Table 1. ANN configurations analysed.

ANN config.	Layers			
	Input node	1st hidden layer	2nd hidden layer	Output node
Config. 1	7	9 neur	-	1
Config. 2	7	6 neur	-	1
Config. 3	7	3 neur	-	1
Config. 4	7	1 neur	-	1
Config. 5	7	9 neur	6 neur	1
Config. 6	7	6 neur	3 neur	1
Config. 7	7	1 neur	1 neur	1

Each training and forecast simulation took, on average, 3 seconds to MLP, 8 minutes to RNN, 16 minutes to GRU and 18 minutes to LSTM (personal computer, 8 GB RAM). The inputs for each ANN were the hour, day, month, year, and average hourly values of the wind speed, wind direction, and temperature. Therefore, the insertion of these meteorological parameters as input data contributes to efficient training of the ANN. In this sense, a descriptive statistic regarding the wind speed at different heights is shown in Table 2.

Table 2. Descriptive statistics for the wind speed.

Height [m]	Hourly average speed [m/s]	Standard deviation [m/s]
101.8	7.21	3.00
81.8	6.81	2.74
25.7	4.98	2.21
10.0	4.01	2.08

The output vector is the predicted wind speed for the next hour. The measuring height for the wind speed and wind direction is divided into four cases: 101.8 and 60.8 m; 81.8 and 60.8 m; 25.7 and 60.8 m; and 10.0 and 60.8 m. The total amount of data is $8.760 \times 7 = 61.320$ (100%), and the amount of data used for training and validation is $6.133 \times 7 = 42.931$ (70.01%). Once the best model for reproducing the real data is obtained, it is important to verify its accuracy by utilising data outside the training sample. Thus, the last 2.627 h are not considered during the training of the ANN. Therefore, the amount of data used for the forecast simulation is $2.627 \times 7 = 18.389$ (29.99%). Each of the aforementioned ANN configurations was trained, validated, and tested to determine which was the most efficient for short-term (1, 3, 6, 9, and 12 h) wind speed forecasting.

The activation functions, which define the outputs of the neurons in terms of their activity levels, that were inserted in this simulation were the sigmoidal function, in the form of the hyperbolic tangent function (continuous, increasing, differentiable, and nonlinear), for the hidden layers on all configurations, the linear function for the output layer on MLP and Softplus activation function for the dense output layer on RNN, GRU and LSTM (the Softplus is enticingly smooth and differentiable; experiments show that the deep neural networks with Softplus units get significantly performance improvement). To perform the prediction, the first step is to identify what ANN architecture can best perform the 1 h forecasting of the wind speed for each height. Then, this predicted wind speed value is assigned as the input for the second hour of forecasting, while the other input parameters used at the start of the forecasting are kept unchanged (e.g. wind direction and air temperature). Thus, the forecast of the wind speed for the second hour is calculated. This procedure, which is shown in Figure 2, is repeated until the nth hour of forecasting is reached.

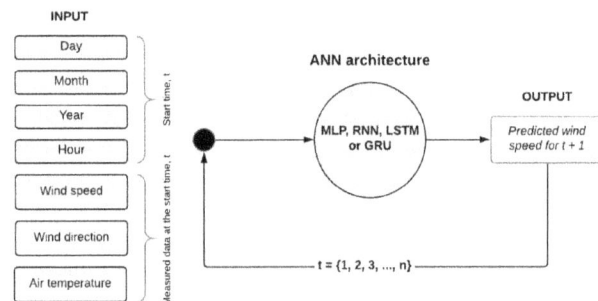

Figure 2. Schematic of the procedure used for wind speed forecasting for 1, 3, 6, 9, and 12 h after the start time.

As the prediction horizon increases, the quality of the predicted wind speed is expected to decrease, which is evaluated in the next section.

3. NUMERICAL RESULTS AND DISCUSSIONS

The statistical indicators employed to analyse the results are the Root-Mean-Square Error (RMSE), Mean Squared Error (MSE), Mean Absolute Error (MAE), Mean Absolute Percentage Error (MAPE), coefficient of determination (R^2 or R-squared), and Pearson's correlation coefficient (r or Pearson's r). Values close to 0.0 are adequate for the MAE, MSE, and RMSE, values close to 0.0% are adequate for the MAPE, and values close to 1.0 are adequate for the R-squared. The Pearson's correlation coefficient ranges from -1.0 to 1.0. A value of 1.0 implies that a linear equation perfectly describes the relationship between matrices **A** and **B**, with all the data points on a line for which **B** increases as **A** increases. A value of -1.0 implies that all the data points are on a line for which **B** decreases as **A** increases. A value of 0.0 implies that there is no linear correlation between the variables.

Each ANN architecture presented in Section 2 was trained, validated, and tested using the input vector for each hour, with the wind speed of the next hour as the desired output vector. The use of a large number of hidden layers is not recommended, because the error measured during training is propagated to the previous layer. The number of neurons in the hidden layers is generally defined empirically and depends strongly on the distribution of the training and validation patterns of the network. When connected and trained in multiple layers, the ANN model can represent any nonlinear function [14]. An advantage of the ANN model is that it can learn the relationship between complex, nonlinear inputs and outputs [15]. The best ANN configurations for Colonia Eulacio are presented in Table 3. The aforementioned ANN architectures that were identified as the most efficient for the 1 h forecast for each height were applied in the computational simulation to predict the wind speed for 3, 6, 9, and 12 h in Colonia Eulacio at all the heights tested. The best MLP architecture was defined in [22].

Table 3. The best ANN configurations.

ANN / heights	101.8 m	81.8 m	25.7 m	10.0 m
		Best ANN configuration		
MLP	7	4	7	4
RNN	1	3	7	5
GRU	7	6	6	5
LSTM	6	5	1	1

The results for the MAE, MSE, RMSE, MAPE, R-squared, and Pearson coefficients for 1, 3, 6, 9, and 12 h wind speed forecasting in Colonia Eulacio are presented in Table 4 for a height of 101.8 m. The lowest values of the MAE, MSE, RMSE, and MAPE, as well as the highest Pearson's correlation coefficient and R-squared values, were recorded for the 1 h forecast for all the analysed heights (101.8, 81.8, 25.7, and 10.0 m). The mean R-squared and Pearson's r for 1 h wind speed forecasting were 0.843 and 0.918, respectively. The lowest MAPE value was 15.840%, for a height of 101.8 m and a prediction horizon of 1 h.

Table 4. Performance indices of forecasting results obtained by different models on the case study (for the height of 101.8 m).

Prediction Horizon [h]	MLP				
	1	3	6	9	12
MAE	0.89	1.67	2.24	2.59	2.87
MSE	1.40	4.68	7.95	10.3	12.38
RMSE	1.18	2.16	2.82	3.22	3.51
Coefficient: r	0.92	0.73	0.54	0.43	0.34
R^2	0.84	0.53	0.30	0.18	0.11
MAPE (%)	15.84	30.13	39.19	43.65	47.10
RNN					

Prediction Horizon [h]	1	3	6	9	12
MAE	0.93	2.64	7.29	7.78	7.94
MSE	1.53	9.77	60.99	68.97	71.43
RMSE	1.23	3.12	7.81	8.30	8.45
Coefficient: r	0.91	0.70	0.40	0.25	0.17
R^2	0.84	0.49	0.16	0.06	0.03
MAPE (%)	17.58	63.56	173.12	183.97	187.0
GRU					
Prediction Horizon [h]	1	3	6	9	12
MAE	0.91	1.96	6.41	8.49	8.85
MSE	1.45	5.92	47.56	80.69	87.04
RMSE	1.20	2.43	6.89	8.98	9.33
Coefficient: r	0.91	0.71	0.47	0.03	0.03
R^2	0.83	0.50	0.22	0.001	0.001
MAPE (%)	18.35	45.84	149.54	197.63	204.7
LSTM					
Prediction Horizon [h]	1	3	6	9	12
MAE	0.89	3.45	5.85	6.08	6.13
MSE	1.43	16.15	42.22	45.03	45.71
RMSE	1.19	4.02	6.49	6.71	6.76
Coefficient: r	0.91	0.63	0.13	0.10	0.09
R^2	0.84	0.39	0.01	0.01	0.01
MAPE (%)	17.33	88.09	146.65	151.25	152.4

The results in Table 4 indicate that as the wind speed forecasting load increases, the quality of the output data of the ANN prediction decreases. Thus, a longer forecasting time yields a larger error. As explained in the previous section, these results were expected, as the adopted procedure uses input data from the start of the forecasting, in addition to the wind speed computed in each forecast hour, to predict the wind speed for the nth hour, leading to an accumulated error. This result is in accordance with the literature, e.g. [16], [17], [18], and [19]. Figure 3 presents a graphical comparison of the RMSE and Pearson coefficient for different ANN model. The graph lines are of 101.8 m. The graph indicates that as the prediction horizon [h] increases, the RMSE increases, indicating that the error between the actual and predicted values increases.

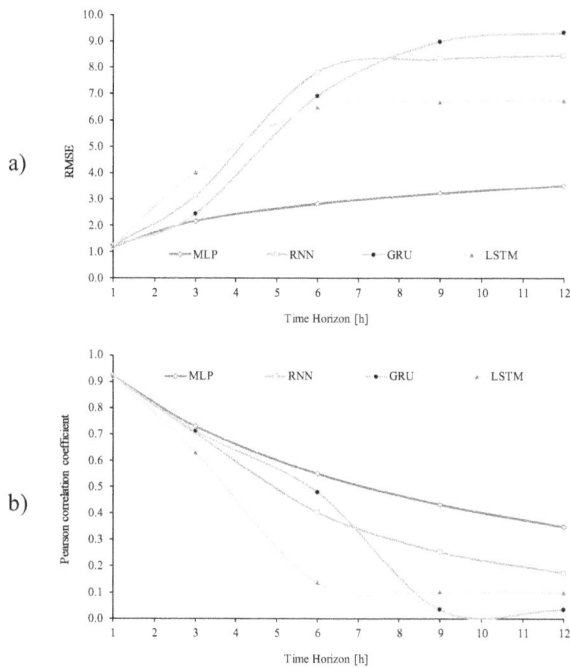

Figure 3. a) Graphical comparison of the RMSE and b) Pearson

coefficient at different prediction horizon for different ANN models (height = 101.8 m).

By definition nowcasting refers to short lead time weather forecasts. The U.S. National Weather Service specifies zero to three hours, though forecasts up to six hours may be called nowcasts by some agencies. Nowcasting is usually made with techniques that differ significantly from normal numerical weather prediction models [24]. Figure 4 shows the comparison of the statistical results for the RMSE at different heights to predict the wind speed at 6 h ahead (this is important to nowcasting to short lead time wind speed forecasting) using different ANN. The best results are recorded for the MLP network, followed by LSTM neural network.

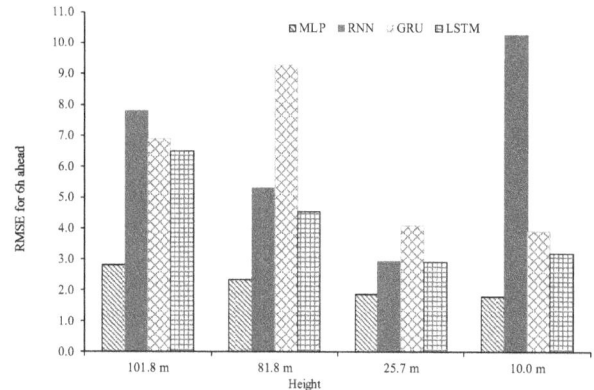

Figure 4. RMSE for 6 hours ahead using MLP, RNN, GRU, and LSTM in different heights.

Figure 5 shows the dispersion between wind speed anemometer and wind speed predicted 6 h ahead.

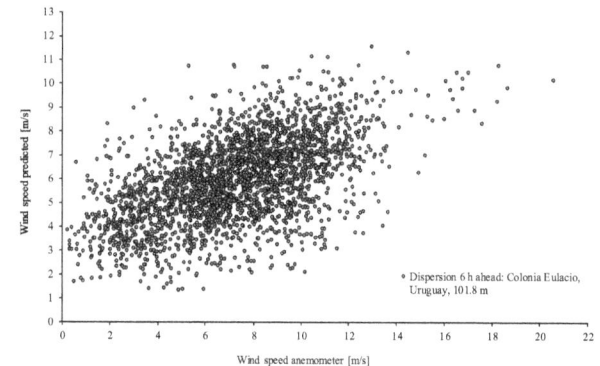

Figure 5. Dispersion's results at 101.8 m for forecast 6 h ahead.

Figure 6 presents a comparison of the results of the ANN wind speed forecasting at 6 h through MLP designed in [22], with real data, which were recorded at Colonia Eulacio with an anemometer height of 101.8 m. The ratio between the wind speed predicted by the ANN model and that measured by the anemometer can be observed with respect to time and the measured wind speed. The middle lines in the plots indicate one-to-one correspondence, and the outer lines indicate difference by a factor of two.

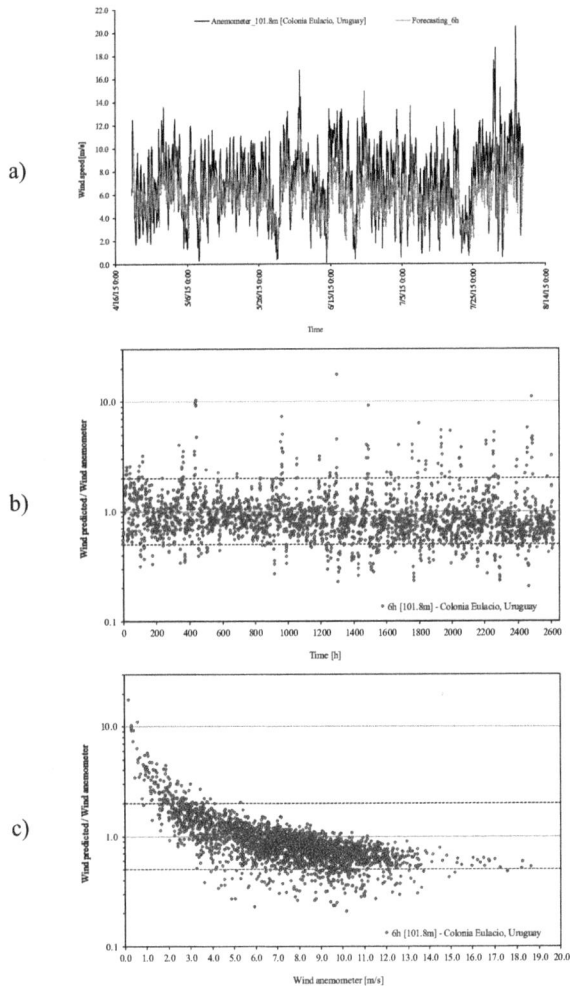

	1 h	97.79%
	3 h	93.71%
	6 h	56.92%
	9 h	43.58%
	12 h	40.69%
LSTM	1 h	98.29%
	3 h	76.94%
	6 h	60.70%
	9 h	59.05%
	12 h	58.39%

The results in Figure 7 indicate that on average, the MLP ANN has better results than the Persistence model for a prediction horizon of 1 h.

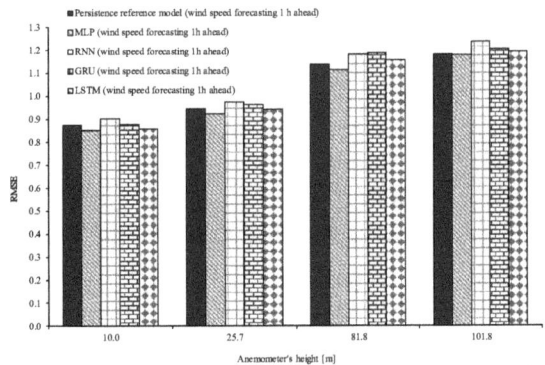

Figure 7. Comparison between the ANN models and the Persistence reference model for wind speed forecasting 1 h ahead.

The investigation of mechanisms that aid the short-term wind speed forecasting, as performed in this study for 1, 3, 6, 9, and 12 h for the generation of energy in wind farms, has been critical to ensure the proper functioning of traditional energy systems. Accurate prediction of the short-term wind speed output helps system operators to adjust scheduling plans in a timely manner, make correct decisions, reduce the standby capacity, reduce the operational costs of the power system, and mitigate the adverse effects of wind power fluctuation.

4. CONCLUSIONS

According to the statistical results of this study, the application of artificial intelligence is a viable alternative for the prediction of wind speed and thus wind power generation, mainly owing to the low computational cost. However, an ANN architecture that is appropriate for the project must be selected, and the data fed to the network must quantitatively and qualitatively be analysed, as these variables directly impact the results of the forecast. This work is relevant because it is a first step in the application of the MLP, RNN, GRU and LSTM models to wind speed prediction, and there are no previous studies on the application of artificial intelligence using deep learning through such neural networks for this region. The statistical results for the prediction horizons of 1 to 12 h, for each anemometric height, exhibited predictable behaviour similar to that for short time ranges. These results are novel because no other studies have used this computational model to predict the wind speed for 1, 3, 6, 9, and 12 h in Uruguay. The application of the MLP and LSTM for wind speed forecasting at different heights was adequate. From the analysis, it was found that the MLP model was superior to the other neural network's models, as they were able to achieve a relatively lower prediction error. The MLP approach here introduced uses a differentiated process of forecasting based on inference. The surprising result is that the simplest model architecture, a

Figure 6. Wind speed forecasting at 6 h: a) The results of six-step predictions of the wind speed series. b) Comparison data of a factor of two (wind predicted/wind anemometer versus time) of the results obtained with the forecast model (six-step predictions) and the real data. c) Comparison data of a factor of two (wind predicted/wind anemometer versus wind anemometer) of the results obtained with the forecast model (six-step predictions) and the real data.

In this study the degradation of the forecast can also be observed by noting that as the forecast horizon increases, the predicted curve moves away from the real curve. Table 5 presents the percentage of the data of a factor of two (fraction of data [%] for $0.5 \leq$ Wind predicted/Wind anemometer ≤ 2.0) to height of observed data = 101.8 m. This showed that MLP and LSTM models were the only ones that maintained results above 50% within the factor of two.

Table 5. Percentage of the data of a factor of two [height = 101.8m].

ANN model	Prediction horizon	Percentage of the data of a factor of two
MLP	1 h	98.44%
	3 h	93.29%
	6 h	88.29%
	9 h	82.43%
	12 h	77.44%
RNN	1 h	98.21%
	3 h	84.64%
	6 h	50.67%
	9 h	47.90%
	12 h	46.69%
GRU		

multilayer perceptron (MLP), with only two hidden layers of one neuron in each of them works best among the considered architectures. This result allows one to suspect that deeper neural network architectures, ensemble or other models may be more beneficial. The 1 and 3 h forecasts were particularly accurate, and as the forecast time increased, the accuracy of the results decreased, as expected. However, this degradation did not make the forecasting results for longer prediction horizons useless; thus, the proposed technique can produce satisfactory short-term wind speed forecasts (up to 12 h) with low computational costs to help wind-farm operators with decision making. This study contributes to the scientific community by providing wind speed forecasting information for a country of South America with high wind power potential (Uruguay), considering the interest of private companies and UTE in the energy sector. The suggestion is that futures works can be developed studying the Wavelets decomposition in the weathers data and be applied to the deep learning technology to wind speed forecasting.

5. ACKNOWLEDGEMENTS

We thank SENAI CIMATEC and FAPESB for their computational and financial support, as well as UTE.

6. REFERENCES

[1] Cheng, W.Y.Y.; Liu, Y.; Bourgeois, A.J.; Wu, Y.; Haupt, S.E., 2017. **Short-term wind forecast of a data assimilation/weather forecasting system with wind turbine anemometer measurement assimilation.** Renewable Energy 107, 340-351. DOI: https://doi.org/10.1016/j.renene.2017.02.014

[2] Jiang, P.; Wang, Y.; Wang, J., 2016. **Short-term wind speed forecasting using a hybrid model,** Energy (2016). DOI: http://dx.doi.org/10.1016/j.energy.2016.10.040

[3] Lia, C.; Xiaoa, Z.; Xiab, X.; Zoua, W.; Zhanga, C., 2018. **A hybrid model based on synchronous optimisation for multi-step short-term wind speed forecasting.** Applied Energy 215 (2018) 131–144. DOI: https://doi.org/10.1016/j.apenergy.2018.01.094

[4] Huang, C.; Li, F.; Jin, Z., 2015. **Maximum Power Point Tracking Strategy for Large-Scale Wind Generation Systems Considering Wind Turbine Dynamics.** IEEE Transactions on Industrial Electronics. 2015. DOI: 10.1109/TIE.2015.2395384

[5] Watts, J., 2015. **Uruguay makes dramatic shift to nearly 95% electricity from clean energy: Keep it in the ground Renewable energy.** 2015. Link to Access: <https://www.theguardian.com/environment/2015/dec/03/urugu ay-makes-dramatic-shift-to-nearly-95-clean-energy>. Access in: 01/11/2019.

[6] REN21. 2017. **Renewables 2017 Global Status Report** (Paris: REN21 Secretariat). ISBN 978-3-9818107-6-9.

[7] Liu, H.; Mi, X.; Li, Y., 2018. **Wind speed forecasting method based on deep learning strategy using empirical wavelet transform, long short-term memory neural network and Elman neural network.** Energy Conversion and Management 156 (2018) 498–514. DOI: https://doi.org/10.1016/j.enconman.2017.11.053

[8] Peng, H.; Liu, F.; Yang, X., 2013. **A hybrid strategy of short term wind power prediction.** Renewable Energy 50, 590-595. DOI: https://doi.org/10.1016/j.renene.2012.07.022

[9] Zhang, J.; Wei, Y.; Tan, Z.; Wang, K.; and Tian, W., 2017. **A Hybrid Method for Short-TermWind Speed Forecasting.** Sustainability 9, 596. DOI:10.3390/su9040596

[10] Lucas, E.A.; Arce, A.M.G.; Moraes, M.R.; Boezio, G.C.; Ottieri, J.C., 2016. **Statistical description of diurnal cycle of wind profile in the first 100 meters of height of the Planetary**

Boundary Layer, in Colonia Eulacio Uruguay. Ciência e Natura v.38 Ed. Especial-IX Brazilian Micrometeorology Workshop 2016, p. 426– 434. DOI: http://dx.doi.org/10.5902/2179460X20308

[11] Russel, S. and Norvig, P., 2010. **Artificial Intelligence: A Modern Approach.** Stuart J. Russell and Peter Norvig. Third Edition. Pearson Education, Inc., 1153p.

[12] Haykin, S., 1999. **Neural Networks: A Comprehensive Foundation.** Simon Haykin. Second Edition. Pearson Education Inc. Hamilton, Ontario, Canada, 823p.

[13] Mori, H. and Umezawa, Y., 2009. **Application of NBTree to Selection of Meteorological Variables in Wind Speed Prediction.** Transmission & Distribution Conference & Exposition: Asia and Pacific, Seoul, Korea, 2009. DOI: 10.1109/TD-ASIA.2009.5356831

[14] McGovern, A.; Elmore, K.L.; Gagne II, D.J.; Haupt, S.E.; Karstens, C.D.; Lagerquist, R.; Smith, T.; Willians, J.K., 2017. **Using Artificial Intelligence to Improve Real-Time Decision-Making for High-Impact Weather. American Meteorological Society.** DOI: https://doi.org/10.1175/BAMS-D-16-0123.1

[15] Quan, D. M.; Ogliari, E.; Grimaccia, F.; Leva, S.; Mussetta, M., 2013. **Hybrid Model for Hourly Forecast of Photovoltaic and Wind Power.** Politecnico di Milano, Dipartimento di Energia. Via La Masa 34, 20156 Milano - Italy, 2013. DOI: 10.1109/FUZZ-IEEE.2013.6622453

[16] Kusiak, A.; Zheng, H.; Song, Z., 2009. **Short-term prediction of wind farm power: a data mining approach.** IEEE Trans. Energy Convers. 24 (1), 125-136. DOI: 10.1109/TEC.2008.2006552

[17] Blonbou, R., 2011. **Very short-term wind power forecasting with neural networks and adaptive Bayesian learning.** Renew. Energy 36, 1118-1124. DOI: https://doi.org/10.1016/j.renene.2010.08.026

[18] Carpinone, A.; Giorgio, M.; Langella, R.; Testa, A., 2015. **Markov chain modeling for very-short-term wind power forecasting.** Electr. Power Syst. Res. 122, 152-158. DOI: https://doi.org/10.1016/j.epsr.2014.12.025

[19] Filik, Ü. and Filik, T., 2017. **Wind Speed Prediction Using Artificial Neural Networks Based on Multiple Local Measurements in Eskisehir.** 3rd International Conference on Energy and Environment Research, ICEER 2016, 7-11 September 2016, Barcelona, Spain. Energy Procedia 107 (2017) 264 – 269. DOI: https://doi.org/10.1016/j.egypro.2016.12.147

[20] Lucas, E.A.; Arce, A.M.G.; Moraes, M.R.; Boezio, G.C., 2017. **Vertical wind profile simulations in the planetary boundary layer with the WRF-ARW model.** Scientia Plena 13, 049913 (2017), vol. 13, num. 04. DOI: http://dx.doi.org/10.14808/sci.plena.2017.049913

[21] Skamarock, W.C.; Klemp, J.B.; Dudhia, J.; Gill, D.O.; Barker, D.M.; Huang, X.Y.; Wang, W.; Powers, J.G., 2008. **A Description of the Advanced Research WRF Version 3 (NCAR Technical Note), Mesoscale and Microscale Meteorology Division do NCAR.** Boulder, Colorado, USA.

[22] Zucatelli, P.J., Nascimento, E.G.S., Aylas, G.Y.R., Souza, N.B.P., Kitagawa, Y.K.L., Santos, A.A.B., Arce, A.M.G., Moreira, D.M., 2019. **Short-term wind speed forecasting in Uruguay using computational intelligence.** Heliyon, Volume 5, Issue 5, May 2019, e01664. DOI: https://doi.org/10.1016/j.heliyon.2019.e01664

[23] Kingma, Diederik P and Ba, Jimmy Lei, 2014. **Adam: A method for stochastic optimization.** arXiv preprint arXiv:1412.6980, 2014.

[24] I. Kuikka, 2009. **Wind nowcasting: optimizing runway in use.** Technical report, Systems Analysis Laboratory, Helsinki University of Technology, 2009.

Techniques of Cognitive Neuroscience in the Assessment and Measurement of Environmental Public Service Announcements Effectiveness

Anna BORAWSKA
Faculty of Economics and Management, University of Szczecin
Szczecin, Mickiewicza 64 71-014, Poland

Mariusz BORAWSKI
Faculty of Computer Science and Information Technology. West Pomeranian University of Technology Szczecin,
Szczecin, Żołnierska 47 71-210, Poland

Mateusz PIWOWARSKI
Faculty of Economics and Management, University of Szczecin
Szczecin, Mickiewicza 64 71-014, Poland

ABSTRACT

To raise awareness and engage the society in realization of environmental goals one needs instruments that could change internal attitudes. For this purpose, public awareness campaigns are used. Public service announcements (PSAs) in the context of such campaigns require not only remembering the content, but also understanding the importance of behavior that is being promoted. Before launching, such PSAs are tested for their effectiveness, mostly using questionnaires and interviews. Due to the development of technology, other methods, i.e. cognitive neuroscience techniques are currently available. Their usage is still not very common, but they are promising in obtaining unconscious preferences of the audience. The article aims to show, how cognitive neuroscience methods can be applied to enhance the survey on public service announcement and what kind of results may be achieved by merging the questionnaire and neurophysiological data. As a case study, two Polish PSAs were chosen. The described procedure of research can be used for testing PSAs that have not been yet launched for the public.

Keywords: cognitive neuroscience techniques; public service announcement, public awareness campaign.

1. INTRODUCTION

Modern times pose a great challenge for the environment and increase substantially the need for the constant protection and care that should be performed in order to preserve the current state and, when possible, to reverse the damage. These objectives are very often a matter of policy making – both globally and locally. The success of such initiatives, however, depends mostly on people. Their personal approaches and opinions and their understanding of problems are vital to introduce positive changes. Authorities have their tools to enforce the desired behaviors (e.g. law regulations), but in order to really engage the society in the realization of the common goal, that is environment protection, the instruments that could change the internal attitudes are needed. For this purpose, public awareness campaigns (PACs) are widely used. Due to their reach and the accessibility of message that they carry, if they are prepared carefully, they can accomplish great results.

The scope of topics for such campaigns is very wide and it concerns a variety of ecological issues. These can be generally divided into three categories: concerning human awareness and behavior, regarding the well-being of animals and referring to the environment/nature as a whole. Such division is arbitrary, because most of the problems occurring in the scope of ecology can be assigned to more than one category. Exemplary topics of existing PACs are shown in the table 1.

Improving the effectiveness of such campaigns may therefore have a very tangible effect on many aspects of life – both for individuals and for whole societies. Public service announcements (PSAs) in the context of such campaigns require not only remembering the presented content, but also understanding the importance of behavior that is being promoted. An effective message should engage the recipient and shape his consciousness, as it can significantly increase the impact of public awareness campaign. Therefore, the need arises to acquire a knowledge of the relationship between public service announcements, and the emergence, spread and durability of awareness concerning the ecological behavior promoted in the campaign.

Every public service announcement that is designed to achieve this goal has to be carefully tested before it is launched. The costs of airing the advertisement that misses its purpose is too large to risk the failure. The methodology of research that is conducted in order to study the reception of such announcements is mostly taken from the commercial marketing toolbox. This includes both quantitative and qualitative methods. In this first group we may find all kinds of surveys and questionnaires, while the other incorporates mainly individual interviews and focus groups [1, 2]. In recent years, however, in the field of marketing it is becoming increasingly common to use the tools of cognitive neuroscience in order to know the unconscious opinions of recipients [3, 4]. Methods of this kind offer access to data that cannot be obtained as a result of the survey [5]. It is caused by the fact that people are sometimes not able (or do not want to) explain their real preferences when asked; as human behavior can be driven by processes that are below the level of conscious awareness and subject's feelings are often inaccessible to the interviewer that uses traditional techniques [6, 7].

This is the reason the tools of neuroscience are becoming increasingly popular in commercial marketing. That also lead to the emergence of a new field of science described as neuromarketing [8, 9, 10, 11]. In the scope of social marketing, in the evaluation of public service announcements in public awareness campaigns, apart from a few exceptions (e.g. [12, 13, 14]) such methods were not commonly used so far. The presented article aims to show, how cognitive neuroscience methods can be applied in order to enhance the survey on public service announcement (video ad) and what kind of results may be achieved by merging the questionnaire and neurophysiological data. As a case study, two Polish PSAs were chosen. They are both concerning the topic of energy saving. The next section justifies the choice of case studies and the following one explains the research procedure and experiment conditions. Then the results of data analysis are presented and discussed. The paper ends with some conclusions.

Table 1. Examples of ecological PACs topics.

Area	Detailed topics
Climate change	• raising awareness of climate change • reduction of CO2 emissions, • stopping deforestation, • promoting alternative sources of energy, • promoting the use of transportation other than cars.
Biodiversity	• protecting biodiversity, • support for endangered species, • preserving the nature.
Animals	• promoting responsible animal breeding, • promotion of adoption of animals from the shelter, • prevention of maltreatment of animals, • stopping tests on animals.
Diet/nutrition	• promoting to drink water, • promotion of vegan/vegetarian diet.
Consumption of goods	• promoting of saving water, • promoting of saving energy, • recycling and use of reusable items, • discouraging to buy leather products, • stopping excessive paper consumption.
Waste reduction	• taking care of the cleanliness of the environment, • waste segregation.

2. MATERIALS AND METHODS

Public awareness about sustainable use of energy is a very important issue in modern world. Due to the growing demand, there is increasing need to adapt the ways in which energy is used in homes in order to reduce its consumption. It is a burning issue, since most of the energy nowadays is still obtained from fossil fuels such as oil and gas. Public awareness campaigns are therefore needed in order to encourage and involve people in energy saving measures, thus contributing actively to the reduction of energy use and to climate change slowdown. Most commonly, such interventions focus on economics incentives, since it is the most convincing way to influence people's behavior. Since the people's consumption patterns have mostly habitual character, in order to induce a change, the habits of individuals must be questioned. This can be done by information, education and awareness raising measures with the final goal to [15]:
Remove incentives that support the old consumption patterns,
Make consumers aware of their behavior and consumption patterns by tools and measures,

Enable them to avoid or control the negative outcomes and provide positive alternative.
An important tool of every energy saving campaign that aims to realize these objectives is usage of public service announcements. A popular approach to such PSA is to present positive patterns of behavior and to shape proper habits. Two examples of public service announcements of this kind will be presented in the article as a case study. Both were run in Poland in autumn 2012. First one was financed by energy company Energa and second one – by Ministry of the Environment1.
Energa campaign, beyond raising awareness about the need for rational use of energy, was aimed to improve the image of the enterprise as the most ecological energy supplier in Poland. The leading roles in the advertisement play pets – cat, dog and canary. They show how to save the energy by simple, everyday activities: switching off unnecessary light or turning off your playing TV and working computer [16]. In 2013 this announcement was distinguished by award of Marketing Communication Association in Poland [17].
The second campaign used in the experiment was prepared to encourage people to protect the environment and climate by rational use of energy. This campaign relies on authorities – two famous Polish professors – Jerzy Bralczyk (linguist) and Zbigniew Lew-Starowicz (sexologist) [18]. In a humorous and light way, they explain that it is very easy to save money and environment by saving the energy in the first place. Apart of their commentary, announcements also show people that present desirable behaviors [19]. The slogan for this ad is "Turn off power, turn on savings".
Both PSAs were chosen for the analysis in the experiment because they share some similarities (topic, aim, light and humorous appeal). Conducted research procedure with the use of cognitive neuroscience techniques will aim to answer the question, which of them was more effective in the terms of inducing memorization, interest and emotions among the viewers and how the neuroscience techniques can contribute to the PSAs assessment.
To achieve the objective formulated in the paper, research procedure consisting of four main steps was conducted. This involved recruiting the participants, performing the recordings of their neurophysiological signals and questionnaire answers, data pre-processing and analysis. Details of the procedure and methods used to conduct it are presented in the following subsections.
Subjects that took part in the experiment watched a 30-minutes movie. It was a popular science documentary with two commercial breaks. Each interruption was formed by six commercial video clips of 30'' or 60'' length. Among the commercial ads, two public service announcements concerning energy saving were placed. During the video the electroencephalographic (EEG), heart rate (HR), and galvanic skin response (GSR) were collected from the subjects. After watching, participants took part in a questionnaire regarding the content they have just seen. At this stage, the experimenter asked the subjects to recall spontaneously the video clips that they memorized. Then, the experimenter verbally listed the sequence of advertisements presented within the documentary asking the subjects to tell which advertisement they remember. Successively, the researcher showed on a paper several frame sequences of each advertisement inserted in the movie. During these two stages, the experimenter also presented several names

---

and pictures related to advertisements that were not inserted in the commercial break (distractors). Finally, the experimenter asked subjects to give a score ranging between 1 and 10 according to the level of appreciation they perceived during the observation of each remembered ad (1 – lowly pleasant; 5 – indifferent; 10 – highly pleasant).

Participants of the experiment were recruited via word of mouth. Tests were conducted for a group of 29 persons, which is the common sample for neuroscience research [20]. Participants were from 19 to 51 years old. The mean age was 29.38 (±10.67). All participants (except one person) were right-handed. The sample consisted of 14 women and 15 men. Informed consent, which was approved by the local institutional ethics committee, was obtained from each subject after explanation of the study.

The cerebral activity was recorded with the use of g.Nautilus device with the sampling rate of 500 Hz. For the needs of the examination, electrodes have been installed on the scalp in compliance with the guidelines of the 10-20 system [21]. In the area of the frontal part of the frontal lobe only 7 electrodes were taken into consideration (Fp1, Fp2, F7, F3, Fz, F4 and F8). The EEG signals have been band pass filtered to remove data with frequencies below 0.4 Hz and above 50 Hz [22]. Then, artefacts have been removed with the use of Blind Source Separation (BSS) technique. The main method which have been applied is wavelet Independent Component Analysis (wICA, [23]), which has been proven very useful for suppression of artefacts in EEG recordings, both in the time and frequency domains. By using discrete wavelet transformation (DWT) function, the signal for each channel have been decomposed into five different frequency bands (alpha, theta, beta, gamma and delta) depending on Daubechies 8 wavelet function [24]. These EEG traces have been then segmented to obtain the cerebral activity during the observation of the public service announcements and that associated with the documentary (baseline period). The HR and GSR were recorded with the Neurobit Optima 4 system with sampling rate of 10 Hz. The electrical cardiac activity was recorded from the left wrist of all subjects and skin conductance was registered by electrodes attached to the palmar side of the middle phalanges of the second and third fingers of the subject's non-dominant hand. Signals were then appropriately filtered [25, 26].

Taking into account the data recorded during the period without commercial stimuli (baseline), EEG, HR and GSR signals registered for two chosen PSAs were standardized using the Z-score. The standardized EEG, HR and GSR values were then used to compute three different indices: Memorization Index (MI), Approach-Withdrawal Index (AW) and Emotion Index (EI).

Memorization Index is established in compliance with the formula:

$$MI = \frac{1}{N_Q}\sum_{i \in Q} x_{\theta_i}^2(t) =$$
$$Average\ Power_{\theta_{left,frontal'}} \qquad (1)$$

where: x_{θ_i} represents the i-th EEG channel in the theta band that has been recorded from the left frontal lobe, Q is the set of left channels, N_Q represents its cardinality. The increase of the MI value is related to enhanced memorization [27, 28, 29].

Index of approach-withdrawal (AW) is calculated based on the formula:

$$AW = \frac{1}{N_P}\sum_{i \in P} x_{\alpha_i}^2(t) - \frac{1}{N_Q}\sum_{i \in Q} y_{\alpha_i}^2(t) =$$
$$Average\ Power_{\alpha_{right,frontal}} - \qquad (2)$$
$$Average\ Power_{\alpha_{left,frontal'}}$$

where: x_{α_i} and y_{α_i} represent the i-th EEG channel in the alpha band that have been recorded from the right and left frontal lobes, respectively, P and Q are the sets of right channels and left channels, N_P and N_Q represent their cardinality. The value of the AW index is related to the increase of interest, it drops together with the decrease of interest. The AW signal measured has been transformed and averaged in such a manner so as to obtain the averaged course [29, 30].

Emotional Index (EI) is established according to the dependency:

$$EI = 1 - \frac{\beta}{\pi}, \qquad (3)$$

where:

$$\beta = \begin{cases} \frac{3}{2}\pi + \pi - \vartheta & if\ GSR_Z \geq 0, HR_Z \leq 0, \\ \frac{\pi}{2} - \vartheta & otherwise. \end{cases} \qquad (4)$$

GSR_Z, HR_Z represent the Z-score variables of GSR and HR respectively; $\vartheta - arctan(GSR_Z, HR_Z)$. The angle β is defined in order to obtain the EI varying between [−1, 1]. According to the Eq. (3) and (4), negative and positive values of the EI are related to negative and positive emotions [29, 31, 32].

3. RESULTS

Memorization index (MI) was established for each second of the both advertising spots, for each of the participants of the experiment. Next, the averaged values for all the persons have been calculated. For Energa advertisement it is continuation of the research [33]. Figure 1 presents the chart of the averaged values of memorization index for Energa advertisement.

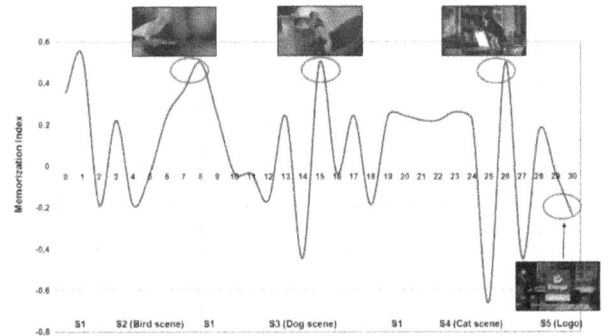

Figure 1. Averaged values of MI for Energa advertisement.

The signal reflecting the MI shows that three frames, in which the animals intend to or are about to switch off electrical devices were memorized in particular. The first substantial increase of the index value occurs for frames: 8 (the bird is switching off the TV set), 15 (the dog is climbing up the cabinet to turn off the light) and 26 (the cat is closing off the laptop). As it is depicted on the chart, the memorization index for frames showing the logo of the electricity supplier (Energa) is low, and that can make the advertiser be concerned as the intention of the company is to promote its brand.

Memorization index for the next advertisement, as shown in Figure 2, has only one main peak that indicates a scene especially remembered by the participants. It is the frame 15 showing a man asking his partner, if he should switch "everything" (all electronic devices) off. The curve of MI for this spot shows also that the frames presenting the slogan of the campaign: "Turn off power, turn on saving", have the lowest values of memorization. It could indicate that the message that is promoted is not "catchy" enough to be remembered.

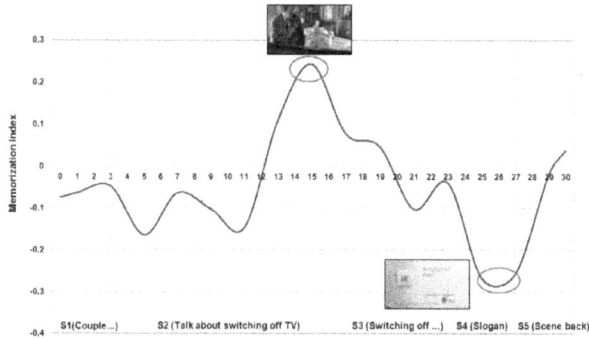

Figure 2. Averaged values of MI for "Turn off power, turn on savings" advertisement.

As the next step, the index of approach-withdrawal (AW) and its averaged value, was calculated for all participants of the experiment. Figure 3 presents values of AW for the Energa spot. Analyzing the signal shown of the chart one may conclude that while broadcasting the advert, the interest tendency of the viewers was slowly increasing. There were two main peaks on the chart regarding the AW value. The first occurred for frame 19, when the advertisement presents the shot of the dog switching off the light and the second one for frame 26 when the cat closes down the laptop is shown. From the next frame after this scene there is a clear decrease of the interest, that lasts till the presentation of the logo of the company.

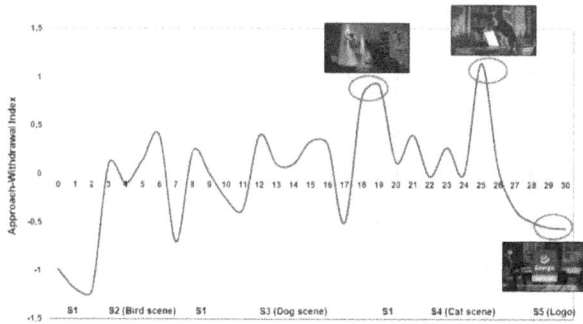

Figure 3. Averaged values of the AW index for Energa advertisement.

Figure 4 presents AW index curve for "Turn off power, turn on savings" advertisement. There are three frames in the signal that show particular interest of the participants. First peak occurs around frame 5 (woman requesting her partner to switch off the TV in standby mode). The second one, as in the case of MI, is concentrated around frames 15-17 (man asking his partner, if he should switch everything off). The highest value of AW index is induced during the scene that shows turning off the radiator (frame 23). This frame comes from a sequence of shots presenting different methods of saving the power. No other image presented in this context caused such interest. Moreover, the frame 19 (turning off the computer monitor) that is shown shortly before was found the least interesting of the whole advertisement.

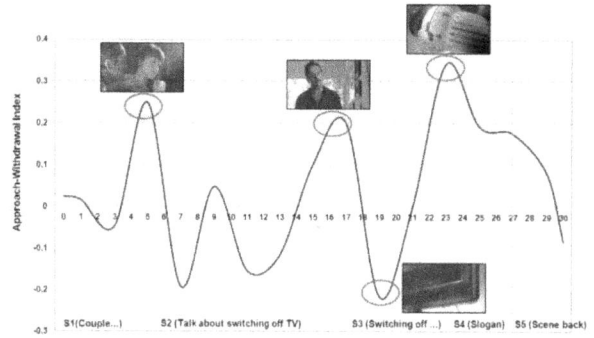

Figure 4. Averaged values of the AW index for "Turn off power, turn on savings" advertisement.

Moreover, emotions evoked by the advertising spots regarding energy saving were examined. The above mentioned was executed on the basis of registered GSR and HR signals. The GSR signal was standardized and it was analyzed for individual persons taking part in the study, together the averaged value. This signal for the Energa spot has been presented in Fig. 5.

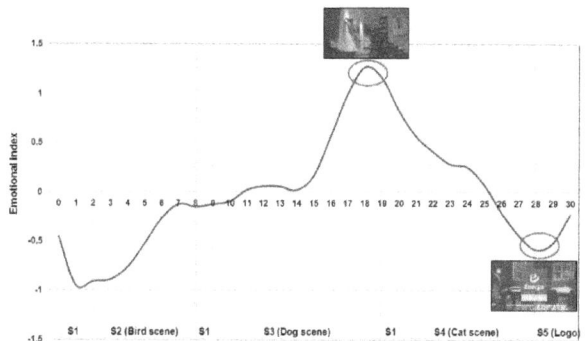

Figure 5. Averaged EI for Energa advertisement.

From the beginning of the advertising spot there was a slow growth in the value of the emotional index. The signal remained on more or less the same level between frames 7-14. These are scenes when the bird switches off the TV set, and then the dog gets out of bed and watches the lights tuned on. A substantial increase in the value of the signal appears with the scene when the dog switches of the light in frames 18-19. A further part of the ad demonstrates a significant decline in the value of the signal, with a short moment of its maintenance when the cat's approaching to the open laptop (frames 24-25). Remarkably, the last scene of the film (frames 28-29), in which the logo of the Energa company appears, demonstrates a relatively low value of the signal; however, it prevents the value from further decrease. On the basis of the analysis of the EI value one may conclude that the biggest emotions among experiment participants were evoked by the scene in which the dog stands on its hind legs and switches off the light. Similar behaviors of other animals did not induce such emotions, although the higher emotional level in such scenes was maintained for a while.

Emotion index curve for the second advertisement (Figure 6) shows the largest negative values at the beginning and at the end of the clip. These are the scenes (frames 1-3 and 28-30) suggesting light erotic overtone in relation between the couple starring in the spot. For other frames (4-28) EI oscillates around zero. Only two scenes generate a little bit higher peaks than the others: removing the phone charger from the socket (frame 22) and man asking, if he should switch everything off (frames 15-17).

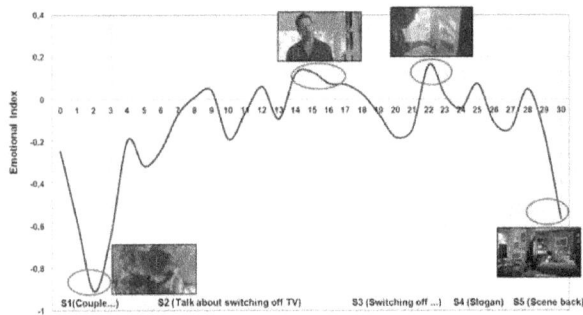

Figure 6. Averaged EI for "Turn off power, turn on savings" advertisement.

The analyses shown in Figures 1-6 present overall results for the whole advertisement, pointing out the most and least memorable, interesting and emotional scenes. Considering the purpose of such spots, which is mainly promoting the change in behavior of their recipients, further examination focuses on these parts of both advertisements that show desired actions. For the ads choses for this research these are the scenes in which one can observe switching off the electronic devices. In Energa advertisement these are frames: 7, 18 and 26. For "Turn off..." it is a sequence of frames from 18 to 23.

Figure 7 shows that in terms of interest and emotion greater effect was achieved for Energa scenes. Average memorization for this ad was at the lower level. It may suggest that that animals used in the Energa advertisement were slightly more effective in terms of evoking emotional response. It did not result in remembering of the spot better. A few short scenes showing desirable behaviors included in the "Turn off..." advertisement, perhaps due to their accumulation in one part of the clip, triggered stronger neuronal reaction connected with memory.

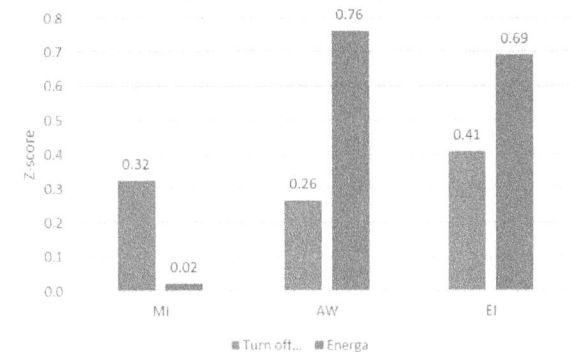

Figure 7. Average Z-score for chosen scenes (indices: MI, AW and EI).

Despite the observed inequality of results, conducted T-tests showed that there is no statistically significant difference between the mean values of indices for both commercials' scenes.

The presentation of experimental stimulus was followed by the questionnaire that was created to collect the responses about the advertisements' recall and appreciation. This part of the research was conducted in order to check, if there will be difference between the conscious replies of the subjects and their psychophysiological reactions. As mentioned before, for the questionnaire, participants responded to three questions concerning spontaneous and aided recall of advertisements. They had an opportunity to express their appreciation for the ads in terms of 1 to 10 scale assessment.

When it comes to spontaneous recall, only 4 people out of 29 (13.8%) remembered examined ads (both of them, there were no such cases, that a person memorized only one advertisement of interest). The participants that spontaneously recalled these spots, have memorized mostly the topic of social campaign (saving the energy). They haven't paid attention to the fact, who was responsible for emitting the ads (only one person has mentioned Energa) and to the slogan that was used for promoting the idea. When it comes to the recall of the plot, they have referred only to the "Turn off power, turn on saving" advertisement in more detailed manner (2 out of 4 subjects remembered a couple discussing the need of saving). Aided recall with the use of stills taken from the PSAs gave the same results: both ads were recalled by 19 persons out of 29 (65%).

Appreciation assessment given by the subject was normalized (Z-score for every person was computed) and the average value for whole group of participants was calculated. Conducted T-tests showed that there is no significant difference in the scores for Energa (M = 0,0683; S = 1.0407) and for "Turn off..." (M = -0.1315; S = 0.9405) advertisements; t = 0.3744, p = 0.7103.

4. CONCLUSIONS

Obtained results show that both public service announcements are comparable in terms of their perceived reception. It was both seen in the questionnaires and in neurophysiological data. Conducted experiment has not exactly shown which elements could be particularly effective in PSAs promoting energy saving. But it allowed to determine which parts of both PSAs induced some greater mental processing. In any questionnaire filled by the participants of the research this was not revealed.

The study was intended mainly to show what are the possibilities of using the cognitive neuroscience techniques in studying the effectiveness of environmental public service announcements. There is plenty of possibilities how the experiment can be enriched in order to give researchers and decision makers more valuable results that will allow for improving the message addressed to the recipients. Better results could be obtained for example by increasing the size of the subjects' group and introducing additional experimental variables (sex, age, self- or non-payment of energy bills, etc.) as it was done for example in [34, 35].

Interesting outcomes could be obtained in case of testing PSAs that have not been yet launched for the public, because the assumption that neuroimaging data would give a more accurate indication of the underlying preferences than standard market research studies may be really useful avoiding expensive mistakes. If this is indeed the case, advertising concepts could be tested rapidly, and those that are not promising were eliminated early in the process. This would allow more efficient allocation of resources to develop public service announcements that could have the greatest impact on audience.

5. FUNDING

The project was financed with the National Science Centre funds allocated according to the decision DEC-2016/21/B/HS4/03036

6. REFERENCES

[1] P. Shukla, **Essentials of marketing research**, Bookboon, 2008.

[2] S.M. Smith, G.S. Albaum, **An introduction to marketing research**, Qualtrics, 2010.

[3] M Lindstrom, Buyology: **Truth and Lies About Why We Buy**, New York: Doubleday, 2008.

[4] R. Ohme, M. Matukin, B. Pacula-Leśniak, "Biometric Measures for Interactive Advertising Research", **Journal of Interactive Advertising**, Vol 11, No. 2, 2010, pp. 60-72.

[5] D. Ariely, G.S. Berns, "Neuromarketing: the hope and hype of neuroimaging in business", **Nature Reviews Neuroscience**, Vol. 11, 2010, pp. 284–292.

[6] G. Calvert, M. Brammer, "Predicting consumer behavior: using novel mind-reading approaches", **IEEE Pulse**, Vol. 3, No. 3, 2012, pp. 38–41.

[7] G. Zaltman, **How Customers Think: Essential Insights into the Mind of the Market**, Harvard Business School Press, 2003.

[8] C.E. Fischer, L. Chin, R. Klitzman, "Defining Neuromarketing: Practices and Professional Challenges", **Harvard Review of Psychiatry**, Vol. 18, No. 4, 2010, pp. 230-237.

[9] L. Zurawicki, **Neuromarketing: Exploring the Brain of the Consumer**, Berlin Heidelberg: Springer-Verlag, 2010.

[10] C. Morin, "Neuromarketing: The New Science of Consumer Behavior", **Society**, Vol. 48, No. 2, 2010, pp. 131-135.

[11] S. Agarwal, T. Dutta, "Neuromarketing and consumer neuroscience: current understanding and the way forward", **Decision**,Vol. 42, No. 4, 2015, pp. 457–462.

[12] J. Zelinková et al., "An evaluation of traffic-awareness campaign videos: empathy induction is associated with brain function within superior temporal sulcus, **Behavioral and Brain Functions**, 2014, pp. 10-27.

[13] M. Mauri, A. Ciceri, G. Songa, F. Sirca, F. Onorati, V. Russo, "The effects of social communication: a research study on neuroscientific techniques application", **Proceedings of International Conference Measuring Behavior**, Wageningen, The Netherlands, August 27-29, 2014.

[14] E.B. Falk et al., "Functional brain imaging predicts public health campaign success", **Social Cognitive and Affective Neuroscience**, 2015, pp. 1-11.

[15] E. Csobod, M. Grätz, P. Szuppinger, "Overview and Analysis of Public Awareness Raising Strategies and Actions on Energy Savings" **INTENSE Project**, 2009. Available online: http://www.intense-energy.eu/uploads/tx_triedownloads/INTENSE_WP6_D6 1_final.pdf (accessed on 01 April 2018).

[16] Wirtualne media. Available online: https://www.wirtualnemedia.pl/artykul/po-prostu-wlacz-zwierzeta-w-kampanii-grupy-energa-wideo (accessed on 01 April 2018) [in Polish].

[17] Portal polskiej reklamy wizualnej. Available online: https://www.signs.pl/nagroda-ktr-dla-kampanii-Energa.-po-prostu-wlacz,18579,artykul.html (accessed on 01 April 2018) [in Polish].

[18] Środowisko. Available online: https://www.srodowisko.pl/wiadomosci-i-komunikaty/wlaczamy-oszczedzanie-58473-10 (accessed on 01 April 2018) [in Polish].

[19] Konkurs Kampania Społeczna Roku. Available online: http://konkurs.kampaniespoleczne.pl/kk_kampanie.php?e dycja=2012&kk_id=470&action=szczegoly (accessed on 01 April 2018) [in Polish].

[20] H. Plassmann, V. Venkatraman, S. Huettel, C. Yoon, "Consumer neuroscience: Applications, challenges, and possible solutions", **Journal of Marketing Research**, Vol. 52.4, 2015, pp. 427-435.

[21] P. Jaśkowski, **Neuronauka poznawcza. Jak mózg tworzy umysł**, Warszawa: Vizja Press, 2009 [in Polish].

[22] J.B. Nitschke, G.A. Miller, E.W Cook, "Digital filtering in EEG/ERP analysis: Some technical and empirical comparisons", **Behavior Research Methods, Instruments, & Computers**, Vol. 30, No. 1, 1998pp. 54–67.

[23] N.P. Castellanos, V.A. Makarov, "Recovering EEG brain signals: artefact suppression with wavelet enhanced independent component analysis", **Journal of Neuroscience Methods**, Vol. 158, No. 2, 2006, pp. 300–312.

[24] M. Murugappan, R. Nagarajan, S. Yaacob, "Discrete Wavelet Transform Based Selection of Salient EEG Frequency Band for Assessing Human Emotions", In: **Discrete Wavelet Transforms-Biomedical Applications**, InTech., 2011.

[25] G.G. Berntson et al., "Heart rate variability: origins, methods, and interpretive caveats", **Psychophysiology**, Vol. 34, 1997, pp. 623–648.

[26] W. Boucsein, **Electrodermal activity**, Springer Science & Business Media, 2012.

[27] M. Werkle-Bergner, V. Muller, S. Li, U. Lindenberger, "Cortical EEG correlates of successful memory encoding: implications for lifespan comparisons" **Neuroscience and Biobehavioral Reviews**, Vol. 30, No. 6, 2006, pp. 839–854.

[28] C. Summerfield, J.A. Mangels, "Coherent theta-band EEG activity predicts item-context binding during encoding", **NeuroImage**, Vol. 24, No. 3, 2005, pp. 692–703.

[29] G. Vecchiato et al. "Neurophysiological Tools to Investigate Consumer's Gender Differences during the Observation of TV Commercials", **Computational and Mathematical Methods in Medicine** 2014.

[30] R.J Davidson, "What does the prefrontal cortex 'do' in affect: perspectives on frontal EEG asymmetry research", **Biological Psychology**, Vol. 67, No. 1-2, 2004, pp. 219–233.

[31] L. Astolfi et al., "Neural basis for brain responses to TV commercials: a high-resolution EEG study**", IEEE Transactions on Neural Systems and Rehabilitation Engineering**, Vol. 16, No. 6, 2008, pp. 522–531.

[32] I.B. Mauss, M.D. Robinson, "Measures of emotion: a review", **Cognition and Emotion**, Vol. 23, No. 2, 2009, pp. 209–237.

[33] M. Piwowarski. "Cognitive Neuroscience Techniques in Examining the Effectiveness of Social Advertisements", In: **Neuroeconomic and Behavioral Aspects of Decision Making, Proceedings of the 2016 Computational Methods in Experimental Economics,** Springer Proceedings in Business and Economic, 2017, pp. 341-352.

[34] G. Cartocci et al., "Neurophysiological measures of the perception of antismoking public service announcements among young population", **Frontiers in human neuroscience**, Vol. 12, 2018, p. 231.

[35] G. Cartocci et al., "Antismoking Campaigns' Perception and Gender Differences: A Comparison among EEG Indices", **Computational Intelligence and Neuroscience**, Vol. 2019, 2019.

Holistic Development of Undergraduate Students – Concept Cartoons to Authentic Discovery

Kausik S. Das[1*], Larry Gonick[2], Monica Mitchell[3], Charles G Baldwin[4] and Moses Kairo[1]

[1]Department of Natural Sciences, University of Maryland Eastern Shore
Princess Anne, MD 21853

[2]247 Missouri Street, San Francisco, CA, 94107

[3]MERAssociates LLC, 8000 Towers Crescent Drive, Vienna, VA 22182

[4]Deapartment of Education, University of Maryland Eastern Shore,
Princess Anne, MD 21853

*Corresponding author: kdas@umes.edu

ABSTRACT

This paper describes a holistic pedagogical approach for classroom engagement. The project translates theory and fundamental classroom knowledge to authentic application with cutting edge research implemented by undergraduates at a Historically Black University. In our project, we developed and assessed cartoons custom designed for classroom instruction and evaluated student engagement while using the cartoons. We further report on student successes achieved through undergraduate research projects.

Keywords: custom cartoons, student engagement, undergraduate research

INTRODUCTION

This paper discusses the first year results of the Targeted Infusion Project (UMES-TIP) at the University of Maryland Eastern Shore (UMES) funded by the National Science Foundation (NSF). There are five aspects to the UMES-TIP project to be evaluated, but only two aspects served as the evaluative focus in the first year of implementation during the 2017-2018 academic year. First, the project developed and cartoons custom designed for the project, assessed student views regarding the cartoons and evaluated student engagement with the cartoons. Second, the project looked at the first year success of an undergraduate research requirement.

If the United States is to retain its historical prominence in science and technology, this nation must produce more science, technology, engineering and mathematics (STEM) graduates. Towards this end, the President's Council of Advisors on Science and Technology has called for a 33% increase in STEM majors per year (1). Unfortunately, of the approximately 300,000 students who enter college annually to pursue STEM majors, only 40% complete a STEM degree. Moreover, we need the increased participation of underrepresented populations (e.g. blacks and Latinos) in STEM fields as they are less likely to pursue STEM degrees than their majority counterparts.

The UMES-TIP grant enables UMES to respond to these urgent STEM needs by introducing innovative teaching methods tailored to the needs of Historically Black Colleges and Universities (HBCU) students to advance a rigorous, state-of-the-art STEM curriculum in physics. The UMES-TIP project targets student engagement in physics. The goals of the project are to improve student learning in physics and to increase student retention. Supporting these goals are five objectives: 1) increase student interactions through group learning, 2) better align labs and lecture content, 3) develop physics cartoons which elucidate key physics concepts, 4) utilize physics cartoons with classroom clickers and 5) implement a senior year research project. This paper discusses the first year results addressing objectives three and five.

Background and Context

UMES is a historically black university and the 1890 Land Grant Institution for the State of Maryland, centrally located on the Delmarva Peninsula. It accepts approximately half of the undergraduate applicants each year. In the fall of 2015, the median SAT score of all entering first-time undergraduates was 861 (50%=840, 75%=920), and the average high school GPA was 2.78. Based upon quantitative admissions criteria, UMES is regarded as among the least selective institutions of higher education (IHE) within the University of Maryland system. Undergraduate first-time, full-time second year retention has varied between 64% and 71% over the past ten years.

Physics courses are taught within UMES's Department of Natural Sciences (DNS). In the fall 2015, DNS was home to 522 undergraduate majors in Chemistry, Biology, Biochemistry and Environmental Sciences and 48 graduate students. At that time, 61% of DNS undergraduate students were African American as were 37% of the graduate students. Typically, 48% of all undergraduates receive Pell Grants.

Theoretical Framework

The President's Council of Advisors on Science and Technology (2012) claims high performing students frequently switch majors because of uninspiring introductory courses. Many students, particularly underrepresented minority students, cite an unwelcoming atmosphere created by STEM faculty as a reason for their attrition (2).

Recently, Wanzer et al. (3) advanced the instructional humor processing theory (IHPT), an integrative theory that draws from the elaboration likelihood model of persuasion (4). For humor to facilitate learning, the IHPT asserts that students need to do two things; first perceive and second resolve the incongruity in a humorous instructional message. The IHPT proposes that the recognition of humor will increase students' attention. Wanzer et al. (3) concluded that the humor related to course content may increase learner motivation and his/her ability to process messages. Further, the researchers found relevant humor does not distract from the instructional message. Humor reinforces learning by making the information more memorable and positively affects levels of attention and interest. Appropriate humor positively influences learners' affective responses (5). However, using humor to support learning has its challenges. Finding high quality cartoonists with sufficient artistic skills and in-depth knowledge of STEM disciplinary content difficult. Consequently, this obstacle has likely restricted the use of cartoon associated humor in science classrooms. As an additional challenge, one of the first author's experiences at UMES suggests that many students struggle to visualize word problems; this, in turn, confounds students who lose interest in the material and/or become lost within the content. Preliminary data from an unpublished pilot study indicated that in a class of 30 students, only two students attempted to answer a question. We believe the low response rate stems from the students' failure to visualize the problem. Yet the same question combined with a supporting cartoon created a clear picture of the scenario. The cartoon humorously depicting a physics problem created interest and fomented discussion.

Our preliminary results suggest that the students see themselves within the context of the practice questions and that stimulates enthusiasm and class engagement. We believe the cartoon supports students' visualization of the question and the students are better prepared to engage a conceptual difficulty concept and are more likely to develop a correct response.

Cartoon Use in STEM Undergraduate Education

Several lines of research show the potential of cartoons in science education. Naylor and Keogh (6) developed, evaluated, and refined the use of concept cartoons as an engagement tool for STEM students. They have also found that the concept cartoon approach minimizes classroom management problems by promoting focused discussion and student motivation (7). Chin et. al. and Ekici et. al. report that teaching via concept cartoons enhances conceptual

understanding by clarifying misconceptions and motivating students (8, 9). Additionally, several aspects of concept cartoons make them relevant to promoting argumentation in science courses (10).

METHODS

Cartoons

The project affiliated cartoonist created 30 cartoons which illustrated concepts central to the fundamental laws of motion. These cartoons were developed over an exploratory phase, where the Principal Investigator (PI) and the cartoonist worked together in an iterative process to assure the successful and conceptually accurate development of cartoon content. They then used the first year to collect data on initial perceptions and feedback on cartoon use from students enrolled in introductory physics courses.

The PI introduced cartoons in three physics courses during the 2017-2018 academic year: General Physics I – Mechanics and Particle Dynamics, Introductory Physics II, and General Physics III – Electrodynamics, Light Relativity and Modern Physics. Sixty-three undergraduate students were enrolled in these three courses and were taught with the use of the cartoons. By introducing the cartoons in three courses, the PI was able to explore the use of cartoons with a cross-section of students which in turn allowed for a refining of the cartoons and their subsequent use in different courses.

18. Usha swings on a vine hanging from point O. As she swings through point A, consider four possible forces:

1. A downward force of gravity
2. A force in the direction of Usha's motion
3. A force exerted by the rope pointing from A to O
4. A force pointing from O to A

Which of those forces is (are) acting on Usha at point A?

A) 1 only
B) 1 and 2
C) 1 and 3
D) 1, 2, and 3
E) 1, 2, and 4

Table 1. Cartoon Assessment Student Survey: Assessment Domains and Corresponding Survey Items

Student Learning Domain	Student Affect Domain	Coherent Presentation Domain	Appropriate Design Domain
The cartoons help in showing the concepts we are learning in class.	The cartoons engage my interest in learning physics.	The cartoons are easy to understand.	The humor in the cartoons is appropriate.
The cartoons help me better understand concepts in the course.	I enjoy answering the cartoon questions.	The language used in the cartoon is easy to understand.	Cartoon pictures are easy to understand.
The cartoons help me remember the material taught in class.	I like using the cartoons to help me learn physics.	The questions are clearly stated.	The cartoons are culturally appropriate.

Table 2 Cartoon Survey Items: Ranking by Mean Score

Survey Item	μ	SD
The humor in the cartoon is appropriate.	3.00	0.00
The cartoons are culturally responsive.	3.00	0.00
The cartoons engage my interest in learning physics.	2.96	0.19
I like using the cartoons to help me learn physics.	2.96	0.19
The cartoons help in showing the concepts we are learning in class.	2.93	0.26
Cartoon pictures are easy to understand.	2.93	0.38
The language of the cartoons is easy to understand.	2.89	0.31
The cartoons help me remember the material taught in class.	2.89	0.42
The cartoons are easy to understand.	2.86	0.45
The questions are clearly stated.	2.82	0.48
I enjoy answering the cartoon questions.	2.81	0.48
The cartoons help me better understand the concepts in the course.	2.79	0.51

The project developed a cartoon assessment survey to collect students' perception on the use of cartoons in their physics courses. The survey examined four domains: student learning, student affect, coherent presentation, and appropriateness of design. Student respondents used a three-point Likert scale (1 – disagree, 2 – neither agree nor disagree, 3 – agree) on survey items in each of the four assessment domains. See table 1 for all survey items.

Undergraduate Research

During the 2017-2018 academic year, the project provided 30 students with undergraduate research experiences, of which, 13 participated for the entire academic year. Seven additional students participated as part of their independent studies in the Physics III lab.

The project administered an online version of the NSF-funded Undergraduate Research Student Self-Assessment (URSSA) survey instrument to collect data on students' experience with the undergraduate research experiences. Eleven of the 13 STEM students who participated in undergraduate research for the full academic year responded to the online survey (69.2% response rate). Most of the respondents were engineering majors, followed by two chemistry majors and one biology major. Only two respondents were female students.

Four core constructs of the URSSA establish acceptable subscale reliability (14). These constructs describe the extent to which students experienced increased cognitive skills and affective learning. The constructs and associated reliability include: thinking

and working like a scientist – $0.88 \leq \alpha \leq 0.90$; personal gains – $0.90 \leq \alpha \leq 0.91$; (research) skills – $0.91 \leq \alpha \leq 0.92$; and (research) attitudes and behaviors – $0.83 \leq \alpha \leq 0.84$.

RESULTS

During the spring 2018 term of exploratory implementation, students enrolled in (PHYS161) took the cartoon assessment survey towards the end of the semester. Twenty-one of the 61 (34%) total

students introduced to the physics cartoons in the spring 2018 semester completed the survey. The cartoons received an overall mean rating of 2.65 (SD = .13), which indicates positive student feedback on the use of the cartoons in physics instruction. Among the survey constructs, students rated the appropriateness of the design of the cartoons the highest with a 2.76 mean (SD = .12), followed by student learning, coherent presentation, and student affect with respective 2.68 (SD = .15), 2.63 (SD = .12), and 2.53 (SD = .05) means (See Figure 1). The high ratings on the appropriate design domain are particularly important since this subscale measures students' perception of the cultural appropriateness of the cartoons. Given the HBCU context and the focus of the project on broadening STEM participation of underrepresented minority students, explicit attention in the cartoon design was given to reflect diverse representation in characters and subject matter to avoid demeaning and disparaging stereotypes. In fact, the survey item asking if "the cartoons are culturally appropriate" had the highest mean score, $M = 2.9$:

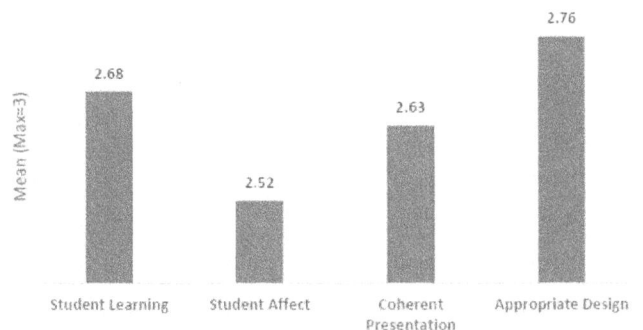

Figure 1. Student Cartoon Assessment - Exploratory Phase

Students also rated the cartoons highly for their contribution to student learning. The second highest-rated survey item, $M = 2.81$, indicates the extent to which the cartoons elucidate physics concepts: "The cartoons help in showing the concepts we are learning in class." After physics content, the next highest rated survey item, $M = 2.76$, focused on the difficulty level of the language used in the cartoons: "The language used in the cartoons is easy to understand." The fifth highest mean score, $M = 2.71$, corresponded to two survey items. One on student learning focused on content retention: "The cartoons help me remember the material taught in class," and the other focused on the humor associated with the cartoons: "The humor in the cartoons is appropriate."

Undergraduate Research Experience

Students responses on the URSSA instrument assessed the extent to which they made individual gains in undergraduate research based on their response to each survey item on a five-point Likert scale where 1 = no gain and 5 = great gain. As shown in Figure 2, students reported experiencing considerable gains in each of four core areas. Students experienced the greatest growth in personal gains (e.g., developing patience with the slow pace of research), followed by gains in their attitudes and behaviors (e.g., feel a part of a scientific community), and finally, experiencing equal gain in research skills (e.g., keeping a detailed lab notebook), and in thinking and working like a scientist (e.g., understanding the theory and concepts guiding my research projects.) Interestingly, female students experienced greater gains in all four core areas than their male counterparts. However, this finding is viewed with caution given the small sample size.

Figure 2. Student Growth: Undergraduate Research

Students were asked about the motivations behind their desire to participate in undergraduate research. The leading reasons included: to explore their interest in science, to gain hands-on experience in research, to clarify whether to pursue scientific research as a career, for the intellectual challenge, and to work more closely with the PI. In fact, students rated the research mentoring from the PI very highly (4.4), as well as the nature of the research (4.4), and the culture of working with other students on the research team (4.5). Students attributed the high quality of the research experience to the project PI as represented in the following comments from two different students. A pseudonym is used in reference to the individual mentioned within the quote below.

My professor Dr. Smith personally asked me to do research. He is single-handedly the greatest professor I have very had and I knew I couldn't give up this opportunity. (Male Engineering Major)
Excellence advice from my mentor and the great sense of doing work as a researcher. (Male Engineering Major)

Students reported that the undergraduate research experience also positively impacted the likelihood of whether they will pursue STEM pathways. Among the STEM pathway options, 50% of the respondents reported that they are extremely more likely to enroll in a Master's program in STEM. The majority are much more likely to enroll in a joint MD/PhD program (62.5%), a Masters program in STEM (62.5%), and a PhD program in STEM (50%). As a caveat, these students likely possessed an interest in scientific research prior to the undergraduate research experience, but the project heightened their interest in pursuing graduate STEM programs. The following student comments capture the direct influence of the research experience on prospective STEM pathways.

My research has been the foundation of my entire undergraduate experience. It has greatly help[ed] me put my life into perspective and help[ed] me determine what I want to do in my future career. (Male Engineering Major)

It made me really consider grad school and I was intrigued by my new found knowledge. (Female Engineering Major)

My research experience opened my eyes as graduate school actually is and how it feels to doing research. I decided to go to graduate school after being involve[ed] in research projects. (Male Engineering Major)

Students had few comments on improving the undergraduate research experiences. The suggestions included having the opportunity to receive a stipend instead of or in addition to one academic credit, more time to do the research in the lab, and the opportunity to attend more conferences. One student said, "It's pretty great the way it is."
The prolific dissemination of manuscripts, posters and conference presentations indicates the robust nature of the research component with undergraduates. The level of scholarly activity in collaboration with students is an important strength of the project in its first year of implementation.

DISCUSSION AND CONCLUSION
Cartoons
This study examined cartoon development and implementation in the project's first year. The study found that the 30 physics cartoons are culturally-responsive, represent high quality in design and presentation, and amenable to improve student learning and student affect. Additionally, the high rating for the question asking about cultural appropriateness indicates that the cultural relevance and

sensitivity of the cartoons are in alignment with the HBCU context of educating underrepresented minority students.

Undergraduate Research

The project successfully provided undergraduate research experiences to underrepresented minority students. While the project provided undergraduate research experiences to 30 students, the study focused on the experiences and results of the 13 students who worked directly with the PI outside of physics classes. The results from the survey on undergraduate research as reported by students (69.2% response rate) reveal positive student outcomes in cognitive and affective learning. Considerable personal growth was seen in students (e.g., developing patience with the slow pace of research), attitudes and behaviors (e.g., feel a part of a scientific community), research skills (e.g., keeping a detailed lab notebook), and thinking and working like a scientist (e.g., understanding the theory and concepts guiding my research projects). Female students experienced greater gains than their male counterparts. However, this finding is viewed with caution given the small sample size.

In addition to the student growth in cognitive and affective learning seen in the first year of implementation, the undergraduate research experience also positively influenced student interest in graduate study in STEM. Several students credited the PI for the self-realization to pursue STEM pathways at the graduate level. The involvement of undergraduate students in the robust level of scholarly activity and dissemination will serve them well in graduate school readiness and preparedness. Gender differences will continue to be examined as the project moves forward in its second year.

ACKNOWLEDGEMENT

This work was partially supported by the National Science Foundation (HBCU-UP Award #1719425) and the Department of Education (MSEIP Award #P120A70068).

REFERENCES

[1] Olson, S., & Riordan, D. G. (2012). Engage to Excel: Producing One Million Additional College Graduates with Degrees in Science, Technology, Engineering, and Mathematics. Report to the President. **Executive Office of the President**

[2] Plourde, P. M. (2016). Increasing STEM degree attainment for underrepresented populations. **Ph. D. Thesis.** Northeastern University.

[3] Wanzer, M. B., Frymier, A. B., & Irwin, J. (2010). An explanation of the relationship between instructor humor and student learning: Instructional humor processing theory. **Communication Education**, 59(1), 1-18.

[4] Cacioppo, J. T., & Petty, R. E. (1986). The elaboration likelihood model of persuasion. **Communication and persuasion,** Springer, New York, NY, 1-24.

[5] Chabeli, M. (2008). "Humor: A pedagogical tool to promote learning." **Curationis**, 31(3), 51-59.

[6] Naylor, S., & Keogh, B. (2013). Concept Cartoons: what have we learnt? **Journal of Turkish Science Education**, *10*(1).

[7] Keogh, B., & Naylor S. (1999). Concept cartoons, teaching and learning in science: an evaluation. **International Journal of Science Education,** 21(4), 431-446.

[8] Chin, C., & Teou, L. Y. (2009). Using concept cartoons in formative assessment: Scaffolding students' argumentation. **International Journal of Science Education**, 31(10), 1307-1332

[9] Ekici, F., Ekici, E., & Aydin, F. (2007). Utility of Concept Cartoons in Diagnosing and Overcoming Misconceptions Related to Photosynthesis. **International Journal of Environmental and Science Education**, *2*(4), 111-124.

[10] Weston, T. J., & Laursen, S. L. (2015). The Undergraduate Research Student Self-Assessment (URSSA): validation for use in program evaluation. **CBE—Life Sciences Education**, 14(3), ar33.

The Outlines of an Art Machine

Tirtha Prasad MUKHOPADHYAY
Department of Art and Management, Universidad de Guanajuato
Salamanca, 36885, Mexico

Victor Hugo JIMENEZ
Department of Art and Management, Universidad de Guanajuato
Salamanca, 36885, Mexico

ABSTRACT

In this paper we propose to examine the cognitive aspects of artistic creation. Art objects are supposed to elicit emotional responses in the viewer. Behavior related to the making of art objects are analysed. Both visual art and artistic verbal expressions are considered for analysis. Emotional appraisal is claimed to be indispensable to artistic creativity, as opposed to appraisal objectives in design cognition where structural variation and the resulting innovations produced could well be emotively neutral in their appearance. The authors propose a heuristic and connective-functionalist thesis of machine art following identification of responsive elements for art as they are laid down in precepts of different philosophical traditions. The insights deriving from ancient and contemporary traditions demonstrate that innovative variation in art presupposes the presence of a set of corresponding variations in visual patterns or linguistic expressions that typify a range of expectations for target objects. A database of categorically defined 'genre' of art should exhibit visual or verbal preferences in interactions. Binary operations may be domain specific depending on the kind of art that is under scrutiny, but from a philosophical perspective, emotional representation must be assumed to be indispensable across generic requirements.

Keywords: Art, Cognition, Emotion, Connectionism, Functionalism, Heuristics

1. INTRODUCTION

How could we describe cognitive behaviors that regulate the making of art works, especifically within the domain of arts disciplines, like painting or sculpture, or as it may appear in more contemporary expressions like illustrations and videos, as much as it occurs in all the new media arts. We may also consider the literary arts, involving verbal expression, as a means of artistic innovation where human language acts as a medium of innovations. We could also, more importantly, think of 'art' broadly, as a generic activity and hope to isolate its tokens from other processes that have innovation as a key element of motivation. Of course, artistic processes quite evidently involve representations that are visible in innovative functions of complex systems. Simon (1988) explains that the search for innovation is an intrinsic behavioral tendency for human beings and that, as such, it drives creative people to produce more and more complex representational systems [1]. But much less has been stated about the extra-representational aspects of the 'arts', namely, its affective demands on the spectator. Even though arts are recognized as an important social or cultural activity where innovations determine the end-product and the success of consumption, there is no dedicated discussion on how the arts should function for human observers. Efland refers to the uneasy connection that exists between arts and psychology and makes a case in favor of integrating visual arts in the curriculum of cognitive sciences [2].

In this context we wish to ask if 'artistic cognition', like in its associated discipline, 'design cognition', should also function like a modular process within our neural systems, just as Taylor explained all creative activity in terms of empirical psychology [3]. The notion of modularity emerged later in the writings of Jerry Fodor [4]. Further, a computational acount of 'artistic cognition', distinct from 'design cognition' has not been explored in any detail. The closest study that helps us find some parallels is to be found in Visser's account of developments in design studies, in its turn towards more situative analyses of design processes [5]. We do acknowledge that certain studies explain how specific aspects of feedback behavior in design studies may be partially relevant to our understanding of artistic cognition but generally the arts have not been singularly identified as a unique cognitive process, not at least generically, and neither in terms of what we shall posit as the defining element in artistic cognition, namely as an emotive process.

2. FUNCTIONAL ADAPTATION

We could start by asking how the brain picks chunks of information and incorporates them in syntactic structures that are either 'visual' (as in case of visual formats like sketching or architectural planning) or 'aural' (as in case of music for instance). Methods of visual representation that involve cognitive priming and selection have been studied by Margolin and Buchanan (1995), Choueiri (2003) and Zainal Abidin and colleagues (2011): findings suggest that the design process involves 'conceptualization' of a problem and negotiating visual alternatives in a spiral of constant feedback [6]][7][8]. Experiments have been used to check whether the brain functions in pre-established circuits of information so as to generate anticipated results [9] [10]. The effect of novelty is produced by means of simultaneous matching and differentiation involving structural analogies with given objects. Now, design cognition provides insight into the ontology of simulated shapes and patterns, yet it also shows how the designer tends to adapt representations with emerging syntactical requirements. Some case studies indicate what in cognitive science we call 'functional' adaptation of design commands. Cognitive functionalism allows us to consider the nature of adaptive behavior that is crucial to planning and creation of innovative maps. Last but not the least, how human innovators make functional decisions may itself be a heuristic exercise. The theory that creativity or design actions should also utilize heuristic models is imperative [11]. Both functionalist as well as heuristic variations are intertwined in artistic solutions.

3. EMOTIVE TEMPLATES

Classic studies thus show that creativity arises out of improvisatory thinking on prexisting templates of information [12] - an idea that seems to provide a backbone for the splay of experiments on how design functions are realized in practice. Designers' decisions help in unfixating the mind from a prision of memory even as they have a mental stock of a very wide range of pre-existing structures of work. Expert innovators are constrained to use these former models for changes and adaptation in novel contexts so that free and ingenious forms of mimesis could emerge in the world. In this sense, 'art' constitutes a functional subdivision of design cognition since any artistic activity depends on improvisatory adaptation. But it would be wrong to classify artistic representations solely under the rubric of adaptive behaviours. We would refer towards an epistemological shift in our understanding of the arts since behavior that is specific to art inescapably comprises emotive triggers. This *a priori* distinction defines the exclusive nature of the arts.

Design cognition would have to involve emotions in order to qualify as artistic cognition. That design employs elements of emotive stimulus is evident for an entire range of products that occur in sports and design of animated games. Th potential for design emotions is already implicit in social media, commercials, and opinion analytics [13] but how would mood reinforcing games differ from emotional deep states typical to 'artistic' expression. Historically, the 'arts' are known to elicit strong or deep emotions involving human norms and transgressions. Thus, Plato said in *The Republic* that arts feed or water the passions. Classic texts of Eastern cultures say that art consists of emotive appraisal of histrionics, gestures or representations [14]. Greek theater uses emotive masks of facial and figural gesticulations that elicit specific classes of feelings in spectators – this is also wonderfully visible in the artistic masks of Japanese theater, like *noh* or *kabuki*. The origins of such emotive representations appear out of deeper evolutionary reflexes that the performer incarnates for the audiences' contemplation. Hence, we have stories of incest, death and survival, or the anxieties and frustrations of contemporary individualism in modern novels or films. Bharata the sixth century Indian aesthete suggests in the *Natyashastra* that arts have specific goals – and have their place only within goal-oriented behaviors [15]. Artistic cognition is something specific to arts-like improvisation rather than non-art design, since art creates emotive surge. Bharata also formulated a taxonomy of basic emotive states, and a taxonomy of secondary emotions which are triggered in the context of these spectator-oriented histrionics.

The effects of art may thus be examined in the context of artificial emotive systems. The question is no doubt tricky. Could we separate cognitive design from more emotively bracketed design acts that are intrinsic to art? Are not the boundaries blurred? We ask if in its extreme cases, is design cognition capable of being conditioned by independent emotive content just as proponents of autonomous emotive states like Zajonc predicted [16]? That for artistic cognition overbearing emotive appraisal is more imminent and necessary is not in doubt.

Design, in general, is emotively neutral, even though it may have a broader range of material or industrial application and even if it may need to satisfy a broader consumer base. At the same time it is important to understand that there can be no independent and formless emotive cognition - since the arts, by definition, employs aspects of design thinking in their pursuit of tradional historical forms and manifests, but what makes such manifests unique is the definite goal that it tries to achieve, namely its appraisal of emotive states or feelings involving all the basic passions.

4. COGNITION AND EMOTION

In what ways could we thus approach computational issues in artistic cognition? Standard approaches based on the AI paradigm, include a neural-network paradigm which is again subdivided when it comes to specific steps in the process, like memory and adaptation. We have a GOFAI approach to basic understanding of cognition as a systemic process [17]. Moreover, both neural networking thesis and GOFAI (Good Old Fashioned Artificial Inteligence) derive from the approach to understanding cognition in terms of "belief boxes". We would like to propose a theory of "emotion boxes" as part of that schema, wherever emotional appraisal is in focus. Hence, we could define the origin of emotions epigenetically in terms of a network of triggers and appraisals from which the artistic intentions would naturally fire and create all those super-moments that are valued in the traditional arts and rituals in all human societies.

Artistic cognition implicates a possibly dualistic or double-phase cognitive-emotive network. Antonio Damasio famously disapproved the erroneous attitude in neuroscientific psychology, namely the one of considering the so-called higher order cortical decision-making processes as being distinctly superior to subcortical emotional processes [18]. Indeed, this does not make sense in the context of recent findings based on MRI and PET scans of the brain during its more attentive problem-solving states. Artistic cognition invites cognitive science to reconnect cognition and emotion in one immanent network of rules that would integrate in *gestalt-like* clusters or moments: we could probably describe them as emotive quirks. The ancients had these ideas - Sanskrit aesthetics speaks of *anubhava* or *rasa* and *sadharanikaran*. Whereas the *anubhava* or *rasa* is a quantific experience or quirk of feeling, the latter, that is *sadharanikaran* (translated as 'collectivisation') dictates how artistic creations elicit not just personal but interpersonal states of feeling in collectives of spectators and could unite several or countless persons in a stream or timeline, such as occurs in cinema audiences, stadiums or performance venues, and responses in mass culture diasporas, like TV audiences spread across different contextual environments and spaces. It is one of the pre-conditions of artistic cognition that they can sweep and somatically involve participants or spectators in their modes of presentation. The Chinese notion of the *dao* is similarly a completely amodular state in its moments of revelation - *wu wei* means an action bereft of intentionality, in the sense that it is supraintentional, but at the individual level it may retain some kind of intentionality [19]. A quick translation would be like the meaning embodied in the phrase 'go with the flow'. The Chinese idea of non-intentionality however is primarily also emotionally viable.

5. THE SOMATIC MARKERS OF ART

Consider the foundation of emotive sciences as it is laid out by Antonio Damasio [20]. Damasio stridently divides the entire substratum of emotions - he speaks of the presence of basic emotions or primary emotions that are caused by excitability of the limbic system, which he calls innate emotions. Damasio also speaks of 'secondary' emotions or 'acquired' emotions that depend on how emotional receptors get activated by the primary emotions. The model has been conducive to the development of algorithms in reinforcement learning, which considers emotive levels in decision making processes [21]. Damasio also speaks of bodily manifests of emotions – the fact that we can understand emotions only as they are incarnated in the human body, as 'somatic markers' as he calls them. What the theory of somatic markers helps us in understanding is the way results of emotion-based decisions are projected on the human body or face, especially in situations involving interaction and adaptation between individuals or collectives. The paradigm, we suggest, is especially helpful for understanding design-like cognition but especifically artistic behaviors as they are manifestly visible in the representations of the bodies of painting or portraits for example.

We might think of instances from pre-historic rock art - in the visual systems on petroglyphs, in which visual stimuli create iconic effects resembling images of the body. One of the reactions, among others, that this kind of semiotics inspires, even for a viewer situated in a different or distant time and space, is the feeling that is elicited by the indexical power of the bodily gesture, like a dancing human or a human with raised arms. Peirce and Peircian semioticians would like to suggest that this visual power is an emotive tweak [22]. Creative effects illustrate improvisation on biomimetic iconography, like in the shapes of anthropomorphs or zoomorphs which appear repeatedly inside the *umwelt* of cave paintings. Bharata, the ancient Indian philosopher likewise speaks of an emotional substratum of basic states and defines the finer artistic emotions as products of interrelated stimuli generators. Damasio speaks of the art of comedians who induce realistic settings and gestural or facial incongruencies typical to comedy and involve both the performing subject and audience. Damasio's somatic markers are all visible in comic art, as well as tragic arts, which represent grief and fear. The performance space resembles the neural map of immersive and interactive secondary emotion environments.

Damasio's theory of emotional appraisal would lead us to believe that emotions are perceived on the body and then create feedback loops. This principle is exactly what reinforcement learning algorithm captures - in its episodes of programming which either generates a reward or a punishment, that is an accumulation or redaction of a 'reward' depending upon a decision that is made by an emoting agent. If this happens for emotions in general then it is obviously true for 'artistic cognition'. Creative decisions are naturally goal oriented [23]. If considered from a functionalist perspective, a creative task that is also artistic, will consider if the decisions also lead to greater emotive satisfaction in the end products of that flow chart.

6. INTENTIONALITY IN ART COGNITION

Thus, what do we learn from the ancients? What the ancients taught us, and what we also learn from Damasio's philosophy of emotion is simply this: creativity should be an organic, improvisatory process as much as a connectionist-functionalist (thai is, adaptative) episode. It is both adaptive and perhaps also non-intentionalist [24] [25]. Indeed, what about the most conservative question in relation to artistic *praxis* - as opposed to much of design thinking in contemporary discussions? Conservative opinion in cognition favors the subjective role of the artist but for a more functionalist definition art cognition starts with given templates from material culture and supports a

memory-based modularity of some sort. Even in very recent postmodern explanations which suggests the arts completely break down pre-existing rules and grammars, the role of the artist as an individual, intentional creator is not completely ignored. Can we accept this model of intentionality for the artistic process?

Gopnik and others have tried to demonstrate that first-person intentionality, similar to what we call 'authorial' intention, is constructed around age three and a half when children begin to develop insights into the so called transparent nature of object - and their "objectivity". Gopnik locates intentionality in the growing child's negotiations with a real world filled with objects and inter-objective relationships in a causal way [26]. Gopnik even goes to the extent of suggesting that intentionality is a direct result of the causality implicit in the child identification of construal and formation of objects in the real world [26]. This attitude solidifies into the subsequent concept of a first-person intentionality. Perhaps Gopnik shares, in principle, the same kind of connected perceptive environmental evolution of what Dennett calls the 'intentional stance', a human tendency to ascribe agency to objects and identities. In the history of arts societies have also in a sense upheld and deified the artist as an intentional entity. In case of assuming a theory behind artistic cognition we can consider the challenge posed to intentionality by a strictly computational view of artistic production. How could databases predict an artistic configuration? Is machine art ever going to happen? Is it not the same question as the robotic typewriter getting to be successful in ultimately writing a Shakespearean sonnet? While this is computationally feasible, let us look at the various hierarchies of interactions involved - in an example like of literary creativity.

7. METAPHOR

Something of this paradox can be explained in the example of the effect metaphor has on the human mind. We remember in this connection that metaphors, as Lakoff and Johnson showed are dependent on physically embodied actions. The "journey" metaphor: "Life is a journey", shows how journey is metaphorically linked to life, as an event laid out in time, just as all journey are. The journey metaphor captures the analogy of the interests and dangers of a real journey. The analogy holds for life as well with its sequence of shocks and surprises. Indeed, the semantic networks that activate these two different metaphorical experiences create an emotive effect because of the interplay between cognitively appraised experiences as well as emotional experience. The happiness associated with the journey through life, which is full of experiences is emotively equal in maps of both life and journey. From the computational standpoint the problem precisely lies in recognizing the moment in which parallels consummate an emotive quirk in the equivalences of these two separate cognitive maps. There is a certain degree of uniqueness in the intertwined narratives of the metaphor discussed here.

But again, in case of metaphors, we ask why is one set of analogy preferred over another? In any artistic engagement these interplays are crucial - the manner in which the tokens of experience are interchangeable and validated or valued. Like chunks in visual clusters, artistic moments will have to rest finally on whether the chunk turns into a quirk. Now more and more evidence suggest that such emotive analogies are heuristically apprised. There is a good deal of evidence to argue in favor of a heuristic art machine, since the arts involve long and complex acculturation with chunks of experience but in practical engaement all associations are rendered into an emotive channel very rapidly. It turns out that a word may be used in an emotive way - it is also true that that the reverse - that counting the number of emotive usages of single words will not necessarily create metaphors that automatically elicit the same effects on the listener. Consider the case of dead metaphors that pass on into language. Dead metaphors are dead precisely because they fail to evoke emotive states after a period of usage and decay. Similarly, 'art' - produced on an industrial scale can die from usage and mechanical reproduction. There is no way of finding out except by means of feedback from the contexts of meaning that are available for the moment. These are some of the complex questions implicit in artistic computation. In any case the undivided singularity of the experience gives us a clue.

8. CONCLUSIONS

There is no way in which we could evade around the question 'what is 'art'? In as far as we are concerned here we cannot consider any definition of art that does not take into account the function of art achieving a certain goal, which we just showed from ancient analogies, is not simply a cognitively realized goal. Art is the only activity that aspires to a goal in which the goal itself does not need to have a reference to the product, other than eliciting an emotion. Since the goal of art is emotive, cognition either does not play a role in its improvisatory stages or is subservient to emotive effects or remains at best intra-relational between levels of processing and attitude building. The arts, as we said, seek to capture what Confucius called a *wu wei* or the Indian grammarians called *rasa*. The *wu wei* or *rasa* can create bodily feedback and engender a sense of well-being.

9. ACKNOWLEDGEMENT
Rectoria, PUAC, DICIS, Universidad de Guanajuato

10. REFERENCES

[1] Simon, Herbert A, Simon, "Creativity in the Arts and the Sciences." **The Kenyon Review** Vol. 23, No. 2, 200, pp. 203-220.

[2] Simon, Herbert A, Simon, "Creativity in the Arts and the Sciences." **The Kenyon Review** Vol. 23, No. 2, 200, pp. 203-220.

[3] C. W. Taylor, (1988). "Various Approaches to and Definitions of Creativity". **The Nature of Creativity**, 1988.

[4] Fodor, Jerry A. "Fodor's guide to mental representation: The intelligent auntie's vade-mecum." **Mind** Vol. 94, No. 373, pp. 1980, pp 76-100.

[5] W. Visser, **The Cognitive Artifacts of Designing**, CRC Press, 2006.

[6] Margolin, Victor, and Richard Buchanan, eds. **The Idea of Design**, MIT Press, 1995.

[7] L. S. Choueiri, "Diagrams of the Design Process", In **Proceedings of 5th European Academy of Design Conference**, 2003.

[8] Zainal Abidin, Shahriman Bin, Anders Warell, and Andre Liem. "Understanding styling activity of automotive designers: A study of manual interpolative morphing through freehand sketching." In **DS 68-9: Proceedings of the 18th International Conference on Engineering Design (ICED 11), Impacting Society through Engineering Design, Vol. 9: Design Methods and Tools pt. 1, Lyngby/Copenhagen, Denmark**, Vol 15, 2011.

[9] A. Chakrabarti, Prabir Sarkar, B. Leelavathamma, and B. S. Nataraju. "A functional representation for aiding biomimetic

[10] N. Crilly, "Fixation and creativity in concept development: The attitudes and practices of expert designers." **Design Studies** Vol 38, 2015, pp. 54-91.

[11] S. Abdelmohsen, Ayman Assem, Sherif Tarabishy, and Ahmed Ibrahim. "A Heuristic Approach for the Automated Generation of Furniture Layout Schemes in Residential Spaces." **Design Computing and Cognition'16**, Springer, Cham, 2017.

[12] N. RF. Maier, "Problem Solving and Creativity: In Individuals and Groups", 1970.

[13] R. S. Sutton, and Andrew G. Barto, **Introduction to Reinforcement Learning**, Vol. 135. Cambridge: MIT Press, 1998.

[14] M. Thirumalai, "An introduction to natya shastra-gesture in aesthetic arts." **Language in India,** Vol 1, No. 6, 2001, 27-33.

[15] M. Ghosh, "Natyashastra (ascribed to Bharata Muni)", *Chowkhamba Sanskrit Series Office*, 2002.

[16] R.S. Lazarus "On the Primacy of Cognition", 1984.

[17] M. A. Boden, "4 GOFAI." The Cambridge Handbook of Artificial Intelligence, 2014.

[18] A. R. Damasio, **The Feeling of What Happens: Body and Emotion in the Making of Consciousness**, Houghton Mifflin Harcourt, 1999.

[19] E. Slingerland, **Effortless Action: Wu-wei as Conceptual Metaphor and Spiritual Ideal in Early China**. Oxford University Press, 2007.

[20] A. R. Damasio, **The Feeling of What Happens: Body and Emotion in the Making of Consciousness**, Houghton Mifflin Harcourt, 1999.

[21] J. Velásquez, "A computational framework for emotion-based control." **Proceedings of the Workshop on Grounding Emotions in Adaptive Systems; International Conference on SAB**, 1998. pp. 62-67.

[22] M. Lefebvre, "The Art of Pointing. On Peirce, Indexicality, and Photographic Images." *Photography Theory*, 2007.

[23] R.W. Wilson, Frank C. Keil, eds. **The MIT Encyclopedia of the Cognitive Sciences,** MIT Press, 2001.

[24] P.M. Churchland, and P.S. Churchland, "Functionalism, qualia, and intentionality." **Philosophical Topics**, Vol 12, No. 1. 1981, pp. 121-145.

[25] A. Gopnik, Alison. "How we know our minds: The illusion of first-person knowledge of intentionality." **Behavioral and Brain Sciences** Vol 16, No. 1, 1993, pp. 1-14.

[26] A. Gopnik, Alison. "How we know our minds: The illusion of first-person knowledge of intentionality." **Behavioral and Brain Sciences** Vol 16, No. 1, 1993, pp. 1-14.

and artificial inspiration of new ideas." **Ai Edam**, Vol 19, No. 2, 2005, pp. 113-132.

AUTHORS INDEX

VOLUME I

www.ingramcontent.com/pod-product-compliance
Lightning Source LLC
Chambersburg PA
CBHW081532220326

41598CB00036B/6408